**Reinhard H. Schmidt, Hans Dieter Seibel, and Paul Thomes
From Microfinance to Inclusive Banking**

Edited by
Sparkassenstiftung für internationale Kooperation

Reinhard H. Schmidt, Hans Dieter Seibel, and Paul Thomes

From Microfinance to Inclusive Banking

Why Local Banking Works

Edited by
Sparkassenstiftung für internationale Kooperation

WILEY

WILEY-VCH Verlag GmbH & Co. KGaA

All books published by **Wiley-VCH** are carefully produced. Nevertheless, authors, editors, and publisher do not warrant the information contained in these books, including this book, to be free of errors. Readers are advised to keep in mind that statements, data, illustrations, procedural details or other items may inadvertently be inaccurate.

Library of Congress Card No.:
applied for

© 2016 Wiley-VCH Verlag & Co. KGaA, Boschstr. 12, 69469 Weinheim, Germany

All rights reserved (including those of translation into other languages). No part of this book may be reproduced in any form – by photoprinting, microfilm, or any other means – nor transmitted or translated into a machine language without written permission from the publishers. Registered names, trademarks, etc. used in this book, even when not specifically marked as such, are not to be considered unprotected by law.

British Library Cataloguing-in-Publication Data
A catalogue record for this book is available from the British Library.

Bibliographic information published by the Deutsche Nationalbibliothek
The Deutsche Nationalbibliothek lists this publication in the Deutsche Nationalbibliografie; detailed bibliographic data are available on the Internet at <http://dnb.d-nb.de>.

Printed in the Federal Republic of Germany
Printed on acid-free paper

Gestaltung: pp030 – Produktionsbüro Heike Praetor, Berlin, Germany
Coverdesign: Christian Kalkert Buchkunst & Illustration, Birken-Honigsessen, Germany
Cover Photography: Philip Ruopp (© Sparkassenstiftung)
Typesetting: inmedialo UG, Plankstadt, Germany
Printing: CPI books GmbH, Leck, Germany

Print ISBN: 978-3-527-50802-0

Table of Contents

List of Abbreviations	IX
List of Figures	XIII
List of Snapshots	XV
List of Tables	XVII
Foreword	XIX
Preface	XXI

I. INTRODUCTION: REFLECTIONS ON MICROFINANCE

1 Microfinance – banks – savings and cooperative banks 3
   1.1 Microfinance: From humble beginnings to hype and disenchantment 3
   1.2 Banks as providers of microfinance services 7
   1.3 The relevance of savings banks and cooperative banks 8
   1.4 Conclusions and consequences 10

2 Basic definitions 13
   2.1 Why precise definitions are desirable but difficult to provide 13
   2.2 Terms that need to be defined 14

3 The broader context of social and development-oriented banking 21
   3.1 How new forms of financial institutions emerge and survive 21
   3.2 The role of the state and other "third parties" 23
   3.3 The art of financial institution building 25
   3.4 The objectives of socially-oriented, inclusive financial institutions 31

4 Does history matter? 35
5 Our main propositions 39

II. GERMAN SAVINGS BANKS AND CREDIT COOPERATIVES – A BLUEPRINT FOR INCLUSIVE FINANCE?

1 Objectives – Why a historical perspective? Why credit cooperatives and savings banks? Why Germany? 43
2 Saving and borrowing – A socioeconomic historical approach 49
   2.1 Satisfying needs – A vital challenge 49
   2.2 Saving and borrowing – An everyday exercise 53
   2.3 Winds of change – Pawnshops, widows' and orphans' funds, and savings and loan societies as innovative inclusive instruments of change management 55
   2.4 Savings as a fundamental condition for change and growth 56

3 "Out of the box" – An international comparative survey of 19th century savings-based microfinance trends ▪▪▪▪▪▪▪▪▪▪▪▪ 59
4 The emergence of the German savings bank model – Inclusion from the beginning ▪▪▪▪▪▪▪▪▪▪▪▪▪▪▪▪▪▪▪▪▪▪ 65
   4.1 Divergence and convergence – Comparing the early savings banks 68
   4.2 Diffusion in the wake of early industrialization and growing incomes 72
   4.3 The Prussian Savings Bank Regulations of 1838 – A legal template for future development 77
   4.4 Urgent need for profound change – Towards the economic takeoff 81
   4.5 The savings business around 1900 – Cradle-to-grave incentives 84
   4.6 The credit business – A fluctuating and attractive combination of microfinance features 95
   4.7 Debit and credit – Reserves and non-profit appropriation 107
   4.8 Administrative and organizational success factors – Supervision, skill enhancement, and networks 108

5 Case study – The Aachen Association for Promoting Industriousness [*Der Aachener Verein zur Beförderung der Arbeitsamkeit*]: A holistic local inclusion approach ▪▪▪▪▪▪▪▪▪▪▪▪ 111
   5.1 "Money and Intellect" – An integrated welfare concept combining insurance, savings, and education 112
   5.2 The savings bank of the Aachen Association – A successful experiment 116
   5.3 The end – The disastrous consequences of World War I 124
   5.4 Evaluation – The holistic concept as a role model? 125

6 "Out of the box" – An international comparative survey of 19th-century credit-based microfinance trends ▪▪▪▪▪▪▪▪▪▪▪▪ 131
7 The emergence of the German credit cooperative model – Tradition meets innovation ▪▪▪▪▪▪▪▪▪▪▪▪▪▪▪▪▪▪ 135
   7.1 The liberal approach – Schulze-Delitzsch and his "Volksbanks" (People's Banks) 137
   7.2 The Christian charity approach – Raiffeisen and his fight against rural usury 144
   7.3 Dispute over principles – Jockeying for position and an optimization process 147
   7.4 Wilhelm Haas and other agents of change – Salt in the soup? 150
   7.5 Case study – The Hachenburg Credit Cooperative [*Vorschussverein Hachenburg*] 153
   7.6 Volksbanks and Raiffeisen cooperatives – A remarkable success story 158

8 Savings banks, credit cooperatives, and commercial banks –
Complementarity versus rivalry ▪ ▪ ▪ ▪ ▪ ▪ ▪ ▪ ▪ ▪ ▪ ▪ ▪ ▪ ▪ 163
9 Summary, conclusions, and outlook – Are there lessons to be learned
from the History Lab? ▪ ▪ ▪ ▪ ▪ ▪ ▪ ▪ ▪ ▪ ▪ ▪ ▪ ▪ ▪ ▪ ▪ ▪ 169
 9.1 Organizational findings   169
 9.2 Practical findings   171
 9.3 Connecting past and future   174
 9.4 Overview – Constitutive elements of local banking in Germany:
   From microfinance to inclusive banking   177

III. GLOBAL DEVELOPMENT AND CURRENT STATUS OF MICROFINANCE PRACTICE

1 An overview of institutions, concepts, and approaches ▪ ▪ ▪ ▪ ▪ ▪ 183
2 The spectrum of microfinance institutions ▪ ▪ ▪ ▪ ▪ ▪ ▪ ▪ ▪ ▪ ▪ 187
 2.1 A typology of microfinance institutions   187
 2.2 Informal microfinance   190
 2.3 Community-based microfinance, or village "banks"   198
 2.4 Cooperative microfinance: What role for government?   212
 2.5 Microfinance banks   226
3 Sources of data on access to finance ▪ ▪ ▪ ▪ ▪ ▪ ▪ ▪ ▪ ▪ ▪ ▪ 265
 3.1 Self-reporting by individual institutions   266
 3.2 Global reporting by networks of financial institutions   269
 3.3 Global data sets   274
 3.4 Market saturation   280
4 Microfinance as a field of international aid and cooperation ▪ ▪ ▪ ▪ 283
 4.1 Early forms of development finance and the emergence
   of microfinance   284
 4.2 The turn towards modern microfinance   292
 4.3 Strategies for creating efficient and sustainable microfinance
   institutions   296
 4.4 Commercial microfinance and its challenges   308
 4.5 Why microfinance is losing its clout   314

IV. LOCAL FINANCIAL INSTITUTIONS – LEARNING FROM THE HISTORY OF SAVINGS BANKS AND COOPERATIVE BANKS FOR DEVELOPMENT POLICY TODAY

1 Summing up the historical survey ▪ ▪ ▪ ▪ ▪ ▪ ▪ ▪ ▪ ▪ ▪ ▪ ▪ ▪ 321
2 The general relevance of the historical survey for the design of
development projects ▪ ▪ ▪ ▪ ▪ ▪ ▪ ▪ ▪ ▪ ▪ ▪ ▪ ▪ ▪ ▪ ▪ ▪ ▪ 325

3 The direct relevance of the historical survey for the design of development projects 331
4 A concluding comparative remark and a plea for diversity of banking structures 337
5 Summing up: Insights and recommendations for national and international decision makers based on 200 years of inclusive microfinance and local banking history 343

References 347

List of Abbreviations

ACPC	Agricultural Credit Policy Council of the Philippines		[German Association of Savings Banks]
ADB	Asian Development Bank	DTMFI	deposit-taking microfinance institution
ADEMI	Association for the Development of Microenterprises	DTVF	deposit-taking village fund
AFI	Alliance for Financial Inclusion	DZ Bank	Deutsche Zentral-Genossenschaftsbank
AG	Aktiengesellschaft [stock company]		German Central Cooperative Bank
APMAS	Andhra Pradesh Mahila Abhivruddhi Society	EACB	European Association of Co-operative Banks
APRACA	Asia-Pacific Rural and Agricultural Credit Association	EBRD	European Bank for Reconstruction and Development
avg.	average	EDC	electronic data capture
BAAC	Bank for Agriculture and Agricultural Cooperatives of Thailand	eG	eingetragene Genossenschaft [registered cooperative]
BaFin	Bundesanstalt für Finanzdienstleistungsaufsicht [German Federal Financial Supervisory Authority]	eGmbH	Genossenschaft mit beschränkter Haftung [registered cooperative with limited liability]
BMZ	Bundesministerium für wirtschaftliche Zusammenarbeit und Entwicklung [German Federal Ministry for Economic Cooperation and Development]	eGmuH	Genossenschaft mit unbeschränkter Haftung [registered cooperative with full liability]
		EU	European Union
BoG	Bank of Ghana	EUR	Euro
BoL	Bank of Lao	FAO	Food and Agriculture Organization of the United Nations
BPD	Bank Pembangunan Daerah		
BPR	Bank Perkreditan Rakyat	FAS	Financial Access Survey
BRI	Bank Rakyat Indonesia	FINCA	Foundation for International Community Assistance
CAMELS	Capital Adequacy, Asset Quality, Management Quality, Earnings, Liquidity, Sensitivity to Market Risk	FMO	Netherlands Development Finance Company
		FS	financial services
CAR	capital adequacy ratio	G20	Group of Twenty
CARD	Center for Agriculture and Rural Development	G8	Group of Eight
CCF	Cooperative Central Fund	GASCA	Greater Accra Susu Collectors Association
CEO	Chief Executive Officer		
CGAP	The Consultative Group to Assist the Poor	GCSCA	Ghana Co-operative Susu Collectors Association
CMAC	Cajas Municipales de Ahorro y Crédito [Municipal Savings and Credit Banks]	GDP	gross domestic product
		GIZ	Deutsche Gesellschaft für Internationale Zusammenarbeit [German Agency for International Cooperation]
DFID	Department for International Development of the United Kingdom		
DGRV	Deutscher Genossenschafts- und Raiffeisenverband [German Cooperative and Raiffeisen Confederation]	GPFI	Global Partnership for Financial Inclusion
		GTZ	Deutsche Gesellschaft für Technische Zusammenarbeit [German Agency for Technical Cooperation]
DM	Deutsche Mark [German Mark]		
DOEN	The DOEN Foundation		
DSGV	Deutscher Sparkassen- und Giroverband	HIID	Harvard Institute for International Development

ICBA	Independent Community Bankers of America	OECD	Organization for Economic Co-operation and Development
IDB	Inter-American Development Bank	OJK	Otoritas Jasa Keuangan [Financial Services Authority of Indonesia]
IDR	Indonesian Rupiah		
IFC	International Finance Corporation	ORP	operational restructuring plan
IFI	international financial institution	PACS	Primary Agricultural Credit Society
IFPRI	International Food Policy Research Institute	PCF	People's Credit Fund
IKP	The Indira Kranthi Patham poverty reduction program	PCH	ProCredit Holding AG & Co. KGaA
ILO	International Labour Organization	PISCES	Program for Investment in the Small Capital Enterprise Sector
IMF	International Monetary Fund		
IPC	Internationale Projekt Consult	PLPDK	Pembina Lembaga Perkreditan Desa Kabupaten
IPO	initial public offering		
JLG	joint liability groups	PPP	Public Private Partnership
KfW	Kreditanstalt für Wiederaufbau [German Reconstruction Loan Corporation]	PR	public relations
		PSBC	Postal Savings Bank of China
		RBI	Reserve Bank of India
KGaA	Kommanditgesellschaft auf Aktien [partnership limited by shares]	RCT	randomized control trial
		ROA	return on assets
km²	square kilometer	ROE	return on equity
KWG	Kreditwesengesetz [German Banking Act]	ROI	return on investment
		ROSCA	rotating savings and credit association
LAK	Laotian Kip		
LDR	loan-to-deposit ratio	RWTH Aachen University	Rheinisch-Westfälische Technische Hochschule Aachen [Rhenish-Westphalian Technical University of Aachen]
LPD	Lembaga Perkreditan Desa		
LWU	Lao Women's Union		
MACS	Mutually Aided Cooperative Society		
		SAVIX	Savings Groups Information Exchange
MCID	Micro Credit Innovation Department	SBFIC	Savings Banks Foundation for International Cooperation [Sparkassenstiftung für Internationale Kooperation]
MENA	Middle East and North Africa		
MF	microfinance		
MFA	microfinance association		
MFI	microfinance institution	SBV	State Bank of Vietnam
MIS	management information system	SCI	Service Corporation International
MIV	microfinance investment vehicle	SCU	Savings and Credit Union
MIX	Microfinance Information Exchange	SDC	Swiss Agency for Development and Cooperation
mn	million	SERP	Society for Elimination of Rural Poverty
MRI	Mutually Reinforcing Institution		
MSEs	micro and small enterprises	SG	savings group
MSMEs	micro, small and medium enterprises	SHG	self-help group
		SHPI	self-help-promoting institution
NABARD	National Bank for Agriculture and Rural Development of India	SKS	SKS Microfinance Limited
		SMEs	small and medium enterprises
NBFI	non-bank financial institution	SWOT	Strengths, Weaknesses, Opportunities and Threats
NDTMFI	non-deposit-taking microfinance institution		
		TSB	Trustee Savings Bank
NDTVF	non-deposit-taking village fund	UGX	Uganda Shilling
NERI	National Economic Research Institute	UN	United Nations
		UNCDF	United Nations Capital Development Fund
NGO	non-governmental organization		
NPL	non-performing loan	UNDP	United Nations Development Programme
NRLM	National Rural Livelihood Mission		

US	United States	VO	village organization
USAID	United States Agency for International Development	VSLA	village savings and loan association
		WGZ	Westdeutsche Genossenschafts-Zentralbank [West German Cooperative Central Bank]
USD	United States Dollar		
VAPCF	Vietnam Association of People's Credit Funds		
VF	village fund	WOCCU	World Council of Credit Unions
VND	Viet Nam Dong	WSBI	World Savings Banks Institute

List of Figures

1: Circle of microfinance sentiments – "old" role models – "new" role models. 4
2: Microfinance as a change management instrument 37
3: Holistic institutions matrix – STEPLE approach 44
4: Stages of growth and change according to Rostow 45
5: Economic megatrends 46
6: Phase shift of industrialization. 51
7: Berlin City Hall 1818, business location of the Municipal Savings Bank of Berlin 74
8: Savings passbooks and savings in Prussia, 1880-1913. 85
9: Powerful alliance: Headquarters of the Aachener Verein. 111
10: "Mens agitat molem" (Mind drives matter), RWTH Aachen University 115
11: Holistic change management scheme – smoothing the process of industrialization. 116
12: Credit portfolio of the Delitzscher-Vorschussverein, 1854 and 1858. 140
13: Cooperative networks 152
14: Parameters for the achievement of above-average results 172
15: Impact of microfinance institutions around 1900 172
16: Number of savings banks and cooperative banks and their balance sheet volumes 174
17: Mobile analog banking in a digitalizing world 175
18: Structure of the German banking market 177
19: The evolution of financial depth in the LPD sector, 1999–2012 210
20: Key balance sheet data for the PCFs, 1995–2013 224
21: Key balance sheet data for CCF/CoopBank, 1995–2013 224
22: Total deposits and loans outstanding for the BRI microbanking units, 1984–2012. 246
23: Financial access by data source for sub-Saharan Africa 268
24: Data of the Microcredit Summit Campaign on MFI outreach compared with
    World Bank data on poverty, by region, 2010 269
25: Credit unions, during and after the crisis 273
26: Global Findex (2014): Adults (age 15+) who do not have an account with a
    formal financial institution. 277

List of Snapshots

1: Feasibility assessment in historical perspective.. 36
2: Typology of savings banks in Germany... 66
3: Benchmark data for the Savings and Loan Bank of Kiel, 1796 67
4: Savings objectives... 69
5: First Prussian municipal savings bank – the Municipal Savings Bank of Berlin, 1818..... 72
6: Microfinance-relevant aspects of the Prussian Savings Bank Regulations of 1838 78
7: Microfinance-relevant structural parameters in the late 1840s 80
8: Diffusion process in Germany... 81
9: Savings Bank of the Aachen Association, 1850....................................... 82
10: Forerunner of cellphone banking? Savings machines: First installed in the city of Padua, Italy... 86
11: Complicated but safe – agency banking of the District Savings Bank of Saarbrücken, 1888/89.. 87
12: Doorstep collection of deposits by savings banks in Germany 88
13: "Awakening a spirit of thriftiness among the working-class population": Instructions from the management of the Rhineland-Westphalian gunpowder factories, 1884 89
14: Various savings models.. 90
15: Nominal wages, cost of living and real wages in industry, trade, and transportation, 1871–1913... 90
16: Wages in an industrial region around 1900 – The spread of wealth 91
17: Lending operations of the District Savings Bank of Saarbrücken according to the bank charter of 1857 96
18: Public fire insurance companies as an instrument of social change..................... 98
19: Bank service instructions for processing mortgage applications, 1889.................. 98
20: The first loan issued by the District Savings Bank of Saarbrücken, April 24, 1858........ 100
21: Credit regulations for personal loans at the District Savings Bank of Saarbrücken, 1858 .. 101
22: Decision of the Executive Board of the District Savings Bank of Saarbrücken, 1911 104
23: Interest trap – A call for action, 1887.. 105
24: Thrift... 119
25: Impressive decennial balance sheet, 1844 120
26: The bonus bank, 1909.. 122
27: Institution building – networks and apex institutions 127
28: The Rochdale Principles for the operation of cooperatives 133
29: Systematic analysis of changes – current analogies are obvious 138
30: Credit terms and conditions for craftsmen – abuse of savings banks 139
31: Sustainable savings incentives 140

32: Mission of the German Cooperative Bank of Soergel, Parisius & Co. 142

33: Raiffeisen's ideals: freedom and independence 144

34: "Agricultural Association for the Rhine Province" 145

35: System comparison around 1870: Two approaches and one goal. 149

36: Supervision and organizational design in the German Cooperative Act of 1889. 152

37: Balances of early credit cooperatives, 1862 to 1865 155

38: Aachener Bank, Urban Craftsmen Credit Cooperative, 1900 157

39: Success factors identified in the History Lab 167

40: If governance fails: the role of the board 208

41: Internal control and supervision of the units 242

42: Facts and figures about ProCredit Holding 259

43: How financial cooperatives performed before and after the global crisis 273

44: Some facts and figures about funding sources of microfinance institutions. 283

List of Tables

1: Top ten savings banks in Prussia in 1849 82
2: Ability to save of urban, low-income households, first half of 19th century 83
3: Savings banks density in selected German states, 1905 84
4: The average annual wages of employees in industry, trade, and transportation* 91
5: Average interest rates of the savings banks in Germany during the period 1820–1910 ... 92
6: Graded interest rates, District Savings Bank of Saarbrücken: 1900–1914 92
7: Savings accounts in Prussia, 1850–1908 94
8: Financial sponsoring statement of the Aachen Association, 1834–1909 116
9: Account balances of Customers of the Aachen Association bonus bank, 1834–1921 123
10: Key indicators of the Aachen Association in peace and wartime, 1912–1921 124
11: Savings deposits of savings banks and credit cooperatives in Germany, 1850–1910 164
12: Savings bank locations in the Prussian Rhineland province by government district as of 1912 165
13: Constitutive elements of local banking in Germany: from microfinance to inclusive universal banking 178
14: BRI's loan portfolio and non-performing loan ratios (≥1 day) by business segment, Dec. 2012 245
15: Data on the ProCredit Group 259
16: MIX market microfinance data by region, 2011 266
17: WSBI retail savings bank data, 2011 270
18: Financial cooperatives: credit unions (2011) and cooperative banks (2010) 272
19: Credit unions by market penetration of region 272
20: VSLA membership in facilitated groups (as of October 2013) 274
21: Access to formal financial institutions 278

Foreword

Half of the world's population lives and works in the informal economy – not by choice, but by necessity. In the language of economists, poorer families in developing countries are consumption-smoothing households and capital-consuming, self-employed entrepreneurs at the same time. As a result, they need a broader range of financial services to manage inevitably irregular income and expense spikes, accumulate working capital, build assets, and mitigate risks. Lacking better alternatives, they often resort to informal financial mechanisms, such as moneylenders, pawnbrokers, and rotating savings clubs, which can be very unreliable and expensive.

At the same time, an increasing body of evidence shows how appropriate financial services can help improve household welfare and spur small enterprise activity. There is also macroeconomic evidence that economies with deeper financial intermediation tend to grow faster and reduce income inequality.

Against this backdrop, policy makers around the globe are embracing formal financial inclusion as an important soft infrastructure ingredient for social and economic progress. The G20 has made financial inclusion one pillar of its development agenda and some 50-plus countries have made explicit financial inclusion commitments. More recently, the World Bank Group has called for universal access to basic transaction services as a building block for economic development by 2020.

As emerging markets countries develop and deepen their financial systems, there may be lessons to be learned from the formalization of financial intermediation in today's highly industrialized countries. The German Financial Inclusion story is one example. There, new types of local, community-based financial institutions started serving customers in the very late 18th century for the same reasons we have seen microfinance institutions and other non-conventional providers emerge much more recently in developing countries: because the predominant commercial banks of their time pretty much catered to government, big business, and wealthy patricians, leaving the vast majority of the working population excluded.

The German *Sparkassen* (loosely translated as savings and loans institutions) and somewhat later the *Genossenschaftsbanken* (cooperatives) introduced a safe way for farmers, artisans, low-income workers, domestic employees, traders, budding entrepreneurs, and everybody else to deposit money and get credit. Early on they introduced long-term savings to help provide for older-age in the absence of the yet-to-be introduced public pension systems. They accompanied the Industrial Revolution throughout the 19th century, built trust and capital through three regional wars, predating modern German unification in 1871. Laws were written, regulations introduced and by 1913, before the outset of World War I, every single German family had a savings and transactions account.

As they draw lessons from this experience, the authors of the study presented below highlight the importance of decentralized inclusive financial systems, anchored in the community, understanding their customers, and lubricating the local economy. They point to the historic economic success that this system has brought about and to the recent, relative stability it ensured. About 70 percent of German retail deposits today remain with these local, community-based institutions that continue to be at the center of economic life in small towns and municipalities.

The world has of course changed since the rise of the German *Sparkassen* and *Genossenschaftsbanken*. New institutional set-ups and technologies allow for new ways to reach people faster and more cheaply. But, the underlying imperatives to understand and serve customer needs, to be trusted in the community, and to serve the larger purpose of helping people improve their lives and realize their economic potential remain the same.

Read on and draw your own conclusions about the elements of the German story that might be applicable to the financial inclusion challenges in a different time and under different circumstances.

Washington, July 2015 *Tilman Ehrbeck, former CEO of CGAP, now a partner at Omidyar Network*

Preface

Microfinance is a diverse and difficult socio-financial phenomenon. It is difficult to define, to understand, to perform, and to implement. The last decade in particular has seen the gamut of emotions regarding it, from hype to disenchantment and from microcredit to microfinance – the latter term having been coined back in 1991 by Hans Dieter Seibel, one of the authors of this book. Another landmark was the establishment of the Consultative Group to Assist the Poor (CGAP) in 1995 as a think tank first of the microcredit movement, then of the microfinance movement which succeeded it. The topic entered the global arena of public and scientific discussion upon the awarding of the 2006 Nobel Peace Prize to the Grameen Bank and its founder, Muhammad Yunus.

In fact, the more promising an approach is, the ruder the awakening will be when disappointment sets in, and the more difficult it becomes to evaluate existing institutions. In the extreme case, insiders today generally negate the suitability of the microfinance approach; others assume the position that organizations aiming to provide inclusive financial services can be successfully run only as nonprofit enterprises, operating on permanent subsidies. For some time these evaluations have been prompting the microfinance community to consider new ways to diversify and optimize the original business model. Nevertheless, it seems that, in general, too little systematic knowledge has flowed into the design of microfinance models and projects.

This study on microfinance represents the findings of an interdisciplinary team of authors. It picks up on past experiences, describes and analyzes them, and merges them into a fresh interpretation of microfinance, widening the scope in the sense of the CGAP graduation approach. In doing so, it seeks to learn from the past, presents options, and tries to define parameters of success and failure. The authors have studied the subject in manifold ways. Hans Dieter Seibel, a retired professor of sociology at the University of Cologne, and Reinhard H. Schmidt, a retired professor for international banking at the University of Frankfurt, have worked in the field for many years, both as practitioners and as theoreticians with long publication lists. To extend the scope of observation and add a long-term perspective, Paul Thomes, a professor at RWTH Aachen University and an expert in banking history, has added a comparative analysis of examples from the era of European industrialization. At that time, savings banks and credit cooperatives started to play an important role in change management, especially in Germany, with the emergence of these institutions being a kind of microfinance revolution in its own way. Of course, the historical case studies must not be seen as a template to be adopted one-to-one in the present day, although attempts have been made to copy historical European role models and they often have been cited (uncritically) in the microfinance literature. But the present time is different indeed, and so are cultures and people. However, the latest trends in microfinance, especially in the context of the discussion about sustainability, seem to confirm that it is well worth looking at all the different methodological solutions and models that the past and the present have at their disposal.

The authors are convinced that their holistic approach has the potential to deepen general knowledge about microfinance and to generate among the parties involved a better mutual understanding, which has frequently been obstructed in the past by cultural and other differences. Financial participation, understood in the context of its importance, intentions and effects, is comparable to people participating in energy supply and transportation infrastructures. In light of the current global challenges, the ultimate objective must be inclusive and reflective societies which address challenges together in a partnership of equals. Optimized microfinance concepts – in the sense that they are better culturally adapted – might contribute to the achievement of this ambitious aim.

Designing, structuring, and writing the present text was a joint endeavor. However, roles have been assigned, reflecting the three authors' main fields of interest. The main author of Chapter I, which offers a general introduction, clarifies concepts and provides an economic background of today's microfinance, is Reinhard H. Schmidt. Chapter II, on the history of savings and cooperative banks in the long 19th century, is the domain of Paul Thomes, the historian among the trio of authors. The main contributions to Chapter III, which is essentially a collection of case studies of large microfinance institutions and programs that aspire to be inclusive and development-oriented, were authored by Hans Dieter Seibel, with Reinhard Schmidt as an additional contributor. The final chapter, Chapter IV, which provides a summary and outlook, is then indeed a joint endeavor. In spite of this assignment of roles, all chapters have been jointly discussed among the authors at great length in order to create coherence in terms of substance and, to some extent at least, also of style.

The work underlying this book has been generously funded by the German Federal Ministry for Economic Cooperation and Development [*Bundesministerium für wirtschaftliche Zusammenarbeit und Entwicklung*] and two organizations belonging to the German Savings Banks Finance Group, namely the Savings Banks Foundation for International Cooperation [*Sparkassenstiftung für Internationale Kooperation*] and the Academic Sponsorship of the Savings Banks Financial Group [*Sparkassen Wissenschaftsförderung*]. For their confidence in us and for their financial support, we owe a great debt to these two organizations.

The person who oversaw the work at the Savings Banks Foundation is Dr. Ilonka Rühle. Her continual support and encouragement, as well as her valuable contributions to the substance of our text, are by all standards outstanding. We are grateful for all she has done to bring this book into being and, as we hope, with successful results at that. Our gratitude to Dr. Rühle goes far beyond what would be due merely to her formal role.

Since we are not native English speakers, we also needed support to improve the linguistic and stylistic quality of our original manuscript. We were really fortunate to have Ms. Grace Tasch and Mr. George McElheny to help us out in this respect. Their competence both as translators and editors with a long-time focus on microfinance made them our ideal partners. We are deeply indebted to them for their outstanding work.

Bonn, March 2016 *Reinhard H. Schmidt, Hans Dieter Seibel and Paul Thomes*

I.
INTRODUCTION: REFLECTIONS ON MICROFINANCE

1 Microfinance – banks – savings and cooperative banks

1.1 Microfinance: From humble beginnings to hype and disenchantment

What is today called microfinance is the outcome of a stunning process of institutional development and innovation that started in the 1970s and 1980s. The beginnings of modern microfinance – with a more social orientation in Bangladesh, a more commercial orientation in Indonesia and a more political orientation in Latin America – were shaped by high ambitions and noble intentions and spurred by the growing insight among experts that the old concepts of development finance, focusing on state-owned development banks, that had been favored by national and multinational aid donors since the 1950s, were unsuccessful, politically counterproductive, and economically inefficient.

However, calling microfinance new is not really correct, since it would merely reflect the rather one-sided perspective of an observer who comes from the Western world and is, moreover, not very conversant with the history of banking in the part of the world from which he or she comes. In truth, what is now widely known as microfinance has existed in almost all parts of the world for decades, if not for centuries, and has been the core business of savings banks and cooperative banks in Germany and a number of other European countries since the 18th and 19th centuries respectively. We emphasize the one-sidedness of the belief that microfinance is a new phenomenon precisely because it is one of the main objectives of this study to make our readers aware of the important role that savings banks and cooperative banks have played in the provision of microfinance services over the course of some two hundred years. However, two things are indeed new: firstly, the interest of policy makers and development experts in microfinance and in a policy of supporting microfinance in developing countries in a big way, and secondly, the use of the term "microfinance". Both of these new phenomena are addressed in more detail later on in this study. Given that there is a difference between older forms of providing financial services to relatively poor people and those that have emerged in the last half-century and are now called microfinance, we use the attribute "modern" for the latter where confusion might arise.

Early modern microfinance was not only ambitious, but by necessity highly innovative as well; new ideas, insights, and concepts were generated and tried out in practice. The idea that poor people are creditworthy, that they could take out loans, use them wisely and subsequently repay them was a new and hardly credible one for the advocates and practitioners of the old strategies of development finance that had been practiced for decades and for conventional bankers. But due to a combination of personal intelligence and charisma on the part of some of the protagonists, notably Muhammad Yunus; numerous important and convincing academic studies, notably those from a research center at Ohio State University; and favorable macro-political circumstances, notably a policy of lifting interest restrictions in most countries, the new form of development finance later called microfinance was given a chance.

However well-intentioned and heart-warming it may have been, early microfinance was not particularly effective. The scale of operations of most early providers of microloans and their high costs severely limited the outreach and impact they could achieve.

Microfinance matured in the 1990s and in the early years of the new millennium. The growth of microfinance in the years up to 2007 was part boom and part hype. It reached its peak in 2005, when the UN launched the International Year of Microcredit, and 2006, when the uncontested leading figure in microcredit, Muhammad Yunus of Bangladesh, and Grameen Bank, the poor people's bank that Yunus had founded, were awarded the Nobel Peace Prize for developing and implementing new ways of providing credit for the poor. What had made Yunus and his bank so well-known and so highly respected all over the world was his ambitious vision that microcredit would be able to eradicate abject poverty from the face of the earth (Yunus 2006/2007).

In the 1990s and the early 2000s, lending technologies were developed that were new to development experts and bankers and that really made it possible to reach poor clients and to get back the money lent out in the form of loans, and ways had

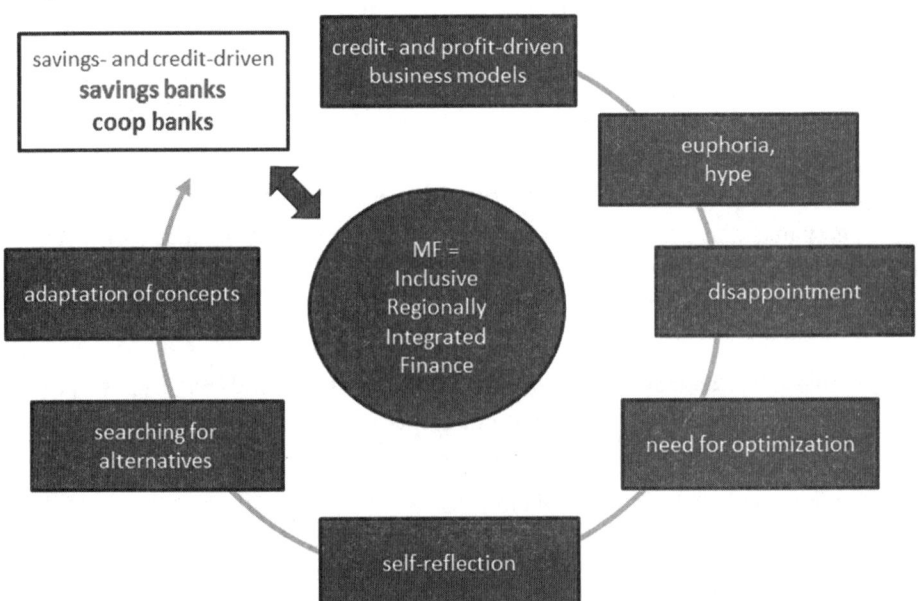

Figure 1: Circle of microfinance sentiments – "old" role models – "new" role models

been found to lower the cost of providing loans to the poor and to their small business undertakings. Moreover, a number of institutions that had formerly only granted small loans funded by governments and foreign donors also began taking deposits from their clients and offering payment transfer facilities – in other words, they were converted from microcredit institutions into genuine microfinance institutions (MFIs) offering both savings and credit facilities and other financial services as well. Based on these developments, microfinance expanded greatly in scope and sophistication and started to have an impact that was really worth talking about.

During these years, a new concept of managing MFIs emerged that became known as the commercial approach. Its early message was simply that the cost of granting very small loans can be reduced substantially by introducing appropriate operating procedures, and that it is possible to charge interest rates both high enough to cover the full costs of the institutions that provide the small loans and low enough to be borne by the typical microcredit client.

For the early advocates of the commercial approach, it was clear that microfinance has a dual objective: achieving strong social and developmental impacts, and at the same time establishing MFIs that are profitable and stable ("sustainable") and therefore able to expand their services and generate yet more developmental impacts. This was a grand vision, but it appeared to be realistic. By the middle of the 1990s a few MFIs had indeed achieved financial sustainability of their ongoing operations – a great success by any standard[1] Not surprisingly, the success of these showcases of efficient and sustainable MFIs raised the interest of policy makers, investors, and the general public and led to more funds flowing into microfinance. Early success was feeding ongoing success. This positive feedback cycle, which reached its peak in 2007, the point at which the financial crisis broke out, led to the widely held conviction that if done properly, microfinance can be both socially valuable and at the same time profitable.

However, the early triumph of the commercial approach to microfinance around the turn of the century also had negative effects at a later point in time. Some established banks and MFIs seem to have only seen the profit potential, forgetting the development side of the equation. As far as targeting and reaching poor clients was concerned, they did start to imitate what genuine MFIs with a dual objective of developmental impact and financial sustainability had done. But these new players had only one objective: to serve their own financial interests.[2]

Two MFIs that went public by issuing shares to institutional investors and the general public are particularly noteworthy examples of an excessive emphasis on a commercial orientation. One of them is the Mexican MFI Compartamos, which

---

[1] The first institution to adopt this approach very early on, in the mid-1980s, was BRI in Indonesia in its micro-banking units.
[2] See Business Week (2007).

undertook a financially very successful initial public offering (IPO) in 2007. This IPO triggered strong criticism among microfinance experts, because the high price at which the shares were issued was most probably due to very high profits generated by exorbitant interest rates. As Muhammad Yunus put it, institutions like Compartamos were taking over the role of loan sharks instead of fulfilling what he regarded as the supreme mission of MFIs, namely to drive the loan sharks out of the market and to eliminate exploitative interest rates for the poor.[3]

The other case was the microlender SKS in India, which went public in 2010. Like a few other private MFIs, SKS had expanded at an unprecedented and clearly unsustainable rate. Many poor families served by the institution ended up borrowing much more than they could ever repay. This microcredit institution reacted by using strong-arm methods to enforce repayment. Under the pressure exerted by the institution's money collectors, a number of borrowers committed suicide. These tragic events attracted worldwide attention and started a process of rethinking the economic and ethical merits of microfinance.

Possibly alerted by these two cases, microfinance experts started to undertake a thorough and critical investigation into the reality of microfinance,[4] and they found further grounds for concern. A one-sided and excessively commercial orientation, microlending that served to finance consumption instead of income-generating activities, multiple borrowing by clients and consequent over indebtedness were found to be more widespread than had previously been thought. Moreover, a number of academic studies questioned the ability of microfinance to pull microfinance clients out of poverty, as Yunus had made the world believe[5]. Other critics argued that the typical expenditures that most MFIs finance do not contribute to economic development in the respective countries, but rather keep them trapped in underdevelopment.[6] Then came a book that reported extensively and in a highly critical tone on certain MFIs whose management and staff were allegedly cynical and incompetent, and some of their supporters even more so.[7] Though the author did not explicitly say so, this book created the impression that deficient organizations were a widespread problem in the world of microfinance.

All of this did great damage to the former uniformly positive reputation of microfinance. At the least, it made microfinance look much less promising than before. Whether these recent developments are merely the sobering realization that the former hype was excessive and that former expectations were overblown, or whether they have put an end to microfinance or microcredit as it has been

---

3 In Business Week Online, December 2007, Yunus was quoted as having said, "Microfinance was created to fight the moneylender, not to become the moneylender."
4 See the programmatic title *Due Diligence: An Impertinent Inquiry into Microfinance* of Roodman's influential book from 2012, which addresses these issues at great length and in a very balanced way.
5 See Roodman and Murdoch (2009) and Roodman (2012).
6 See Bateman (2010, 2011 and 2013) and, even earlier, Dichter and Harper (2007).
7 See Sinclair (2012) and a number of related publications by the same author.

known to date, remains to be seen. However, even though the hype is over and some of the criticism is justified, most observers remain convinced that microfinance is a positive phenomenon.

1.2 Banks as providers of microfinance services

One consequence of the transformation of microfinance in the late 1990s – from a well-intentioned but extremely small-scale and amateurish development aid activity to an important element of the financial sector of the respective host countries – was the need to find suitable forms for the institutions involved. How could they best provide financial services to people who formerly did not have access to financial institutions? Building good financial institutions suited to providing microloans and other financial services was a great challenge during these years. Acknowledging the importance of this challenge gave birth to what has been called the institution-building approach, a conceptual twin of the commercial approach which looks so similar that an observer might hardly see a difference, since in order to pursue a commercial approach you need an appropriately structured and managed MFI, and any sound MFI must operate in a commercially sound way.

Once a certain degree of liberalization in the host countries made it possible, several MFIs that had formerly been organized as not-for-profit institutions or non-governmental organizations (NGOs) were incorporated and converted into formal and licensed banks, while in other cases new MFIs were set up as banks from the start.[8] There are many reasons why MFIs should become licensed banks subject to normal banking regulation and supervision. The most important one is that only licensed, regulated and supervised banks can take voluntary and withdrawable deposits, thus providing an important service to their clients and at the same time attracting funds that can be converted into small loans[9].

Several years after the beginning of the most serious banking crisis since the Great Depression, one may wonder whether the move towards corporations and formal banks that are completely and exclusively driven by shareholders' interests in profit maximization is really all that convincing. Have not banks lost much of their former clout and credibility in the crisis? And is the integration of microfinance into the larger context of financial markets[10] too dangerous for a type of financial activity that traditionally did not aspire to be under too much pressure to be profitable? Don't the Compartamos and SKS IPOs argue against the exposure to capital market pressure, given that in both cases hedge funds and private equity

---

8 See Chapter III, section 4 on different ways in which this institution-building problem has been resolved.
9 In some countries, there are by now special rules and regulations for MFIs that are permitted to take deposits, and these are typically more restrictive than those pertaining to non-deposit taking MFIs.
10 Wagner and Winkler (2013) have recently shown empirically that this integration has already gone very far over the past few years.

firms have played a highly problematic role?[11] These questions must be answered with great caution. Strong capital market pressure may indeed lead to a one-sided focus on profitability and the erosion of social and developmental concerns. However, if they aspire to have an impact and to serve their clients well, MFIs must grow and remain stable at the same time. To do so, they need to raise deposits, since a strong deposit business makes them relatively independent of funding by international financial institutions such as the World Bank, regional development banks or other investors. A lesson worth remembering from the peak of the financial crisis is that the resources of public and private banks are limited and that in times of crisis their support may prove less reliable than funding via a stable deposit base – which presupposes the formal status of a licensed deposit-taking bank. Furthermore, an earlier crisis, the Asian financial crisis of 1997/98, already taught the important lesson that appropriate regulation and effective supervision are crucial for any financial institution, and this benefit can best be achieved if MFIs are formal banks or other licensed deposit-taking financial institutions.

The new microfinance or small business banks that started to become important players in microfinance during the 1990s and before were all meant to have two features in common: Firstly, they should be target group-oriented, that is, they should focus their activities on a clientele of small businesses and relatively poor people in general who formerly did not have access to financial services from existing banks. And secondly, they should pursue the dual objective of achieving a substantial social and developmental impact and at the same time operating as stable and profitable enterprises. In other words, they would have to be profit-oriented but not profit-maximizing. Profit making should not be their only objective. The burning question was what legal and institutional forms, what legal regime and what ownership structures were available to banks with a social and developmental mission, and which of them would best facilitate the provision of microfinance services?

1.3 The relevance of savings banks and cooperative banks

Evidently, there are several institutional forms with various possible ownership and governance structures that can be considered for microfinance and small business finance. Among the financial institutions that have always pursued a dual objective and that were at one time created with intentions quite close to those that inspired the creation of MFIs over the past 40 years, two are particularly noteworthy: savings banks and cooperative banks. J.D. Von Pischke (2009), an early advocate of microfinance and the commercial approach, started a recent state-of-the-art survey article with the following words:

---

11 The lawmakers in Indonesia had anticipated this lesson when they passed a law on rural banks in 1988 which barred local microfinance banks (BPR) under central bank regulation and supervision from accepting foreign investments.

Microfinance has developed steadily and rapidly over the past 20 years. Its antecedents include cooperative and community endeavors in Germany and elsewhere in Europe. Today these institutions and their offspring around the world continue to provide a large volume of credit and other financial services to households and tiny businesses. These inspirations are reflected in the objectives of microfinance, which include the use of credit and savings to create better lives for the poor and others of modest means, and a certain style of leadership by activists and social entrepreneurs.

Interestingly, Von Pischke not only mentions the tradition of German savings banks and cooperative banks of being "dual bottom line" institutions, with both a financial and a developmental and social mission, but also the specific leadership and governance features of these institutions. Therefore it seems highly appropriate that we intend to analyze in this study whether savings banks or cooperative banks may be suitable legal and institutional forms for microfinance vehicles. Of course, this question cannot be answered with a simple yes or no. We therefore discuss which of their features might be worth incorporating into the design of MFIs. For this purpose, we try to systematically determine whether lessons for the design and management of today's MFIs – and if so, what lessons – might be drawn from the history of savings and cooperative banks in Germany and other parts of Europe during the so-called long 19th century. Their history will be described in detail in Chapter II, and lessons will be derived there and developed in more detail in the concluding chapter of this study, Chapter IV. As we will point out in Chapter III, which covers current developments in microfinance, there have already been numerous adaptations of the German models in many parts of the developing world.

Analyzing the possible role of savings and cooperative banks as they emerged in Germany in the 19th century as a model, or at least as a source of inspiration, presupposes a precise notion of what constitutes a savings bank and a cooperative bank. As we will show in more detail in Chapter III, establishing a precise definition turns out to be a challenge, especially in the case of savings banks. Suffice to say here that both savings banks and cooperative banks in Germany are formal financial institutions that share four main features:

1. They are locally rooted financial institutions with a high degree of local autonomy.
2. They are "inclusive" institutions in that they cater to broad segments of the population, including those who may have, or at least had, serious problems of access to the well-established, privately owned and predominantly profit-oriented banks.
3. They pursue a dual objective which includes being profitable as business enterprises and at the same time promoting the welfare and business success of their clients and the local area they cater for.

4. They are members of close networks of similar institutions, which enables them to combine the advantages of scale and of decentralization in a very specific way.

1.4 Conclusions and consequences

Irrespective of all definitional problems, we conclude and summarize this introductory section with the following statements and indicate our conclusions for the structure of our study:

1. Modern microfinance has evolved over the last 40 years as a promising option in the field of development and development policy.
2. Modern microfinance started about 40 years ago in a modest way and was initially driven by high ambitions of poverty alleviation. However, the early MFIs hardly achieved the scale and the efficiency of operations that would permit significant outreach and impact.
3. This started to change with the advent of the so-called commercial approach to microfinance. As part of this approach, a number of MFIs were converted into licensed and regulated banks or were even started as banks, and this conversion had very positive consequences for the clients that the institutions aspired to benefit.
4. However, the institutional form of a formal bank can also have drawbacks, especially if a microfinance bank is a corporation with private owners who are mainly or even exclusively interested in the profit generated by the bank as a business enterprise.
5. Therefore, it seems appropriate to investigate the potential of savings banks, defined broadly, and cooperative banks – or at least certain features and aspects of these types of banks – to serve as models or at least as a source of inspiration for designing and managing MFIs in developing countries and supporting them in the framework of foreign and international cooperation, as is the purpose of this study.

The structure of this study is based on these considerations. The topic of the next chapter is an account of the history of savings banks and cooperative banks in Germany in the course of the extended 19th century, that is, from the late 18th century, when the first savings banks were founded, to the beginning of World War I in 1914.

Chapter III is dedicated to modern microfinance and its potential and challenges. It starts with a brief classification of the various institutional forms of MFIs. We then present a series of detailed case studies giving examples of informal finance arrangements, local savings-led institutions, financial cooperatives, and banks focused on serving relatively poor people and small and very small businesses.

1.4 Conclusions and consequences

The chapter continues with a critical look at the various data sources available with regard to microfinance and inclusive finance and their main messages, and it concludes with a section on microfinance as a field of international aid and co-operation.

In Chapter IV we offer a brief summary and outline a set of tentative policy conclusions as to how microfinance should best be supported. The conclusions are, of course, based on our account of history in Chapter II, as well as on the lessons that can be derived from the case studies in Chapter III. They lead us to the overarching question that has motivated this study: Are savings banks and cooperative financial institutions suitable institutional forms for providing financial services to broad segments of the population in the less developed parts of the world, and if so, how and under what conditions can and should they be supported in the context of international cooperation?

2 Basic definitions

2.1 Why precise definitions are desirable but difficult to provide

For any serious study, it is important to clarify to the greatest extent possible the meaning of the most important terms used in the study. Up to this point, we have left the definition of some key terms to the imagination and intuition of our readers, assuming that they have some idea of what the terms savings bank, cooperative financial institution or cooperative bank, and MFI mean and that these ideas are largely the same for most readers. In an introduction, this use of vague and undefined terms is appropriate, but at some point it is necessary to be more precise; and we have now arrived at that point.

In general, definitions are rules for the use of language. In the social sciences, definitions have a dual role. They specify to what object a term refers, and they contain an element of description of the phenomena to which they refer. A given definition may be better for one role and not as good for the other. A way out of this dilemma is to be explicit in distinguishing between narrower and broader definitions and to be as explicit as possible concerning what the descriptive content of a term shall be and which aspect of a phenomenon it is intended to evoke. Since, in the context of this study, the classes of phenomena to which the terms refer are heterogeneous, one is well advised to characterize *types* of phenomena. For instance, one can speak of a typical cooperative institution, implying that there are other financial institutions that may in some respect differ from the prototypical cooperative institution, but that also belong to the broader class of cooperative financial institutions.

The problem of establishing precise definitions of the terms used in this study results from the fact that the common use is in constant flux. And there are two reasons for this. One is that the phenomena to which terms refer change over time. To illustrate, take the terms "microfinance institution" and "savings bank". The organizations which we call MFIs today are vastly different from those called MFIs 30 years ago. To give just two examples: the MFI FINCA of today is a large international group of companies that hardly resembles the small local institutions such as ADEMI, an MFI founded with substantial support from USAID in the Dominican Republic in 1983. Should the term microfinance institution only be used for those organizations that resemble the old ADEMI of 1983, or should its meaning be broadened to also cover large international organizations like FINCA in 2010 or Banco ADEMI of today? And should the term savings bank be defined narrowly, so that it only reflects what is still called a savings bank in Germany today, or should it be defined in a much broader way?

The second reason is that there are differences relating to the local perspective and the cultural backgrounds of different readers and users of language. A financial cooperative in present-day India differs from one in 19th-century France, and the same term may evoke vastly different ideas in an Indian and a French reader.

Narrow definitions have the advantage of being more precise and also quite descriptive. But they have the drawback of often failing to capture the broader class of phenomena to which the speaker or author wishes to refer. For example, there are cases in which the speaker might wish to make a statement about a broad class of savings banks. This would require having a correspondingly broad definition of the term savings bank. But such a definition may then be so broad and so unspecific that it is not clear what is covered by it and what is not.

Changes in the use of terms and the phenomena that they designate, as well as changes in the contextual background which terminology reflects, are important. This is why we go beyond mere definitions of terms in this section on several occasions. With these caveats in mind, we now present working definitions for certain important terms used in this study and supplement them with brief basic descriptions of the phenomena they designate and the context they reflect.

2.2 Terms that need to be defined

(1) Microfinance. As it is commonly used, the term microfinance refers to activities that aspire to make financial services available to people of relatively limited income and wealth and business undertakings of limited size and complexity. An additional feature of the clients or customers or beneficiaries of microfinance is that they would not have access to financial services from existing, established banks if microfinance were not available.

Microfinance encompasses the following: loans of small denominations to certain client groups, known as microloans; savings facilities for small deposit amounts, known as microsavings; money transfer services; and microinsurance. What size categories define loans, savings, and insurance as "micro" depends on the conditions of time and place.

In a narrower sense, one can define microfinance as financial services for very small and small businesses or as microenterprise finance, thus excluding consumer lending from the concept. But even though consumer finance for poor people has recently earned a bad reputation for being irresponsible and exploitative and for being used by the clients for "unnecessary" consumption expenditures[12], one should not throw the baby out with the bathwater and stigmatize consumer finance as being generally less valuable than small business finance. It has always

---

12 Though it may be problematic in general to label consumption expenditures as unnecessary, there are egregious examples which are beyond any doubt. Zeitinger (2008) cited the example of a Ukrainian bank that advertised on TV by showing a man next to his Porsche and a woman in an elegant fur coat as clients of the bank who were able to fulfill their wishes by taking out a microloan.

been a function of finance to smooth out income over time, and enabling this income smoothing is by all standards a socially and economically valuable function of finance.[13]

In search of a definition, David Roodman (2012: 75, 76) rightly states that "[d]efining the boundaries of microfinance turns out to be surprisingly difficult," and continues by stating that "microfinance is by and large that which connects rich-country donors and investors with poor-country clients" and adding that "[T]he most famous form of microfinance entails making loans to small groups of people, usually women". This is intuitive and plausible, but much too narrow, as it does not cover savings or any other components of microfinance, and it is certainly not what was originally meant by the term. When what is now called microfinance was "invented" as a form of development aid around 40 years ago, the narrow definition was largely appropriate, since at that time, and for some 20 years thereafter, the focus was almost exclusively on small and very small loans. In retrospect, we now call this "microcredit".

The term microfinance, which was coined in 1990 and first publicly used in 1991,[14] was introduced with the aim of highlighting the fact that microfinance is more than microcredit. The widespread adoption of the term indicates a paradigm shift that was getting underway at that time. There were two dimensions to this shift: from "credit delivery only" to financial intermediation between savers and borrowers, and from mostly unsustainable providers of microcredit (such as credit-granting NGOs and development banks) relying on donor and government funds to self-reliant institutions which mobilize their own resources to a large extent locally and from private sources, and allocate them to their local customers in the form of loans.

In a much broader sense, the term microfinance is used to refer not only to financial services provided to people of low wealth and income by MFIs, but also to finance[15] or financial activity undertaken and organized by the local people themselves, for instance in the form of self-help groups (SHGs) or informal finance.

(2) Inclusive finance. In recent years, this term has been introduced to replace the term microfinance. To the best of our knowledge, it was first used in 2004 by CGAP (CGAP 2004: VIII) and has gained widespread acceptance since that time.

---

13 The role of microfinance for income smoothing and stabilization has rightly been emphasized in numerous publications of the International Food Policy Research Institute (IFPRI), see for example Zeller (1999) and Meyer and Zeller (2002).
14 See Seibel (1991) and also Seibel (1996a, 2006).Vogel's paper on "Savings Mobilization: The Forgotten Half of Rural Finance" from 1984 served as an inspiration for the "invention" of the new term (Vogel 1984).
15 *Finance*, the main component of the term microfinance, refers to operations and decisions regarding the allocation of scarce resources (money, labor, grain, livestock) at different points in time. This includes savings accumulation and deferred investment, credit and deferred savings to repay the loan, aspects of risk management and payment operations. Many financial operations are monetary transactions, though this is not part of the definition.

CGAP noted: "The term 'inclusive financial systems' refers to the integration of microfinance into formal financial systems to ensure permanent access to financial services by significant numbers of poor people." A joint publication of CGAP and IFC contains a more precise definition: "Financial inclusion refers to a state in which all working-age adults have effective access to credit, savings, payments, and insurance from formal service providers" (Ardic et al. 2012:3).

Once more, the change of terminology marks a change of policy, in this case abandoning the former narrow focus of CGAP and most donor organizations on unregulated providers of microfinance services in the form of NGOs that were largely disconnected from the general financial system. On the very first page of its 2003 annual report, CGAP presented its vision of how microfinance should develop in line with the change in terminology: "The term 'microfinance' will no longer be necessary as we remove the walls – real and imaginary – that separate the microfinance community from the much broader world of financial systems, markets, and development." However, this is not meant to signal a demise of the social and developmental mission that the activity now referred to as inclusive finance pursues. Consequently, CGAP's next five-year strategy, 2014–2018, is entitled *Advancing Financial Inclusion to Improve the Lives of the Poor*.

There does not seem to be an ideal and unambiguous term. This also applies to the understanding of inclusive finance: Its initial focus was on a narrowly defined target group, such as women and the poor, that was to be "included" or no longer left out, but excluding other market segments such as men and the non-poor. We call this narrow concept *discriminatory inclusive finance*. In contrast, *non-discriminatory inclusive finance* refers to access to finance for all without any bias, but of course including the poor and their businesses as well as the businesses of the non-poor who do not have access to "normal" banks.

For the purpose of our study, this change of terminology is welcome, since "non-discriminatory inclusive finance" has for a long time been what savings banks and cooperative banks have aspired to offer. However, in our understanding this is already implied in the term microfinance. Therefore, in the following, we will nevertheless use both terms as equivalent as long as doing so does not lead to misunderstanding.

(3) Financial institutions. Financial institutions are organizations that specialize in providing financial services to other elements of an economy. The most important and best-known type of financial institution is the *bank*, defined as a financial institution which offers deposit and credit facilities and payment or money transfer services, which typically has access to a central bank, and which is subject to regulation and supervision by the competent national authorities. Other types of financial institutions include insurance companies, leasing firms, investment and pension funds and many more. They are *non-bank financial institutions* which are not subject to banking regulation, but rather to other regulatory regimes. *Credit-*

granting NGOs, which play an important role in microfinance, are either non-bank financial institutions or completely unregulated institutions. In most countries, savings banks and cooperative banks are banks in the sense defined above, while in others they are non-bank financial institutions.

(4) Microfinance institutions. This term designates financial institutions that specialize in providing microfinance services. Some MFIs are stand-alone institutions, some are parts, for example subsidiaries or divisions, of larger financial institutions, and some belong to international networks or groups of MFIs. Some MFIs are licensed as banks, while others are not. Accordingly, for some MFIs the range of products and services is more restricted, for instance to lending, i.e. they are credit-delivery-only institutions, while others are "universal banks"[16] for small businesses and their owners and other people of limited means.

While it is easy to characterize a typical MFI, it is almost impossible to draw a dividing line between organizations that are MFIs and others that are not, even though they may be strongly dedicated to offering their services to people who would hardly be welcomed as clients of most private banks in their countries. To what extent must a financial institution be specialized in providing microfinance in order to qualify as an MFI? How high must the share of microloans in the loan portfolio be, and how small do small loans or small businesses have to be for a "real" MFI? For purposes of the present study, the precise delineation of MFIs seems to be of some relevance, because it is not clear whether one can classify the cooperative and savings banks of today as MFIs. But perhaps this question is irrelevant as long as it is accepted that in the 19th century these institutions were definitely what one today would call MFIs.

(5) Related terms such as *microbanks* refer to MFIs set up as licensed and supervised banks. In keeping with the spirit of inclusive finance, a number of banks that were formerly almost exclusively focused on a clientele of poor people and very small businesses have recently turned to serving smaller mid-sized firms as well, and some have even decided to discard the terms microfinance and microfinance bank for themselves. One group now calls its member institutions "neighborhood banks".[17]

(6) Savings banks. Defining savings banks is a real challenge, because today the features of financial institutions that are called savings banks (or something similar) differ enormously between countries and in some cases even within a country.[18] Formerly this was not the case. Only some 30 years ago, the savings banks

---

16 The term universal banks is used here to emphasize the difference to financial institutions that only provide loans or only deposit and payment facilities. In the general finance literature, it is used for banks that provide at the same time both commercial banking services and capital market related services. Evidently, this broader notion is not relevant in the context of microfinance.
17 Namely the ProCredit Banks, which we will discuss at greater length in Chapter III.
18 If one looks at the list of members of the World Savings Bank Institute, an organization that represents savings banks serving the general public, this diversity or heterogeneity becomes obvious.

in most Western European countries had the following features that characterized them as a special type of institution and that clearly set them apart from other financial institutions:

- They were public institutions set up and monitored by a state, city, county, or region.
- They had a mandate to support the local economy and to foster social cohesion.
- They had a limited profit orientation and the dual objective of being financially successful banks and of contributing to general welfare at the same time.
- In many cases, they were legally independent, locally rooted and locally active institutions that were nevertheless embedded in national networks of similar institutions.
- For historical and other reasons they emphasized the importance of savings for their clients and of deposit mobilization for themselves.

Over the course of the past 20 years, most national savings bank systems in Europe have been transformed substantially. In some cases, savings banks were privatized, some were integrated into one single national bank, and others even disappeared completely. Some are no longer part of networks, and some even no longer declare that they have a dual mission and are committed to furthering the common welfare[19] Nevertheless, what we have described above is still the prototype of a European savings bank. Interestingly, the German savings bank system is the only one in Europe that today still exhibits all of the features listed above and is at the same time fairly successful and an important element of the German banking system. These two features make it particularly interesting to take a very close look at how German savings banks emerged and developed in the 19th century, as we will in the next chapter of our study.

There have always been some financial institutions, such as postal savings banks, that call themselves savings banks, yet show only some of these characteristics of a "typical" savings bank. This is true of the former British savings bank[20] and of the Japanese Postal Savings Bank, for instance. The latter, like the British savings bank during its period of operation, is a large centralized institution that is hardly involved in granting loans at all and instead channels the funds it collects to the national treasury, by investing in government bonds, or to other banks, which use them for their lending operations.

In many developing countries, the institutions called savings banks or postal savings banks do not conform to the traditional model of decentralized and locally rooted institutions that used to exist in continental Europe, but rather follow the British (and Japanese) model of being government-controlled centralized institutions and de facto "small denomination retailers" of government debt.

---

19 For a comparative view of how savings banks have developed in various European countries over the course of the past 20 years, see Bülbül et al. (2013).
20 This institution, known as Trustee Savings Bank (TSB), was sold to Lloyds Banking Group in 1995.

Therefore it is impossible to provide a common characterization that both describes savings banks well and at the same time sets them apart from other banks, apart from their features of openness to the general public and a special focus on savings and deposit taking. When we use the term savings bank in the following, we tend to refer to typical savings banks as they used to be in continental Europe some years ago. Where this is not appropriate, we instead use another term: savings-based or savings-led institution, since it is closest to what most readers can be assumed to think when they read the term savings bank.

In contrast to widespread perceptions in the microfinance community, the most popular forms of microfinance are *savings-based institutions*, ranging from millions of informal institutions and large numbers of financial cooperatives all over the world to the microbanking units of BRI in Indonesia, with some 25 million active deposit accounts and 5.5 million loan accounts (2012), the Postal Savings Bank of China (PSBC) with 478 million depositors (2014) and a rapidly expanding credit business since 2008, and vast numbers of other savings-led institutions, large and small, non-profit or for-profit. In a very broad sense of the term, they are all savings banks.

(7) Cooperative financial institutions. These are institutions with the legal form of a bank or of a special financial institution, commonly called credit unions in the English-speaking world, whose common characteristic is that there is, at least to a certain extent, an identity of owners and customers. This so-called "principle of identity" means that, in the legal and institutional form of a cooperative, the customers are the owners and, conversely, it is only, or at least mainly, the owners who can be customers of the institution. It is generally assumed among adherents of the cooperative concept that as a consequence of this "principle of identity," each owner – typically called a member – has only one vote in the regular meetings of members or owners, irrespective of the number of shares held, and in most countries this one-person-one vote rule is also an essential part of the laws and regulations pertaining to cooperatives. Thus the defining feature of cooperative or mutual banks is their ownership and governance structure. We will later discuss the implications of this structure in greater detail.[21]

Almost without exception, cooperative financial institutions are largely decentralized and locally rooted. Like the prototypical savings banks, most of them are a part of more or less complex networks of related institutions. This network structure allows them to benefit from economies of scale in certain banking operations. In contrast to the savings banks, most European cooperative banking systems have largely retained their traditional structure, even though they have also been transformed to some extent recently.

---

21 See section 3.3.

In developing countries cooperative finance is widespread. Its manifestations range from millions of informal cooperatives to modern semi-formal cooperatives that can be classified as non-bank financial institutions, or even as completely formal cooperative banks. The modern cooperatives in developing countries have been introduced by Western missionaries, advisors and development aid organizations, as is often the case in Africa, or they have at least been inspired by models from Western countries, as for instance in India, a case that we will take up at greater length in Chapter III.

Since this study focuses on savings banks and cooperative banks, we will provide later on, in Chapter II, a table with a list of features that shows the differences and commonalities between these two types of financial institutions (Table 13).

(8) Socially-oriented banks, social banks or alternative banks. We also use these summary terms to designate the class of financial institutions which share the features of being set up and run with the intention of providing financial services to small and very small businesses and their owners and other people of limited means, who are not regarded as desirable clients by established private banks, and of not being exclusively profit-oriented. This class of institutions comprises savings banks, cooperative banks, most development finance institutions, and some other public banks with a special mandate to foster social inclusion and to promote economic development and the public welfare. Truly private banks are typically not part of this class, since most of them are purely for-profit institutions and/or they only offer services to established or even wealthy clients. However, there are exceptions to this rule. Some banks are private in terms of their ownership and governance structure but at the same time subscribe to a developmental or social mission. This hybrid form can occasionally be found in developed economies and is quite frequent in the world of microfinance.

(9) Microfinance providers is an even broader term which, in addition to the institutions listed above, also includes non-specialized NGOs and non-specialized government agencies that provide financial services to broad segments of the population.

3 The broader context of social and development-oriented banking

The general and overarching purpose of our historically-based and interdisciplinary study is to look at savings banks and cooperative banks in Germany and, to a limited extent, in other European countries during the process of industrialization and at similar organizations in today's developing world in order to gain insights that will allow better solutions to today's problem of designing, managing, regulating, and supporting MFIs. The specific purpose of this section is to reflect our search for issues that we will address as recurrent and overarching themes in the following chapters, and thus establish a list of the main general propositions that we want to formulate and examine in our study.

3.1 How new forms of financial institutions emerge and survive

The questions of how new institutions or new types or forms of institutions come into existence, and why they remain in existence over a long period of time, are clearly important ones in the case of the three types of institutions that this study primarily addresses, i.e. savings banks, cooperative banks and other types of MFIs. After all, savings banks have been in existence for around 200 years, cooperative financial institutions for more than 150 years and other types of MFIs for some 40 years. This calls for an explanation.

The emergence of new institutional forms typically results from two main causes or factors and also their interaction, i.e. both of them must be present in parallel. The first factor is the demand for institutions that solve certain problems, typically problems that are themselves novel. The second is the political and ideological or intellectual developments of the time which make it possible to devise a given institutional response to the need and/or opportunity.

This was the case in Europe when, starting in the late 18th century, the traditional agrarian economies of Northwestern Europe became industrialized. This process was accompanied by severe socioeconomic problems and migration to urban centers. It was a multilayered process that took around 100 years. Savings banks and credit cooperatives came into being as a means of cushioning the negative impact of these radical changes.

As will be described in greater detail in the next chapter, the first German savings banks were founded around 1800, a time that was shaped by the existential problems of the feudal *Ancien Régime* and the French Revolution and their political repercussions in Germany. The events in France fostered the awareness among politically minded people that there were indeed social and political problems that needed to be addressed by various means, including the creation of financial institutions for the "lower classes".

Cooperative banking in Germany started around 1850. Here as well, a situation had arisen in which acute socio-economic problems coincided with a window of opportunity. In the late 1840s, the last major period of famine in Germany affected large parts of the country's rural areas, while the growing urban population engaged in petty trade and commerce or working in the skilled trades suffered from the rising industrialization. This coincided with a wave of political activism associated with the brief episode of bourgeois revolution in 1848. The creation of the first cooperative financial institutions was, politically and ideologically, a timely response to an acute problem.

The situation in many developing countries at the time when modern microfinance first started was to some extent similar. Migration to urban centers, the transformation of society and the economy and the manifestations of globalization created enormous problems of unemployment and poverty and scope for political radicalism. Something had to be done, and microfinance was conceived as a means of combating poverty and of creating employment for poor people in the fast-growing slums on the outskirts of big cities in the so-called Third World.

The political situation of the time was conducive to the beginnings of microfinance for various reasons. Most importantly, the end of colonial regimes in several parts of the world and the end of the Vietnam War made it urgent from the perspective of Western countries to win over people's hearts and minds and, motivated by a combination of bad conscience and the need to provide compensation, to devise forms of development aid that directly – and visibly – addressed the needs of the poor people. Large-scale development funding, which had dominated development aid in the preceding years, was no longer politically acceptable, since experience had shown that if it spurred development and growth at all, it typically led to dualistic development.[22]

The change in development policy was ushered in by the famous Nairobi speech, in 1973, of Robert McNamara, then President of the World Bank and formerly Secretary of Defense of the US, in which he declared "the end of trickle-down" and called for direct poverty-related aid strategies. Early microfinance, in the form of microcredit, fitted this concept perfectly. Only a few years later the deregulation of the financial systems in most of Latin America and some other parts of the world and the free market ideology of the Reagan–Thatcher era lent support to the spread of microfinance as a new concept of development finance that was at the same time poverty-oriented and business-oriented – and that largely bypassed host country governments.[23]

Of course, explaining why certain institutional innovations occur at a given time by showing that they can be regarded as a response to an urgent and serious prob-

---

[22] The well-known exceptions to this general rule are South Korea and Taiwan. For a harsh critique of the older form of development aid, see Easterly (2001).
[23] For details, see Schmidt (2010).

lem or crisis, combined with a specific political situation and powerful ideological trends, is not enough to allow an understanding of why some new institutional forms subsequently survive and even prosper for many years. For this purpose, it is necessary to show that they have survival value as institutions, which means that they provide certain services in a way that leads their clients and those providing funding, labor, and other necessary resources to remain committed to them; that they are not swept away by the competition; and that they are able to withstand crises and adapt to changing conditions. The survival aspect will also be the focus of later chapters.

3.2 The role of the state and other "third parties"

The second topic that comes up time and again in our discussion of socially-oriented banking is the role of governments, states and other "third parties". The term "third parties" refers to entities or people who do not belong to the target population served by MFIs or banks. Their role in the emergence and development of poverty-oriented and "inclusive" financial institutions is important by any standard. It would be naïve to assume that financial institutions that serve relatively poor people are simply manifestations of market developments emerging spontaneously under the pressure of market forces.

In the case of savings banks, this is self-evident, since in most cases savings banks are public institutions. They are almost always created by public sector entities, most of them are in some sense publicly owned, and in some cases, such as that of the German savings banks, they operate under a public law regime. Irrespective of the details, which vary considerably from case to case, savings banks always have close ties to state or municipal authorities.

Third parties are also important for cooperative, i.e. member-owned financial institutions, at least if one disregards ROSCAs and other forms of informal finance. In Germany and other European countries, the early financial cooperatives were founded by socially minded and well-intentioned citizens as institutions intended to support and benefit others – the poor and less educated, or, as one might call them today, the target population. An active role on the part of third parties has remained a feature of the governance structure and the business model of most financial cooperatives.

In almost all developing countries as well, cooperative finance has been introduced by the respective governments, by benevolent, educated and relatively wealthy citizens or missionaries, by development aid organizations and their staff, or by cooperative organizations from other countries.

Finally, almost all of the so-called MFIs we observe today are the result of third party activity and initiative. Modern microfinance in developing countries is mainly a brainchild of development aid, raised on foreign funding and foreign technical expertise and supported by foreign experts. In fact, the very concept of microfinance has been imported into most host countries by international or foreign national donor organizations or consultants hired by these organizations. Even if there were some local roots on which MFIs were built, the bulk of the support needed to make them grow into efficient organizations has typically come from foreign sources.

Third party intervention was also behind the creation and the subsequent growth of several well-known modern MFIs that appear to be homegrown. One example is the famous Grameen Bank. Even though he is a native of Bangladesh, in terms of social background and education Muhammad Yunus, the founder of Grameen Bank and a former economics professor, certainly does not belong to the poor classes in his country. Similarly, the bankers, public administrators, and foreign advisors who helped Bank Rakyat Indonesia (BRI) transform its former village units into commercially operated microbanking units were not members of the target population of the BRI Unit system. One of the early MFIs in Latin America, Fundación Carvajal in Colombia, was created by a scion of one of the richest industrialist families of that country. In a sense, all of these founders of MFIs had roles and ideas similar to those of the bankers, wealthy farmers, public servants, pastors, and doctors who helped to set up savings and cooperative banks in 19th century Germany.

Third parties are important not only for the creation of MFIs but also for their growth and development and their survival as institutions. Their role consists to some extent in continual funding and the provision of expertise, but even more so in monitoring the institutions and safeguarding their integrity. Likewise, the role of states and governments is important, as they must provide the legal and financial infrastructure that MFIs need: an appropriate legal framework within which they can operate; regulation and supervision to assure their proper functioning; and a safety net which will be accessible to them when needed. Providing this infrastructure is clearly a function of states and their governments and parliaments.

The involvement of third parties can also have negative effects, and experience has shown that this is quite frequently the case. Relying on the support of foreign or other donors and supporters tends to weaken the incentives for local people to help themselves and to assume responsibility. For instance, in a number of cases massive foreign funding has dulled the incentives to grant loans with due caution and only to those who are able and willing to repay, or to put sufficient effort into the mobilization of local savings.[24] In some cases, for example in cooperative systems in Africa and Asia, substantial inflows of foreign funds have undermined the morale and the coherence of complex local cooperative financial systems, since

---

[24] The classic account of these negative effects is the collection of essays in Adams, Graham and Von Pischke's appropriately titled book *Undermining Rural Development with Cheap Credit* from 1984.

control over foreign funds typically resides with higher-level organizations such as cooperative associations and weakens the role of the local cooperatives and their members.[25] Moreover, ample external funding may prevent MFIs from evolving from mere distributors of credit, as many of them are in the beginning, into true financial intermediaries, which is what they should strive to become. The long and sad history of many development banks that never bothered to mobilize deposits illustrates this danger well. Interestingly, there was no significant state funding for savings banks and cooperative banks in 19th century Europe.

Ongoing state support can be particularly problematic. The development of cooperatives in India, originally self-financed during the first decades of the 20th century, is a good example, which we will present as a case study in Chapter III. When state governments started providing funds to the cooperatives on a massive scale, they ruined what had previously been a vibrant and healthy system. The general reason for caution is that governments very rarely provide support without expecting some form of influence and power in return, and they may well be inclined to use their power to abuse local financial systems for political purposes such as influencing who receives loans, imposing loan forgiveness programs, and appointing political allies to influential positions. In such cases, what first appears to be a giving hand easily turns into a grabbing hand.

3.3 The art of financial institution building

The next general and overarching topic concerns the institutional design of financial institutions that have the mandate or mission to serve the lower end of the market: What are the design features of good MFIs?

Over time, various institutional forms are "invented" that exhibit quite different features. However, sooner or later, those that are not suited to fulfill their functions tend to disappear again. In a certain sense, the process of elimination and thus the "selection for survival" of institutional forms is based on competition in a broad sense, which refers equally to hard facts such as costs and revenues, efficiency and profits, and to aspects such as the ability to garner ongoing support, political patronage and the like. Institutional forms can also lose their relevance when they are no longer adopted by newly created organizations or when existing organizations change their legal and institutional form, as has happened in the case of MFIs that converted from NGOs to corporations.[26]

Scholars who follow the new institutional economics approach to the study of institutions[27] explain observable features of existing institutions by showing that

---

25 For an illustration see the study of a cooperative financial system in Burkina Faso in Gounot (2001).
26 These changes are described and assessed in Nair and Von Pischke (2007).
27 For a general overview of the new institutional economics approach, see Furubotn and Richter (2005).

these features enable an institution to fulfill its functions and demonstrating how and in what specific sense they do so, assuming that institutions that have remained in existence for some time have explicitly been designed with a view to their functionality, even though this assumption may be simply wrong.[28]

So what makes a specific form of MFI successful and able to survive? The answer depends on a number of factors. One of them is the overarching function that such an institution is supposed to perform. As discussed above, MFIs have typically been created with the objective or mission of generating benefits for their clients, that is, for people other than those who have created them. An institutional-economics analysis of MFIs[29] is based on the insight that, like any other organizations[30], they are organizations to which many people are related in various capacities: as borrowers and depositors, as lenders, as employees, as managers, and owners or members of a supervisory board or some similar body. All of these so-called stakeholders have to make decisions, and taken together these decisions are the determinants of success or failure.

It is important to understand that all stakeholders have a certain freedom in deciding how they play their respective roles given that perfect control is impossible, in an MFI even more so than in most other organizations.

For an institution to achieve lasting success, clients must decide to become and remain clients and, if they take out loans, must be willing and able to repay them; staff members must perform their respective functions carefully and diligently; managers must be able and willing to provide leadership and to work hard; depositors and other lenders must be willing to entrust their money to the institution; members of the supervisory body must take their monitoring role seriously; and finally, equity providers or those in a similar position must accept the risk and reward structure that the institution offers. If everyone did what he or she was expected to do, any institution would most likely prosper, irrespective of its institutional design. But assuming that everyone will perform perfectly, out of a sense of duty and fairness, or simply because they wish to, would be unrealistic.

Standard economic theory assumes that by and large, most people are acting in their own interests, that they are dishonest, unfair and uncooperative, and that they will behave accordingly if this serves their purposes. Depositors and lenders are fickle and might withdraw their funds at will and at inconvenient times,

---

[28] Alchian (1950) discusses the applicability of the Darwinian concept of "natural selection" to the study of institutions and argues that institutional forms can be analyzed by invoking the (counterfactual) assumption that they have explicitly been designed with a view to their "survival value".

[29] The following argument was first developed in Schmidt and Tschach (2002), who, following Fama and Jensen (1983), analyze "microfinance [institutions] as networks of incentives".

[30] Here we use the terms "institutions" and "organizations" in the everyday sense of these words. In the relevant academic literature, the meaning of these two terms is not the same. For North (1991) and others, who make a terminological distinction, "organizations" are complex organizational forms (or institutions in the colloquial sense) such as firms or governments or MFIs, whereas the term "institutions" refers to building blocks such as rules or incentive systems.

or refrain from lending in the first place. Once they have received their loans, many borrowers will avoid repaying on time or even at all if they can get away with it. Once they have a job in an MFI, staff members, managers, and even board members might prefer to put in less time and effort than they are expected to provide; loan officers might choose to issue loans to their unreliable buddies rather than to those who should receive them. And finally, owners or those making strategic decisions might be inclined to turn away from a difficult-to-serve clientele in favor of serving other client groups and extracting as much profit or other private benefit from the institution as they can. Again, the outcome of this behavior is easy to predict: An institution would certainly fail.

Comparing the good and the bad extreme scenarios, one thing can be seen: When others are performing their respective roles well, it seems to be more attractive for everyone to do the same; and if everyone else is acting in an uncooperative manner, it is more likely that any one individual will do the same. Therefore, behavioral patterns that prevail in organizations are interdependent.

However, this is not the whole story. Organizations are not the passive victims of how people affiliated with them choose to behave. Instead, they have a wide spectrum of options to influence the behavior of those with whom they work and on whom they depend. They can design and implement rules, define decision rights, provide rewards and apply sanctions, make information available that encourages cooperative behavior, and instill a sense of responsibility and fairness in all those who belong in some way to the organization or are closely related to it.

The totality of these means of influencing and even shaping behavior is the essence of an organization's institutional structure. Even though there are of course exceptions[31], one can assume that in most cases their own shortsighted interests will make uncooperative behavior appear more attractive to all the individuals involved. Therefore an organization can, and should, try to substitute the short-term incentives not to cooperate with long term incentives that encourage cooperation.

One can easily demonstrate this substitution in the case of MFIs: The almost natural short-term incentives for borrowers not to repay their loans can be counteracted by a more or less explicit promise that borrowers who repay their loans fully and on time will be able to obtain new loans at better terms when they apply for them later; however, for this incentive to function properly, the lending technology must be designed in a suitable way. Loan officers who might be inclined to take a short-term view and provide loans to their unreliable buddies can be given an incentive to perform better if they have good prospects of keeping their jobs or

---

31 The exceptions are people whose behavior is driven by altruism, a sense of fairness or ethical values, or religious convictions, and therefore they may not be all that rare. Recently, economists have started to take account of these behavioral patterns, which conventional economic theory has largely ignored. For an overview, see Fehr and Gächter (2000).

even of promotion to better jobs; for this incentive to function, human resources policies must be designed in a suitable way. The short-term incentives for managers to shirk their duties can also be counteracted by good and reliable prospects of long-term employment and advancement, and potentially lazy board members can be induced to take their role seriously if being a board member of a successful and respected organization adds to their social standing. Finally, the short-term incentive for owners to extract as much profit from the institution as possible can be counteracted by creating the expectation that keeping equity in the institution will be more attractive in the long run.

This is more than a list of examples; it is the simplified description of an incentive system – or an institutional design – whose elements are interrelated and complement each other: If the lending policy does indeed offer incentives to borrowers to pay back their loans properly and if loan default rates are therefore low, the work of the loan officers is more attractive and they will be more inclined to take a long-term perspective and to cooperate. If lower-level staff perform well and in accordance with expectations, employment and advancement opportunities for managers are better, and therefore their own incentives to cooperate and perform well are also stronger. If lending operations are sound and staff and management performance is good, it is much more likely that board members will also regard it as rewarding and prestigious to take their roles seriously and to simply do what is expected of them and what benefits the organization; and finally, if things are going well at all levels within the institution, the owners' prospects of benefitting if they do not pull out large amounts of money are also stronger.

Incentive effects are interrelated, both in the positive case of a system of properly aligned incentives and in the negative case in which dysfunctional incentives at one level trigger a vicious circle which makes the whole edifice crumble and break down. As one can also easily see, all of the positive longer-term incentives rely on a common premise: that the institution offers good prospects of surviving economically as an institution. If this condition were not fulfilled, the short-term incentives would retain the upper hand and the institution would indeed find it hard to survive. Thus expectations are to a certain extent self-fulfilling: Positive expectations lead to positive results and vice-versa.

Successful financial institution building is based more than anything else on a proper understanding of how incentives function, how the different incentives used in an organization are related to each other and how they depend on the organization's long-term prospects, and thus on its strategy. This is a general proposition applicable to all organizations.[32] But it is of particular importance for MFIs for two reasons which are specific to microfinance: One of them is the fact that

---

[32] The relevant literature in which this interrelationship is explained and used most notably includes Milgrom and Roberts (1992), Brickley, Smith and Zimmerman (1996/2008) and, for the special case of human resource management, Baron and Kreps (1999).

the creditworthiness of small and very small firms and of poor and often self-employed individuals is difficult to assess, and therefore the performance of loan officers is also difficult to monitor. The second is that the typical MFI is supposed to pursue a dual objective of operating successfully as a business and of benefitting its clients. Having more than one objective opens up room for discretion to management and supervisory boards. Therefore, their performance is also difficult to monitor and assess. Whenever direct monitoring and performance measurement are difficult, proper incentives are all the more important.

As we will later argue, considerations like those presented here also have a direct bearing on the question of what constitutes a suitable ownership and governance structure for MFIs. Since we will have more to say about this at a later point, a few brief and general remarks will suffice at this point.

Among the most important issues in institutional design are who has the right to make high-level decisions and how this right is defined and delimited. Since supreme decision rights are in many cases closely connected with the role of being an owner, the issue of allocating and defining supreme decision rights is closely related to the question of who should be the owner of an MFI.

Supreme decision rights in an MFI, and possibly the role of owner as well, should be assigned in such a way that the institution can achieve its dual objective. Therefore, decision rights and the ownership role should be assigned to people or entities that can be expected to be loyal to the mission of the institution even if circumstances change, and that have the competence and the motivation to act as true and responsible owners who will do what is necessary to strengthen and protect their organization. Ideally, owners should see themselves as trustees of the institution and its clients and should act accordingly.

However, such perfect owners are difficult to find. Therefore, some institutional forms – such as foundations and associations, the legal forms of not-for-profit organizations – do not include the role of owner in their design. To a certain extent, this is also the case for savings banks in some countries, including Germany, where most savings banks are governed by a public law regime in which the role of owner does not exist. Not having owners can be dangerous because it entails the risk that nobody really feels responsible for the organization and its stability and development or will take action when action is needed.

The owners of most cooperatives have very limited powers, which can also be dangerous because it leaves the institution's managers in a strong position, which they might be tempted to abuse. The limitation of the ownership rights of the members of cooperatives derives from two specific features of the cooperatives' ownership and governance structure: (1) In most cases, owner-members are not permitted to sell their shares to other people at a freely determined price which would in some way reflect their economic value. Instead, they can only redeem their shares by giving them back in exchange for the amount of money they invested (plus accumulated profits). And (2) in most cooperatives, owner-members have only one vote in the general assembly, irrespective of how many shares they might own. Taken together, these two features have a positive and a negative consequence. The positive consequence is that there are only weak incentives or possibilities for owner-members to put pressure on a cooperative's management to act in a way that would increase profit *at the expense of economically and socially weaker members*, and therefore the danger that some members will be exploited remains limited, which corresponds to the institutional logic of cooperatives as self-help organizations that also operate in the interest of their weaker members. The concomitant negative consequence of the prohibition on selling shares at their economic value and on accumulating voting rights is that it also gives owner-members only limited incentives and opportunities to sanction a management that does not do a good job, operates without the required care, does not make enough effort, or even abuses its position and acts in its own interests. Owner-members who see that the management is not performing its functions properly do not have an economic incentive to do anything to remedy the deficiency, because they would hardly benefit from having a better management, at least as long as the sheer continued existence of the cooperative is not in jeopardy. And as no member is able to have more than one vote, it would be difficult to vote an incompetent or self-serving management out of office, or even initiate something like a hostile take-over.[33]

Finally, having genuine owners with strong ownership rights might be good for the organization as an institution, because true owners tend to look after their assets and care about the institution's costs, revenues and profits, but here the relevant danger is that these owners might not care about the interests of the target clientele of an MFI.

Which of the three dangers is greatest and has to be given most weight in the design of MFIs is a question for which there is no general answer. In any given case, the answer depends on the specific situation in which an ownership regime has to be determined or assessed and on the way in which the ownership regime, which is a part of an institution's governance system, interacts with the other elements of that system.

From a purely intellectual or political standpoint, this agnostic result may appear disappointing. However, as far as our objective of understanding the potential and the weaknesses of savings banks and cooperative banks as institutional forms of MFIs is concerned, it also holds a positive, encouraging message, for the following

---

33 The argument presented here is explained at greater length in Ayadi et al. (2010: 33 et seq.). But evidently, it applies to (European) public savings banks as well (see Ayadi et al., (2009), pp. 14-30), since economically speaking, (European) savings banks do not have genuine owners but merely trustees. A similar argument pertaining to foundations and associations as the legal forms used by most microfinance NGOs can be found in Schmidt and Zeitinger (1996).

reason: It is quite clear – and will be shown in more detail later – that it is a weakness if institutional forms do not have strong and responsible owners at all or their owners are largely powerless. This deficiency would make savings banks and cooperative banks appear to be bad choices for institutional forms of MFIs. However, if there is no other ownership regime that is a priori better and if the merits of a given ownership regime depend strongly on the entire governance system, then savings banks and cooperative banks may still qualify as good institutional forms for microfinance. Whether and under what conditions this is the case will be discussed in the concluding chapter of our study.

3.4 The objectives of socially-oriented, inclusive financial institutions

Given that socially or developmentally oriented financial institutions, including MFIs, have more than one objective, the following questions arise: How are the different objectives reconciled or weighted, and what is the substance of their social and developmental objectives?[34]

Objectives can be defined on a more general or strategic or on a more operational level, and they can be defined with respect to shorter-term or longer-term horizons. Irrespective of the timeframe involved, there are two objectives that are of strategic relevance for socially-oriented, inclusive financial institutions, namely the social and developmental objective or, as one could also call it, the value that is created for others; and the business-oriented or organizational objective, and thus also the value that is created for the organization itself and for those who provide their resources to the organization. In a long-term perspective, the social and developmental objectives play, or at least should play, the dominant role. Having or being or running a successful business is only a necessary precondition for achieving the overarching objective of creating value for someone. In a short-term perspective, the relative importance of the two objectives is the inverse. Business concerns play the dominant role and determine decisions and actions, and the social and developmental objective only provides an orientation and acts as a constraint with regard to the decisions and actions which can be taken. It is a positive consequence of the shift toward the commercial approach in microfinance, already mentioned briefly above, that the importance of the business objective has been properly understood. In the early years, when MFIs and their leaders and supporters did not bother about cost containment, cost coverage or financial sus-

---

[34] Even though they are often closely related, social and developmental objectives may be distinct. Social objectives consist mainly in helping the poor and those in need, while developmental objectives may refer to creating employment, contributing to the growth of the local economy or improving infrastructure.

tainability, it was rarely acknowledged how important fulfilling the business objective is for the stability and the proper functioning of an MFI.[35]

And what exactly is the content of the social and developmental objective? All participants in the debate seem to agree that socially and developmentally oriented banking should aspire to do two things: to improve the lives of people who are in some sense economically and socially disadvantaged, and to provide access to financial services for those who have not had access before. This was once the aspiration behind the creation of early savings and cooperative banks, and it is the aspiration behind the endeavors in the field of microfinance of today. Beyond this point, disagreements start.

One point of disagreement concerns the question of what defines the so-called target population, i.e. the clientele for whom MFIs are supposed to create benefits. Some argue that ultimately the members of the target population are just "poor people"; and this often goes hand in hand with the claim that microfinance has the strategic objective of lifting poor people out of poverty by granting loans to them. This definition of the target population and of the objective of microfinance activity is rather restrictive; it implies focusing exclusively on "poor people," and it is a rather one-sided, lending-focused definition.

Others argue that the target population of microfinance should be defined more broadly and at least to some extent differently. As far as lending to finance income-generating projects is concerned, it should mainly target very small (or micro), small and not-so-small businesses. Thus, it is the owner of a small village bakery who should receive loans – who is not really poor by local standards, but in many developing countries does not have access to the loans of established conventional banks – and not the really poor part-time sales person working in the bakery. As far as other services, including deposit taking, payment services and emergency loans are concerned, MFIs should simply be "inclusive," an approach that has proven its value in the past in Europe: They should offer their products and services to a broad and general population, but without by any means excluding low-income households, who might not otherwise have access to any kind of banking services or might not be treated respectfully by other banks.

Among the well-known examples of MFIs, Grameen Bank represents the focus on the narrow definition of the target population, while BRI's microbanking unit network adheres to the broader, non-targeted definition.

Why would good microfinance be expected to provide benefits to its target population and especially the poorer strata of society? And what, based on plausible assumptions, should be the immediate or tactical content of the social and developmental objective? For a long time it has been taken for granted that *receiving loans*

---

[35] As we explained in the last section, the incentive system of a good MFI is based on the institution being successful as a business.

is in itself helpful for those whom microfinance serves, including the really poor. The underlying assumption was that poor people would have the ability to put credit to good use. This may indeed be true, even though the empirical evidence on this point is mixed.[36] However, one should not forget that taking out a loan has a negative side: it implies having debt that needs to be repaid, as Dale Adams, one of the grand old men of development finance, has pointed out again and again, criticizing the general euphoria about "credit to the poor". Borrowing money and then spending it unwisely can be disastrous, especially for poor people, as recent events in India and other places have drastically demonstrated. In contrast, the welfare-enhancing effects of other financial services for the poor, notably access to savings facilities, seem to be beyond doubt and are empirically well confirmed.

If one accepts the position of those who have doubts about the direct benefits of loans to really poor people, the question arises as to wherein benefits might lie from their point of view. If loans go to the woman who owns a small village bakery instead of her sales person, she can expand and stabilize her business, produce better bread for the clients, and offer more, and more stable, employment. These are positive direct effects for the borrower, who by Western standards is also quite poor, though perhaps not by local standards, and at the same time yield positive indirect effects for her clients and employees, including those who are really poor by any standard. There is an even more indirect, but no less important economic impact: Steady and reliable access to credit and other financial services for small and medium businesses is a main determinant of economic growth and development, which also tends to benefit the poorer parts of a country's population through job creation and income generation.

Microfinance or inclusive finance can make a difference to the quality of a country's financial system,[37] and as many econometric studies[38] have confirmed, financial sector quality is a major determinant of growth, stability, and economic and social development. The fact that in most countries MFIs at present contribute barely 5 % of total financial sector assets is no contradiction. The field is developing, and development takes time, as can be seen from the history of Germany's savings banks and credit cooperatives, which today have a combined market share of over 50 % of retail business. What makes financial sectors better is that financial

---

[36] Direct evidence that really poor microfinance clients benefit directly from having received a microloan is scarce and unreliable; see Roodman (2012a) for an excellent summary of this debate. The indirect and case-based evidence which is offered in the brochures of most MFIs is not reliable, since individual cases are not representative and reflect the biases of those who present them.

[37] At an early stage of the modern debate about microfinance, Von Pischke (1991) and Jackelen and Rhyne (1991) propagated a "financial systems approach" to microfinance. They argue that microfinance should first and foremost aspire to improve the efficiency and the openness of developing countries' financial sectors. Evidently, this is not in any way a contrasting position to the institution building approach (Krahnen and Schmidt, 1994) and the commercial approach (Otero and Rhyne, 2004), but rather complements it conceptually.

[38] For a very competent and complete overview of these studies, see Levine (2005).

institutions exist, that they are themselves stable and offer access to broad segments of a country's population, that they make responsible lending decisions which take borrowers' debt capacity into account, and that they treat their clients from all social strata fairly and respectfully.

We want to summarize this section by expressing our doubts about the direct benefits of loans to really poor people and thus, by implication, about the objective of poverty alleviation that is so often used in publicity for microfinance. There are in all likelihood also positive effects that help to pull poor people out of abject poverty – or at least prevent them from falling into it – but these are indirect effects which only become visible over a longer time span and are attributable to a multitude of factors. Access to finance is only one of them, and economic growth is probably a more important one. Instead of poverty alleviation, the main objectives of microfinance or, more generally, of socially and developmentally oriented finance should be to improve "democratic" access to finance, strengthen small businesses and their employment-creating capacity and improve financial sector quality.

By ensuring access and fair treatment of clients, a more developed financial sector enables small firms to grow and create more jobs and income, and increases the willingness of their owners to aspire to growth for their businesses. This is because, in the absence of reliable access to finance, many owners of small firms that have the potential to expand would refrain from even aspiring to do so, due to a fear that once their business has grown and its demand for credit has grown as well, they might not get the loans they would then need, and the strategy of growth would turn out to be a costly failure.[39]

---

[39] In a complex formal model that extends the theory of credit rationing put forth by Stiglitz and Weiss (1981) to the case of microfinance, Ingo Tschach (2002) has shown that the main economic role of MFIs might be to bridge the gap between informal finance and the credit supply of established conventional banks and thereby remove a very important obstacle to the growth of small firms.

4 Does history matter?

Time and again microfinance experts and historians have referred to the German financial cooperatives as precursors of modern microfinance. A particularly enthusiastic and particularly kind example of this can be found in the book *Finance at the Frontier* by J.D. Von Pischke (1991)[40]. Roodman (2012a), the author of one of the most important recent books on microfinance, also draws this historical connection, though with some caveats. As we show in the third chapter of our study, covering current developments in microfinance, there have indeed been quite a number of borrowings of the German approach worldwide – and usually with limited success.

What is missing, however, is a systematic and critical analysis of the historical role models. The current book tries to close this gap. It takes present and historical perspectives seriously and links them in a critical, systematic, and interdisciplinary way and thereby, we hope, contributes to eliminating deficits in the relevant literature and the corresponding discourse. The conviction behind our approach is that collecting and processing data, facts, and experiences in the "History Lab" can help us to gain deeper insights and uncover essential features of reality and to make us wiser. History thus matters – because we can learn from it.

However, when we say that one can learn from history, and more specifically from the 19th century history of German savings and cooperative banks, we are by no means suggesting that the "German way" of setting up and organizing inclusive financial institutions should be regarded as a blueprint to be followed precisely, merely because it has been successful over a long time span. If it were to be attempted at all, a precise replication of what the presumed blueprint represents would almost certainly fail; even expecting it to work would be a kind of neocolonial way of addressing modern challenges with the solutions of 200 years ago, transplanted to a different context.

Nevertheless, our approach holds the promise of stimulating new ideas and arguments that will hopefully lead to a new, objectives-oriented definition and a new practice of microfinance which will prove that microfinance concepts can inherently work sustainably and on a long-term basis without ongoing external capital injections.

In fact, there are good reasons for integrating a historically-based approach into the analysis. Despite all the differences, there are indeed correspondences between today's developing countries and the European countries at the time of their early industrialization, as Chapters II and III will show at length. Moreover, a retrospective approach generally allows a better understanding of current events in

---

[40] In a footnote on page 43 Von Pischke even provides instructions to his English-speaking readers on how to pronounce the difficult German name Raiffeisen: "… *rai* as in rise, *feis* rhymes with pies, and *sen* as in send".

that it places present experience in a broader context of development processes. In this way, the interrelationships and differences between patterns and structures such as path finding, path dependencies and lock-ins, and transformation processes or traditions, as well as discontinuities and disruptive situations, can be recognized more easily. The resulting gain in knowledge can be exploited as an additional tool for evaluating and improving current approaches. In other words, the central aim is to perceive history as a dialogue of the present with the past about the future aimed at generating additional awareness and knowledge.

The theoretical basis of this endeavor is a historical-hermeneutic approach. The core of this approach is to understand individuals, actions, and developments by themselves and in relationship to one another. This explicitly includes incorporating the general socio-economic and socio-technological context in order to identify, comprehend, and evaluate interrelationships. Thus, the approach brings together micro and macro perspectives. This, in turn, is fully in keeping with the microfinance concept, whose objective is to sustainably and efficiently organize processes of structural change. In addition, we make use of such economic concepts as institutional economics, change management, and private-public partnership research. In the light of the present socio-economic challenges worldwide, this approach might contribute a creative methodological approach for the general transformation research that has increasingly gained in importance as well.[41]

The historical survey focuses in particular on structural change processes in the various German states, which were largely independent at that time, without losing sight of European developments. Looking out of the box, so to speak, helps one to find explanations. As far as the time perspective is concerned, our observation period extends from the end of the 18th century up to the beginning of World War I in 1914. In the second half of the 18th century, the industrialization process began to dissolve the archaic-agrarian social and economic structures which had evolved over many centuries. At the time, the northwestern part of Europe constituted an emerging market, to use modern terms, which resulted in a highly industrialized society at the beginning of the 20th century. Parallel to this process of modernization, savings banks and cooperatives evolved as financial institutions specifically conceived to address this change.

The historical survey in this book thus addresses the role of savings banks and cooperative financial institutions in the industrialization process under aspects of microfinance for the first time. It aims to investigate whether the German savings and cooperative bank models might inspire the current discussion about sustainably optimizing microfinance concepts – even for the Western world.[42] The historical perspective may help us to understand how people and institutions han-

---

41 Cf. among others https://www.ifw-kiel.de/forschung/p1fb1/globale-muster-des-strukturwandels
42 See for example the German-language article "Unilever prepares itself for poverty in Europe"; http://www.t-online.dewww.t-online.de, 27 August 2012, 9:49.

dled certain challenges and change processes in the environment in which they operated and to assess whether these actions and reactions were wise or unwise. Such an understanding may serve as a template for today's decisions.

What helps this process is the large number of publications on German savings bank and credit cooperative history. Often missing from these sources are refer-

---

Snapshot 1: Feasibility assessment in historical perspective

| 18th/19th century Europe | 20th/21st century developing countries |

CORE CHALLENGE:

Limited or no financial access / Exclusion of large social groups

SHARED GENERAL CHALLENGES:
Fast-growing populations
Rural exodus – urbanization
Structural change from agrarian to industrial/service society
Collapsing social institutions
Pauperism
Infrastructure
For individuals: poverty, lack of finance, insecurity
=> MANY SIMILARITIES

Figure 2: Microfinance as a Change Management Instrument (Lewin/Schumpeter/Thomes)

Kurt Lewin (1890-1947), *Frontiers in Group Dynamics* (1947), http://www.kurt-lewin.com
Joseph Schumpeter (1883-1950), *Theorie der Innovation / The Theory of Economic Development* (1912/ 1934)

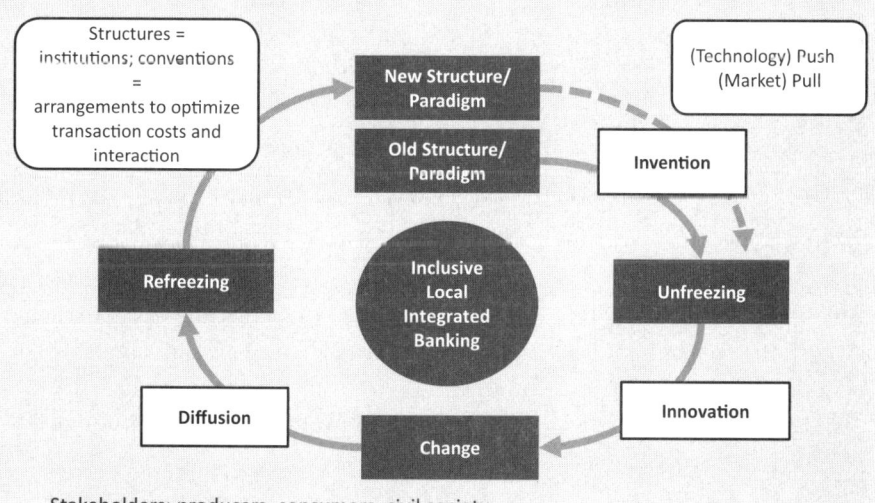

- Structures = institutions; conventions = arrangements to optimize transaction costs and interaction
- New Structure/ Paradigm
- Old Structure/ Paradigm
- (Technology) Push (Market) Pull
- Invention
- Refreezing
- Inclusive Local Integrated Banking
- Unfreezing
- Diffusion
- Innovation
- Change

Stakeholders: producers, consumers, civil society
Framework: environment, law, politics, culture, technology, science

ences to modern microfinance, which limits their value for understanding the challenges of today's microfinance. However, these publications shed light on how a system of "inclusive" emerging financial institutions with a social mission developed over time and drew on options that resulted from its own growth and from changing economic and political circumstances, and the way in which these two factors interacted. One can thus draw valuable lessons on how socially-oriented financial institutions emerged, how they solved the problems inherent in providing financial services to a clientele that had not so far been served by existing financial institutions, and how they evolved and were transformed as institutions over time to finally become a very important part of the German financial sector. The historical case study thus becomes highly instructive even though the savings banks and cooperatives of 19th-century Germany cannot serve as a global blueprint for setting up effective and efficient inclusive financial institutions in the 21st century.

5 Our main propositions

As noted above, some influential Western authors who have expressed their views on microfinance and the direction in which it should develop, whether some time ago or recently, seem convinced that it is in some sense helpful to look at history, in particular that of inclusive banking in Germany in the 19th century. A look at history will allow a better understanding of the potential and the challenges of advancing finance at "the small end of the market" and, as J.D. Von Pischke (1991) puts it, of "shifting the frontier of formal finance outward" so that more people can benefit from having access to good and affordable financial services. Unfortunately, Von Pischke does not refer to the development of cooperative finance in Germany after the early years in which the first cooperative financial institutions were founded, a task that he leaves to historians. We are convinced that the later years, in which cooperative banks matured and became stable financial institutions that serve millions of people, are equally important, since this part of history may hold lessons concerning what makes inclusive financial institutions gain and maintain survival value.

As far as the literature on microfinance and on banking history is concerned, English-language references to the early savings banks in Germany and other European countries and the development of their systems over time are more difficult to find. However, there are extensive studies by German historians on savings banks[43]. Their findings show that the history of savings banks is equally instructive for today's microfinance. As in the case of financial cooperatives, these analyses yield valuable lessons on how poverty-oriented financial institutions emerged, how they solved the problems inherent in providing financial services to a clientele that had not so far been served by financial institutions, and how savings banks as institutions evolved and were transformed over time to become a very important part of the German financial sector. And as several authors have seen it in the case of cooperative banks, the history of savings banks may also be highly instructive.

But regardless of whether the frequent references to early inclusive banking in Germany in the microfinance literature reflect a sufficiently broad perspective or not, they clearly imply a conviction which we share and which we therefore restate here as our first proposition:

The history of inclusive local banking, especially that of German savings banks and cooperative banks, might offer illuminating lessons on how to create, transform and support financial institutions that subscribe to a mission of creating benefits for people of limited means and for networks or systems of such institutions.

---

[43] These sources will be quoted extensively in the next chapter.

These lessons from the History Lab go both ways. Some of them show what can be done to create value for the clients or customers, what factors contribute to the success of socially-oriented financial institutions, and what may have been responsible for their survival as institutions. But history also shows what the main dangers are for financial institutions that differ in important respects from what is often regarded as the "normal" institutional form, that of a bank, namely a shareholder-owned, large, and highly centralized institution.

A corollary of our first proposition is that the historical lessons are valuable irrespective of any assessment as to whether savings banks or cooperative banks are good and replicable models of how to organize inclusive banking in today's developing and transition countries.

In addition to this first and predominant proposition, there are three other propositions which we will develop and test in the course of this study. The first is that saving is very important for any individual, family or country. This suggests that it is equally important that today's MFIs – and those "third parties" that support and to some extent shape them – place a high value on providing savings instruments for their clients and, very much in line with the tradition of the savings banks in Western countries, consider it an important part of their social role to "inspire thriftiness". The history of savings banks, and also the contrast between their history and that of other financial institutions which do not offer deposit or savings facilities, suggests that saving, was once called "the forgotten half of development finance" (Vogel 1984), and may in fact be the more important half.

The second additional proposition is that the institutional design of financial institutions is of overriding importance for their economic survival and their continuing ability to provide benefits for individuals other than their owners. This refers to the two issues addressed above: the loyalty of an organization to its mission and the design of incentives at all levels of an organization.

Another aspect of organizational design – and our third additional proposition – relates to the design and the role of networks or federations of financial institutions. We claim that these networks are of paramount importance. Their importance is easy to recognize when looking at the German savings banks and cooperative banks in the 19th and 20th centuries. We see good reasons to argue that the clever design of their respective networks has been one of the main reasons why the German cooperative and savings banks have been quite successful in the past, why they have survived over the years and why their market position is still so strong today. In microfinance, networks are now already very important, and our reading of the history of savings and cooperative banks suggests that their importance may increase still further in the years to come.

II.
GERMAN SAVINGS BANKS AND CREDIT COOPERATIVES – A BLUEPRINT FOR INCLUSIVE FINANCE?

1 Objectives – Why a historical perspective? Why credit cooperatives and savings banks? Why Germany?

The current book takes present and historical perspectives seriously and links them in a critical and interdisciplinary way and thereby, we hope, contributes to eliminating deficits in the relevant literature and the corresponding discourse. The intention behind this approach is to exploit the experiences and data collected in the History Lab – with the help of critical, systematic analysis – in order to gain insights that will support current objectives in developing and highly developed economies. In doing so, due care will be taken to ensure that the results are translated to current conditions. In no way does it mean that the historical way is the only way to tackle current challenges.[1]

This interdisciplinary approach, which explicitly links the past, present, and future in a reciprocal way, might serve to stimulate new ideas and arguments that will help lead to a new, objectives-oriented definition and practice of microfinance which conclusively proves that microfinance concepts, whether they take the form of for-profit or non-profit institutions, can inherently work sustainably and on a long-term basis.

In fact, we are not the first to have looked for historical precedents of modern MFIs, as will be shown in detail below. And there are good reasons for integrating a historically-based approach into the analysis.

There are obvious analogies between the interrelationships we are seeing today and the developments in the European industrialization process.[2] Moreover, a retrospective analysis generally enables a better understanding of current events in that it roots the present experience to the historical context and places it in the context of process developments. In this way, the interrelationships between patterns and structures such as path finding and transformation processes or traditions, as well as discontinuities, disruptive situations and the resulting changes, can be recognized. The resulting gain in knowledge can be exploited as an additional tool for evaluation and optimization.

Thus, the aim of this chapter is to systematically identify microfinance relationships in the historical context of industrialization as well as to describe and understand these relationships and critically interpret them with respect to their present applicability. In other words, the aim is to perceive history as a kind of dialogue of the present with the past about the future.

---

1 http://ineteconomics.org/video/30-ways-be-economist/barry-eichengreen-why-economics-needs-history.
2 For details see the historical analysis further on.

The theoretical basis is a holistic historical-hermeneutic, argumentative, and explanatory approach, as dicussed in detail in chapter 4.[3] The key results will be summarized at the end of each chapter on the basis of a strengths/weaknesses and opportunities/threats (SWOT) analysis.

The historical study focuses on structural change processes in the German states, without losing sight of European developments. Looking out of the box, so to speak, helps one to find explanations. As far as the time perspective is concerned, the phase under observation extends from the end of the 18th century up to the beginning of World War I in 1914. In the second half of the 18th century, the industrialization process began to dissolve traditional archaic-agrarian social and economic structures. At the time, the northwestern part of Europe constituted an emerging market, to use modern terms, which resulted in a highly industrialized society at the beginning of the 20th century.

Parallel to this modernization process, savings banks and cooperatives evolved as financial institutions specifically conceived to address this change. They became widespread, evolving into universal banks and integrated components of the financial system. Nevertheless, they adhered firmly to their original business model. This section analyzes their role in the industrialization process under aspects of

Figure 3: Holistic institutions matrix – STEPLE approach

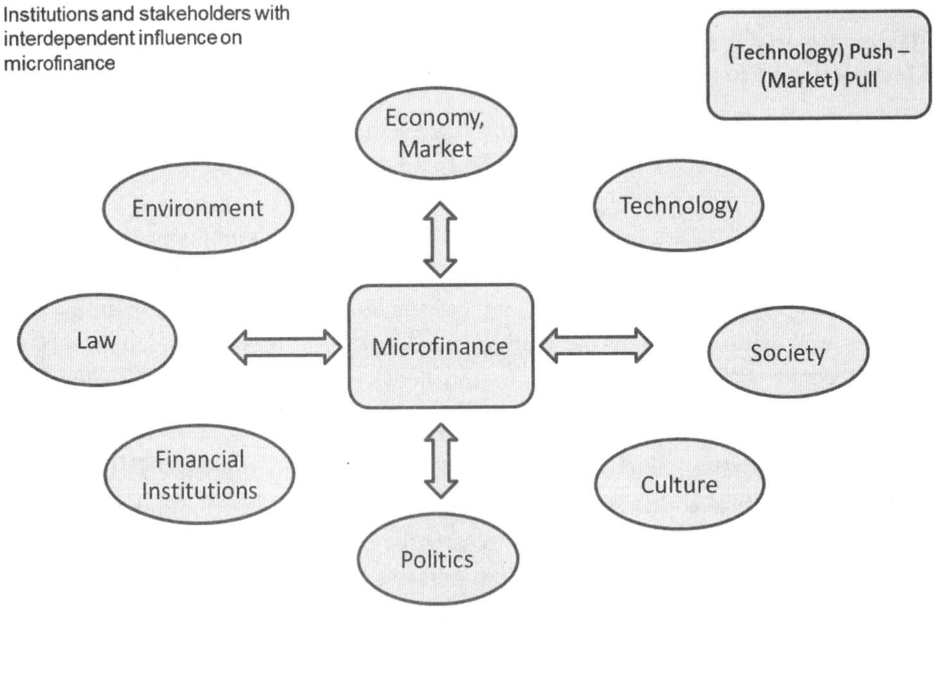

Institutions and stakeholders with interdependent influence on microfinance

(Technology) Push – (Market) Pull

- Economy, Market
- Environment
- Technology
- Law
- Microfinance
- Society
- Financial Institutions
- Culture
- Politics

---

3   See, among others, https://www.ifw-kiel.de/forschung/p1fb1/globale-muster-des-strukturwandels. The focus of research would need to be broadened accordingly.

microfinance. Using these historical case studies, it will be systematically investigated to what extent cooperatives and savings banks might serve as blueprints of the current microfinance approach. In particular, the business models and their development will be analyzed, and criteria for success and failure will be defined that may be applicable for optimizing present microfinance concepts in developing and developed economies.

What is remarkable as far as the developed world is concerned is that the normal full-time work relationship, arising during industrialization and defined by stable and adequate work conditions, nowadays is eroding in developed economies. As a result of globalization and digitalization, it has given way to precarious part-time jobs, with many workers in the low-wage and small business sectors no longer fully socially insured. Exaggerating somewhat, one could say that the situation in the Western postmodern era has reverted back to pre-modern structures. Consequently, the risk of poverty is also increasing in the Western world, for history has shown that poverty is only overcome by consistent, adequate employment and income conditions.

In addition, there is another challenge. At the beginning of the 21st century, the Western world sees itself on the path to the age of life sciences. The society is aging rapidly. Once more there is a fundamental change to handle. Old-age provisions are taking on a new meaning. Meanwhile, the current financial crisis has once again pushed regionally-based financial institutions and microfinance banking models to the global forefront. It is here that another circle is closing between historical and current analysis. We will see to what extent the thesis applies that

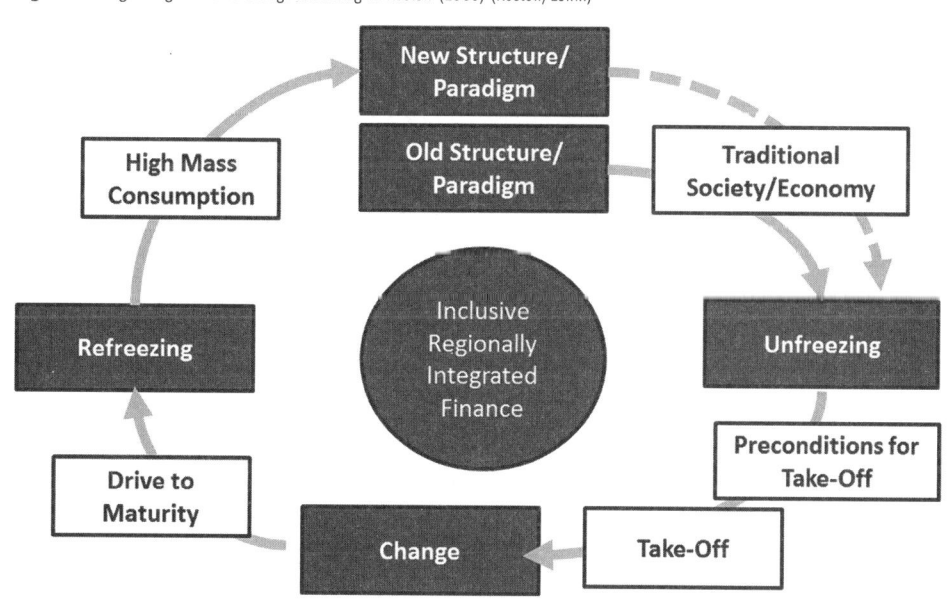

Figure 4: Stages of growth and change according to Rostow (1960) (Rostow/Lewin)

Figure 5: Economic megatrends

Socio-economic Supercycles

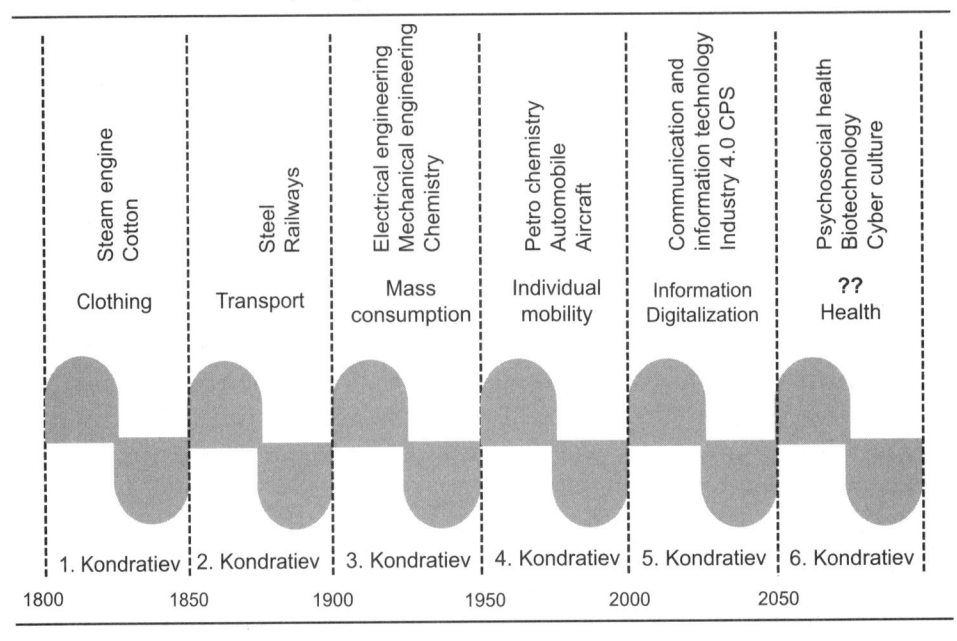

1. Kondratiev	2. Kondratiev	3. Kondratiev	4. Kondratiev	5. Kondratiev	6. Kondratiev
Steam engine, Cotton	Steel, Railways	Electrical engineering, Mechanical engineering, Chemistry	Petro chemistry, Automobile, Aircraft	Communication and information technology, Industry 4.0 CPS	Psychosocial health, Biotechnology, Cyber culture
Clothing	Transport	Mass consumption	Individual mobility	Information Digitalization	?? Health

1800 — 1850 — 1900 — 1950 — 2000 — 2050

the current processes of change can be positively influenced by microfinance concepts, even in developed societies. The focus of interest is on the question of whether new institutions or formats like crowdfunding are needed for this, or whether proven institutional forms – i.e. credit cooperatives and savings banks – can assume these tasks – if they wish to do so and are able to assimilate.

Food for Thought

The following points deserve consideration:

- Poverty is linked to high uncertainty.
- Financially precarious households need access to savings and credit opportunities with transparent terms and conditions.
- The benefit of credit alone for poor households is doubtful. Loans do not structurally lift the poor out of poverty.
- The political sphere plays a central role in shaping financial infrastructures through intrinsic engagement, regulation, and the establishment of incentives and subsidies (smart subsidies for institution building, not subsidized interest rates).
- Strict state intervention is in no way ideal.
- The effects of market mechanisms need to be constrained by institutional guidelines.
- Social and financial targets need to be harmonized.
- The incomes of the poor are more volatile than those of the wage earners. At the same time, however, the 'normal state of work' is eroding in the Western world (Collins et al 2010; Hardach 2006).
- The earning capacity of poor individuals depends strongly on their health, which is in turn fragile due to a lack of adequate nutrition and the fact that they not always insured and have only limited access to medical care.
- Structural uncertainty calls for opportunities to save money in relatively good times and disciplined behavior accordingly; this is easier said than done.
- Uncontrolled currency devaluation combined with zero or negative interest rates renders savings-based enhancement/enablement models ineffective.
- Private pension and healthcare plans can only supplement, and not replace, a socioeconomic safety net.
- The aims of development are: freedom in the sense of self-determination, access to education, advancement of gender equality and diversity, financial incentives, competition between institutions and models, and promotion of entrepreneurship.

2 Saving and borrowing – A socioeconomic historical approach

2.1 Satisfying needs – A vital challenge

Since the dawn of human history, people have been striving to satisfy their needs and deal with risk. For centuries, people of all cultures have lent and saved using all suitable instruments and methods available to them. For just as long a time, institutions, in the sense of traditions and rules, must necessarily have existed in order to further these aims, whether the institutions were informal, semiformal or formal in nature; and which also, in the sense of MFIs today, covered even the smallest transactions and transfers carried out to fill people's needs. Credit in the sense in which we know it today was an integral component of everyday life in the past and permeated every layer of society, even more so than today.[4]

Thus, there is real reason to assume that such patterns are universal and timeless and can be adapted to reflect the respective sociocultural, socioeconomic, and sociotechnical environments. There are numerous historical examples of such adaptations, which strengthens the plausibility of the historical comparison attempted here. Moreover, there is no absolute best practice per se. However, one can assume that the more precarious people's living conditions are, the more informal their savings and credit customs are – although it should be noted that in general, informal finance has always involved a very complex web of arrangements.

In European preindustrial life, the most threatening factors causing uncertainty were firstly seasonal and structurally induced hunger and secondly disease.[5] Both factors were everyday phenomena and were closely interrelated. In those days, most people in Europe lived at the subsistence level, even though they were mainly employed in producing food. When sources from the Middle Ages or early modern period speak of famine, it means not just that people were hungry, but that they were literally dying of starvation. This ever-present constellation of threats led to the development of safety mechanisms which were generally anchored in social networks, whether they consisted of family, the village community, or feudalistic structures incorporating various relationships of personal dependency, up to and including loss of personal freedom. In this regard, there are many analogies to the conditions in developing and emerging economies. It was the Agrarian Revolution, preceding the Industrial Revolution, which first created leeway to overcome these dire conditions. This revolutionary transformation can be thought of as a secular process spanning several generations. Why? Consider-

---

[4] See Braudel 1967/79, vol. 1; Collins et al 2010; Seibel 1978, 1980, 1984, 2003, 2010b; Sahlins 1974.
[5] For the following see Bass 1991; Braudel 1967/79, vol.1; Abel 1978, 1986; Klein 1973, 1982; Wehler 2005, vol.1.; Persson 2010. The potato harvest was about four times higher per unit area measured in calories than that of cereals, and it grew on poor soils; potato monoculture, however, was responsible for the great Irish famine of the late 1840s.

ing the variety of, at times, competing interests on the part of stakeholders, the dissemination of new technologies also requires changes in laws and in the norms embodied by the term 'tradition'. Despite numerous catastrophic famines, it took many centuries until the potato, for example, as a revolutionary agricultural innovation, engaged the minds and stomachs of European consumers as a staple foodstuff. This and other innovations were an important prerequisite for the Industrial Revolution of the $18^{th}/19^{th}$ centuries, whose workers normally stemmed from the agrarian sector and needed to be fed.

It is well known that England was the pioneer of industrialization, because it could build on an advantageous set of circumstances: a comparatively modern societal order without feudalism, a consitutional monarchy, an efficient transport infrastructure (partly due to its island location), and forest and coal resources for energy, ore resources and a growing population. Population growth provided cheap workers whose numbers increased still further through the Enclosure Movement, which converted public farm and grazing land to private ownership and drove peasants off their land. Last but not least, England had extensive overseas colonies which it exploited to import inexpensive foodstuffs and raw materials, while trade surpluses significantly accelerated the accumulation of capital.

It is no coincidence that the steam engine was invented in England, and disseminated from there, during the second half of the 18th century. The steam engine's innovative power-generation concept heralded the mass production of machines. Truly revolutionary schools of thought and behavior evolved, coupled with Adam Smith's market economics and combined with the central role of the individual, of labor and the division of labor. Thus, the Enlightenment, with its new view of the world and the human being, undermined the seemingly immutable societal traditions based on subservient relationships and the lack of personal freedom (Braudel 1979).

The extent of the Enlightenment movement was revealed by the emergence of numerous bourgeois circles and societies. Not only did they intensively communicate with one another throughout Europe and across the Atlantic, they also generated an enormous amount of literature, including encyclopedias, which made available contemporary knowledge.

In 1848, Malchus, the first chronicler of the European savings banks system, pointedly and rightly described its intention as "a philanthropic attempt of humanistic individuals."[6] Using a holistic approach and working within the scope of the existing social order and work ethic, the philanthropists aimed to support people's advancement, yet also expected of individuals themselves that they strive to better their own condition. Widespread poverty was the most obvious driving force motivating the philanthropists' efforts. Parallel to this change in thinking,

---

6 Malchus 1838/1994; for the quotation see Trende 1957, 21.

2.1 Satisfying needs – A vital challenge 51

Figure 6: Phase shift of industrialization according to Rostow (1960)

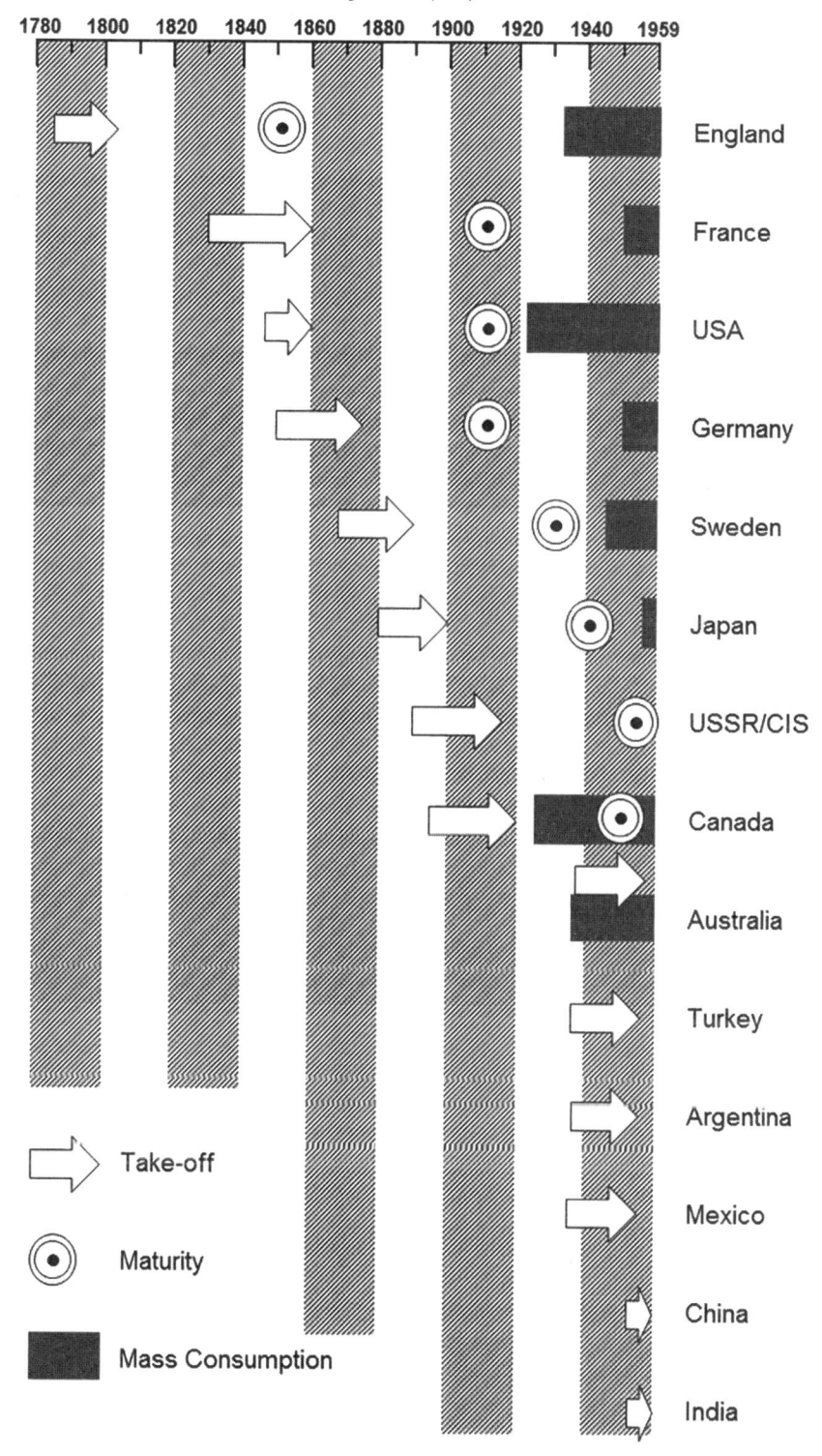

⇨	Take-off
⊙	Maturity
■	Mass Consumption

Countries (top to bottom): England, France, USA, Germany, Sweden, Japan, USSR/CIS, Canada, Australia, Turkey, Argentina, Mexico, China, India

Timeline: 1780, 1800, 1820, 1840, 1860, 1880, 1900, 1920, 1940, 1959

the concept of mercantilism, which was oriented to the needs of the state, lost its attractiveness and acceptance (Beaudoin 2007; Geremek 1994).

On the European continent, the changes outlined above unfolded as a kind of 'catching up' process, and were thus even more compressed in terms of timeframe and even more revolutionary in nature. Many factors converged at the turn of the 19th century and were enormously accelerated by the French Revolution. Since 1789, this revolution had radically overwhelmed the continent and had claimed many victims with its call for "freedom, equality, and fraternity", which was scandalous to the ears of the power elite. This revolutionary call triggered huge tensions and set previously unimaginable impulses free – as evidenced by the eradication of feudal reign and the abolishment of tradesmen's guilds. These changes meant personal freedom, including the freedom to choose one's occupation, production methods and organizations as well as place of residence. These freedoms, in turn, spurred the mobility of land ownership and capital as the inalienable prerequisites for progress.

Meanwhile, the Agrarian Revolution created the nutritional foundation for the Industrial Revolution by introducing more intensive management systems, combined with the use of mineral fertilizers and new agricultural products. The pessimistic-deterministic demographic trap prophesied by Thomas Robert Malthus, based on the thesis that the population would grow exponentially while increases in crop yields remained linear, therefore failed to materialize.[7]

Consequently, the path was open for the change from agricultural to industrial society. The difficult transition phase, marked by structural mass poverty (pauperism), was ultimately due to the fact that the emerging industrial commercial production was not yet capable of making the necessary workplaces available, while at the same time the traditional social safety nets were crumbling. All in all, complex processes were underway which made it difficult for contemporaries to recognize the ex post unmistakable material advances to come, given the limited span of the average human lifetime.

These conditions still prevailed in the 1830s and 1840s when, in the German states[8], the twin developments of the customs union (*Zollverein*) (1834) and the introduction of the railroad (1835) led to the creation of larger markets, an important prerequisite for growth. Ultimately, the Revolution of 1848 is to be understood as a reaction to the inherent economic problems still prevailing at that time. The famine of 1846/47, which preceded the political events of 1848, was the last agrarian-triggered economic crisis and a further decisive driving factor behind the expansion of the savings bank system as well as the founding of the first financial cooperatives.[9]

---

[7] Broadberry and O'Rourke 2010; Federico 2005; Wehler 2005, vol.1; see also the following pages.
[8] There was a federal national state only from 1871.
[9] See the following chapters of this book.

It was not until the second half of the 19th century that the strains of the modernization process first began to ease. Industrialization accelerated, prosperity gradually spread to broader segments of the population, and both social structures and the economic basis of life began to re-emerge in new forms. It is worth noting here, however, that these processes took more than 60 years and spanned three generations – unbearably long for those concerned. Perhaps this is exactly the same feeling engendered in the critical viewer today – some 200 years later – when observing the painful processes underway in developing and emerging economies, especially in light of the enormous economic possibilities of the world community of today as opposed to earlier times.

2.2 Saving and borrowing – An everyday exercise

As sociocultural framework conditions changed, so did financial transactions. As we have pointed out, credit was an integral part of everyday life and permeated all strata of society, perhaps even more so than today. Common reasons for assuming long-term credit were marriage and inheritance cases, while short-term credit was taken up to meet acute vital needs and to cover temporary financial shortfalls related to unemployment, illness and the death of individuals or livestock. Moreover, credit was used to finance business inputs such as seed or animals. People saved on an informal basis to cover these needs; however, once they took out loans, paying off the debt required a more structured savings process. To put it in modern terms, credit involved efficient, dynamic cash-flow management.[10]

In a society where illiteracy was widespread, credit dealings were generally conducted orally and sealed by a handshake or tallied on a tally stick. Even the Napoleonic Code mentioned the tally stick as the typical document of debt; the Bank of England worked with so-called tallies until 1823. Tallies remained in use until their abolishment in 1834 (Chatfield 1996).

Members of families or village communities acted as financial intermediaries. Moreover, foundations, monasteries, orphanages, landlords, and itinerant merchants, the latter often denoted as Jews or usurers, were all involved in the savings and loan business – thus making up an extremely fragmented market. To counter usury and help borrowers, the Catholic Church founded the *Monti di Pietà* (*montes pietatis*) in Italy in the latter part of the 15th century. These institutions functioned along the lines of pawnbroking establishments and formed only the tip of the enormous pre-modern iceberg of credit institutions. The Banca Monte dei Paschi di Siena, founded as a *Monte di Pietà* in Siena in 1472 (Klein 1982; Trende 1957), is currently listed as the oldest bank in the world – a remarkable proof of the sustainability of such credit institutions, even though a financial scandal shook this bank in 2012/2013.

---

10 Braudel 1979, vol.1. Deneweth et al. 2014; Collins et al. 2010.

These and other financial intermediaries slowly gained increasing importance in Europe from the 15th century on. On the one hand, population growth was responsible for this development, even though the Black Death had ravaged parts of Central Europe during the 14th century and the Thirty Years' War in the 17th century wreaked havoc on the German states, causing an average 40 % decline in population levels. On the other hand, the prohibition of interest, traceable back to Aristotle and rooted in canon law, began gradually disappearing from European legal codes from the 16th century on in light of changing ethics which reflected economic realities. Up to then, the prohibition on the taking of interest had burdened every kind of financial transaction and increased its price.[11]

With regard to the types of business transactions carried out, in Europe all financial instruments as we essentially know them today were formed at the beginning of the early modern period. These even included speculative instruments such as the pre-harvest sale of crops ("on the stalk"); even ordinary consumers used these instruments to optimize the harvest cycle – albeit often without the expected success, due to information asymmetries. Guaranteed and collateralized loans as well as cash credit, for instance in the form of "chalking up" debts for later payment, were also known. Last but not least, the era even saw visions of a new cashless society, such as those articulated by Sir Thomas More in the early 16th century.

Even so, the natural daily exchange of goods and services dominated everyday life. Such barter exchange hampered neither credit and savings transactions nor the need to acquire collateral, but it did cause relatively high costs. It is no coincidence that the spread of the monetary economy accelerated from the 16th century on. Apart from the convenience of coins, the discovery of silver deposits in Europe and imports of rare metals from the New World were the essential determinants leading to the increasing monetary valuation of everyday goods and services. These developments allowed coins to increasingly reach all areas of the world, and thus created new framework conditions for savings and credit, including exchange losses as the result of coin depreciations,[12] and new options as well.

These few highlights should suffice to allow at least a basic understanding of the situation at the European transition to the Modern Era. In a distant analogy, the structures and the processes of that time indeed resemble the current situation in developing and emerging economies. Rudimentary cash-flow management takes place among the broader masses, while the transition from informal to formal banking, now as then, strongly correlates with rising individual incomes.

---

11 Ashauer 1991, 25 ff.; Braudel 1979, vol.1; Wilson 2009, chapter 3; for details concerning usury, see also below.
12 Hollow 2012; Klein 1982; Roodman 2012, 36 ff.; Vilar 1976/2011.

2.3 Winds of change – Pawnshops, widows' and orphans' funds, and savings and loan societies as innovative inclusive instruments of change management

Looking at European financial institutions from the mid-18th century on, we see a variety of credit and savings forms within the framework of the sociocultural processes described already. As they are today, business dealings were based on some form of collateral and/or mutual trust. Pawnshops were a widespread form of early formal institution which included low-income individuals in their clientele, and in this sense, these institutions can be considered precursors of current models of MFIs. During the mid-18th century, pawnshops could be found in every larger city of Central Europe. Moreover, many individuals and organizations engaged in charitable lending, one prominent example being the Irish writer Jonathan Swift, who lent amounts of £5-10 pounds to "industrious tradesmen" in Dublin during the 1720s, signed for by two guarantors and initially interest-free, as a "charitable loan system."[13]

In the German states as well, the 18th century saw the heyday of pawnshops in the tradition of Italy's *Monti di Pietà*, which sought to offer an alternative to the inherent legal insecurity of dealing with usurers and carrying out private credit transactions. After older pawnshops disappeared during the Thirty Years' War, this business model experienced a renaissance in the form of a pawnbroking institution first operated by a French merchant in Berlin in 1692. This pawnshop mainly gave collateralized loans to small tradesmen and merchants who were thus able to reliably finance their businesses – a main objective of modern MFIs as well. A moderate interest rate was set of initially 6% p.a. The Hanau Lehn-Banco, founded by the Earl of Hesse in 1738, aimed, very much in the mercantilist tradition, to aid merchants and manufacturers as well as to help the needy in an inexpensive way. Another objective was to enable well-off patrons to safely invest their wealth and earn interest (minimum investment 100 Florins; after 1828 10 Florins; interest rate 4% p.a.). The institution still exists today as the Hanau Savings Bank [*Sparkasse Hanau*]. Moreover, the Princely Savings and Loan Bank of Detmold [*Gräflich-Lippische Leihekasse zu Detmold*], founded in 1786, was likewise open to "the needy, farmers and manufacturers."[14]

These institutions were financed through endowments of the owners or deposits of wealthy citizens. As the high minimum deposits indicate, social concerns regarding the importance of saving did not play a direct role here. Viewed in this light, these financial houses competed with private bankers and foundations or orphans' funds for savings business. In general, these established practices also applied in the 19th century. Over time, some credit banks integrated the small-scale

---

13 For further information see the chapter discussing the international context.
14 Ashauer 1991, 39ff., including case references to Braunschweig (1765) and Detmold (1786); Wysocki 1980; with regard to Hesse, see Strube 1973.

savings business, or they cooperated with savings banks to obtain the funds needed to finance their credit operations.[15]

From the point of view of microfinance, several points are worthy of note here. State decrees aimed at greater standardization, such as the Prussian Pawn and Loan Regulations of 1787 and the corresponding Napoleonic decrees of 1801, increased transparency. In a broader mercantile context, the socioeconomic inclusion or transfer approach aimed to advance entrepreneurship and fight poverty through methods which did not exclude the wealthy. Likewise of interest is the fact that over 200 years ago, transparent access to credit was intended to extract the "evil of usury" by its roots, even before small-scale savings transactions became a specific focus (Ashauer 1991, 47 ff.; Wysocki 1980).

The orphans' funds that likewise originated in the mid-18th century operated on comparable principles. They were primarily concerned with the safe investment of trust funds accruing interest, i.e. fairly large amounts of money. They lent the funds directly, cooperated occasionally with pawnshops and savings banks, developed into saving banks themselves or merged with savings banks. One of the oldest of these institutions in Germany is the Orphans' Fund of the Salem Monastery [*Ordentliche Waisenkasse des Klosters Salem*], founded in 1749. In 1838, it evolved into a municipal savings and loan bank; thus, it is considered to be the oldest German credit institution resembling a typical savings bank (Trende 1957).

2.4 Savings as a fundamental condition for change and growth

Formal institutions that would accept small-scale interest-bearing deposits were, however, missing. And thus the savings banks emerged as financial innovations motivated by the mercantile need for reform to address this deficit. These banks explicitly catered to the lower class. In this regard, one might ask: Aren't poverty and saving inherently mutually exclusive? As it ultimately depends on how these terms are defined, one should take care not to project the modern European understanding of these terms onto other cultures.[16] In 1850, German writer Theodor Fontane remarked in this connection: "The Englishman, even the common man, is fastidious in his requirements, and when he speaks of 'eating potatoes', means going hungry; in Saxony's Erzgebirge Mountains, however, 'eating potatoes' means being rich, enviably rich." (Fontane 1963; Trende 1957). This quotation also illustrates the time lag in the European process of modernization. Again, savings banks evolved with the changing times and simultaneously helped to shape this change. In fact, it was actually presumed that the "poor" were at least periodically able to accumulate savings.

---

15 Führer 1992; with reference to orphans' funds, see following page; with reference to cases of cooperation, see Thomes 2008, 2010.
16 For more details, see the international review further on; Geremek 1994; Murken 1995; Trende 1957, 19 ff.; Wysocki 1980, 114 ff.; Wysocki and Wehrmann 1986. *Wissenschaftsförderung* 1996.

As far as we know, this business model was first implemented in France by Hugues Delestre in the 17th century, and was also discussed in Italy, and later in England, most notably by Daniel Defoe; it was first implemented in England at the turn of the 19th century.[17]

The innovative and distinguishing feature of savings banks was that these institutions accepted, for the first time, relatively small interest-bearing deposits comparable to a day's wage of a laborer. This meant that they offered fair participation in institutional financial systems. Individuals who had little money, and until then had to resort to storing it under the mattress, now had the option of earning interest and keeping their money safely on deposit.

Both private individuals' finances and the economy at large profited from the savings banks thanks to the improved liquidity. To put it simply, more money flowed into the system, which is of particular importance in coin-based currency regimes. This, in turn, benefited everyone, especially since businesses were based locally or regionally.

These points again highlight the relationship between savings and growth. Savings have always been a fundamental prerequisite for the triggering and shaping of innovative processes and change – just as access to credit has been.

With only a few exceptions German savings banks combined the savings business with the loan business from the very beginning. This fact essentially differentiated the German savings banks from the English and French models, which mainly dealt in state credit, thereby rendering the latter ineligible as role models for integrated microfinance. The same temporarily applied in the German states of Bavaria and Württemberg; this might be a reason for the delayed industrialization of the economic structure of these states, even though credit cooperatives promoted private credit from the 1860s on. Should these assumptions hold true, they would also deliver a first historical proof for the regional economic impact of MFIs.[18]

The institutionalized saving of small amounts of money that accrued positive real interest rates seems to go hand in hand with an overall steady increase in the income of broad segments of the population. Thus, the success of savings banks was preprogrammed, while their existence simultaneously propelled economic growth. This conclusion is substantiated by the fact that the savings banks also expanded the available range of transparent credit opportunities (Hardach 2003; 2006).

---

[17] For more details, see further on.
[18] Mura 1996; *Centralverein* 1864; see also the next chapter.

3 "Out of the box" – An international comparative survey of 19th century savings-based microfinance trends

The international exchange of ideas and its effects on institutional savings systems has already been mentioned. Many scholars cited English savings banks as archetypes of the European savings banks movement. This was true even for Germany, where, after the Congress of Vienna in 1815, it was widely assumed that the savings banks operating in Germany were based in Great Britain – a strong indication of the prevailing confusion in the revolutionary French era. This chapter adds a German perspective to the tale.[19]

France definitely exerted a notable influence as well, beginning with Hugues Delestre, who had published a proposal for a holistic socioeconomic reform scheme in 1611, at the beginning of the mercantile era. One aspect was an institution along the lines of a "Monte di Pietà," which propagated the idea of an integrated, universal financial institution which would boost overall wealth and include the underprivileged. As a distinctly inclusive concept, this reform scheme explicitly offered formalized access to financial services to those who did not yet have it, and at the same time invited wealthy individuals to participate as well. Although it was not apparent at the time, this model was very important since it incorporated all the basic ideas of microfinance. Moreover, it is the model that was implemented starting from the end of the 18th century in German savings and loan banks; in other words, Delestre's blueprint formed the basis of the savings bank movement in Germany.[20]

The main features of this approach were as follows:

- Everyone could make deposits.
- As a social component and an incentive for the poor, however, underprivileged working-class individuals such as laborers, farmhands, and maids and other domestic servants received a higher interest rate of 5.88 % p.a. on their deposits, while all others received 3.33 %.
- The credit business was based on pawnbroking.

The next approach worthy of note dates back to 1791, when French polymath Count Mirabeau once more introduced the topic of savings banks in political discourse. Again, however, no specific project was implemented in the 18th century – perhaps due to the outbreak of the French Revolution.[21]

---

19 For a detailed overview of the beginnings in Europe, see Malchus (1838); for a modern European perspective, see Mura (1996); for the beginnings in Britain, see Roodman (2012), 53.
20 Wysocki 1984; including the scheme.
21 Ashauer 1991, 31 ff.; Klein 2003, 50 ff. Malchus (1838); Mura 1996.

Analogous developments took place in Switzerland, where the first savings bank was founded in Bern in 1787 and was followed by a similar institution in Basel in 1792, probably based on the German prototype. An interesting feature of the Basel institution was that the city's 20 wealthiest citizens served as guarantors for the bank, once again underscoring the inclusive aspect. During the 1820s, the same business principles were observable as in German savings banks, namely, a combined savings and credit business in one and the same institution. Nonetheless, some Swiss institutions, such as Neuchatel in 1812, later influenced the founding of savings banks in parts of southern Germany. Thus, one could call this a type of reciprocal dissemination.[22]

As regards the emergence of British savings banks, David Roodman (2012) has recently provided a concise summary of their development from a modern microfinance perspective. Therefore, we will discuss the topic only briefly here, highlighting some specific aspects.

The development of savings banks – so-called parish or provident banks – in England, Scotland and Ireland seems to have lagged behind the development of analogous institutions in Switzerland. This may be somewhat surprising for the first mover of industrialization, especially given that Great Britain's social problems were more apparent than those in continental Europe. Even so, there are many intertwined roots.[23]

The earliest initiatives in England were the so-called "Friendly Societies," or mutual charitable associations, which dated back to the 17th century and, as some scholars argue, spawned the English savings banks system. Daniel Defoe may have sown the seeds for such schemes as early as 1697 in his famous essay entitled "An Essay on Projects." He proposed that all individuals, while young and able, should save small amounts of money to help themselves in case of emergency, in old age, or to help others. In short, this piece represented a self-help tool for paupers. Jonathan Swift was another early sponsor, setting up a charitable loan system in Dublin starting in the 1720s. In the 1790s, polymath and social reformer Jeremy Bentham, drawing on his past experience with the Friendly Society model and other ideas, reinterpreted the concept.[24] Some years later, Thomas Robert Malthus promoted Bentham's scheme as a means of slowing down population growth. He complained about the lack of institutions that would pay interest on the small-scale savings of the poor, and at the same time extend to them full liberty to withdraw their savings whenever they wished, which he saw as basic prerequisites for saving in general. From about this period on there is a record of the founding of various types of savings and loan institutions.

---

22 For details, see Malchus 1838, 251–303.
23 Roodman, 2012, 36 ff., 42–45, 48 ff.; in general Horne 1947; Irish savings banks followed the English path, so they are not discussed separately here.
24 Trende 1957, 75 ff. citing Scratchley 1860. Roodman gives an overview, 45 ff.

In Ireland, the so-called "loan funds" model, initiated by Jonathan Swift, reportedly covered 20% of households by around 1850. This constituted a remarkable success, on the one hand; however, on the other, the model failed during the catastrophic Irish potato famine. In its specifics, the Irish business model had many features analogous to practices observable in modern microfinance: social pressure, weekly payments, high interest rates on loanes, short loan terms, and rigid penalties for defaulting borrowers.[25]

Friendly Societies and other types of benefit clubs embraced a holistic socioeconomic agenda that covered savings, insurance, loans, education, and other services for the common people. In 1798, Priscilla Wakefield, a wealthy philanthropist and feminist, took the initiative in her role as a leader by combining the Tottenham-based "Friendly Society for the Benefit of Women and Children" with a savings branch called the "Benefit Club." While the savings branch had initially collected children's savings, in 1801 it expanded its business to take deposits from adults as well. The "Frugality Bank," as it then became known, paid 5% p.a. interest on savings deposits exceeding £1 – a considerable sum of money at that time. At the beginning of the 19th century, there were about 9,000 Friendly Societies with a total of 700,000 members – representing a huge potential, but the individual societies were always threatened by bankruptcy due to their small scale and weak organizational structures.[26]

Another savings bank pioneer was the Scottish reverend Henry Duncan, who, through his dedication and drive, accelerated the savings movement from 1810 on. Duncan founded the first Scottish savings bank, called the "Savings and Friendly Society," which quickly became a prototype for such institutions throughout Great Britain. It did no credit business, but cooperated with the Edinburgh-based British Linen Company Bank, founded to promote the regional linen industry. As far as regulation of the savings bank movement was concerned, in 1807 the British Parliament rejected a bill proposing a nationwide savings and insurance institution. The ruling was not against savings banks per se, but rather against state intervention, in accordance with Adam Smith's liberal economic ideas. Unlike in Germany, there were only a handful of influential British actors promoting change through exclusively mutual private initiatives such as those of Priscilla Wakefield. Generally, the British financial landscape consisted of "banks" organized by aristocrats acting as independent trustees and guided by motives of philanthropy, paternalism, and ultimately by a self-serving desire to maintain the status quo, as the French Revolution had triggered fear among the upper class regarding their status. Developments in France also followed a different path than in Germany; charity was a primary motivation and there was an absence of any small-scale lending business (Mura 1996).

---

25 Roodman, l.c.; citing Swift's approach.
26 Trende 1957, l.c.; Malchus 1838, 333ff., Gosden 1996, 152f.

In 1815, a cultural sea change took place in England with the establishment of the Provident Institution of Bath, considered to be the country's first trustee savings bank. In 1816, there were actually 78 savings banks for "the industrious." For mainly practical reasons, the banks invested local savings in government bonds. In modern terms, this marked the beginning of a regional financial drain. To regulate all these activities, England enacted a savings bank law as early as 1817: the "Bill for the Protection and Encouragement of Provident Institutions, or Banks for Savings." This law was extended to include Scottish savings banks in 1835. It codified the typical British non-profit trustee scheme into law, giving the trustees a central financial role locally without providing for any systematic supervision of their institutions.

This law led to a boom in the founding of savings institutions. In 1820, there were around 500 trustee savings banks in Scotland and England. However, the trustee system was subject to rapidly rising deficits, prompting further regulation such as the stipulation of strict maximum deposits. One reason for the deficits was that the wealthy were obviously "abusing" the banks, given the high interest rates their deposits accrued. Moreover, widespread mismanagement was reported. Consequently, though promising grass-root initiatives had emerged, paternalistic actors and governmental manipulation consistently undermined the system, thereby systematically preventing the initiatives from developing their full potential. Thus, it is not surprising that this financial movement did not spread rapidly in the mid-19th century in Scotland and England (while in Germany, in contrast, the general crisis of the late 1840s led to accelerated dissemination of the savings bank concept and the emergence of loan cooperatives). By 1861, there were only around 650 trustee savings banks, due to the limitations of this concept (Gosden 1996).

The year 1861 also saw the founding of the English post office savings bank – again a national institution under direct government control that could offer obvious advantages. There were almost 3,000 post offices providing banking services. The interest rate of 2.5% p.a. on savings was far below market rates; however, in 1888, by decree and to eliminate competition, the English government reduced the trustee savings bank interest rate to the same level. To compensate for this, some trustee savings banks set up "special investment departments" which invested in municipal bonds and paid 4% interest. However, the decline in trustee savings banks could no longer be stemmed. By around 1900, the post office savings bank had five times more clients than the trustee savings banks. Not until 1904 were the trustee savings banks granted more freedom regarding assets.

From a modern microfinance perspective, this system of trustee and post office savings banks would seem to be a sound idea, as evidenced by the regional focus, the acceptance of small savings deposits, the partly regional focus and the establishment of close personal contacts among the stakeholders – all combined with non-profit elements. However, the system also had inherent handicaps. Strict regulation led to stagnation, thus stifling creative potential, and kept the system separate from the financial market. Small savers were exploited to finance government needs at low interest rates. The fact that the trustee and post office savings banks did not have a direct local credit business moreover caused a local financial drain. The same thing occurred in France where savings banks also mainly acted as capital collectors for the public authorities, excluded certain societal groups, and operated in a dual structure with post office savings banks (Moster and Vogler 1996; Klein 2003).

Presumably, this might be one reason for Great Britain's loss of industrial leadership at the end of the 19th century and for the delay in French industrialization. The centralized deposit collection schemes catered to the needs of the central government and big industries at the expense of start-ups and MSMEs, whose growth lagged behind. Thus, the local economy lacked important instruments to finance innovation and growth. As Roodman observed as well, this was not ideal and led to "underexploited opportunities," as the contrasting German case will demonstrate (Roodman 2012).

In summary, it has not been the objective here to decide who invented savings banks – a question quite difficult to answer and not important for our purposes. Rather, the aim has been to show that there was an urgent need for savings and loan institutions during industrialization and that a variety of concepts emerged in response, some of which stressed credit, while others focused on savings. Nonetheless, all of the schemes described above were initiated and managed by the upper class or the government. The roots of a modern, integrated savings and credit bank scheme certainly emerged in France parallel to mercantile schemes, but they were not taken up. England's role may have been overestimated, even though business models existed there early on and saving capacity grew faster in England than on the continent. Ultimately, the British approach failed to create fair and regional inclusion. This becomes especially obvious when it is compared to the German model, which is presented in the following section.

4 The emergence of the German savings bank model – Inclusion from the beginning

The German approach explicitly combined aspects of savings and credit on a local basis from the very beginning. Up to the outbreak of World War I, this concept enabled savings banks to develop into regionally focused, quasi universal banks that financed structural, social, economic, and technological change. To this day, the savings banks continue to make up one of the three pillars of the unique German universal banking system.

As far as we know today, the first German savings banks to be set up as such, rather than evolving out of pawnshops or orphan's funds, were established in Hamburg in 1778, in Oldenburg in 1786, in Kiel in 1796, in Goettingen – the first municipal institution – and in Altona in 1801, and in Darmstadt in 1808. The institutions in Kiel and Goettingen operated explicitly as savings and loan banks. This finding refutes the commonly held opinion that the credit business emerged with time; on the contrary, this view is merely apocryphal.[27]

With the founding of these banks, the missing step from innovation, as sketched above, to implementation was finally taken. As far as the institutions' mission and vision was concerned, the establishment of all six banks was motivated primarily by "poverty alleviation" through enablement or empowerment with the aim of socioeconomic convergence. We will now assess whether these banks achieved their objective.

The charter of the so-called "*Ersparungs-Casse*" (savings bank) established in the Duchy of Oldenburg [*Herzogtum Oldenburg*] in 1786 precisely defines the aims of its savings business. According to the charter, "persons of the lower class ... have the opportunity which they lack as yet, to safely deposit, on an interest-bearing basis and without the risk of loss, the small profit which they have earned by modest means through diligence and work in order to satisfy their future needs" (Wysocki 1980). Thus, this bank offered the secure, interest-bearing deposit of smaller amounts that lay outside the scope of interest of the established financial intermediaries.

By contrast, in 1796 the Savings and Loan Bank of Kiel accepted the deposits of any customer who "desired that some of their wages and otherwise honestly earned acquisitions be set aside and saved (...)." Thus, the Kiel bank consciously competed with the existing institutions; it enabled savings of the wealthy to be transferred to the needy, not on the basis of charity, but in the form of loans issued within the framework of a sustainable business model. The credit business was seen as an integral part of the concept. The following statute states the mes-

---

27 Salem, mentioned above, founded in 1749, became a public savings bank in 1838; for the discussion and concepts, see Ashauer 1991, 51–64; Böer 1998; Ott 2006; Trende 1957, 29 ff.; Klein 1982 300 ff.; Wysocki, 1980; Roodman 2012, 48 is not up to date concerning Germany; see Trende 1957, 8 f.; Ashauer 1991, 41–49, 74 f., 90 f.

sage explicitly: "With the... savings bank, we have... as a second and equally important institution of aid for mitigating poverty, associated a credit bank to facilitate our working class citizens in carrying out their trade or art by enabling them to purchase materials or tools, or make any other considerable expenditure, by means of a moderate credit or advance payment, without pledge, but under the responsibility for timely and consistent repayment within short and easily manageable periods." (Wysocki 1980).

> **Snapshot 2: Typology of savings banks in Germany**
>
> There are two main types of savings banks: public and private.
>
> **Public** savings banks comprise
>
> - municipal savings banks (*Stadtsparkassen*), which were the start of the public savings banks movement (Göttingen, 1801). They are run mainly by cities and serve a predominantly urban clientele.
> - district savings banks (*Kreissparkassen*) were intensely promoted by state administrations after the crises of 1846/48 to cover rural areas. They are run by counties and serve a predominantly rural clientele.
>
> The local outreach of the public savings banks generally correlated with the boundaries of the administrative districts or municipalities which they served.
>
> **Private** savings banks are run by private institutions and organizations. Among them is the *Hamburger Sparkasse*, today the largest savings bank in Germany.
>
> Due to mergers, the number of savings banks fell from an all-time high of 3,072 in 1910 to 421 in 2014, of which 416 were public and five private (see chapter 9.3).
>
> In 1871, Germany became a federal national state with the form of a constitutional monarchy, made up of 25 states. Prussia was by far the largest among them, accounting for well over 50% of the total population and economic power, followed by Bavaria, with about 10% of the population. Deriving from this federal structure, which is still in existence today, the individual German states each have their own savings banks laws. The Prussian law of 1838, valid until 1945 (see chapter 4.3), served many other states as a template.
>
> The savings banks (*Sparkassen*) did not come under banking regulation until 1934.

In principle, this embodied a kind of cash credit scheme for tradespeople that enabled short-term loans to be issued flexibly, with a minimum of bureaucracy, and with no collateral required. The provisions of the charter seem pioneering in that credit seekers had to demonstrate the innovative potential of their endeavor or the effect of the loan on the continuation of their business. Explicitly listed among the permissible loan purposes is the redemption of materials or tools pledged in the pawnshop in order not to endanger production. Another characteristic compo-

Snapshot 3: Benchmark data for the Savings and Loan Bank of Kiel, 1796

Sponsor:	A private association known as the Society of Voluntary Friends of the Poor [*Gesellschaft freiwilliger Armenfreunde*], founded in 1792
Aim:	To alleviate poverty

Provisions of the charter of the Savings and Loan Bank of Kiel:

Savings business:

Deposits:	Minimum deposit: 5 Schillings (currency of the duchy of Schleswig)
Maximum deposit:	100 Marks; more in exceptional cases, or after an investment consultation
Interest rate:	Interest paid as from a sum of 50 Schillings: around 4% p.a.
Interest period:	Quarterly, plus an 8-day waiting period (to facilitate the calculation)
Period of notice:	4 weeks prior to the end of the quarter
Savings objectives:	Precautionary and purpose-specific savings
Incentives:	Savings for old age, household goods, dowry, master's equipment, journeyman's uniform, to bridge periods of unemployment, for example seasonal unemployment in the winter months

Loans:

Eligible:	Those citizens operating a trade or business in the city of Kiel
Prerequisite:	Performance audit, with an assessment of the innovation potential of the proposed investment and, conversely, the worst-case scenario which would endanger the sustainability of the business and the profitability of the enterprise
Benefits:	Opportunity to finance tangible goods such as materials and tools, to obtain cash in the case of a liquidity shortfall, and to redeem items pledged to a pawnshop as security for a loan
Credit amount:	Generally 5 to 100 Marks, exceptions possible
Credit interest rate:	4%
Opening times:	Wednesdays 11 a.m. 12 noon and by appointment
Administration:	Voluntary staff consisting of clerks, professors, lawyers, merchants; a salaried accountant; two auditors responsible for carrying out an annual audit
Financing:	Through interest revenues and an endowment of 500 Taler

Support:

- Shares in the form of deposits denominated in Taler, in amounts divisible by 10
- By the subscription of corresponding sums with which possible losses were covered accordingly, either for a particular period or yearly (Wysocki 1980).

nent was equal nominal interest rates for credit and savings; an interest period less favorable to the customer concerning savings contributed to financing the operation costs. In addition, a start capital of 500 Taler[28] was provided by a sponsor. Moreover, there was the possibility of support through stock options or certain sums that could be used to offset possible losses and were made available for at least one year. Voluntary experts managed and audited the bank. For good reason, the accounting officer, however, had a salaried position. He was available to the clients on a daily basis by appointment. The entity owning the bank was an association comparable to the British Friendly Societies.

In all, these savings and loan banks represented a comprehensive microfinance concept in the tradition of Hugues Delestre, one which would make some modern microfinance approaches look truncated and rudimentary. In any event, it contained all the elements necessary for a sustainable implementation of the institutions' objectives.

The bank charter even provided information to the users about possible savings strategies and the degree of deposit security. This information was appropriate in light of the clientele's lack of experience with such modalities and thus increased customer acceptance of the new services offered. For historians, these clues provide a wealth of information about the way in which people thought and carried out their business dealings at that time. For example, tables showed the development of assets with respect to a single, one-time deposit, such as an amount received as a present or in the form of a tip, and for regular savings up to a period of 30 years. Everyone could decide for himself whether frugality early on in life would be worth it in old age – namely, "how one, through his own resources, could secure a decent income for his old age."

The charter also pointed out the possible use of the savings facility as an old-age pension plan: A weekly deposit of one Schilling starting from the 30th year of age would yield, after the 60th year of age, a weekly "subsidy" of 8 Schillings for ten years, to be understood as a contribution to their living expenses. Thus, the concept revealed surprising similarities to current pension strategies.

4.1 Divergence and convergence – Comparing the early savings banks

Even though a systematic comparison of the six "primary savings banks" that had been founded by 1808 reveals a certain degree of variation among them, with the Kiel institution as a reference model, these deviations were not large[29]. Notably,

---

28 Designation for the silver coinage in widespread use in the northern German states from the 15th to the 19th centuries, and the etymological root of the word "dollar" (500 Taler = equivalent to about 1,500 to 2,000 daily wages of a day labourer, 1 Taler = 24 Groschen until 1821, later 30 Silbergroschen.
29 Wysocki 1980, 24; for the statutes, see 197–216.

there was again a certain degree of convergence between these strategies and the approaches of modern MFIs.

The parameters of the business model of these precursors of modern savings banks are outlined below:

Mission and vision:
Institutionalized support to encourage the propensity to save, the formation of savings, and the financial welfare of broad segments of the population.

Sponsors:
In the case of three of the institutions, associations which today would be called non-governmental organizations (NGOs);
In the case of the other three, public funding bodies: the Duchy of Oldenburg and the municipalities of Goettingen and Darmstadt.

Administration:
Voluntary and professional; regular supervision by auditors.

Target groups:
Defined by various social, age-related and geographical criteria; underprivileged "non-banked" groups such as "low-income diligent persons of both genders" or "everyone, including all low-income individuals";
The Kiel savings bank was open to all interested individuals. The Goettingen bank charter explicitly addressed the city's citizens. In the Darmstadt bank charter, children were specifically mentioned, with emphasis on the fact that trust funds or gifts were intended for investment and not for consumption.

Minimum deposits:
Very small sums were accepted, but did not bear interest; interest accrued as from a sum equivalent to the daily wage of a day laborer.[30]

> **Snapshot 4: Savings objectives**
>
> Precautionary savings for emergencies or periods of illness and old age; purpose-specific savings for marriage, dowry, household items, education and further training, or establishment of a business.

The institutions' business focused on the acceptance of deposits and thus promoted saving. In order to ensure that revenues would be available to cover interest payments, two of the banks integrated a credit business into their operations. In addition to short-term business-oriented lending, the banks financed municipalities, purchased government bonds, and granted mortgage-secured loans. Probably as a safety precaution, the bank charter explicitly ruled out "the needy" as borrow-

---

30 For information about income, see Hardach 2006.

ers. In addition, the savings bank in Darmstadt cooperated with a pawnshop, opened at the same time as the bank, in order to add credit operations.

The interest-bearing minimum deposit corresponded to about the amount of a day's wage or somewhat above. This did not mean "very small sums" verbatim. Rather, the depositors had to start their own individual saving process upstream: The savings banks supported these prospective customers to an extent by "storing" the customers' small savings in the bank without interest until the minimum limit needed to accrue interest had been reached. Likewise, there were maximum limits on deposits, but not throughout the whole system at that time. Many bank charters explicitly anticipated exceptions with the aim of ensuring the necessary flexibility for an innovative enterprise.

From the business parameters that they established, one can infer that savings and loan banks emerged because the existing credit institutions did not supply financial services to certain groups of people. This hypothesis is substantiated by the fact that in many cases conventional bankers were involved in the management of the savings and loan institutions, mostly on a voluntary basis. Thus, from the very beginning, the institutions relied upon expert competence, including that of auditors for the purpose of regular controls. These factors were and have been essential criteria for success, as is also true of today's MFIs.

The wide diversity during the early savings bank phase was mainly attributable to the heterogeneous political structures of the time. Criticizing this heterogeneity fails to give due recognition to the creativity of the founders and overlooks the idea that innovation itself first draws upon a wide range of experiences before it can flourish along suitable paths of development. The fact that political regulatory initiatives were still lacking in Germany can definitely be seen as a positive factor, as the negative examples of France and England in this regard show. There and elsewhere, a restrictive early legal code hampered the development of the institutions and led to adverse results, most notably regional capital drain and the financial exploitation of the poor.[31]

The constellation that arose in Germany can be considered a stroke of luck, for it triggered competition among differing approaches. Moreover, though the chaotic conditions in continental Europe from 1789 led to enormous suffering, the period also spurred many new developments and gave new hope. Undoubtedly, the insecurity of the times increased the willingness to innovate, just as it promoted both intellectual flexibility and flexibility in practical terms under the key catchwords of the French Revolution, "freedom, equality and fraternity."

---

31 See chapters 4.3 and 7.6.

In all, we see a business model with a flexible range of variations allowing the inclusion of hitherto marginalized individuals into the financial market with the aim of socioeconomic convergence – namely, precisely the kind of inclusion that modern MFIs are intended to achieve. Considering the challenges of the time, the early birth of this concept is a remarkable, yet natural consequence.

A political evaluation of the early savings bank phase comes to less favorable conclusions, however. Even though the intentions were convergence and inclusion, maintenance of the status quo – whether in the sense of preservation or reformation – predominated. It is no coincidence that the Establishment was behind the founding of the banks. At that time, the business model did not provide for any participation of the newly included target groups in the organization and management of the bank.

SWOT analysis of early German savings institutions

Strengths:
- Interest accrued on small savings
- Transparent conditions of business
- Inclusive approach
- Audit and supervision

Weakness(es):
- Limited flexibility

Opportunities:
- Poverty alleviation
- Empowerment
- Institution building
- Regional organization
- Absence of incentives to focus on profit maximization

Threats:
- Conservative social approach
- Close links to the authorities

4.2 Diffusion in the wake of early industrialization and growing incomes

After the defeat of France in the Napoleonic Wars, the Congress of Vienna politically restructured continental Europe in 1815. In numerous cases, the old pre-revolutionary conditions again took hold. Even so, that did not deter the savings bank movement, for the concept tended to help sustain the system. Moreover, rapid population growth and a lack of jobs were giving rise to mass poverty. Microfinance concepts were needed more than ever (Wehler 2005; Ashauer 1991).

Nevertheless, the existing savings banks could not kindle the desired interest at first. This is further proof that revolutions need time. Among the first German banks to be established after 1815 were the Württemberg State Savings Bank and the Municipal Savings Bank of Berlin, the first municipal savings bank in Prussia, both of which were established in 1818. Contemporaries also looked to England and Switzerland as models. Among other factors, this might be due to the fact that England was the first country to pass a savings bank law, as discussed above (Trende 1957).

The Berlin institution reveals parameters that are characteristic of the early phase of savings banks. Initial savings generally originated from the "nest egg," which meant that there had been a longer process of saving before the funds were deposited with the bank. Alternatively, the funds placed on deposit originated from a one-time growth in assets in the form of gifts or inheritances, since the mean annual deposit in the first year was at least onehalf of the annual income earned by a day laborer.

> **Snapshot 5: First Prussian municipal savings bank – the Municipal Savings Bank of Berlin, 1818[32]**
>
> Motivation: Savings as a panacea
>
> According to writer Adolf Steckfuss, commenting on conditions in Berlin around 1818, "There was a terrible, suffocating poverty among the lower classes of Berlin, and all endeavors of the city administrators to mitigate it proved to be increasingly in vain, for the means which the city could offer were only meager."
>
> Irrespective of the social echelon of the savers, the motivation for the establishment of the savings bank was stated as follows: "In order to give the city's inhabitants the opportunity to safely deposit their savings on an interest-bearing basis, and thus to help them acquire capital which they can use in the event of marriage, the establishment of a business, old age or in cases of emergency, the city board members have hereby decided to open a savings bank under the guarantee of the municipalities and under the authorization of the Municipality and its supervisors."

---

32 Trende 1957, 83 ff.; www.berliner-sparkasse.de/module/ihre_sparkasse/geschichte-seit-1818.

Below is an overview of the chronology of the founding of the Berlin savings bank and key aspects of its savings and loan business:

Chronology of founding:

July 31, 1817: Adoption by the city board after "much preparation and seeking of expert advice" of a resolution to establish a "savings bank for the poorer class of the city's inhabitants... ." The Prussian state government did not object to the City of Berlin's plans and allowed the city to remain in charge of administering the bank.

April 26, 1818: Adoption of the savings bank charter.

June 15, 1818: Opening at 9 a.m., business location: Berlin City Hall [*Rathaus*], Spandauer Strasse.

Nature of savings business (as announced in the bulletin *"Intelligenzblatt"* 135 of June 6, 1818):

"§ 1. *This savings bank, which is located at the City Hall, and may not be removed therefrom, is hereby authorized to accept sums in hard cash of twelve Groschen[33] up to fifty Taler.*

§ 2. The bank will pay interest on all deposited sums of one Taler and above, with the exception of Groschen, which will not earn interest, with this interest being four and a sixth percent."

Maximum deposits: 50 Taler. This sum corresponded to about the annual income of a daily laborer and therefore represented a fortune. Maximum deposit restrictions were eliminated in 1827.

Credit business:

From the point of view of modern microfinance, the loan business was suboptimal, because the municipal administration, used the savings for its own purposes.

Acceptance:

On the last trading day in 1818, 551 accounts with a total volume of savings deposits of 13,982 Taler were registered, i.e. an average of 25 Taler per account, a modest start.

---

33 Subdivision of the Taler currency. At that time: 1 Taler = 24 Silbergroschen. In today's currency, one Taler was equivalent to about EUR 35.

Figure 7: Berlin City Hall 1818, business location of the Municipal Savings Bank of Berlin (Archives of Berliner Sparkasse)

Sitz der Sparkasse im Gründungsjahr 1818

Also typical was the long time that it took for customers to accept the model. Five hundred accounts opened in the first year is hardly a large volume of accounts for a capital city with around 200,000 residents. But isn't that the normal pattern of an innovation diffusion curve? Moreover, the public savings banks' close links to the authorities may have inhibited the diffusion of innovation. In the worst-case scenario, the savers were reluctant to entrust their savings to the tax collector. Even in the early 1880s, Raiffeisen, one of the promoters of the German cooperative movement, raised the subject of the disadvantages related to the close ties to state authorities and mentioned fears about tax increases connected with savings deposits.[34]

The initial reluctance of the clients to embrace the bank model dissolved, at the latest, when the first interest payments had been made on deposits and people had learned of the advantages via word of mouth or the favorable bank reports. From the client's point of view, the incentive was the safe and interest-bearing savings. The nominal interest rate of over 4% also ensured that inflation would be offset. The positive outcome from an economic point of view was that previously hoarded capital came into financial circulation to help generate workplaces and to accelerate growth dynamics.

As a result, the following years were marked by a wave of new savings bank foundings. In 1825 in the German states, there were 110 such institutions, most of

---

34 For details see chapter 7.2.

which conducted their business under the name *"Sparkasse"*. Twenty-nine savings banks had their headquarters in Prussia, 26 in the Duchy of Schleswig-Holstein and Lauenburg and 23 in Bavaria. The remaining banks were distributed across the other German states. Though the diffusion process picked up speed, it was still in its infancy. By 1836, 281 savings banks were registered, and there was no end to the successful new foundings in sight (Ashauer 1991; Wysocki 1980).

Yet it is important to ask here: In terms of microfinance, what changed after 1808? There were necessarily still many links to the "primary savings banks." The most obvious change was the majority ownership by municipalities or municipal corporations whose principal aim was to reduce burdensome poverty in their areas. There were also further private savings banks, as in Saxony and those of the Aachen Association for Promoting Industriousness [*Aachener Verein zur Beförderung der Arbeitsamkeit*], with its highly innovative and sustainable approach, which will be discussed in section 5 (Centralverein 1863; Thomes 2010).

As before, the target group was primarily, but not exclusively, the lower class. Deposit limits were flexibly changed downward as well as upward; occasionally these limits were coupled with social criteria. In principle, the intended aims remained unchanged. Again worthy of note here was the idea of savings as a prerequisite for professional investments or the start of a new business. This was just as the Berlin savings bank had specified in its public notification on the occasion of its opening in 1818–even though it did not take the further step of also transferring funds to private individuals in the form of loans. The annual interest rates on deposits of 3% to over 4% at least reflected market conditions, thereby offering a considerable incentive for small savers and often for well-to-do savers as well. This was documented by the rise in larger deposits, which must be seen as a positive inclusive development.[35]

The success of the savings business almost automatically led to a systematic credit business. Granted, the various strategies pursued did not fulfill all microfinance criteria. One negative example is the Berlin savings bank – it invested the money exclusively in its own municipal bonds. Meanwhile, the Bavarian savings banks bought bonds of the state of Bavaria, and the situation was the same in Württemberg. As already noted above, there would appear to be an inherent conflict in investing the savings of society's most underprivileged members, at least partly to cheaply finance public projects beyond the area served by the institutions, causing an undesirable regional capital drain in the process (Ashauer 1991).

Nonetheless, most of the institutions built their own credit business based on the typical instruments of mortgages, promissory notes, and guaranteed and collateralized loans. Thus, they covered numerous microfinance targets. The nominal interest rate hovered around 5% p.a., with transparent terms and conditions and

---

35 Trende 1957.

flexible maturity periods. Consequently, in cooperation with the pawnshops, the savings banks made an essential contribution to eradicating the "wretched usurers," as the Prussian Minister of the Interior put it in 1828.[36]

Particularly worthy of note here is the moderate range of interest rates, which was an important prerequisite for the success of the business model and part of what enabled the institutions to achieve an economic impact. In contrast, high interest rates and too-short and inflexible terms to maturity are essential reasons for the failure of current microfinance business models.

The important point is that the promotion of savings and of credit complemented each other as equal objectives. Moreover, the legal authorities of the time also allowed the young institutions much leeway for development. Undoubtedly, this had positive effects since it promoted the development of "best practices." As before, what all savings banks had in common was the concrete, microfinance-specific distinguishing feature of interest-bearing savings deposits in small amounts. Moreover, as another distinguishing feature of microfinance, many of the banks developed a small credit business from the start as well.

The motivations for founding the savings banks mostly concurred, with the exceptions to the rule only serving to confirm the rule. In addition, the founders all stemmed from the politically and financially dominant class. As before, they were motivated by the need to address societal changes within the framework of the status quo. At the same time, the success of the institutions would serve the interests of the upper class, and they provided an increasing amount of support by disseminating information, promoting the establishment of further institutions, providing financial support and, finally, establishing a suitable legal framework. Politics had discovered the savings banks as a panacea for saving the system. Was this a good prerequisite for the achievement of microfinance goals?

In the 1820s and 1830s, the 39 German monarchic states and four Free Imperial Cities *[Freie und Reichsstädte]* were in a state of turmoil triggered by political, social, and economic uncertainties. The population continued to grow, the pace of urbanization accelerated and poverty spread as urban freedom lured the poor peasants to the cities. Yet the cities could not keep pace with the development: There was not a sufficient demand for trades, crafts, and services to satisfy the increasing demand for jobs. "Pauperism" became a key word in political discourse. Nevertheless, politicians and entrepreneurs continued to promote the industrialization process, which ultimately helped to improve living conditions.[37]

Intrinsic conviction combined with the threat of another revolution served to accelerate the pace of change. The year 1828 marked the first German interstate tariff treaties that culminated, in 1834, in the famous "*Zollverein*": the first German

---

36 Trende 1957, 104f.; for more details concerning usury, see the chapter on credit cooperatives.
37 See chapters 2.1 and 2.2 and Ashauer 1991, 65ff.

common market and an initial step towards political unification. One year later, in 1835, the first railway track was laid, and not long thereafter, the economy took off. There was considerable collateral action behind these developments, and the savings banks had a growing role to play among the various instruments for change. Meanwhile, the state strived to consolidate structures in order to achieve economies of scale.

4.3 The Prussian Savings Bank Regulations of 1838 – A legal template for future development

As implied above, the laws established to regulate savings banks must be assessed ambivalently from a microfinance point of view. In the state of Bavaria as from 1816, the savings banks – together with insurers against fire and hail and the pawnbroking shops – belonged to a system of institutions operating within the framework of legislation for the poor (Koch 2012). Yet the decisive change came with the foundation of a public debt cancellation fund in 1823. Among other things, this fund was obligated to pay 5% interest p.a. This freed the municipalities from the task of investing money and indeed led to a more frequent rate of new savings bank establishments. When the state reduced the interest rate to 3.5% – as in England, to lower capital costs and to discourage wealthy individuals from participating in such deposit schemes – the savings banks bought government bonds, which again was not at all in keeping with the aims of microfinance. The Bavarian Savings Bank Act of 1843 achieved a certain degree of flexibility by establishing the following key features:

- Limitation of the target clientele to the lower class ("persons of meager means").
- Reduction of the minimum deposit to 30 Kreuzer (half a Florin), i.e. two to three daily wages.
- Establishment of a maximum deposit amount of 400 Florins.
- The possibility of collaboration of the savings banks with pawnshops and mutual benefit societies.

From a modern microfinance perspective, the positive features of this legislation were the reduced minimum deposit (though it still equaled more than a day's wage) and the possibility of collaboration with a local credit business. However, the law still forced the savings banks into a social niche and limited their range of action. In fact, the forced reduction of their larger deposits caused liquidity problems for many institutions, since the public debt cancellation fund was not always sufficiently liquid to meet its repayment obligations. The economic and political crisis years of 1846 to 1848, which were pivotal in Germany and beyond, even saw a payment stop on the part of the debt cancellation fund, and thus on the part of many savings banks as well. These conditions represented a serious setback for the development of savings banks in Bavaria (Trende 1957). At the same time, they paved the way for new financial cooperatives that operated outside the state's sphere of influence.

Prussia, by far the biggest German state, took a much more liberal approach in many ways. The public savings banks were only subject to specific legislation from the 1830s, and then only indirectly. The earliest legislation dealt with the legal status of the deposits held and the handling of passbooks as bearer or registered securities, a status they had as from 1836.

The debate on the appropriate legal framework led to the first Prussian Savings Bank Act of 1838. This act was important for two main reasons: First, having resulted from a fundamental and controversial opinion-forming process, the law retained its validity for almost a century. Second, it served as a model for other German states in various ways. Both points reflect the law's innovative character. In contrast to the very detailed Bavarian law, the Prussian law merely established a framework regulation which built on typical practices. It provided guidelines for the foundation, organization, and operation of savings banks without stipulating the details. Moreover, the auditing had to be performed in an insightful manner which took the specific nature of the savings banks' operations into account. The highest licensing authorities were now the governments of the Prussian provinces. This implied the acceptance of regional needs, which is a central causal factor in the long-lasting success of the German business model of the savings bank under municipal trusteeship.[38]

The savings business was intended to focus primarily, but not exclusively, on the needs of low-income depositors; the inclusion aspect of microfinance was interpreted reciprocally here. Thus, wealthy savers were by no means an exception, which also attests to the attractiveness of the interest rates earned on deposits. Of

---

Snapshot 6: Microfinance-relevant aspects of the Prussian Savings Bank Regulations of 1838

The minimum deposit should be as low as possible.

"In order to promote the primary objective of the savings banks of enabling the most extensive use by the poorer classes, the minimum deposit which the institution collects should be set as low as possible (...). The maximum of the individual sums as well as the total deposit of each depositor lies at the discretion of the community (...)."

The maximum deposit remained flexible. The prerequisite was that the municipality took care to manage liquidity aspects, in order to ensure that the institution would be able to repay obligations at any time. This was seen as a decisive factor for client acceptance.

---

38 Hahn 1920, 5–13; Mura 1987, 107f.; Thomes 1985a; Trende 1957, 103–113.

course, in 1830 Berlin introduced a "certification" by savers to attest that they belonged to the lower-income classes, which served to exclude wealthy savers.

The stipulations regarding the organization of the credit business were just as flexible. In principle, every "fully safe type" of investment was possible. This made it easy to match investments to varied and changing needs. Explicitly cited were mortgages, national government bonds, mortgage bonds, pawn loans, gilt-edged securities, and accepted bills. This left enough leeway for the activities of an MFI, which the savings banks then took advantage of, with lending strategies influenced by a mixture of expediency and social motivation.

In the 1840s, state-guaranteed railroad shares were added as well in order to facilitate the financing of this epochal investment in the transportation sector. The complementary effects were apparent, in particular, in the coal and steel industry, general construction and civil engineering, and machinery and plant engineering. Municipal loans generated comparable effects. In the 1840s, the Municipal Savings Bank of Düsseldorf, for example, lent around 90 % of its assets to the city, which used these funds not only to finance infrastructural measures such as the development of the Rhine riverbank and the construction of a harbor, but also for the promotion of cultural projects. Once government bonds were included and began to make up an increasing share in the assets of the savings banks, the lower class also played a significant role in co-financing the development of modern public infrastructure. From the very beginning, the personal loan and mortgage business with private individuals, ranging from employees to owners of medium-sized businesses, was likewise a part of the bank's mission statement, however much more effort it entailed (Haas 1976; Pohl 2001). Inherently popular products were investment instruments that curtailed risk, administrative effort, and the amount of expertise needed to deal in them.

Regarding the question of financial and economic interest rates, the Prussian Savings Bank Regulations stipulated the following: The interest rates set for both loans and deposits should cover all costs and allow the formation of a suitable reserve fund. Moreover, the banks were permitted to use surplus profits for charitable funding. In practice, this led to nominal interest rates of maximally 5 %. Not only did these rates allow the formation of a reserve fund, but also the charitable distribution of surpluses, which further boosted interest in the business model and the momentum of development (Wysocki 1980).

Another key criterion for success was the supervision of the banks. The law assigned responsibility for the monitoring function to the municipal supervisory authorities. In addition, it generally called for continued watchfulness on the part of the provincial and regional governments; In particular, documentary proof was to be submitted annually. The publication of annual results was likewise mandatory. Extraordinary audits were possible as well. This bundle of measures contributed decisively to increased customer confidence – a prerequisite for success. The private savings banks subjected themselves voluntarily to the statutory supervisory regime to preclude any competitive disadvantages. Individual legal rulings, where they arose, tended to help simplify the banks' business dealings rather than reduce their flexibility.

> **Snapshot 7: Microfinance-relevant structural parameters in the late 1840s**
>
> Core goal: Collection of interest-bearing small savings deposits combined with lending activities
>
> Initiators: The upper class and the municipal authorities, with the aim of perpetuating the system
>
> Organization: Mostly municipal, regulated by public law, no branches
>
> Personnel: Dual structure consisting of:
> A manager, usually salaried, or a municipal clerk who also handled the city treasury; fixed or variable income
> A board of directors made up of experts (bankers, entrepreneurs, politicians, government officials) working on a voluntary basis
>
> Flexibility: With regard to opening hours, minimum and maximum deposits, interest rates, credit business; flexibility as an important factor to allow the institutions to best comply with regional needs and customs.

SWOT analysis

Strengths:

- Interest-bearing small savings deposits
- Individual credit opportunities
- Professional administration
- Transparency
- Clearly defined terms and conditions
- Security of savings deposits
- Regular auditing and supervision

Weakness(es):

- No or little network
- Concentrated in cities
- Short opening hours
- No mini savings deposits
- Formal processes
- State influence

Opportunities:

- Rising incomes
- Growing acceptance on the part of customers and the founders themselves as familiarity increased
- Establishment of branch networks

Threats:

- Competing newcomers
- Innovation on the part of traditional financial institutions
- State influence on investment policy

4.4 Urgent need for profound change – Towards the economic takeoff

The Prussian Savings Bank Regulations of 1838 initially only slowly began to affect the rate of bank start-ups: In 1839 and 1840, only 10 new institutions were established. The late 1840s, however, then saw the rate of bank foundings begin to pick up. While only 85 banks in all were in operation in 1839, by 1847 there were about 200 banks in operation, holding total deposits of 15.7 million Taler (about EUR 500 million). By the end of 1849, a further 36 savings banks holding total deposits of more than 100,000 Taler had been founded; the institutions located in Aachen[39], Berlin and Lübben held deposits of over one million Taler each. These three institutions maintained a fully operational network of branches, which can be considered a key parameter of success. As of the end of 1849, there were a total of 700 savings banks, not including branches or agencies, operating in the German states. Savings banks were ubiquitous in every city.[40]

This diffusion process was propelled by various factors – namely, the crisis-driven socioeconomic modernization process, political initiatives, and the personal commitment of local individuals. There are very heterogeneous individual findings concerning geographical distribution, organization, and business scope and practices, all of which typically reflect the specifics of regional habits, needs, and legislation. Last but not least, the savings banks did not face any serious competition around the middle of the 19th century.

Snapshot 8: Diffusion process in Germany

In 1825, 110 savings banks; in 1836, 281 savings banks; in 1853, 912 savings banks (Trende 1957).

---

[39] For this private savings bank, see Thomes 2010.
[40] For regional concepts, see Ashauer 1991, 79.

Table 1: Top ten savings banks in Prussia in 1849

City/Region	Savings (Volume in Taler)	Accounts (Number)
Aachen	1,935,840	11,498
Berlin	1,416,560	30,292
Lübben	1,366,369	19,416
Breslau	912,472	14,473
Magdeburg	680,512	12,945
Elberfeld	487,726	7,060
Görlitz	477,971	10,338
Soest	369,704	2,655
Stettin	369,255	9,350
Stralsund	298,046	8,165
Total	**8,314,455**	**126,192**

The ratio between savings and accounts mirrors different savings models and practices (Ashauer 1991; Trende 1957).

At first glance, the balance of this diffusion phase looks impressive. Not without reason did politicians of the time consider savings banks to be "the greatest economic discovery of the modern era."[41] A more precise analysis of the data, however, shows that the impact of savings bank diffusion was still low. From a statistical point of view, per capita assets in Prussia in 1850 amounted to only one Taler. Moreover, deposit levels fluctuated greatly and the main target group needed to be more fully involved in the initiatives aimed at them.

The fact is that the supporters overestimated the capability and willingness of the target group to save during this early phase. The income of the masses often was

---

Snapshot 9: Savings Bank of the Aachen Association, 1850[42]

The savings bank had over 13,000 deposit customers, i.e. there was one savings account for every 35 residents of the area. Total deposits reached 2.2 million Taler or 6.6 million Marks[43] and thus considerably surpassed those of all other savings banks. The average balances in the preferential savings accounts linked to social criteria amounted to 220 Marks, while those in the standard savings accounts amounted to 829 Marks. In 1850, approximately 43% of the Aachen savings bank's assets were attributable to mortgages, 23% to securities, 14% to bills of exchange, and about 6% each to collateral loans and bank deposits – lending operations that were atypical for savings banks at that time.

---

41 Convention of the Bavarian Kingdom, 1843; Ashauer 1991, 116.
42 Centralverein 1863; Kähler 1910, 1912; Aachener Verein 1909; see the special chapter on the holistic and inclusive Aachen Association scheme.
43 Currency of the new German Reich [*Kaiserreich*] founded in 1871; 1 Mark = 100 Pfennige = 0.33 Taler = 0.58 Florin.

Table 2: Ability to save of urban, low-income households, first half of 19th century

	Income in Marks p.a.	Cost of Living in Marks p.a.	Amount available to save in Marks p.a.
Lübeck	340	313	27
Frankfurt	450	450	0
Bremen	377	374	3
Hamburg	389	418	-29

Wilhelm Otto Ludwig Frhr. v. Reden: Vergleichende Zusammenstellung der Preise der notwendigsten Lebensbedürfnisse der handarbeitenden Volksklassen in Hamburg, Bremen, Lübeck und Frankfurt a. M. in: v. Reden (Editor): Zeitschrift des Vereins für deutsche Statistik, vol. 1, Berlin, 1847, p. 1041, 1046; quoted by Böer 1998, 24.

simply still too low and too inconsistent to allow for sustainable saving. The savings banks did offer a financially attractive safe harbor, however, as well as for small assets in the form of gifts or inheritances.

The legendary Silesian Weaver's Revolt of 1844 was not the first example of upheaval in response to the precarious conditions described earlier. The revolt was a drastic measure to draw the attention of the public to the abusive conditions prevailing in this cotton industry, which was widespread throughout the countryside. One direct reaction to the revolt was the establishment of the Central Union for the Welfare of the Working Classes [*Centralverein für das Wohl der arbeitenden Klassen*]. Once again, a coalition of educational and financial experts, individuals and bureaucrats worked towards allowing the growing proletariat a share in the profits of the economic upswing. For this purpose, local associations were supposed to promote the establishment of savings banks, pension funds, health insurance, and support funds. What differentiated them from comparable organizations were their scientific and analytical approaches, as set forth in numerous publications (Centralverein 1863; Reulecke 1998). Notably, no contact took place between these reform-oriented circles and the emerging workers' associations, a fact which again illustrates the social divide that was an inherent aspect of the relationship between the savings banks and their clients. It should be noted at this point that one of the activists behind the founding of the Union was Hermann Schulze-Delitzsch, who was also one of the engineers of the German credit cooperatives and will be discussed further.

Meanwhile, the whole of Europe was steering towards a new crisis resulting from continuously precarious incomes and a still-volatile agricultural production. The leading elite continued to cling to and defend the conventional structures. The entrepreneurs were profiting from the situation, for the problematic factors hindered neither the spread of a productive factory system nor the payment of low wages. Also, the market distributed the benefits and costs of the industrial growth unevenly, in favor of entrepreneurs and the elites.

When the last great European agrarian crisis brought about misery and death in 1846/47, this key event once again led to political revolution. Driven by various

Table 3: Savings banks density in selected German states, 1905

State	Number of agencies	Residents per agency	Area served per agency, in km²
Baden	156	12,889	96.6
Bavaria	983	6,535	77.2
Hamburg	89	9,830	4.7
Hesse	48	25,191	160.2
Prussia	4,964	7,518	70.3
Saxony	421	10,709	35.6
Württemberg	1,922	1,197	10.1
German Reich	9,127	6,644	59.2

Pohl et al. 2005, 30.

interests, the revolutionary political movements aimed to overthrow the old order once and for all. From this point of view, the *Communist Manifesto* published by Marx and Engels in 1848 mirrored the prevailing zeitgeist. In turn, the ruling class tried, as usual, to save the system by distributing grain and initiating employment measures, and, at the same time, to generate "loyal domestics" and "reliable workers" by building the personal wealth of the workers. This constellation of responses is highly familiar from modern-day experiences in emerging economies. History has shown, however, that just making microfinance structures available within a reform-resistant system ultimately merely gives impetus to the societal and political reform process which the microfinance measures are intended to stem. Improved income and living conditions are needed as well as financial institutions (Wehler 2005, vol. 2).

4.5 The savings business around 1900 – Cradle-to-grave incentives

In Germany, approximately 21 million people out of a population of around 60 million – or statistically speaking, every German household – owned a savings passbook in 1913.[44] Thus, it is no exaggeration to speak of a comprehensive geographic dissemination of savings banks and of socioeconomic inclusion, one of the main objectives of the modern microfinance approach. Even though this process took around a century, it would surely have been accelerated under today's socio-technical conditions. The following presents some details of this process which are of interest from a contemporary perspective.

As regards geographic accessibility to savings banks, German Reich statistics for 1913 indicate that there were 3,133 savings banks operating over 6,000 branches for a total of around 10,000 locations. This meant that there was one branch for

---

44 Trende 1957, 291 ff.; Ashauer 1991, 101 ff.; Deutsche Bundesbank 1976.

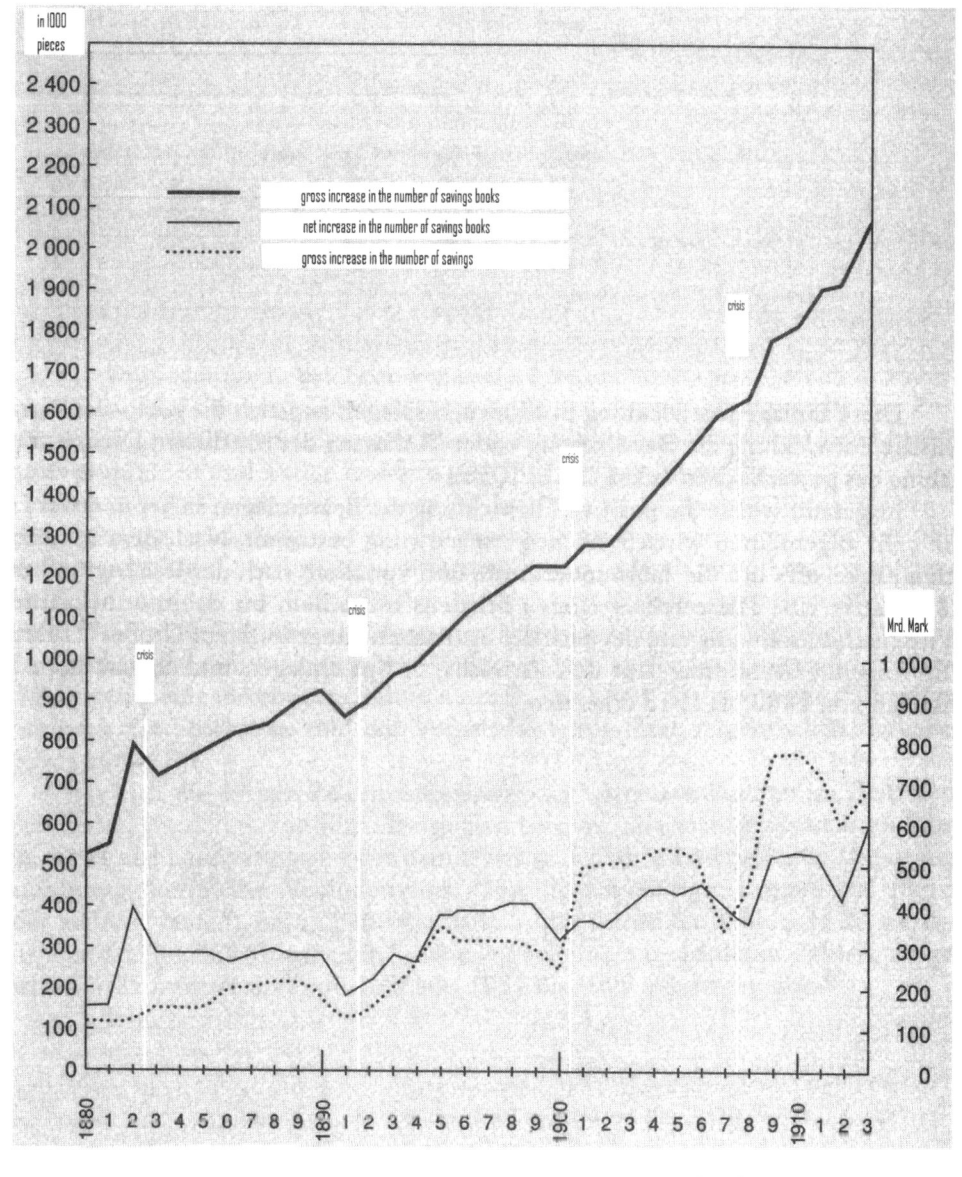

Figure 8: Savings passbooks and savings in Prussia, 1880-1913 (in bn Mark) (Ashauer 1991, 130)

less than every 6,000 residents. In addition, there were thousands of support institutions, i.e. the school, youth, factory, "pfennig," premium, and old age savings banks. These institutions often employed so-called "home savings banks," money boxes, automated saving machines, or savings stamps as well as doorstep collection, i.e. tools that facilitated regular saving. These instruments were more or less spread throughout the German states.[45] In other words, there was a wide variety of opportunities to save. At the turn of the 20th century, everyone in Germany –

---

45 For details, see the following pages.

> **Snapshot 10: Forerunner of cellphone banking? Savings machines: First installed in the city of Padua, Italy**
>
> Around 1895, one Italian bank installed savings machines at eight sites. All you had to do was insert a 10-centesimo coin, turn a crank and receive a voucher. Once you had collected five vouchers, you could open a savings account.
>
> A contemporary reporter's comment: *"You cannot make saving any easier. The machine works very precisely and does not accept bad coins. This idea might find imitators."* (Trende 1957)
>
> Savings machine in a German school, 1908
>
> Source: *Die Sparkasse. Volkswirtschaftliche Zeitschrift*, 626, 1908, p. 139.

whether he or she was an infant, pupil, worker, housewife or pensioner – also had the opportunity to save at literally every corner in town – at the kiosk, shop, train station, school, church, city hall or other government building, workplace or pub.

Even if there was no opportunity nearby or if an individual did not want to make the effort to get there, the minimum deposit amount could be collected door-to-door, as was already the case at the Frankfurt Savings Bank in 1826. The fact is: From the mid-19th century on, the smallest savings deposits gained more attention than ever before, even though (or because) incomes had been increasing consistently, and even after social safety networks became increasingly secure by legislation from the 1880s on. At the same time, the minimum interest-bearing deposit amounts declined.

Another factor contributing to the accessibility and success of savings banks was the so-called "transferability of savings deposits" introduced during the 1880s. This service reflected the needs of a geographically mobile industrialized society. For example, at the beginning of 1884, 59 savings banks of the State District of Düsseldorf [*Regierungsbezirk Düsseldorf*], recognized as a national pioneer in the banking sector and part of the highly industrialized Ruhr area, established this service in their charter. By 1913, this service was standard. It represented an instrument which was of increasing importance in binding customers and enhancing customer loyalty.[46]

Regarding the temporal accessibility of savings banks, from 1900 on most savings banks offered opening hours every workday. Unlike before, when they had opened their doors even on Sundays after church services or in the evenings, the banks were now closed on Sundays and holidays. These opening times also applied, with some variations, to agencies or branches, which were still often connected with shops or pubs and reflected their opening times. Apart from this, in 1913 there were many types of branches. Reusch differentiated two main types in 1908:[47]

- Independent branches that distributed their own savings passbooks and offered deposit and withdrawal facilities in the branch.
- Dependent branches, with account management at the main bank, but with deposit and withdrawal facilities in the branch.

Moreover, there were numerous branches with a combination of characteristics of both types of branch.

> **Snapshot 11: Complicated but safe – agency banking of the District Savings Bank of Saarbrücken [*Spar- und Darlehenskasse für den Kreis Saarbrücken*], 1888/89**
>
> The agents were allowed to accept individual deposits up to a sum of 600 Marks. The amounts deposited at the agencies were transferred by post to the main office of the bank; if these deposited sums amounted to 600 Marks, the transfer to the bank took place immediately. The amounts were registered in the deposit records at the main office, and the savers received an interim receipt.
>
> The agents' compensation for this service was 0.5% of the collected deposits.
>
> The agents were not permitted to execute withdrawals.
>
> The agents processed loan applications and submitted them to the Board of Trustees for their decision.[48]

---

[46] Haas 1976; Thomes 2007; Trende 1957, 412 ff.
[47] Concerning professionalization and agencies, see Trende 1957, 366 ff., 556 ff.; Reusch 1935.
[48] Work instructions for agents 1888; Thomes 1985a.

> **Snapshot 12: Doorstep collection of deposits by savings banks in Germany**
>
> Among other institutions, the Frankfurt Polytechnic Society *[Frankfurtische Gesellschaft zur Beförderung nützlicher Künste und deren Hilfswissenschaften]* in Frankfurt am Main introduced the "doorstep" deposit collection service in its savings department *[Ersparnisanstalt]* in 1826. The private savings society founded in Karlsruhe in 1832 offered this service as well. In 1912, another savings bank, the Nassau State Bank in Wiesbaden, advertised its doorstep deposit collection service for servants – free of charge and with interest paid on the deposits. The service required a membership fee of 0.50 Marks and minimum monthly deposits of 1 Mark for nine months. The members' employers and their family members, including "children, in particular," could participate, too. The Nassau State Bank also suggested that employers should both encourage their servants to join and pay the membership fees of their employees.
>
> After the monetary reform of 1948, the savings banks throughout Germany revived the doorstep collection of savings deposits and thereby gained many new customers.

As the examples show, one literally could not escape from saving; thriftiness and saving were imbued in the society as a virtue and mission in times of modernization, though saving in a way was less necessary than before. The underlying incentive was still to prompt people to regularly save even the smallest amounts. There were many occasions that made long-term saving of such small sums worthwhile, such as first communion, confirmation, education, attainment of master craftsman status, marriage, illness, old age, a death in the family, or any other events entailing one-time expenditures best covered by funds set aside earlier. Such long-term saving greatly diminishing the need for emergency loans which are so widespread in developing countries today.

As before, the initiators and agents were typically prominent local citizens, such as politicians, teachers, ministers, entrepreneurs, etc., and companies. It should be kept in mind that numerous institutions, such as the Prussian Mining Administration, railway companies, or other corporations ran their own savings banks, though unfortunately there is no general statistical data. They also cooperated in many different ways with the public savings banks.[49]

The initiators involved now were still motivated by a combination of intrinsically philanthropic and state-supported ethical convictions and the familiar attempts to mitigate social inequity, and thus to maintain the political status quo. As has become apparent in retrospect, this applied not least of all to the growing strength, since the 1870s, of the Social Democrats, who won seats in Parliament as represen-

---

49 Centralverein 1863, 343; Thomes 1984; Trende 1957, 383 ff.

Snapshot 13: "Awakening a spirit of thriftiness among the working-class population": Instructions from the management of the Rhineland-Westphalian gunpowder factories, 1884

"With respect to humanitarian efforts to improve the lot of the working class – an urgent matter in modern times – the main priority is to awaken a spirit of thriftiness among the working-class population. Today, a skilled, industrious, full-time employed worker earns wages that allow him, in good times, to set aside some money for hard times, provided that he keeps his requirements within the boundaries of his social status. Therefore, to enable this, the worker needs an opportunity to set aside small amounts of his pay and gradually collect them in savings funds, before they are spent on everyday needs. Here, one should help him with good advice, for he is usually inexperienced and awkward with such matters (...). The effect of success is apparent with respect to both economics and morality. First of all, by being thrifty, the worker will be spared from wastefulness and, in particular, from insobriety. Later on, he will have funds in the form of savings that could be used in hard times to supplement any reduced income resulting from the loss of wages. Were he to be spared from calamity altogether, he would have at his disposal purchasing power which, in itself, would elevate his standard of living, even if this involved a greater expenditure. Thus, he would be conscious of the fact that he owes his small fortune to his own work and, thus, instinctively harbors the feeling that his work is profitable and valuable to him. In this way, he will become more devoted to his workplace and less susceptible to indoctrination by agitators. For example, he will find the catchphrase of "the disinherited people" refuted in his very own case."

(Saul et al. 1982)

tatives of the working class: Savings were still an instrument for ensuring political stability and inclusion. Nevertheless, a certain paradigm shift occurred from the 1880s on with the introduction of state-sponsored mandatory social insurance. From then on, saving acted as a strong complementary means of support of the state insurance networks which protected people, at least rudimentarily, against the elementary risks of illness, invalidity, and old age. From this point of view, the modified traditional conservative approach, combined with state-sponsored measures and overall prosperity growth, strengthened the foundation for so-called "German thriftiness," which can apparently still be observed in the present day. After all, the monetary assets of around 82 million Germans today amount to around EUR 5.3 trillion (figures as of 2015).

Meanwhile, the terms and conditions for saving also significantly improved as business routines grew smoother and were increasingly supported by the use of technology. At first, the minimum deposit was lowered in absolute and relative terms. In the 1880s, the minimum deposit was typically one Mark. Based on 300 workdays p. a., this amount corresponded to a little less than one-third of a daily wage, based

Snapshot 14: Various savings models

The total value of savings stamps, which typically had a value of 10 Pfennig each, in circulation in Germany in 1889 amounted to 345,000 Marks. The Munich Savings Bank marketed savings stamps in over 100 stores and automated saving machines and sold almost 700,000 stamps in 1910.

"The savings of each child must begin in the cradle. So long as the child is not able to do so, his family must save for him. Once he enters school, his independence in saving should begin. However, the child should not be externally compelled to save. Instead, he must have an internal drive to save that will be stimulated by emulating the other children of the family." (Friedrich Hofmann, 1865)[50]

In Dresden, there were so-called "Stollen tax" savings plans: In 1893, about 20,000 – 30,000 Marks are said to have been deposited with bakers for the purchase of the traditional Christmas cake known as "Dresdner Stollen."

In the western part of Saxony's Erzgebirge Mountains alone, 300 savings associations with 25,000 – 30,000 members were supposedly in operation at the beginning of the 1890s.

In its decree of June 1, 1886, the district government of Düsseldorf instructed the communities in the establishment of pension savings banks "…and emphasized that only through the creation of such institutions would the actual objective of the saving banks, i.e. to serve the need of the lower class to save, then be completely fulfilled." At this time, there were already 13 pension savings banks that, as an incentive, had obtained subsidies of almost 50,000 Marks from the ordinary savings banks' surpluses that were earmarked for the common good. The deposits were generally available only from the age of 55.

Snapshot 15: Nominal wages, cost of living and real wages in industry, trade, and transportation, 1871–1913[51]

"The real impact of wage fluctuations can only be appreciated when 'nominal' (i.e. actual) wages and changes are accounted for in the cost of living. For example, if a worker's nominal wages rise during a given period, but the cost of living rises even more, then his or her 'real wages' have declined. Table 4 shows how these factors are interrelated. A period of relative economic stagnation occurred after 1873. Here, we can see its effects in the period of 1875–1880: Although the cost of living index declined somewhat over these five years, indicating a period of price deflation, nominal wages declined even more. Hence, German workers' real average annual wages dropped from 578 Marks to 524 Marks, and the index of real average annual wages (taking 1895 figures as 100) fell from 87 to 79 during this same five-year period. This index rapidly rose during the "mini-boom" of the last half of the 1880s, and then more slowly during the "mini-bust" of the early 1890s. Even though these increases may

---

50 For these and other examples, see Trende 1957, 374, 403f., 407.
51 http://germanhistorydocs.ghi-dc.org; source: Desai 1968, 112, 117, 125.

have been small, they were never negative, excluding the five years from 1875 to 1880. Consequently, historians have revised previous assessments that spoke of a 'Great Depression' during these years."

"The period 1873–1896 was both preceded and followed by boom years, leading many contemporary Germans to perceive these intervening years as a time of uncommon hardship. Note the dramatic increases in both nominal and real average annual wages in the period from 1895 to 1913. Nevertheless, these statistics obscure important variations in the earning potential of workers in different economic sectors and regions of the country. They also mask the ever-present danger of catastrophe should unemployment, injury, sickness, or death of the primary breadwinner cause a loss of earnings."

Table 4: The average annual wages of employees in industry, trade, and transportation*

Year	Nominal average annual wages		Cost of living index**	Real average annual wages	
	Marks	1895 = 100	1895 = 100	In 1895 prices	1895 = 100
1871	493	74	105.8	466	70
1875	651	98	112.7	578	87
1880	545	82	104.0	524	79
1885	581	87	98.6	589	89
1890	650	98	102.2	636	96
1895	665	100	100.0	665	100
1900	784	118	106.4	737	111
1905	849	128	112.4	755	114
1910	971	147	124.2	789	119
1913	1,083	163	129.8	834	125

* Not included in the table: farm workers, those employed in cottage industries and domestic service, civil servants, and workers and salaried employees whose annual income was high enough to exempt their employers from the requirement to pay contributions to the mandatory accident insurance fund established by the Accident Insurance Law of 1884 (and its supplements). In most industries, this income limit was 3,000 Marks until 1913. For further restrictions with regard to employees prior to 1886, see Hohorst et al., pp. 107–108.
** In calculating the cost of living, Desai assumes a broader basis than other scholars by including clothing, fuel, and lighting.

Snapshot 16: Wages in an industrial region around 1900 – The spread of wealth

In 1901, skilled workers in the glass industry earned 1,500–2,500 Marks p.a., while helpers earned 800–1,350 Marks p.a.; a bottle maker and his helper earned 1,000–1,500 Marks and 600–900 Marks p.a. respectively.

In 1913, a miner earned around 1,400 Marks p.a. (compared to 720 Marks in 1870); daily wages rose from 2.50 Marks to 4.45 Marks.

Parallel to the growing demand for labor, there was a considerable increase in the number of women taking up industrial and service jobs in order to augment their family income. In addition, women raised food in their gardens, and children also contributed to the family income. Working class women played an important role in accumulating wealth. Nonetheless, there were no special savings institutions targeting women (Banken 2003, 98 ff.).

Table 5: Average interest rates of the savings banks in Germany during the period 1820–1910

1820	1841	1875	1901	1910
3.9%	3.2%	3.7%	3.4%	3.5%

(Mura 1995 II, 25)

Table 6: Graded deposit interest rates, District Savings Bank of Saarbrücken: 1900–1914

1900	3.50% up to 1,000 M	3.00% for higher deposits
1901	4.00% up to 300 M	3.00% for higher deposits
1907	4.00% up to 500 M	3.50% up to 2,000 Marks; 3.00% for higher deposits
1908	4.00% up to 2,000 M	3.50% up to 10,000 Marks; 3.00% for higher deposits
1914	3.75% for all deposits as a consequence of war	

(Thomes 1985a)

on an average annual wage in the German Reich of almost 1,100 Marks in 1913 (compared to around 500 Marks in 1871). Maximum deposit limits, which were intended to exclude wealthy savers and to prevent liquidity management problems, gradually disappeared. From a microfinance viewpoint, these developments must be seen as highly positive because of their inclusive socioeconomic effects.

Savings interest rates, especially in the beginning, often did not directly depend on market demands, but rather on practical considerations. Thus, the originally widely applied interest rate of 3.33% p.a. in the Taler currency area enabled the accrued interest to be easily calculated by customers and bank employees without using technical aids – an efficient and user-friendly approach. The annual interest accrued for one Taler, subdivided from 1821 into 30 Silbergroschen and 360 Pfennig, amounted to 1 Silbergroschen and the monthly interest was 1 Pfennig. After the transition to the decimal system within the scope of the Mark currency as of 1871, the interest rates accordingly became more flexible. This was not always advantageous for savers, for the interest rates could now be more easily adapted to reflect changing market conditions, as was actually the case in the 1890s.[52]

Social aspects, which again are a crucial aspect of microfinance, can be traced throughout all the bank charters in the form of graded interest rates. These interest rates occasionally differed by up to two percentage points or more between small and large deposits in favor of the small ones. It is no coincidence that small deposit sums overall represented the largest group of all assets.

Another key innovation was the payment of interest on a daily basis beginning with the day after the deposit and ending with the day before the withdrawal. This innovation, which required effective cost management on the part of the banks, was offered at most institutions from 1907 on. Also advantageous for the savers were shorter notice periods in the event that they wished to withdraw money.

---

52 Thomes 1985a, 185f.; Trende 1957, 511–526.

This progress resulted from the growth of the institutions and the development of liquidity mechanisms applied among the savings banks themselves and in cooperation with local or state banks (*Landesbanken*).[53]

A further aspect which enhanced the attractiveness of the banks and which was still relevant at the turn of the 20th century was bonuses paid on the deposits of low-income savers. Nevertheless, this feature was not found consistently at all savings banks. The Aachen Association, for instance, was exemplary and systematic in implementing this principle in its savings banks. By contrast, the public savings banks were very reluctant to take up the offer of the Prussian *Landesbanken* to issue a part of their surpluses as bonus payments to "not notoriously rich" savers, despite repeated urging of the regulatory authorities to do so. In 1871, only 61 of 121 savings banks of the Rhine province participated in this endeavor. The District Savings Bank of Saarbrücken made an effort to obtain such funds only from 1867 to 1869. As reasons for this passivity, the institutions cited the high administrative effort, which fueled the aforementioned criticism that the savings banks had turned away from their original aims. Anyway, this service was terminated in 1873. In the 1890s, plans for a bonus lottery under the motto "Saving and Playing the Lottery," which had already existed since the 1830s, were not licensed due to the lottery character of the scheme.[54]

Bonus payments to small savers then experienced a widespread renaissance in 1908/09. As a kind of social compensation for the deposit and current account business that the savings banks were allowed to pursue, they were required to distribute one-third of their net profits from this branch of business in the form of bonuses for underprivileged savers, as a kind of social signal. In another context, the possibility of setting up "locked" savings passbooks, which had been making inroads into the day-to-day business of savings banks since the 1880s, was also relevant from a microfinance perspective. Taking into account overall saving objectives and the concept of long-term private provisions, this service allowed the availability of assets to be restricted to a certain point in time or connected with a specific occasion; such as attainment of the age of majority, start of military service or apprenticeship, marriage, or retirement. In particular, such accounts were used to deposit funds held in trusteeship for minors.[55]

To summarize developments in the period between the last agrarian crisis in 1846–1848 and the eve of World War I: Germany had succeeded in becoming an industrialized economy. Incomes grew and, in a reciprocal process, savings banks offered new savings and payment services culminating in checking accounts as a first step to cashless payments for the masses. The overwhelming majority of sav-

---

[53] Thomes 1985a, 203.
[54] Pohl 1982; Thomes 1985a, 126ff.; Thomes 2010; Trende 1957, 424ff.
[55] For background information, see Trende 1957, 410ff., 440ff.; Mura 1987, 28; Thomes 1985a, 184f., 221f.

Table 7: Savings accounts in Prussia, 1850–1908 (in %)

	up to 60 Marks	60 to 150 Marks	150 to 300 Marks	300 to 600 Marks	above 600 Marks		
1850	34	27	20	11	5		
1855	33	24	20	14	7		
1860	34	23	18	14	8		
1865	33	22	18	14	11		
1870	30	21	17	15	13		
1875	24	20	18	17	20		
1880	24	19	16	15	21		
1885	28	17	15	15	22		
1890	28	16	14	15	23		
1895	28	15	13	15			

					600 to 3,000 Marks	3,000 to 10,000 Marks	above 10,000 Marks
1896	28	15	13	15	22	3	0.4
1897	28	15	13	15	22	3	0.4
1898	28	15	13	15	23	3	0.4
1899	28	15	13	15	23	3	0.4
1900	28	15	13	15	23	3	0.4
1901	27	15	13	15	24	3	0.4
1902	28	14	13	15	24	3	0.4
1903	27	14	13	14	24	4	0.5
1904	27	14	12	14	25	4	0.5
1905	27	14	12	14	25	4	0.5
1906	27	14	12	14	25	4	0.6
1907	28	14	12	14	25	4	0.6
1908	28	13	12	14	24	4	0.6

Ashauer 1991, 125.

ings innovations were microfinance-relevant. These innovations helped to enable the masses to embrace new opportunities and cope with threats by including these people in the formal financial system, the development of which, in turn, was influenced by their needs.

This historical analysis reveals the landmarks of the financial integration process. It shows that transparent savings schedules help to alleviate poverty: The poor can save, and savings are one means among others of overcoming poverty. Nevertheless, rising and regular incomes are a crucial requirement to create sustainable socioeconomic stability, as seen in the case of European industrialization, and they are a prerequisite for sustainable saving. Therefore, it is natural that the savings banks expanded in parallel to industrialization and economic growth. It is also natural that savings opportunities and financial instruments boomed after the state had set up a social insurance network. This development shows that the savings paradigm had changed: No longer were savings used to protect savers from rudimentary risks, but rather as a means of enablement and financial inclusion of the low-income households. It is important in this context that the savings banks opened their doors to all individuals – a visible sign of the inclusion process.

SWOT analysis of the savings business from a microfinance perspective, up to 1913

Strengths:
- Geographic and temporal accessibility
- Geographical transferability of accounts
- Acceptance of very small savings deposits
- Broad range of pre-saving instruments for the smallest amounts
- Graded interest rates favoring smaller savings deposits
- Bonuses for smaller savings
- Broad range of savings products
- Flexible availability of savings

Weakness(es):
- Opening hours on holidays or Sundays (e.g. after church services) reduced or eliminated
- Reluctance to pay bonuses on the savings of small savers
- Slow development of cost management

Opportunities:
- The savings banks becoming universal credit institutions

Threats:
- Competition
- Relinquishing competence in serving small clients
- Neglecting small businesses
- Giving up microfinance ideals

Direct effects: Safe, attractive, interest-bearing, and transparent savings instruments for low-income households; inclusion in the financial system.

Indirect effects: Social emancipation, low interest rates for larger savings deposits of the wealthy, thereby helping to create surpluses which flowed back into charitable measures within the district served by the savings bank

4.6 The credit business – A fluctuating and attractive combination of microfinance features

In light of microfinance's overall objectives, it is intentional that we only now discuss the credit business, after first having analyzed the savings business. The simple reason is: Taking on debt without having equity automatically makes a client

> **Snapshot 17: Lending operations of the District Savings Bank of Saarbrücken according to the bank charter of 1857**
>
> *"The deposited funds will be lent:*
>
> *Provided that they are guaranteed by a secure mortgage on properties. Without necessitating an assessment, such a security is presumed to exist for buildings within the first half of the sum for which they are insured by the Rhine Provincial Fire Society [Rheinische Provinzial Feuerversicherung] and for properties within about the first half of their value;*
>
> *Provided that they are secured, without a mortgage guarantee, by promissory notes that have been signed by two prominent wealthy persons who assume liability for the capital, interest and costs. Such loans conferred to one and the same person, however, may not exceed the sum of 300 Taler. Also in this way, maximally one-third of the total bank assets may be lent. Finally, such loans may be granted with a maximum repayment term of one year...;*
>
> *To the communities of the district of Saarbrücken...;*
>
> *Provided that the granting of the funds under items 1 through 3 is not possible, these funds may be invested at the provincial mutual bank or in national government securities as well as in other safe securities."*
>
> (Thomes 1985a, 304)

less solvent, and thus increases his or her risk of falling into poverty. As has been discussed in previous sections, it was logical that the early savings banks innovatively and intentionally prioritized the savings business. They did also offer loans, but they were certainly not targeted to the poorest of the poor; yet this fact was not an absolute disadvantage to poorer clients, since these transfer processes also benefited the underprivileged. The decisive point in microfinance terms is that loans should be granted at moderate terms and conditions, within the region served by the institution. However, the development of the savings banks' credit business showed convergence with the financial mainstream with time, and the effects this had were ambivalent.

The Prussian Savings Bank Regulations of 1838, as noted previously, gave the savings banks considerable leeway in developing their business, which was not the case with comparable legislation in Great Britain, France or Bavaria. The priority set by the Prussian regulations was security alone – i.e. to ensure "fully safe" deposits. From a microfinance perspective, this meant: Nothing stood in the way of local banking. As the historical sources confirm, the savings banks exploited this leeway and were able to flexibly respond to the economic developments of that time. From the 1870s on, the local characteristics of the banks converged in all German states.[56]

---

[56] For the law, see Hahn 1920.

Despite the transparent and competitive business conditions, the market entry of the savings banks into the local credit business was often a laborious undertaking, because the savings banks were trying to penetrate quite efficient market structures dominated by private and institutional providers. The economic takeoff in the 1850s, which resulted in an increasing need for capital in all sectors – agriculture, industry, and services – then helped the savings banks gain a foothold in the credit business. In general, mortgage credit rapidly developed to become an essential pillar of their credit business, accounting for well over 50 % of accounts receivable. This applied especially to the rural areas, where shares of mortgage credit in accounts receivable of over 80 % were hardly a rarity. In 1903, the savings banks in Saxony had a share of mortgage loans of over 81 % (Thomes 1985a; Trende 1957). Accordingly, other areas of the savings banks' lending operations steadily declined in importance. This trend emerged even though the government authorities placed a high priority on personal loans, which they considered to be an effective instrument to put livelihoods or businesses at risk back on a secure footing; this was exactly the argumentation of the early savings banks and is also a central aspect of modern microfinance in the sense of solidarity groups.

Municipal credit played a more important role, especially since it was possible to lend money to the municipality operating the savings bank. Most municipalities made use of this option. Investment in bonds was also quite strong because of low administrative costs, and it was a good tool for liquidity management. However, at the same time such bond investments turned out to be a risky business. Starting in the 1880s, many savings banks had to absorb losses due to fluctuating interest rates. The share of such bonds in assets was generally about 20 %, though it fluctuated considerably, as did the shares of other areas of the credit business.

4.6.1 Mortgages – the main pillar of the credit business and a universal change management tool

A detailed analysis of the mortgage business identifies a broad variety of microfinance features. In particular, historical notary records reveal the relevant market structures of the time. Respected local families often acted as semi-professional lenders. Average people, too, engaged in lending, mostly to their own relatives. Other important lending agents were foundations, societies, large companies such as the Prussian State Mining Company, and insurance or benefit funds, before savings banks entered the market.

At times this competition even led to an overabundant credit supply. In any case, Otto Beck, at the beginning of the 1860s, stated about the District of Trier [*Regierungsbezirk Trier*] that due to the lack of demand, capital "carried little interest and at times no interest at all." In addition, problematic factors for the savings banks were the typical interest rate of 5 % and the complicated approval process for granting a customer a loan, due to security reasons. Moreover, excerpts from the local land registry, the cadaster, had to be obtained along with proof that a cli-

> **Snapshot 18: Public fire insurance companies as an instrument of social change**
>
> The history of public fire insurance companies dates as far back as the 16th century. The Prussian Provincial Fire Insurance Societies offered standardized fire insurance policies from about 1836/37. Official cooperation with the public savings banks, as well as the expansion of the business to include life insurance, however, began only in the early 20th century. Besides these agencies, there were also public–private partnership companies, such as the fire insurance provider of the Aachen Association, established in 1823, whose profits also financed the local savings bank affiliated with it. Today, German savings banks and credit cooperatives run their own insurance groups.[57]

ent had no outstanding mortgage debt; proof of insurance had to be obtained as well. All of these requirements could lead to costs equivalent to 5–10% of the credit amount. Due to these hurdles, customers gladly acquired credit "through easier means." Over time, however, there was close cooperation between savings banks and underwriters to reduce costs and simplify the granting of mortgages (Beck 1868; Thomes 1985a).

Often the savings banks worked together with credit intermediaries and notaries. If necessary, funds were placed on deposit with such intermediaries in order to speed up the lending process. From time to time, the savings banks also took out short-term loans at other savings banks for intermediate financing if a lucrative lending opportunity happened to arise and they did not have sufficient funds to take advantage of it. In this way, the savings banks rapidly optimized the existing

> **Snapshot 19: Bank service instructions for processing mortgage applications, 1889**
>
> For buildings: Granting of a mortgage up to 50% of the fire insurance sum without additional assessment of the building; higher credit amounts extended with additional assessment of the building by the bank with respect to insurance sums of up to 3,000 Marks; for higher-value buildings, "assessment of an authorized master builder, master bricklayer or master carpenter."
>
> For lots: Granting of a mortgage up to around 50% of the value of the real estate determined by two experts, one of whom may come from the savings bank.
>
> Required documents: Excerpt from the cadaster and fire insurance policy; if required, valuation report with notarized signatures; most recent abstract of title.
>
> Declarations of the applicants: Declaration that the real estate in question is free of liens and that the applicant has full title to the property (Thomes 1985a).

---

57 Koch 2012; Thomes 2010; with regard to the insurance provider of the Aachen Association, see the special chapter. http://www.ruv.de; http://www.provinzial.de; /www.sparkassenversicherung.de

local finance systems (Pohl 1982). The attractiveness of the mortgage business lay in the long terms of such loans, coupled with safety and a stable rate of return. Over the roughly 60-year period from 1850 to 1913/14, mortgage interest rates fluctuated within the range of 3.5–5%.

From the mid-1880s on, lending processes became more professionalized in order to make decision-making more objective. Standardized forms, fixed terms of credit and longer notice periods, and regular loan repayment schedules were all introduced. The issue of regular repayment schedules, in particular, generated considerable criticism among the customers. Nonetheless, up to 1914 there was no widespread amortization obligation, despite repeated political initiatives to introduce it. However, the accounting practices of the banks that had been pretty unfavorable to customers disappeared as a result of efficient auditing, supervision, and public pressure.

Apart from this, loans were granted flexibly and in the customers' interest, for example with respect to credit limits. This was especially the case with rural real estate, which was less affected by economic fluctuations than urban or business real estate. Nonetheless, agrarian loans entailed difficulties of their own in light of price setting via auctions. The savings banks were thus reluctant to pursue this business despite favorable investment returns and high public pressure; they withdrew to an extent from the agrarian credit business, allowing it to become, in many cases, the province of dubious and unreliable businesspeople.[58]

From a microfinance perspective, the composition of the banks' clientele and the uses of loans are especially of interest. The bank clients came from all echelons of society: day laborers, servants, workers, miners, tradesmen, civil servants, entrepreneurs, merchants, industrial bosses, and their employees. Most of them were men; married couples often took out loans together. Women were represented only as widows, i.e. as heads of households. As regards the geographical distribution of bank customers, most of them lived in the vicinity of the bank.

In general, the funds were used to buy, build, or renovate homes and buildings, to refinance debts and finance modernization in SMEs, which will be discussed in a separate chapter. For the building of new homes, the funds were disbursed as the construction of the building progressed. Most of the loans fell in the range of 1,000 to 10,000 Marks; to compare, 1,000 Marks was equivalent to the annual salary of a skilled worker. The rate of defaults was very low due to the standardized credit terms and conditions tailored to the customers' financial situation. If bankruptcy proceedings were initiated and no buyer could be found for the real estate in question, the banks assumed possession of it. Thus, they entered into the real estate management and marketing business, which today is an important line of business for them, with the savings banks often being the largest local marketer of

---

[58] Brüggemann and Henrich 1896; Mura 1995, 70 ff.; Trende 1957, 478 ff.; see also below, and for cases Thomes 2008, 2010.

properties. In general, there were no liquidity risks because of the long-term stable growth of the economy.

4.6.2 Personal loans – Passing up opportunities

The personal loan business offered the savings banks the best market opportunities. As this type of lending was the least transparent, the savings banks acted as the sole serious providers of such services until credit cooperatives emerged – with the exception of credit extended among family members or acquaintances. Before the savings banks entered the personal loan business, the market was dominated, both in cities and in rural areas, by so-called "usurers," who lent money at exploitative terms and conditions. Though their rates appeared modest at first sight, the diverse constraints and requirements employed by these moneylenders – the loan sharks of their day – inflated their relatively moderate nominal interest rates to effective interest rates of 40% p.a. or more.[59] Debtors have never been able to afford to pay an interest rate of even 20% p.a. because of low productivity, and at that time up to 80% of earnings was needed to cover day-to-day living expenses. An additional problem was the short loan terms, comparable with current payday loans.

These aspects show obvious analogies to current microfinance practices in modern developing, emerging, and transition countries. There is, however, a contradiction in the current line of argumentation in favor of high interest rates. As history has shown, it is not that exorbitant credit interest rates are needed to compensate for risk. Rather, the fact is that high interest rates actually drive up the risk. The solid and stable development of the savings banks' business has irrefutably proven this correlation.

In the business operations of the savings banks, "personal credit" generally meant taking out a loan secured by a guarantor. Often one reputable individual to serve as guarantor was sufficient. What boosted the success of this line of business was not only the demand, but also the fact that guarantor and borrower often came

---

Snapshot 20: The first loan issued by the District Savings Bank of Saarbrücken, April 24, 1858

Borrower:	Jacob Kuntz, farmer
Amount:	30 Taler (around 90 days' wages)
Interest rate:	5% p.a.
Notice:	By arrangement, normally four to six weeks
Fees and charges:	Stamp duty
Purpose:	Unknown
Loan period:	5 years

(Thomes 1985a)

---

59 Beck 1868, 125; Brüggemann and Henrich 1896, 47 ff., 62 ff.; Faust 1977, 328–332.

from the same social milieu. Moreover, in practice, the short and impractical maximum term of one year was largely disregarded. Actually the loan terms ran for up to five years, and short delays in customers' interest payments often were not penalized. The typically low default rate, as well as the low average loan amounts reflecting the borrowers' existential needs, confirmed the appropriateness of this approach.

The personal credit business actually made a promising start. With shares of 30 % of assets, it attained remarkable volumes that corresponded to the objectives established at the outset. This mainly applied for Prussia.[60] In addition, the high demand for personal loans signaled a great need for them. The much-cited "little man," whether he was a worker or a businessman, could genuinely have been helped in this regard. The savings banks soon began to neglect this business, however. At least in individual cases, they actually chose to instead provide funding to wealthy moneylenders.[61] The savings banks definitely passed up opportunities here.

Starting in the economically difficult years of the 1870s, at the latest, the personal loan business dwindled, whether for the financing of businesses or other purposes. As a result, the share of this business declined to levels of less than 10 % of assets. Neither raising the loan amounts, nor introducing regular repayment schedules to reduce risk, nor governmental or union initiatives helped to stem the tide. In number terms, personal loans at the large savings banks ranged into the several hundred; in volume terms, however, the percentage share accounted for by these loans fell into the lower single digits. There were of course exceptions, especially in rural areas.

The reasons why the savings banks began to neglect this former core business are quite interesting. There were the high administrative costs, combined with an aversion to risk. Another reason was obviously the emergence of the flourishing

Snapshot 21: Credit regulations for personal loans at the District Savings Bank of Saarbrücken, 1858

The borrower had to have one to two guarantors, depending on the amount of the loan; the maximum loan amount was 300 Taler. With the involvement of the mayors of the district communities, the district council annually established a list of all persons suitable to serve as guarantors. The list contained the name, profession, and residence of the guarantors, together with the guarantee amounts they covered; they were people with a yearly income of about 500 Taler. The first annual list, published in May 1858, included 1,810 individuals with an impressive overall guarantee amount of 293,115 Taler (Thomes 1985a).

---

60 In Bavaria personal loans were only allowed from 1874.
61 For further details, see the section on credit cooperatives.

credit cooperatives, to which the savings banks quietly forfeited their business. In a positive sense, one could interpret this development as a division of labor, especially since the credit cooperatives were often loan customers of the savings banks. For example, in the 1890s the District Savings Bank of Saarbrücken loaned to a local credit cooperative, which had been founded in 1873, the sum of 10,000 Marks, secured by five members of the cooperative acting as guarantors (Fabry 1986; Thomes 2010).

Especially during the 1890s, there was extensive criticism of the savings banks' gradual withdrawal from the personal credit business. The critics accused them of becoming too comfortable, and of systematically neglecting the needs of low-income households and of small communities as well. There was at least one case in which the governmental supervisory board forced a savings bank to favor the credit applications of low-income individuals and of small boroughs. And the bank did so – temporarily.

From the savings banks' point of view, they essentially got rid of an unpopular branch of business. The reason for its unpopularity was primarily the low profit margin; the banks' original mission had apparently been forgotten. From a microfinance point of view, this was a kind of mission drift that was closely related to the success of the credit cooperatives, however.

4.6.3 Financing SMEs – A specialty of savings banks from the very beginning

Financing SMEs has been a specialty of savings banks right from their beginning. The importance of this microfinance-relevant branch of the savings banks' business generally has not been recognized, simply because it was mostly part of the mortgage or personal loan area. These areas of lending supported the needs of industrialization from the very start and responded to growing market demands. In fact, savings banks financed many small craftsmen's businesses that began to mechanize and evolve into industrial producers. As the Saarbrücken case again shows, mortgage clients in the 1880s and 1890s included, for example, manufacturers of faience, pianos, glass, furniture, soap, and spirits, as well as leather and textile merchants and a brewer. All of these business loans were secured by mortgages and thus facilitated the modernization and industrialization of the traditional trades and crafts. A special kind of mortgage was the ship mortgage, which was typically acquired by waterway businesses along rivers and which entailed maximum loans of 10,000 Marks. It shows the ability of the system to adapt to serve even special business needs. The socioeconomic network of the board members was an important factor for success in this regard.[62]

If no property was available to serve as loan collateral, which was quite often the case for start-ups or small enterprises, personal loans then came into question. As

---

62 Karbach and Thomes 1994, 157 ff., 177 ff.; Thomes 2002; Trende 1957, 506. For details concerning the agents, see below.

already mentioned, personal loans were an important focus of the savings banks' credit business from the very beginning. For example: Of 22 personal loans made by the District Savings Bank of Saarbrücken in 1859, eight were granted to tradesmen. Moreover, of 108 personal loans granted in the period from 1858 to 1861, 50 were issued to tradesmen representing 20 different occupations. The trades most represented were blacksmithing, metalworking, carpentry, and bricklaying, accounting for 23 loans in all. In addition, the list of borrowers included 13 small farmers, nine miners, seven teachers, and five wagoners. Other professions listed included those of calculator, clerk, merchant, surveyor, foreman, secretary, day laborer, and technician. Four of the borrowers lived outside the district of the savings bank. No one would call the majority of these people, nor their guarantors, really poor.

Another aspect is noteworthy in this context. Larger loans were increasingly granted to housing cooperatives and credit cooperatives that, in turn, issued loans to their members, another microfinance-relevant feature. Collaboration between savings banks and cooperatives was not uncommon, while the entry of numerous credit cooperatives into the market as from the 1860s reflected a constant demand for small loans.[63] The few examples cited here might suffice to demonstrate the degree to which this balanced policy affected the socioeconomic conditions at that time. Financing SMEs helped to efficiently create the urgently needed jobs for the lower class while at the same time supporting modernization and growth – showing microfinance at its best.

4.6.4 Financing institutions and municipalities – An instrument of structural change

Similarly to mortgage credit, the launch of municipal credit also proved to be difficult for the savings banks. Just as with real estate loans, there were serious competitors in this market, including banks, foundations, and public-sector financial institutions. Other competitors included other cities and, again, insurance companies.

Nonetheless, this type of lending was an obvious match for the savings banks because of their close personal and organizational contacts with the municipalities. In addition, there were clear advantages: On the one hand, the administrative effort was moderate, the supervision by public authorities increased security, and the statutory responsibility for regular repayments, as in Prussia, supported liquidity. Moreover, the attractive interest rate of 5%, which remained at this level well into the 1880s, was a further advantage.[64] On the other hand, the municipalities discovered the potential of "their" credit institutions as an efficient instrument for financing their activities. Thus, the savings banks rapidly turned into

---

63 Fabry 1986, 41 ff.; for details, see the relevant following sections.
64 As from the mid-1880s, interest rates began to fall under 4%, starting to rise again only in the 1890s. For the consequences, see the next section.

house banks that not only solved financing problems but also served as repositories for liquid funds. Moreover, they could use their surpluses to finance municipal loans, provided that these loans were used to finance projects for the public's benefit. It was no coincidence that municipal credit became a mainstay of the savings banks' business.

The central factor influencing the development of the municipal lending business was the exploding financial need of the urban public sector as the result of much more rapid demographic growth compared to that in rural areas. Here, the savings banks stood, as it happens, in direct national competition, because the large cities more frequently began to issue municipal bonds in amounts in the millions. Nevertheless, the business boomed. Up to the early 1870s, the largest savings bank of the District of Trier loaned out almost all of its deposits, for the sake of simplicity, to a local public foundation dating back to Napoleonic times – thus forming an integrated reciprocal financial system, tailored to suit local needs.[65]

Often enough, the savings banks were non-bureaucratic and generous towards their municipalities with respect to loan terms and repayment rates. In urgent cases, the savings banks pre-financed bank loans and put off private customers. Rarely were applications for a public-sector loan denied. And when criticism arose, as in Prussia in the 1890s, the regulatory agencies made sure that smaller communities in the district were not neglected. The idea of spreading risk also meant a boost in security.[66]

Often overlooked is the fact that from a microfinance point of view, municipal lending should be seen as positive, since lending activities in this area essentially contributed towards optimizing the framework conditions for economic enablement of the lower class. This also applies to the areas of education, health, and religion and meeting people's fundamental needs for a place to live and for mobility. Public loans de facto served mainly to finance infrastructure projects. Primarily in industrial metropolitan areas, capital was needed for land development, the construction of community, military and church buildings, and for schools, hospitals,

Snapshot 22: Decision of the Executive Board of the District Savings Bank of Saarbrücken, 1911

"Should the municipal loans, whose conferment seems highly desirable, not attain the market interest rate, it has been decided to confer such loans at a lower interest rate."

(Thomes 1985a, 278)

---

65 Ehmer 2004; Müller 2000; Thomes 1985a, 2007, 2008.
66 Pohl 1982, 2001; Thomes 1985a, 1997. See the next section as well.

slaughterhouses and renovations to existing infrastructure. Moreover, transportation infrastructure such as streets, bridges, harbors, railroads, and streetcar lines had to be expanded. Last but not least, the impressive expansion of the municipal water, power, and gas supply had to be financed. As growth and infrastructural performance were linked, the savings banks were intrinsically involved with this development.

4.6.5 Investment in bonds – Convenient for the saving banks but only partly beneficial for the region

The savings banks were quick to recognize the potential of the bond business. The decisive factors were the low administrative costs, the eligibility of the bonds as collateral and their easy tradability, which helped to ensure liquidity. The rather moderate rates of return and the price risk in the event of premature sale were not considered a problem. For some savings banks, bond investments gradually increased to become the main pillar of business, with peak values of up to 90 % of assets. This was surely not the intent of the savings banks' initiators. Sometimes it seemed as if the executive boards had sacrificed their mission for the sake of convenience.

What advanced the bond business was the fact that in 1884, Prussia gave general permission to savings banks to engage in lending to municipal associations and public-sector institutions throughout the state. This fully opened up new dimensions. First, this extended the savings banks' range with regard to municipal credit to the state level; second, it promoted the interweaving of local capital markets into one statewide capital market. For the municipalities, this facilitated the financing of modernization and expansion of the education, healthcare and insurance, and residential and transportation infrastructures. In turn, the savings banks gladly took advantage of this, especially because municipal lending promised higher rates of return than government bonds. For the sake of completeness, it should be mentioned here that later on, in the 20th century, politicians decreed minimum shares for bonds of up to 25 % of assets in order to broaden the market and lower costs. This move was a quite negative one with respect to the microfinance idea and to the founding mission of the savings banks.[67]

> **Snapshot 23: Interest trap – A call for action, 1887**
>
> *"As I have already informed you most respectfully, ... the district savings bank cannot afford to invest funds at 3.5 %, because the bank is still being forced to pay 3.5 % interest, while ca. 0.25 % administrative costs are still being incurred on every 100 Marks, despite the fact that the administrative costs here are the least expensive of the whole government district. Thus... may I respectfully request... the reduction of the interest rates... so that the district savings bank may be spared from greater losses."*[68]

---

67 See the previous chapter; Hahn 1920; Trende 1957.
68 Letter from the chairman of the board (*Kuratorium*) to the head of the district authority.

A phase of low interest rates, beginning in the mid-1880s, depressed the interest rates on bonds partly below the average interest rate accrued on savings accounts and led to a certain amount of disillusionment. And when interest rates began to rise again in the mid-1890s, it caused the savings banks to incur strong losses for the very first time in their history. Even though the losses were not problematical, their extent had not been expected.[69] From the point of view of microfinance, at least the municipal and railway bonds helped the growing cities to finance their needs and foster mobility and regional integration. It should not be forgotten that bonds were an indispensable instrument of liquidity management and an outlet for money that was not needed locally.

Needless to say, many infrastructure projects would not have been carried out without the savings of the wide base of the population. Without the savings banks, industrialization and the modernization of crafts, too, would have undoubtedly run a different course, with respect to individuals, enterprises, and institutions.

SWOT analysis of the lending business from a microfinance perspective, up to 1913

Strengths:
- Provision of small loans
- Moderate interest rates
- Transparent, flexible, long-term credit forms on the basis of personal loans
- Lombard loans
- Mortgage loans
- Possibility of periodic amortization
- Financing of municipalities, which enabled them to invest in local infrastructure

Weakness(es):
- Preferring big loans over small loans
- Neglecting the original aims and competencies of the savings banks

Opportunities:
- Creating stable market conditions through transparency
- Reasonable loan terms and conditions
- Preventing insolvency
- Promoting asset formation
- Promoting and facilitating structural change by financing infrastructure (transportation, energy, water, education, housing)
- Financing industrialization by supporting the development of SMEs and the modernization of craftsmen's enterprises

Threats:
- Danger of loss of original core customers to competitors

---

69 See the previous and the following chapter.

The savings banks played a decisive role in the financing of growth. From a current perspective, the results also substantiate the great importance of a local orientation as a criterion for the sustainable success of MFIs. Here in particular, sustainability is an important aspect, since the funds with which the savings banks did business were mostly those earned by low-income households.

4.7 Debit and credit – Reserves and non-profit appropriation

To recap: The mission of savings banks was not to maximize profits, but rather to promote the common good. And they often began operation without any funds. Nonetheless, they had to operate profitably and to build up reserves. As soon as they had formed reserves equivalent to a certain share of liabilities, up to 10–20 % in the beginning, a part of the earnings could then be used to sponsor local projects of public benefit.[70]

Perhaps surprisingly, most of the savings banks became profitable within a few years despite the moderate interest margin of about one to three percentage points between debit and credit. In this context, it should be kept in mind that the savings banks had a partly voluntary staff and little or no rental expenditures, or other operating expenditures, during the start-up phase. The savings banks' reserves grew steadily into the 1880s as their management gradually professionalized and decoupled bank administration from municipal administration. Thereafter, as credit interest rates dropped temporarily, with an adverse impact on earnings, interest on savings remained more or less constant. In these years, the mandatory reserve requirement was reduced to 5 % of assets, which, as from the 1890s and in the aftermath of extensive debate on this controversial issue, was eventually accepted as the general minimum requirement, while regional clearing networks secured liquidity. As soon as this reserve requirement had been met, municipalities were allowed to use 50 % of the savings banks' earnings to finance social projects.

This mechanism opened up an alluring option to broaden the scope of municipal operations without increasing taxes and it boosted the founding of savings banks, as mentioned earlier. There were constant and ongoing discussions between the municipalities and the government about the precise meaning of the words "charitable" and "social," yet ultimately there was a common-sense consensus that such projects – i.e. projects for the public benefit – would not have been carried out otherwise. This interpretation prompted a wide range of opportunities and activities. The following social aims were widely accepted: improvement of living conditions, including the support of cooperative housing development; the awarding of bonuses to low-income households; and an increase in deposit interest rates or

---

[70] For details, see the section on early savings banks and Trende 1957, 527 ff.

a reduction in credit interest rates for members of low-income households. Further objectives on record were to support the training or education of needy children; to allow students to attend agricultural schools; to finance the acquisition of seed and fertilizer; and to award incentives for the establishment of compost sites and the cultivation of fruit trees. Other objectives were the founding and support of educational institutions, hospitals, infant care, school health programs, and the purchase of advice books to help people master everyday problems.

In light of such opportunities, the last vestiges of local political reluctance to support public-sector founding of savings banks dissipated. Foundings of new savings banks from the 1890s on were mostly due to this attractive expansion of financial freedom (Thomes 1997). Actually the surpluses enabled or accelerated the implementation of numerous municipal projects. Moreover, they indirectly contributed, to a certain extent, to reducing the tax burden. Everyone profited, but the privileged classes may have indirectly benefited most of all – a constellation which can be said to leave a certain aftertaste. Ultimately, it was mainly the savings efforts of the lower and middle classes that eased the financial burden. Thus, it is no coincidence that the savings banks and their managers occasionally were accused of misappropriation of funds (Knebel Doeberitz 1907; Thomes 1995, 1997).

On the one hand, the historical analysis is not entirely positive with respect to microfinance criteria. On the other, the results underscore the need for an inclusive business model. The savings component of this model should be open to prosperous clients in order to involve them in generating the surpluses that can then be used to support local projects oriented to the common good.

4.8 Administrative and organizational success factors – Supervision, skill enhancement, and networks

From the very beginning, supervision, including elements of auditing and controlling, was essential. As the savings banks were innovative financial institutions, the authorities operating and guaranteeing the banks had a strong vested interest in avoiding financial losses and possibly even bankruptcy. The same was true from the savers' perspective. Thus, supervision was an instrument of self-protection and marketing. Every savings bank charter therefore included provisions regarding this function. The savings bank laws, like the Prussian Savings Bank Regulations of 1838, also stipulated that public authorities, such as provincial and district administrators, act as auditors. As implied above, both these authorities and the owners kept a watchful eye over the business, for any losses incurred would affect them both.

The corresponding historical reports document exact management procedures based on directives issued to the staff. The documents and procedures subject to audits were journals, receipts, accounts, correspondence, and the safekeeping of stocks, bonds, and cash. It is important to keep in mind that the local auditors at the time were normally experts: entrepreneurs, lawyers or even bankers. Although the auditors did uncover violations, they were relatively infrequent due to the strict supervisory regime. If there were indeed losses, the bank managers had to reimburse them. At the least, the savings banks could use the managers' security deposit.

The increasing professionalization of the savings banks becomes apparent here. In addition, a need for special bank control mechanisms evolved. Starting in the 1860s, there were government initiatives to prompt the savings banks to organize an audit system. In some regions, government officials regularly conducted such audits. In the late 1880s, external solutions were sometimes employed due to the increasing complexity and risks of the business. Another important point was that the desire for expert supervision formed one of the main motivations for the formation of regional German savings banks associations. According to the literature, the Hannover Savings Bank Association, founded in 1887, conducted the first association audit in Germany at the District Savings Bank of Hameln.[71]

Established and reputable savings bank experts acted as supervisors. At first, they worked part-time, commissioned by the saving bank associations on the basis of standardized regulations. One result of the bank audits was the expansion of the full-time savings bank personnel to at least two individuals and the introduction of the four-eye principle. Even before this, however, deposit and withdrawal receipts had only been valid with two signatures. Another essential advance was an increase in the quality of customer service. Prior to World War I, independent bank audits were being carried out in all German states, whether by the savings bank associations or the government. Consequently, savings banks rarely experienced any substantial losses due to fraud or security problems, and confidence in the institutions continued to grow steadily.

Given the rapid and intensive pace of change, a professionalization of the banks' business operations was inevitable. This involved replacing governmental accounting with commercial accounting practices and streamlining and simplifying procedures by making use of technology. The savings bank associations took over an important role as mediator and shaper of change. Another important task was to foster training and education programs for bank staff, with initiatives dating back as far as the 1880s. Due to their increasing caseloads and their function as retail banks, the savings banks were early adopters of labor-saving technologies as well. Last but not least regionally-based clearing networks and state banks [Landesbanken] secured liquidity (Trende 1957; Thomes 2011).

---

[71] Hahn 1920; Ashauer 1991, 176 ff.; Deutscher Sparkassen- und Giroverband 1985; Geiger 1992; Löber 1985; Trende 1957, 458 f.; Zweig 1986.

With regard to current expectations of microfinance structures, efficient structures and good governance coupled with expertise are essential criteria for long-term success. The history of the savings banks in Germany shows that these framework conditions do not have to be in place from the very beginning and do not have to be too narrowing in order to sustainably promote success. The essential point is that there was enough leeway for the banks to adapt to changing requirements and, at the same time, to shape this change.

5 Case study – The Aachen Association for Promoting Industriousness *[Der Aachener Verein zur Beförderung der Arbeitsamkeit]*: A holistic local inclusion approach

This association was chosen as a case study to demonstrate the wide range of possibilities available for MFIs beyond the typical German model of a savings bank organized under public law.

In 1824/1825, prominent citizens of the city of Aachen in western Germany established the Aachen Fire Insurance Company *[Aachener Feuerversicherungs-Gesellschaft]* as a joint stock company, together with an association called the Aachen Association for Promoting Industriousness *[Aachener Verein zur Beförderung der Arbeitsamkeit]*, as greenfield projects.[72] The founders included entrepreneurs and politicians. The principal founder and driving force was David Hansemann – a merchant, politician, organizer and networker. He was also a represent-

Figure 9: Powerful alliance: Headquarters of the Aachener Verein, located between the Aachen Chamber of Commerce and the offices of the regional government, 1890; source: Aachener Verein (1909)

Verwaltungsgebäude des Aachener Vereins in Aachen.

---

[72] For the following, see Aachener Verein 1884, 1909; Kähler 1910; Thomes 2010, 2013; Aachen city archives. For details concerning overall political and economic developments, see the earlier sections on the emergence of savings banks and credit cooperatives.

ative of the local chamber of commerce, which had been established under French Napoleonic rule in 1804 as a think-tank to promote the modernization of the economy and society. Even though the Napoleonic era had passed, Hansemann did indeed strive to promote revolutionary ideas in a humanistic modern spirit.

5.1 "Money and Intellect" – An integrated welfare concept combining insurance, savings, and education

The idea of a fire insurance company was nothing new, nor was the idea of founding a social club and savings bank. Yet the innovation here was the interweaving of concepts in the form of an integrated holistic socioeconomic scheme that combined both elements of entrepreneurial profit-seeking and sustainable societal benefit. The concept was designed to fill the vacuum left behind by the French Revolution in the area of social security. In addition, it was an institutional facilitator of industrial modernization. In this sense, the fire insurance company would finance the Aachen Association, which chose a beehive as its symbol, in keeping with the Benedictine tenet *ora et labora* (pray and work).

The scheme worked quite simply. As soon as the fire insurance company had generated sufficient reserves, 50% of the annual surplus of the joint stock company would then be appropriated to the Aachen Association to support public welfare projects. This is exemplary proof of social entrepreneurship at that time. The local scope of the Aachen Association was the district [*Regierungsbezirk*] of Aachen, a territory comprising 3,500 km^2 and about 350,000 residents. So advanced was the scheme that neither donors nor the Prussian king would provide funding to the project to allow an early start. Thus, it was unable to start operations until 1834, when the insurance company transferred 35,386 Taler of its earnings to the Aachen Association, enabling it to start up just in time to help smooth the industrialization process.

The executive board and the association's supporters brought together almost all the distinguished entrepreneurial families and politicians of Aachen. What made the approach innovative was that it was not traditionally paternalistic. Instead, this scheme was a trendsetting, semi-democratic and transparent organization unencumbered by pressures and constraints. It committed politicians, entrepreneurs, and average citizens to embracing its goals; it was truly worthy of the label "inclusive" in a microfinance context.

All stockholders of the fire insurance company who lived in the district were automatically members of the association, as were all clients who owned insured real estate worth more than 12,000 Taler. At the time, one Taler was worth roughly three to five times the daily wage. Smaller insurance clients who had become

Aachen Association members received a discount of up to four Taler p. a. on their insurance premiums. Moreover, any district resident could become a member by paying four Taler p. a.

All Aachen Association officials had unsalaried positions. The directorate reported to a board that represented the members, who, in turn, chose the directorate, decided on the statutes, and approved the budget, among other things. The board was made up proportionally according to the number of residents of the individual counties in the district, with one board member per 6,000 residents of any given county. Moreover, the president and two members of the district government served as honorary members. The board could assimilate as members any individuals who promoted the association's aims. Subordinate to this kind of district-level board were county boards made up of members living in the county as well as honorary members including, by definition, all parish priests, mayors, and the chief administrative officers of the county in question. In fact, these honorary members managed the association's local operations on a voluntary and unsalaried basis. Consequently, the association had vanguard structures combined with transparent decision-making processes and adhered to the idea of a broad network of both privileged and underprivileged individuals.

These structures lasted 50 years. In 1874, the fire insurance company then had to be re-chartered, which did not pose a problem, however, due to its overwhelming success. At the same time, the stockholders separated the fire insurance company from the Aachen Association, because the insurance company had begun to operate nationwide and needed to be positioned so as to utilize its earnings proportionally across the regions. Nevertheless, both institutions continued to cooperate with one another in organizational and in practical terms.

By 1874, the fire insurance company had donated more than 1 million Taler to the Aachen Association. This was a huge sum at that time and served to fulfill the association's aims, which included fostering industriousness and thriftiness, optimizing the education of working-class children, establishing and sponsoring technical, commercial and agricultural schools and, finally, promoting efficient capital management to ensure adequate revenues. Later on the statutes formulated the aims more generally as founding and sponsoring non-profit institutions, a phrasing that spanned the broad variety of means available to boost public welfare.

The original Aachen Association concept, conceived in the 1820s, aimed at improving the living conditions of the poor through the help of "worker colonies," a notion borrowed from a Dutch model, combined with providing poor people with access to education. Further measures were to include establishing savings banks and financing public job-creation schemes to counteract economic crises.

By 1834, when the association was beginning its activities, the initiators had made a pragmatic change of plans. They decided that savings banks would be the most efficient financial instrument for achieving their aims, in terms of both cost-benefit ratios and the broad and beneficial trickle-down effects. The great success of the fire insurance company and the subsequent success of savings banks also permitted the association to finance educational institutions. Later on it began providing financial support for a broad platform of social and cultural activities as well. Thus, the Aachen Association pursued the dual strategy of acting both as a social entrepreneur and as a financial sponsor.

Acting as a social entrepreneur, the Aachen Association operated kindergartens (as from 1839), general schools and home economics schools for girls, and pension and relief funds (as from 1851). The independent and explicitly liberal approach of the institutions was quite unique at that time. Far from stigmatizing the poor, the relief funds were socially inclusive – helping workers to be independent of employer-imposed constraints. In this sense, the Aachen Association scheme aimed to attain a balance between capital and labor. Cost-effectiveness was not a core criterion here. For example, the annual mean cost of placement of a child in a kindergarten was 4 Taler and 15 Silbergroschen; the parents, however, only had to contribute 12 Silbergroschen p.a. toward these costs.

In a second area of activity, the Aachen Association sponsored a variety of social projects, whether aid to veterans and their families, financing of workers' hospital medical costs, or payment of the school fees of poor children wishing to enter provincial agrarian schools. In addition, the association sponsored various clubs, schools, hospitals, recreational and re-integration homes and many other social projects, including penny-saving projects of children throughout the district.

One particularly outstanding example of the Aachen Association's social commitment was the granting of a generous donation to establish a new polytechnic school in Aachen – today known as RWTH Aachen University and with an enrollment of more than 43,000 students.[73] On the occasion of its 25th anniversary in 1859, the Aachen Association earmarked a donation of 100,000 Taler for this project provided that the new polytechnic institute was built in Aachen. In 1864, once the government's decision fell in favor of Aachen, as opposed to its larger neighbor Cologne, the Aachen Association transferred 131,739 Taler (100,000 Taler plus interest) to implement this ambitious project. RWTH Aachen University later became by far the association's biggest donee.

Up to 1913, the last year of normalcy before the outbreak of World War I, the Aachen Association had spent well over 30 million Marks on the abovementioned projects. This sum was equivalent to the annual wages of approximately 30,000 workers at that time. The Aachen Association's self-concept appears to have been cutting-edge: It acted as a type of "innovation laboratory," according to the 75th

---

73 Today RWTH Aachen University is among the universities chosen to participate in Germany's Excellence Initiative in education and research.

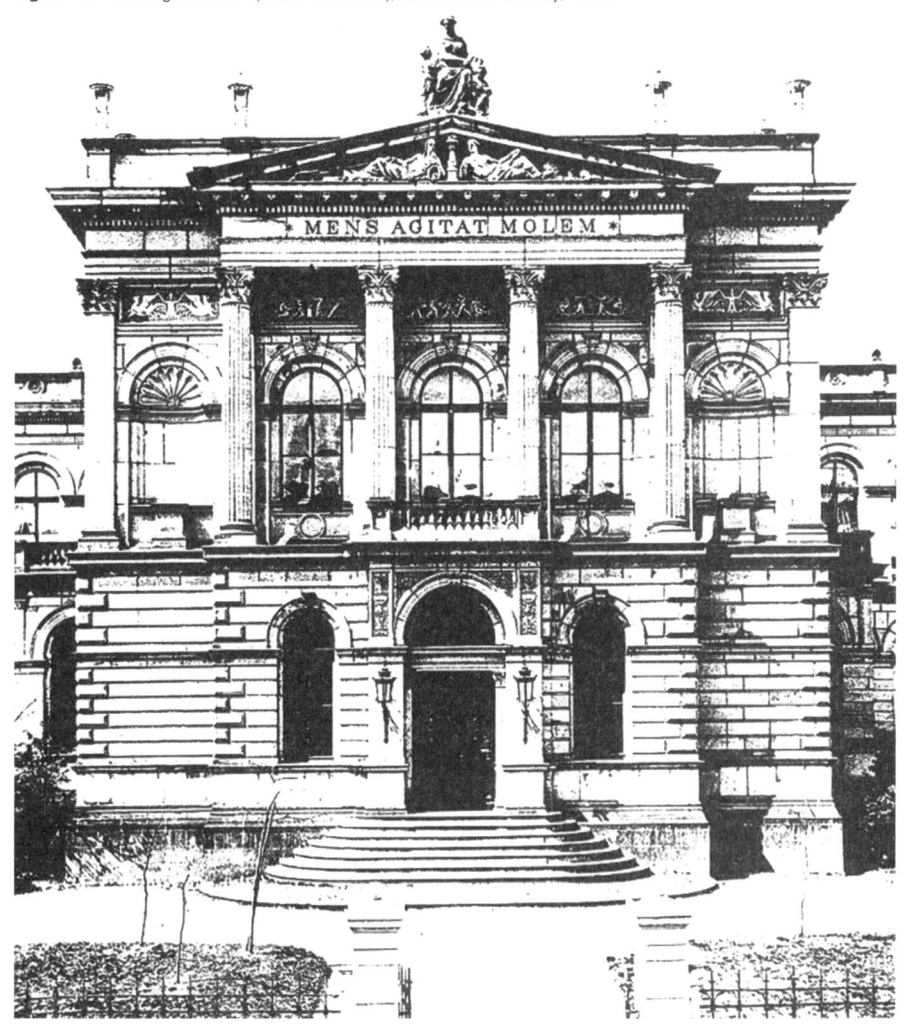

5.1 "Money and Intellect" – An integrated welfare concept combining insurance, savings, and education

Figure 10: "Mens agitat molem" (Mind drives matter), RWTH Aachen University, 1870s

jubilee publication of 1909. Describing the Aachen Association's mission with a certain pride, the publication praised the association as being an innovative medium for creating social capital spanning generations. The association had followed the vision of recombining production factors, financing inventions and innovations and generating common wealth. This holistic, inclusive approach helped to boost local prosperity in a unique and sustainable way. It represented an exceptional scheme of inclusive entrepreneurship on the basis of a public-private partnership.

Table 8: Financial sponsoring statement of the Aachen Association, 1834–1909

1.	Contributions to association's savings banks	14,904,332.44
2.	Contributions to workers' pension savings banks	8,973.42
3.	Childcare and education systems	3,653,764.66
4.	Needlework education at public elementary schools	1,104,040.78
5.	Poor relief	698,772.16
6.	Patriotic purposes	63,750.00
7.	Promotion of welfare system	252,550.00
8.	Health care	595,908.37
9.	Promotion of agricultural issues	143,506.00
10.	Education system	2,784,986.08
11.	**Technical University Aachen (RWTH)**	**1,739,428.90**
12.	Foundations and associations	250,550.00
13.	Contributions to pension funds for civil servants	309,000.00
	Total sponsoring (in Marks)	**26,509,616.81**

From the Aachen Association charter:

§ 1 Purpose of the association

"Furthering industriousness (*Arbeitsamkeit*) among the poor by creating opportunities for self-improvement"

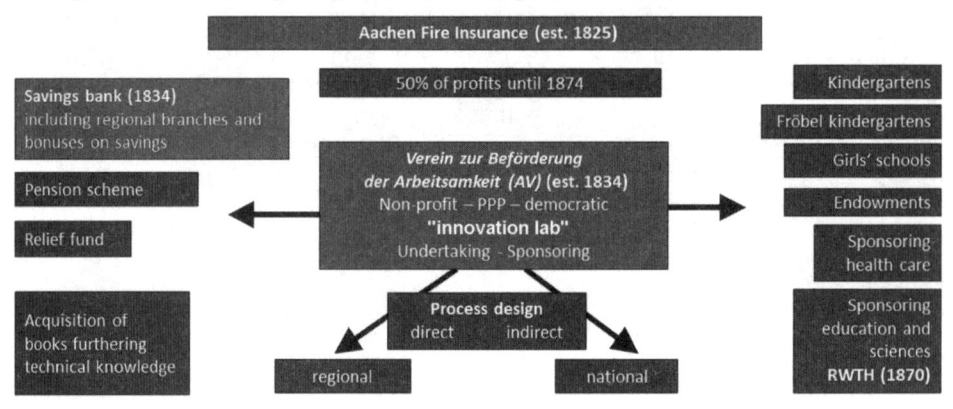

Figure 11: Holistic local change management scheme – smoothing the process of industrialization

5.2 The savings bank of the Aachen Association – A successful experiment

A central factor of success was the extraordinary savings bank of the Aachen Association. Around 1900, this institution served more than 170,000 out of a total of 600,000 district residents as clients. As every household was a client from a statistical standpoint, it had indeed reached financial inclusion. Moreover, the savings bank became a major participant in the financing of local industrialization, even as its earnings flowed into funding the social sponsorship projects of the Aachen Association.

According to its vision, the savings bank always followed a middle course between boosting earnings and maximizing local inclusion. From the beginning, the credit business was locally oriented but structured in line with customary bank practices, while the savings business met the needs of the whole population and was open to all.

It is worth noting that the savings business did not exploit the lower class by offering low interest rates on deposits. In fact, "small savers" could profit from annual interest rates exceeding 10 % if they combined ongoing saving with education – an optimal approach for furthering sustainable wealth management and inclusion for the underprivileged classes.

The concept for the bank was based on four main features: 1) The savings bank would pay interest on small savings; 2) it would pay bonuses on the savings; 3) it would pay interest rates scaled according to social criteria; and 4) branch offices would integrate rural regions into the savings bank's business.

The savings bank model was adopted in part by the Rhine Provincial Mutual Benefit Fund [Rheinische-Provinzial-Hilfskasse], established in 1854 as a state-owned regional bank whose mission included backing up the public savings banks as the central institution for the region. It used part of its earnings to grant bonuses on the savings of underprivileged clients of public savings banks. Many municipal savings banks established thereafter followed suit, a fact which highlights the character of the Aachen Association savings bank as a forerunner and prototype for socially responsible enterprises (Pohl 1982).

5.2.1 Statutes and organization – Innovative, flexible, and oriented to the common welfare

To reach its goals, the Aachen Association divided its business formally and locally into two divisions, the savings bank and the bonus bank. The model even included separate terms for the divisions' clients, who were referred to as "depositors" and "savers" respectively.

The bonus bank targeted the "craftsman class of the population, for whom acquiring, increasing and maintaining small capital is absolutely necessary for promoting and maintaining their welfare." As Article 1 of the charter stated, the bonus bank should foster "incentives and safe opportunity to save." In this context, the bank incurred "considerable sacrifices," since the regular interest rate on savings of 5 % p. a. significantly exceeded revenues. If one again considers the volunteer work, bonus payments and other diverse incentives, the nonprofit inclusion potential of the Aachen Association savings bank model becomes completely clear.

The statutes defined the following persons as being entitled to bonuses: tradesmen without apprentices, tradesmen who were not self-employed, factory workers, miners, daily laborers, servants, and persons who belonged to these groups but who were unemployed due to old age, illness or "lack of work." Again, this demonstrated an inclusive approach.

The bank accepted deposits in the amounts of 10 and 20 Silbergroschen as well as full Talers, with 30 Silbergroschen equaling one Taler. In the Mark currency introduced after the founding of the German Reich in 1871, 10 Silbergroschen equaled one Mark. The minimum deposit then corresponded to around a day's wage, a sum which certainly could not be so easily or regularly set aside. Thus, authorized persons at the bank also accepted smaller sums of money and stored them until a sum of 10 Silbergroschen had been reached. The maximum deposit was 200 Taler, a small fortune at that time. A further savings incentive beyond receiving the 5% interest was that under certain conditions, savers could receive an extra bonus of 3 Taler on the first 20 Taler of savings, provided that their account had been open for at least three years.

The savings bank, in contrast, was open to all individuals and institutions. However, it could reject applicants who appeared "unsuited to the purposes of the savings bank," whatever this meant. The establishment of interest rates followed social principles, too: The smaller the deposit, the higher the interest rate. In 1834, the savings bank paid an interest rate of 3.33% on deposits of up to 600 Taler, while the interest decreased to 2.5% for deposits of up to 2,000 Taler. If the deposit balance rose above 2,000 Taler, the savings bank was entitled to terminate the payment of interest – which it did not do, however. The periods of notice for the withdrawal of funds – although quite client-friendly – were intended to give customers time to think about whether they really needed to withdraw their savings.

The entire assets of the Aachen Association served as security for the deposits. Moreover, financial results were published yearly and included the anonymous account balances of each client so that everyone could check the balance in his/her account without having to make a trip to the bank. The cashiers had to provide a security deposit and their names had to be published – a fact that also represented a type of social control. Changes in the bank charter were first subject to the approval of the district government in order to "always fully ensure that the guarantee made to the savers has been met." This measure was intended to place the private institution on the same level as that of the public savings banks. In fact, the Aachen Association savings and bonus bank was considered to be a safe bank, a vital feature.

The savings business was also subject to clear regulations. In this regard, there was no difference between the savings bank and the bonus bank. A general principle was that the funds should be used "to attain reasonable and secure interest rates," but the executive board always had to obtain the permission of the district commission – a dual control mechanism here as well.

5.2.2 The "Four Percent Savings Bank" – Yield and mission

Founded in 1840, the so-called "Four Percent Savings Bank" was also driven by the association's social mission. The services targeted bonus clients whose deposits exceeded the 200-Taler limit, and they cast an innovative bridge between attractive savings incentives and real estate financing. Deposits were accepted only in the amount of mortgage loans amortized on a regular and annual basis – a unique feature at that time. In addition, there were fixed deposit and credit contingencies. The savings terms and conditions likewise differed from those for normal accounts in that there was a one-year period of notice and the minimum deposit was 25 Taler. Once a mortgage was repaid, the corresponding repayment of the deposits took place via a lottery. The debtors also benefited; they paid only 4.5% interest on the mortgage and thus 0.5 percentage points less than for a loan without regular amortization. In 1844, the volume of such loans came to 38,450 Taler. The Aachen Association, too, profited from the innovation, because this procedure decreased its liquidity management costs, which in turn helped it to achieve the aims of its social mission.

Snapshot 24: Thrift

"Niemals reut:
Selber die gefräßige Maus
Sparet sich in ihrem Haus
Nahrung für den Winter;
Mensch, bleib nicht dahinter!"

"Never regret:
For even the hungry mouse
Saves in his house
Food for the winter;
People, take heed!"

Source: Aachener Verein (1909)

5.2.3 The savings business – Continual growth

The savings bank, with four offices, and the bonus bank, with six offices, started their operations in 1834. In that same year the bonus bank attracted 1,123 individuals, 795 of them men and 328 women, as clients. These clients deposited a combined total of 8,100 Taler, the largest share of which – 4,346 Taler – was deposited by the female clients. In the second year the number of depositors almost doubled, to 2,197. With total deposits of 28,234 Taler, the average account had assets of almost 13 Taler. By contrast, the savings bank, during its first year, could only attract 44 clients who deposited 5,847 Taler. Needless to say, the initiators were disappointed by these results. The poor outcome was attributed to widespread illiteracy, but this was not really the main reason. The association then addressed

> **Snapshot 25: Impressive decennial balance sheet, 1844**
>
> Capital assets: 130,640 Taler; reserve funds: 21,509 Taler
>
> Bonus banks: 9,796 savers; total deposits: 596,997 Taler; withdrawals: 308,610 Taler; balance: 288,387 Taler
>
> Saving banks: 7,277 depositors; total deposits: 3.553 million Taler; withdrawals: 2.526 million Taler; balance: 1.027 million Taler

these poor results through advertising and saving incentives. The expected success then took hold the following year.

In November 1839, Aachen Association opened its first kindergartens [*Kinderverwahranstalten*]. By the end of 1844, around 1,100 children were attending a total of 12 kindergartens. Not only did the Aachen Association introduce kindergartens in the region, but it also again linked this innovation to an attractive savings incentive for the parents: the yearly kindergarten fee of 12 Silbergroschen was waived for children of frequent savers. This scheme acted as a combined socioeconomic incentive by opening up access to education to underprivileged children and simultaneously encouraging their parents to save on a regular basis.

In 1844, there were 15 savings bank offices and 20 bonus bank offices within the district. Even though business was booming, the executive board refrained from expanding the scheme to the entire Rhine province of Prussia that year. Undoubtedly, the success was fueled in large part by people's improving living conditions. Railroad construction in particular caused a local economic boom, creating many jobs and generating increased income. A person can indeed only save once his or her material needs have been adequately met. The relationship between savings and income is thus a reciprocal one on many levels.

5.2.4 Crises and success

What were the effects of the often-cited crisis that gripped Europe during the second half of the 1840s? Triggering social, political, and economic turmoil, this crisis on the one hand prompted the founding of credit cooperatives and accelerated the spread of public savings banks.[74] On the other hand, there were indeed direct negative repercussions. For the first time, the bonus banks had to cope with a drop in business due to the continuous increase in food prices. When the savers had to fall back on their savings to compensate for the rise in food prices, the annual bank report stated that their customers were at least able to use their own resources to combat the unfavorable conditions. The task of bridging short-term risks could indeed be mastered via savings. This situation reflected the precarious balance of the income of the lower class once again. By contrast, the savings bank

---

74 See the relevant sections of this chapter.

experienced a boost in popularity because wealthier people used it as a safe haven for their funds, and in doing so helped it to maintain liquidity in a critical situation.

With Europe embroiled in a revolution once more in the spring of 1848, the Aachen Association bonus bank and savings bank lost almost half of their deposits in the period from March to April of that year. Yet the Aachen Association deftly handled the run. Only a short time thereafter, the funds flowed back to the bank in full. The bank garnered much praise for smoothly managing the crisis. In 1850, the bank had 13,000 savings customers; statistically, this corresponded to one savings account for every 35 residents in the district. The volume of deposits reached 2.2 million Taler. Thus, the Aachen Association's institution far surpassed Prussia's other savings banks.[75]

This success story continued in the wake of the industrial boom. At the end of 1859, the year of the association's silver anniversary, total saving deposits amounting to 5 million Taler meant that every 17th inhabitant out of 450,000 people had a savings account. Prior to this, the association had again to weather the storm due to a second run on its bank offices resulting from the Italian War of Unification, leading to a temporary money drain of 1.4 million Taler. The same applied for the political crises of 1866 and those arising in the aftermath of the Franco-Prussian War of 1870/71. Despite these challenges, the Aachen Association always managed "to punctually honor all of its responsibilities," as an annual bank report boasted – rightly so.

It is clear that this reliability increased the public's confidence, while the stable economic situation at the time strengthened the bank's success. After the foundation of the German Reich in 1871, the dynamics even improved. Noteworthy here is that the "Great Depression" starting in the late 1870s and continuing into the 1880s had only a slight impact on the bank's balance sheets. Meanwhile, the importance of the bonus bank continuously increased, with the average savings account balance rapidly growing as the living conditions of the population improved.

Despite varying market conditions and harder competition, the bonus bank's interest rate remained stable at 5% p.a. for an incredible 60 years until 1894. The bonus system, too, stayed the same until 1900/02 in order to protect savers "from speculative investments," as the annual reports argue – thus, financial security at its best. As most of the bonus clients had been longtime customers anyway, this measure most likely strengthened customer loyalty. In 1872, 38 years after the founding of the bonus bank, about 10% of the accounts opened in 1834 were still active. Over time many clients neglected the rule that they had to leave the institution after having gained financial emancipation. This abuse of the bonus system

---

[75] Trende 1957, 134; see the top ten ranking in Table 1.

was thus prosecuted in the 1880s. The Aachen Association savings bank, however, had to become more market-oriented as it had to serve the bonus bank in a certain sense. The banking instruments used to bring this about were the setting of temporary maximum savings limits, variable periods of notice, and lower interest rates. In any case, customer acceptance of the bank remained as high as ever and did not differ from that of the public savings banks.

The 1890s brought profound changes. The branch network had expanded to 29 offices by 1899. The main motivation was the growing competition. Besides a steadily increasing number of cooperatives since 1869, by 1900 all of the counties had established their own savings banks in imitation of the success of the Aachen Association. These public savings banks now grew to become serious contenders in the market. Nevertheless, in 1905, the Aachen Association savings bank, open to everyone, was administering more than 100 million Marks in deposits with average balances approaching 1,500 Marks per account.

Up to the eve of World War I, both the public and private savings bank systems grew dynamically. This development again reflects the overall sustainable growth in prosperity during these years. At the same time, however, the Aachen Association was able to successfully maintain its position, and in 1913, it held about half of all savings bank deposits in the district of Aachen.

Snapshot 26: The bonus bank, 1909

On the occasion of the association's 75th anniversary, the district was comprised of 664,000 residents. The bonus bank attracted the main share of customers in agriculture and the various trades. Moreover, industrial workers made up 25 % of customers. The maximum deposit amount of 1,000 Marks corresponded to about the annual wage of an industrial worker. Among other aspects, the large share of women savers reflected the high number of industrial jobs for women at that time. Besides, the women also saved for their dowries, a purpose for which the bonus bank offered optimal saving opportunities. By the end of 1908, the bonus bank had around 89,000 accounts with a value of 40.8 million Marks that corresponded to mean assets of 458.79 Marks per account. These bonus accounts offered interest rates that were more than a percentage point higher than those of regular savings accounts. Even more impressive was the fact that over the course of 75 years, about 15 million Marks in bonuses had been disbursed – another impressive example of financial inclusion from a microfinance perspective (Aachener Verein 1909).

Table 9: Customers of the Aachen Association bonus bank, 1834–1921

	Cumulative Total		Year-End 1921	
	Male	Female	Male	Female
Factory workers	51,107	27,551	11,583	5,202
Craftsmen	18,130		4,777	
Railroad workers	6,500	10	1,142	
Tanners	1,181		134	
Printers	1,122		196	
Servants, farmhands	29,291	84,838	4,759	13,888
Seamstresses		27,578		4,587
Daily laborer	25,380	18,651	5,309	3,620
Tradesmen without apprentices	55,980		10,387	
Other workers	16,328	14,662	4,411	3,230
Subtotal	211,019	173,290	42,698	30,527
Total number of clients, male and female	384,309		73,225	

5.2.5 Microfinance features of the credit business

From the very beginning, the Aachen Association's credit business was in line with general banking standards and thus differed significantly from the public savings banks. The first board meeting in 1834 approved the following types of investments:

- Investments of up to 5,000 Taler without a guarantee at banks considered to be wealthy, solid, and financially conservative.
- Mortgage loans of up to 50% of the estimated value for urban real estate and those of up to 2/3 of the estimated value for rural real estate.
- Lombard loans against the pledging of transferable securities.
- Bills-discounted credit with at least two signatures of reputable individuals.
- National and international securities of public issuers up to a maximum of 20% of the Aachen Association investment.

Like the public savings banks, the Aachen Association later invested in government-guaranteed railroad stocks and securities as well as in loans to corporations and institutes. The portfolio reflected the entire spectrum of the contemporary financial repertory. Only the classic personal loan typical of microfinance was missing from it.

The credit business contributed significantly to the industrialization process, in particular, by financing businesses and the development of the transport and supply infrastructure. Acceptance bills and Lombard loans, interbank business and mortgage credits were generally locally concentrated, with a focus on larger

Table 10: Key indicators of the Aachen Association in peace and wartime, 1912-1921 (in mn marks; annual reports)

Year	1912	1916	1921
Total assets	168.5	173.5	271.2
Securities, book value	78.1	100.9	118.3 (nominal: 148.3)
Mortgage credits	60.7	57.6	44.8
Communities, institutions	7.5	7.3	15.1
Current account assets	5.5		
Bill holdings	9.9	0.6	64.6
Fixed assets	0.9	1.03	7.6
Capital reserves	2.8	1.3	0
Liabilities, savings bank	124.3	117.9	213.7
Liabilities, bonus bank	39.1	36.7	38.0
Check deposits	0.9	2.6	16.3
Number of passbooks	85,122	93,005	111,962
Number of bonus passbooks	85,147	82,355	73,225

cities. The rural areas were mostly left out of this business, even though a considerable portion of deposits originated from there. Consequently, there was a certain capital drain from the countryside to city areas. Nevertheless, the money partially flowed back again, since the Aachen Association occasionally provided financing to public loan banks [*Darlehenskassen*] – established in 1854 by the district communes to improve the supply of agrarian credit – and to public savings banks as well.

Mortgage financing for the purchase of small residential homes was the exception, perhaps due to the high administrative expenses. What clearly shows the ambiguity here is that the rate of return was a principal component affecting the potential to finance social initiatives. The ROI-oriented portfolio made a strong contribution in this regard. However, this trend intensified the desire of the communes for their own savings banks. From a microfinance perspective, the resulting regional dual savings bank system can be considered to have had a positive effect. Although the credit business in 1914 cannot be characterized as following typical microfinance objectives as defined by current standards, it did advance microfinance aims indirectly because of its high and consistent rates of return.

5.3 The end – The disastrous consequences of World War I

Even though the outbreak of war catapulted the whole credit economy into a totally new situation, the war initially did not seem to be a threat to operations (Pohl 2001; Pohl et al. 2005). Full employment and tightening consumption intensified the savings business. From 1916 on at the latest, however, the irrationality of the situation became clear. Since the state itself was betting on victory and was mainly financing the war on credit, the money supply exploded. Savings volumes increased exponentially, while sustainable investment opportunities disappeared. Moreover, patriotic duty demanded the purchase of war bonds. Thus, by the end of 1918, about one-third of the portfolio of the Aachen Association consisted of now worthless claims against a non-existent state, because the defeated German monarchy had been replaced by a democracy. The demise of the banking institution was imminent, especially as it was difficult to ascertain the solvency of the other debtors as well. Bank customers and the management alike faced ruin: At first paralyzed, they then found themselves helpless and subject to foreign rule, for the allied troops had occupied the area.

Meanwhile, the Aachen Association board of directors began conducting negotiations after the end of the war about how to address the balance deficit stemming from the drastic loss in value of the war bonds. The institution was not alone in facing this unique problem, but was particularly at risk because of its private character and its lack of membership in bank networks.

The solution was to transfer ownership of the bank to the public sector. The loyalty of its clientele and politics helped the Aachen Association to do so in an orderly manner. In 1923, the State Bank of the Rhine Province [*Landesbank der Rheinprovinz*] took over the bank's assets and liabilities (Pohl 1982). In the next step, the State Bank transferred the savings and other accounts to the public savings banks in the region. Thus, the Aachen Association savings business was transferred to the public sector without harming any of the savers. Above and beyond all of this, however, the hyperinflation which began in 1923 pulverized all assets and claims, and it thus seems, ex post, that the Aachen Association could very likely have continued on a private basis.

5.4 Evaluation – The holistic concept as a role model?

For over 90 years, the Aachen Association's numerous institutions innovatively, sustainably, and significantly shaped the social, cultural, and economic development of the government district of Aachen and beyond. From a microfinance perspective, this case study has led to relevant insights. It shows that:

- A private, local and holistic change management concept, oriented to the common benefit, can function excellently and generate multiple positive long-term impacts.
- A donation-supported enterprise can become an independent and successful business.
- Savings are highly important during processes of inclusion and structural change.
- Utilizing profits locally is highly important.

- Competition promotes the attainment of objectives.
- Institutional networks are necessary, and the lack of networks can lead to failure.
- Supervision, in combination with expertise, which can be acquired gradually, is indispensable.

SWOT analysis of the Aachen Association concept

Strengths:

- Small savings
- Local approach
- Full re-investment of business profits in the region
- Support for the lower class in the form of bonuses, democratic structures, and education
- Financing of local cooperatives, savings banks, and infrastructure projects

Weakness(es):

- No direct microfinance-typical credit operations

Opportunities:

- Holistic, inclusive, nonprofit public – private partnership (PPP) model including customer representation

Threats:

- Private organization
- Competitors backed by the state
- Severe political crises

Today, the public savings banks, the university, and the insurance company are still in operation, as well as some of the foundations established by the Aachen Association and many of the supported hospitals. The savings banks have retained their local business model oriented to the public welfare and are local market leaders. RWTH Aachen University, with more than 40,000 students and around 10,000 employees, is one of the largest universities of the Federal Republic of Germany and has been selected as one of the German Universities of Excellence.[76] The insurance company was acquired by the Italian-based Generali Insurance Company and gave up both Aachen as its headquarters and its original business model some time ago.[77] Out of a holistic microfinance project manifold sustainable societal and economic structures have grown (Thomes 2010).

---

76 http://www.rwth-aachen.de; http://www.tu9.de
77 http://www.amv.de; http://www.generali.de

Snapshot 27: Institution building – networks and apex institutions

Local banking does not work in isolation. History provides many proofs of this thesis. The core reasons why local banks need networks can be summarized as follows:

Reasons: Business: Liquidity, money transfers, investment operations

Market: Competition

Organization: Networking, information, lobbying, auditing, supervision

Instruments: Supra-local banking structures, including apex institutions

Supra-local networks and schemes, including apex institutions

Savings banks

Because of their public top-down structures, the savings banks were able to draw on existing public institutions to meet their needs from the beginning, whether to do business, to implement control mechanisms, or to discuss organizational or legal questions. Thus, provincial banks acted as intermediaries and clearing banks, and local government associations *[Städtetage]* as discussion forums. Specialized internal organizational structures therefore came into being quite late, after the sector had already reached a certain size; only then did savings banks emancipate themselves from the communal structures. Another reason for them to do so was the growing competition from credit cooperatives and private banks, as developing business models began to overlap. Last but not least, diversifying the business required specialized instruments for training and auditing. Those early networks thus emerged as the result of a long-term process. In the framework of current microfinance practice, the process can be shortened, however, and the establishment of networks certainly remains desirable and advisable in a digitalized world, because such structures have proven to be indispensable in making local banking sustainably successful.

Supra-local institutions in the German **savings banks** sector:

1872 Association for the Protection of the Interests of the Savings Banks of the District of Arnsberg [*Verein zur Wahrung der Sparkasseninteressen im Regierungsbezirk Arnsberg*]

1880 Conference of Saxonian Savings Banks

1881 Association of the Savings Banks in Rhineland and Westphalia and Savings Bank Newsletter [*Verband der Sparkassen in Rheinland und Westfalen und Sparkassenzeitung*]

1882 Conference of German Savings Banks [*Deutscher Sparkassentag*]

1884 German Savings Bank Association [*Deutscher Sparkassenverband*]

1887 Savings Bank Syndicate [*Sparkassensyndikat*], the predecessor institution to a national savings bank which was projected but never realized

1888 Ten regional savings bank associations [*Sparkassenverbände*], founded as from 1884

1892 National umbrella organization [*Zentralverband*] as apex of regional networks

1900 Regional informal liquidity and lobbying networks of savings banks

1905 Thirteen regional networks, only a minority of savings banks not included

1908 Giro association [*Giroverband*] of Saxonian cities; others followed

1909 First German savings banks' clearing house, in Saxony; other provinces followed suit

1909 *"Konferenzbezirk der Sparkassen des Saarreviers"* (liquidity management and lobbying association of the savings banks of the Saar region)

1910 *"Geldvermittlungsstelle"* (cash transmission center) covering the larger German cities

1910 First full-time controller (Revisor) for RWSV

1916 German Central Giro Clearing Network [*Deutscher Zentral-Giroverband*]

1924 Merger of the German Savings Bank Association [*Deutscher Sparkassenverband*] and the German Central Giro Clearing Network [*Deutscher Zentral-Giroverband*], including the German Association of Municipal Banks [*Deutscher Verband der kommunalen Banken*], to form the German Association of Savings Banks [*Deutscher Sparkassenverband- und Giroverband*]
Establishment of a national apex institution with the aims of strategy, auditing, education, lobbying, marketing, and scientific research

(Mura 1991; Trende 1957; Pohl et al. 2005; Thomes 1985b; www.dsgv.de)

Credit cooperatives:

Since credit cooperatives were organized privately and on a bottom-up, grassroots basis, they could not draw on existing structures for support. This being the case, cooperatives had to form their own supra-local institutions, which in fact came into existence not long after the movement began to emerge. The motives for establishing supra-local institutions were similar to those noted above with regard to savings banks. What was different is that the shared institutions emerged not only within different regions, but also within the movement's big three competing groups and philosophies. And here competition seems to have hindered efficiency, especially because both the groups and their banks were relatively weak. It speaks volumes that in Prussia the state founded a central bank which was open to all credit cooperatives and achieved considerable success. In organizational terms as well, convergence took place only slowly. All groups had their own apex institutions with structures that worked quite well in the given circumstances. Not until 1972 did the remaining two German credit cooperative apex organizations merge to safeguard their business, interests, and aims more effectively in one apex institution.

Supra-local institutions in the German credit cooperatives sector:

1859 Central Correspondence Office as the first national organizational institution

1864 General cooperative network

1865 Deutsche Genossenschaftsbank as the first cooperative central bank

1895 Central Cooperative Bank, called *Preußenkasse*

1920 German Cooperative Federation [*Deutscher Genossenschaftsverband*] (Schulze-Delitzsch)

1930 National Association of German Rural Cooperatives [*Reichsverband der deutschen landwirtschaftlichen Genossenschaften*] (Raiffeisen)

1972 German Cooperative and Raiffeisen Confederation [*Deutscher Genossenschafts- und Raiffeisenverband (DGRV)*]
National Association of German Cooperative Banks [*Bundesverband der Deutschen Volksbanken und Raiffeisenbanken (BVR)*]
National apex institutions with the aims of strategy, auditing, education, lobbying, marketing, and scientific research

(Guinnane et al 2013; Faust 1977; Gleber et al. 2012; http://www.bvr.de)

6 "Out of the box" – An international comparative survey of 19th-century credit-based microfinance trends

In discussing the origins of the credit cooperative movement, it is only fitting here to begin by again citing a current pacesetter in microfinance research, David Roodman, especially because he has given serious attention to incorporating a historical dimension into his analysis. Drawing a dismal picture of life in central Europe in the mid-19th century, Roodman (2012a) presents the start of the cooperative movement in Germany as follows:

The historical emergence of the credit cooperative movement was a reaction to an emergency, a famine which hit Germany in 1846/47, and to an environment of widespread poverty, usury, and expropriation during the transition from an agricultural to an industrial society. Many people died, indebtedness spread, peasants lost their farms to moneylenders, and small businesses went bankrupt. Initiatives to take action were mostly individual and local; interventions by state government were ineffective.

Undoubtedly, this is a quite accurate synopsis. Even so, it is well worth adding additional aspects to elucidate the process. Recalling the history of savings banks, it is also important to point out that new institutions do not emerge in one fast revolutionary step, but rather as the outcome of a complex dynamic process.

In fact, the origins of cooperative action date back at least to medieval times. The old regime, feudalism, was predestined to foster the evolution of cooperative economic forms. Consider the communally organized agrarian models, such as crop rotation combined with "almende" lands cultivated in common. Such systems were used efficiently to help meet communal needs and minimize risk. In addition, guilds, as cooperative organizations in the areas of commerce and trade were already in existence during the Carolingian era. These guilds aimed to lend members reciprocal support in the event of illness, accident, hardship, old age, death etc. The oldest legal code in which guilds are mentioned is the capitulary of Charlemagne from the year 779 A.D., in which they are cited as giving reciprocal aid in the event of "conflagration or shipwreck." In addition to the donation of money or benefits-in-kind which did not need to be repaid, aid was also provided in the form of loans, whether in the form of money or as payment in kind (Abel 1978; Koch 2012).

Miners' cooperatives were nearly as old; in Germany, the Miners' Benefit Fund [*Knappschaft*] celebrated its 750th anniversary in 2010. The Goslar-based St. John's Brotherhood [*Sankt Johannes Bruderschaft*], for example, supported sick miners as well as widows and orphans. The *Knappschaft* addresses numerous areas of social, health, and financial security (Koch 2012; Greve 2010). Moreover, cooperatives existed in many other fields where there was a need to insure people against risk or to undertake projects jointly: there were funeral home cooperatives, dike cooperatives, fire guilds, and employment associations, to name just a few. And by no means did the new capitalist liberal order of the 19th century make them obsolete. Thus, cooperatives were a part of everyday life and they were also actors on the capital markets.[78] What one sees is the emergence of a European-wide social insurance structure; the insurance aspect should be emphasized here, for insurance is an important component of the microfinance concept, too.

Once again, it is helpful to take a closer look at European developments, especially in Great Britain, the mother country of industrialization starting in the mid-18th century. It was there that Marx and Engels conducted their studies on exploitation; it was also where Robert Owen lived and worked. This self-proclaimed "philanthropist-socialist," as well as entrepreneur and innovator, not only questioned the inhumane conditions in the early factories, but also engaged in holistic experiments aimed at optimizing the living conditions of working-class families – much to the astonishment of many. Owen's tools were manifold: He proposed abolishing child labor, promoting education initiatives, shortening working hours, motivating workers, and offering discounts on consumer items in order to undermine the fatal truck system – the system of paying wages in goods instead of cash – and the extreme exploitation of the workers (Faust 1977; Koch 1991).

Even though Robert Owen's objectives could not ultimately be achieved, his pioneering work was a beacon with respect to entrepreneurial social responsibility. His exemplary ideas influenced organizations such as the Aachen Association for Promoting Industriousness, established in 1823, which has been analyzed above as a prominent example of social entrepreneurship and public-private partnership, foreshadowing Yunus and his movement to a certain extent (Roodman 2012a). Regarding cooperatives, notably Owen animated low-income households to take the initiative to improve their own situation – a radical counter-approach to conservative, paternalistic aid schemes. In fact, Owen was a resolute supporter of producers' and consumers' cooperatives. Moreover, he provided a very good definition of cooperatives: "...a special kind of association which is fundamentally based more on people than on capital and which has not only a financial aim, but also a moral one."

Of course the cooperatives' organizational model had to be adapted to a new capitalist system. The missing link between Owen's entrepreneurial initiatives and workers' self-help are the famous "Rochdale pioneers" who, in 1844, founded an independent consumer cooperative – the Rochdale Society of Equitable Pioneers – with their own money, in defiance of the capitalist dictates of the day. Only one decade later, there were nearly 1,000 British cooperatives inspired by the success

---

[78] Kluge 1991; for more details see further on.

of the Rochdale model. Owen and the Rochdale pioneers have long been considered as the guiding spirit and the executors respectively of "modern" cooperatives. Despite their laudable achievements, however, it has been commonly accepted that the modern history of cooperatives dates back to the 18th century. One example is the establishment, in 1769, of the Fenwick Weavers' Society, whose members pooled their resources to form a consumer cooperative for purchasing bulk food items and even books to set up a library and promote education. The beginnings of this society certainly were in line with the traditional models discussed above. Nonetheless, the Rochdale Principles have left an indelible mark on the idea of cooperatives to this day.[79]

Snapshot 28: The Rochdale Principles for the operation of cooperatives

- Open membership.
- Democratic constitution (one person, one vote).
- Distribution of surplus in proportion to trade.
- Payment of limited interest on capital.
- Political and religious neutrality.
- Cash trading.
- Promotion of education (Kluge 1991).

As with the savings banks, France played a role in the emergence of cooperatives as well. Saint-Simon and Fourier are considered to be the founders of the cooperative theory. As early as 1832, Philippe Buchez, for example, founded a carpenters' cooperative in Paris. Moreover, the idea of the national workshops [*Ateliers nationaux*], founded by the French government in 1848 in an attempt to address high unemployment among Parisian workers, found a certain resonance in the German states, although the experiment proved short-lived in France.[80]

---

[79] Hasselmann 1968, 9; Faust 1977, 103 – 114; Koch 1991, 54 – 58; McFadzean 2008; http://en.wikipedia.org/wiki/Rochdale-Society-of-Equitable-Pioneers; http://thefenwickweavers.coop/frenwick-weavers-society/history; http://www.theguardian.com/business/2007/aug/07/retail.uknews.
[80] Faust 1977, 129 ff., 143 ff., 206; Born 1976, 216; Koch 1991, 59 – 67; Wandel 1998.

7 The emergence of the German credit cooperative[81] model – Tradition meets innovation

Regardless of developments in other countries, Germany is presumed to be the cradle of credit cooperatives and is considered to be an international role model to this day.[82] The world-renowned initiators of the German cooperative movement were Friedrich Wilhelm Raiffeisen, Hermann Schulze-Delitzsch, and lastly Wilhelm Haas, who is perhaps less well known. Other important catalysts of the cooperative idea include Eduard Pfeiffer, Karl Korthaus, and Victor Aimé Huber, considered to be the intellectual father of German cooperatives. Also worthy of note here are Wilhelm E. von Ketteler, Adolf Kolping, and Johann H. Wichern. Even though all these men represented very different points of view, ranging from devout Christian to socialist to liberal, they shared the common idea of improving the precarious situation of broad segments of the population by means of self-help in the form of cooperatives.[83]

In addition, other credit "rivals" had emerged in Germany earlier. In Germany's Harz Mountains, the *Gnadenkasse,* or Mercy Bank, promoted by government authorities in 1743, was turned in 1820 into an agrarian private savings bank [*Privatsparkasse*], which today operates as a credit cooperative under the name *Volksbank im Harz eG* (People's Bank of the Harz). In another example, in 1843, 50 citizens of the city of Öhringen in Württemberg founded a private savings and loan bank as a mutual society that is also operating independently today as the *Volksbank Hohenlohe* (People's Bank of Hohenlohe).[84] In 1845, there were 65 such mutual societies in the crafts and skilled trades sector in Württemberg alone. In that same year, workers also founded a Encouragement Savings and Consumers' Association [*Spar- und Konsumverein Ermunterung*] in the city of Chemnitz in Saxony. Since most of these cooperatives did not survive the political and socioeconomic upheaval of the crisis of 1847/1848 and had had no prominent leaders, the personalities Schulze-Delitzsch and Raiffeisen garnered fame as the "visionary heroes" of the cooperative movement in Germany.[85] In any case, the history of credit cooperatives has remained dynamic, not only in Germany.

---

81 Cooperatives in Germany have used many different trade names over time including "societies," "associations," "unions," "banks," etc.; in this chapter we use the term "credit cooperatives" as an umbrella term. Some original trade names are given in the text to give an impression of the diversity. In the English-speaking world the term "credit unions" is a familiar synonym. See chapter III.
82 See the sections of this chapter discussing current problems.
83 Faust 1977, 167 ff.; Kluge 1991; Koch 1991, 67–84; Roodman 2012, 53 ff; Schramm, 1982; Zeidler 1893.
84 See http://genossenschaftsgeschichte.info/volksbank-hohenlohe-oehringer-privatspar-und-leihkasse-182.
85 Gleber et al. 2012, 12 f.; Hasselmann 1971, 47; Kluge 1991, 43 ff.; Roodman, 2012, 54.

Indeed, the longstanding cooperative traditions once again became particularly relevant during the famine of 1847/1848. On the one hand, there were certainly heavily government-financed relief measures such as job creation schemes and food aid at that time; moreover, many savings banks and other institutions provided credit and other assistance. On the other hand, the political problems that had triggered the crisis needed to be addressed as well through the alternative solutions of grassroots and democratic self-help.

Journalists such as Victor Aimé Huber – a conservative, as it happens – attempted to systematically disseminate knowledge about self-help organizations. As a result, for the scholars, the question remains as to whether one should differentiate between pre-modern and modern types of such organizations.

In any event, cooperative ideas in Germany took on an unexpected momentum – again similarly to the development of savings banks. As Roodman (2012a, 54), citing Tucker, supposes, the identity-building effect of particularly dense German social structures, with a strong community spirit in small village groups, may have helped to enable the huge success of the cooperative concept. Yet the savings banks attained similar success with an alternative concept. Undoubtedly, after the collapse of the preindustrial social networks – a process that was still taking place in many rural areas in the 1840s – there was an urgent need for novel instruments. The political failure that had prompted the socioeconomic crisis of 1847/1848 doubtless encouraged some people to assume responsibility themselves and begin handling their affairs locally. There were enough competing models available, as we have seen. It was no coincidence that Faust remarked that by 1850 "actually all kinds of cooperatives had been tried out."[86]

As was the case with the savings banks, the initiators of the cooperatives were mostly members of the educated middle class – and not members of the target group. These initiators were often involved in managing the cooperatives on a voluntary basis as well; and at least in the beginning, they were indispensable because of their know-how. Thus, all three distinguished founders of German cooperatives had their professional roots in public administration. Yet, unlike the initiators of savings banks, the promoters of the cooperative movement were more strongly motivated by their philanthropic and pragmatic principles and less by conservative political ideas. Self-initiatives by the target group, i.e. peasants and the working class, were mainly hindered by their low level of education and the illiteracy that was widespread around 1850, as many historical documents confirm. Closely related to this was also a general deeply rooted aversion to innovations and a strong orientation towards the tried and familiar.[87]

---

[86] Faust 1977, 206, 323 ff.
[87] Kluge 1991, 42 ff., 55 ff., 98 ff.; Faust 1977, 328–332, including exceptions; Schramm 1982; Wehler 2005, vol. 1 and 2.

Although both the savings banks and cooperative movements sprung from crises and tried to overcome them, the divergence of these approaches reflects the state's mistrust of the cooperatives. The government at first tried to undermine the cooperative movement through bullying, prohibitions, and refusals to grant concessions. But this mistrust eventually dissipated when politics realized that cooperative aims were indeed in line with state interests: By promising stability at the margins of society, the cooperative objectives, in effect, also promised political stability (Kluthe 1985).

7.1 The liberal approach – Schulze-Delitzsch and his "Volksbanks" (People's Banks)

The approach of Franz Hermann Schulze-Delitzsch (1808–1883) was thoroughly liberal.[88] A mayor's son and a well-educated lawyer, he had worked as a state administrator since 1838. From 1841 he served as a *Patrimonial-Richter*, a post somewhat resembling the traditional post of justice of the peace in England. In this function, he came into contact with the members of many strata of society and became thoroughly acquainted with the precarious conditions in which much of the population lived. In 1846 Schulze-Delitzsch was engaged in southern Prussia, 25 km north of the industrial city of Leipzig, Saxony, to fight distress. In a densely populated and industrially well-developed area, he dealt, like Raiffeisen, with the procurement of grain and foodstuffs to mitigate suffering in the aftermath of a crop failure. This initiative brought together fully traditional commercial and charitable elements as well as all members of the community – an integrative approach to ameliorating the effects of the crisis.

Faust outlined the situation as follows:

…There, Schulze-Delitzsch organized an aid scheme for the poor population in which almost all the wealthy citizens of the city took part as well as authorities and neighboring villages. Collections were organized which brought in considerable revenues. One individual leased a mill and a bakery and had the purchased grain made into bread to be distributed to the needy either at reduced prices or, when necessary, for free (Faust 1977, 197).

One year later, Schulze-Delitzsch organized a mutual benefit fund for workers and craftsmen. In 1848 he served as a left-liberal representative to the Prussian National Assembly, where he chaired a commission handling questions concerning craftsmen. There he was called upon to give his expert opinion on around 1,600 documents and petitions – a task that revealed to him the drastic socioeconomic deficits, but at the same time showed him opportunities for solutions that motivated him to promote change. It was no coincidence that Schulze-Delitzsch

---

88 Aldenhoff 1984; Faust 1977, 193 ff.; Förderverein 2008; Kluge 1991, 46 ff.

was also a member of the Union for the Benefit of the Working Classes *[Centralverein für das Wohl der arbeitenden Klassen]* – founded to address social problems in the aftermath of the Silesian Weavers' Revolt of 1844.

Meanwhile, with the failure of the 1848 revolution, he was forced to leave politics and government service. Perhaps it was for this reason that he even more pointedly emphasized models other than the government-subsidized self-help scheme, and why he distanced himself from the other intellectual cooperative pioneers. As an economic liberal, he aimed to support small-scale entrepreneurs in adapting to the demands of industry. By honing their skills to gain a competitive edge, they could avoid falling into poverty and the social destitution of the proletarian working class. His main objective was to encourage small-scale entrepreneurs to be carried by the wave of economic change, as he so poignantly put it. This was truly an innovative approach in light of the times. As a certain degree of assets was a prerequisite, Schulze-Delitzsch's concept did not apply to the fully impoverished.

The departure from his profession and from politics spurred Schulze-Delitzsch to realize his ideas together with others sharing similar convictions. In 1849, he helped establish health insurance and burial funds as well as trade cooperatives for carpenters and shoemakers, "associations," as he called them. Whereas the former were hybrids of external aid and self-help, the latter were purely self-help organizations. The method of financing of these schemes is of particular interest for this current discussion of microfinance aspects: The requisite capital stemmed from so-called entrance fees, members' deposits, loans as well as the cooperative health insurance and burial funds, which had to invest the deposited insurance fees at a profit. These were elements of a revolving system including insurance instruments and implicit saving incentives for the members. Schulze-Delitzsch recognized that, apart from acquisition and marketing, another problem for small businesses lay in the unsatisfactory credit terms and conditions, resulting from non-transparent market conditions mentioned already above.

Snapshot 29: Systematic analysis of changes – current analogies are obvious

"Instead of lamenting about the influences of the factory, commerce, or about the superiority of capital, one should rather seize the opportunities of industrial production, business and investing capital." (Westdeutsche 1984, 7)

"The craftsman was formerly a technical worker, working for a number of families close to him. By contrast, nowadays the selling of ready-fabricated goods is gaining priority: The craftsman has to purchase the materials, maintain a storage hall and speculate with supplies. For this, he needs capital, commercial training and a higher social position. A considerably smaller number of big firms will take over what earlier had been done by a large number of masters working on a small scale together with the housewives."[89]

---

[89] This and the following according to Faust 1977, 205f., 208f.

Snapshot 30: Credit terms and conditions for craftsmen – abuse of savings banks

"...The principal had already been paid back twice and thrice, but always in the form of interest that amounted to as much as 30–40%. Moreover, the repercussions of the famine years 1846/1847 were still being felt. Nonetheless, there was an institution in Delitzsch that could have helped the suffering craftsman – the savings bank. But the bank demanded a guarantee... This aid, however, was only reserved for his more fortunate and richer neighbor who used this privilege to withdraw larger sums from the savings bank in order to subsequently lend these funds, as a "humanitarian" gesture, to the needy at about 30% interest." (Faust 1977, 209)

There had indeed been a savings bank in the city of Delitzsch – Schulze-Delitzsch's hometown and base of operations – since 1848. However, this bank apparently did not grant small personal loans, even though this was principally its mission and was basically permitted.[90] The deficits of this system were obvious, especially because, at least in individual cases, the savings banks let themselves be "abused" by "usurers" (Snapshot 29). What is again remarkable from a microfinance perspective is that the business models of the moneylenders of the 19th century are in some ways comparable to current microfinance business models.

In 1850, Schulze-Delitzsch therefore founded a credit cooperative with the explicit intention of making up for the deficits of the public savings bank in Delitzsch. It was supposed to help small businesses attain credit under cheaper conditions. Since these small entrepreneurs could not raise the necessary capital stock themselves, the idea was to combine a commercial and a charitable approach. The cooperative was set up as follows: Besides the member fees, the capital stock was mainly provided through donations and interest-free loans of wealthy individuals, and the donors were made honorary members. In addition, the association was liable to its creditors only in the amount of its assets. Non-members could also receive loans. Small loans were interest-free, but payment of a one-time fee was required. For bigger loans the typical interest rate of 5% p.a. applied – indeed, a socioeconomic inclusive local approach. Possibly due to the limited liability aspect, this scheme was not very successful, in addition, there were too many loan defaults and the donations dwindled. Such developments are not unknown in microfinance as it is practiced today.

Meanwhile, liberal like-minded friends of Schulze-Delitzsch, namely the physician Anton Bernhardi and the master shoemaker Ernst Bürmann, likewise founded another credit association in Eilenburg, which was 20 km from Delitzsch and also had a public savings bank that had been established in 1843. This association, opened in 1851, was based purely on self-help and the solidarity of the members, who guaranteed the loans: the first genuine credit cooperative. The operating vol-

---

90 For details see earlier; Centralverein 1863, 222 ff.; in 1858 a district savings bank was founded, as well.

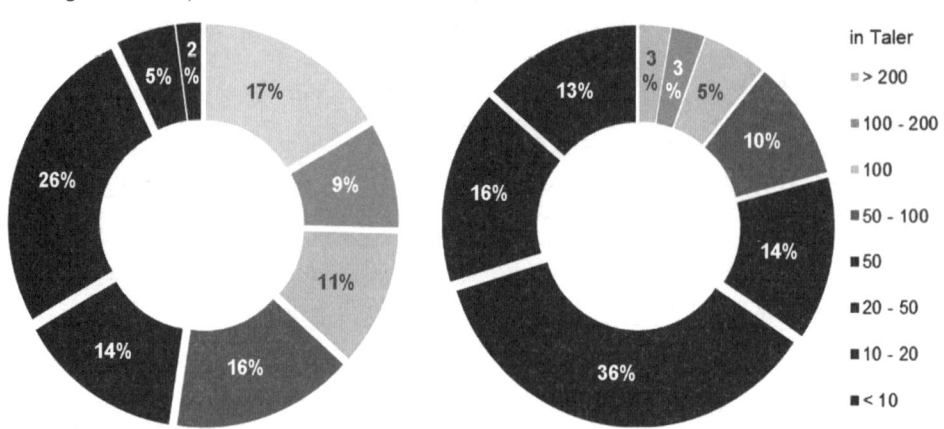

Figure 12: Credit portfolio of the Delitzscher-Vorschussverein, 1854 and 1858[91]

in Taler
- > 200
- 100 - 200
- 100
- 50 - 100
- 50
- 20 - 50
- 10 - 20
- < 10

ume could be expanded through the loans and savings deposits of non-members. In addition, there was a reserve fund against loan defaults.

Even though the credit interest rate of around 14% p.a. was relatively high compared to that of the savings banks, this interest rate was far below those charged by the moneylenders. In connection with attractive credit products and savings opportunities for all, the principles of self-help, self-responsibility, and self-administration could be realized – principles which might also be important for future microfinance initiatives. Since this scheme worked, in 1852 Schulze-Delitzsch restructured his association accordingly. He outlined the principles for extending credit as follows: "The decision to accept or refuse a potential applicant should be made only by taking into account the personality and conditions of this applicant so that there is a high probability that he can repay his loan. The main criteria are profession, skill and a sense of orderliness and accuracy." At first he retained the honorary memberships, mainly in order to strengthen the reserve funds through donations. Yet in 1855, Schulze-Delitzsch declared this as obsolete and argued for a regular membership of the honorary members.[92] In other words, the specific changes he made and his overall approach exemplified "learning by doing" in the context of inclusive finance.

Snapshot 31: Sustainable savings incentives

If members could not put forward their share capital, they could deposit monthly sums of money until their share had been saved up. Every member received a dividend based on the deposited assets. If his share capital had not been fully reached, this dividend was deposited towards meeting this aim – an example of self-financing as a savings incentive.

(Faust, 1977, 218)

---

91 See http://genossenschaftsgeschichte.info/delitzscher-vorschussverein-volksbank-delitzsch-263.
92 Schramm 1982, 75 ff.; for the quotation Faust 1997, 210; see also Kluge 1991, 46 ff.

The business model of both associations interpreted the cooperative credit undertaking as an instrument for financing small businesses, coupled with the possibility to save small amounts on an interest-bearing basis. It incorporated elements of social inclusion by permitting interest-free and interest-bearing deposits of the wealthy. The History Lab shows: Charity can be sustainable in certain cirumstances, and it can help combat usury and indebtedness provided that it is utilized in the right way. As mentioned, the founders had the savings bank as a local model, and Schulze-Delitzsch was even prepared to cooperate with the savings bank on a long-term basis – namely, he planned to acquire operating funds via this institution. In return, he offered the city magistrate extensive participation in the administration of the cooperative. This plan failed, however, and Schulze aborted the idea of an institutionalized cooperation and did not again waver in his convictions (Kluge 1991).

Undoubtedly, the refusal of the savings bank thwarted a major opportunity. One can certainly speculate about the long-term effects of such an institutionalized cooperation between the savings banks and credit associations. This constellation offers fascinating perspectives, especially in the context of the current discussion about future structures of the credit business. Today, both concepts, which exist specifically only in Germany, are in a defensive state on the European level despite their resiliency against shocks and despite their merits in financing start-ups and SMEs. Nonetheless, it is highly probable that from the 19th century onwards the growing competition generated profits for the common benefit.

Success rapidly went hand-in-hand with demonstration effects, which, in turn, accelerated the overall dynamics. To mention a few important milestones: The first credit cooperative in Saxony was established in 1853. Schulze-Delitzsch published his work entitled "Credit Associations as People's Banks" [*Vorschuss- und Kreditvereine als Volksbanken*] in 1855. This work was intended as a guideline for establishing and operating such credit institutions and as a handbook for entrepreneurs, and, moreover, it established the terminology used – i.e. "*Volksbanken*" ("People's Banks"), which will be referred to as "Volksbanks". Meanwhile Schulze-Delitzsch published in all media of that time and toured through the German states, eloquently professing his vision, in his articles and his lectures, "that the time was soon approaching when the credit cooperatives, through their sheer number of institutions and of involved small businesses, would boldly compete with the large banks." This vision, once again, illustrated the socioeconomic inclusion approach that would complement the existing financial structures.[93]

---

[93] Faust 1977, 221.; Gleber et al. 2012, 16; Westdeutsche 1984, 11.

Pursuing his principles, Schulze-Delitzsch organized the "first conference of the German's Savings and Credit Cooperatives, founded by small and medium-sized entrepreneurs for the purpose of extending self-help to those needing loans" in Weimar in 1859.[94] Twenty-nine cooperatives – out of a then total of over 100 – with an overall membership of more than 20,000 took part in this workshop. "The Cooperative of the Future" – a title linking the past with the future – was chosen as the overarching theme of press communications, and a "Central Correspondence Office" was created as the contact and communications center. This marked the early beginnings of the important national association of the movement.

Regional sub-associations had been in existence since 1860. In 1865, the German Cooperative Bank of Soergel, Parisius & Co. [*Deutsche Genossenschaftsbank von Soergel, Parisius & Co.*] opened its doors in Berlin as the first central bank for cooperatives. Both bankers, Soergel and Parisius, were involved in the cooperative movement from the very start. Several cooperatives and Berlin merchants had raised the impressive capital stock of 270,000 Taler. Among the members of the supervisory board was Adalbert Delbrück, one of the later co-founders of Deutsche Bank – another reflection of the aim of complementarity between the cooperative bank and commercial bank systems (Guinnane et al. 2013).

> **Snapshot 32: Mission of the German Cooperative Bank of Soergel, Parisius & Co., § 1**
>
> *"Operation of all kinds of bank and commission businesses; however, its task is, in particular, to best meet the need of German cooperatives to seek bank credit."* (Pohl 1982, 339)

The issuance of a Cooperative Act in Prussia and in the North German Confederation in 1867/68 – generally considered to be attributable to Schulze-Delitzsch – then established the long overdue status of legality that, up to that point, had to be realized through the liability and guarantees of individuals. The law was extended to nationwide validity in 1871 and 1873. It did not contain a licensing stipulation.[95] Legal status remains a crucial issue today as well, as any grassroots movement tends to raise the suspicion of governments, especially in non-democratic or rudimentarily democratic societies, as historical examples have shown. In 1870, shortly before the founding of the German Empire, there were 740 credit cooperatives with a combined total of around 315,000 members. This was quite an impressive achievement, and especially in light of the fact that the politicians still mistrusted their activities. The German Chancellor, Otto von Bismarck, who in 1866 had derided the cooperatives as "war funds of Democracy," did not like

---

94 Pohl 1982, 206; Schäfer 1994; for the development see further on.
95 See among others Faust 1977, 227f., 536ff.; Kluge 1991, 259f.; Pohl 1982, 337ff.

SWOT analysis of the Schulze-Delitzsch approach

Strengths:

- Local, transparent credit business for small-scale entrepreneurs
- Savings or investment incentives in the form of a shareholding in the company
- Regular payment schedules
- Independent structures

Weakness(es):

- Small mono-structured units in terms of number and background of members
- Lack of member solidarity in crises

Opportunities:

- Complementary refinancing options which expanded and improved local financing structures

Threats:

- Economic instability
- Reservations on the part of the political sphere

their liberal character. After Schulze-Delitzsch returned to the political arena in 1859, the two men ultimately became ardent opponents.[96]

Schulze-Delitzsch's advanced, holistic approach focused on self-determination is also reflected in his chairmanship of the Society for Disseminating People's Education [*Gesellschaft zur Verbreitung von Volksbildung*], established in 1871 and which he directed until his death.

Its mission was to "teach the German people about the position of human beings in the society, state, and church and to foster independent thinking about higher interests which will make us open to freedom, the highest objective of civilization" (Faust 1977, 229).

What a poignant motto also for the current microfinance movement. Undoubtedly, Schulze-Delitzsch had truly earned the honorary doctorate degree conferred on him by the University of Heidelberg in 1873 for his systematic approach and for his resolute implementation of his innovative concept in the face of all controversy and opposition.

---

[96] Guinnane et al. 2013, 47, 64 ff.; Faust 1977, 224 ff.; Pohl 1982, 207; for further details see below; Förderverein 2008 estimates around 1,000 institutes in 1865.

7.2 The Christian charity approach – Raiffeisen and his fight against rural usury

In the person of Friedrich Wilhelm Raiffeisen (1818–1888), in a certain sense Schulze-Delitzsch had a congenial counterpart who also shared the common aim of solving social challenges – even when they were unable to cooperate with one another. In contrast to Schulze-Delitzsch's liberal approach, Raiffeisen was motivated by Christian charity and the commandment to "love thy neighbor". As a civil servant, Raiffeisen was a political conformist, but like Schulze-Delitzsch, an activist and innovative. A mayor's son who was rejected for military service due to health reasons, Raiffeisen himself became mayor of Weyerbusch, a rural agrarian village in Westerwald, located around 70 km north of Koblenz on the Rhine, the seat of government of the Rhine Province of Prussia. In this village, he, like Schulze-Delitzsch, was also confronted by the precarious conditions under which the rural inhabitants lived.[97]

> **Snapshot 33: Raiffeisen's ideals: freedom and independence**
>
> *"Mutual help and collaboration do more to secure the freedom and independence of the people than state support… ."*
> *"One for all; all for one!"* (Koch 1991, 9)

Out of conviction and like many others, Raiffeisen initiated a relief campaign during the famine year of 1846 in order to establish a local food supply in the form of a "Bread Cooperative" which operated a bakery as well as acquiring seed for grain and seed potatoes. It sold the bread to the poorer residents, also on credit, at a price that was 50% below the market price. To acquire the funds, Raiffeisen actively drummed up the support of the whole community. He explicitly included "favorably predisposed residents," at first acting against the dictates of his superior, the district administrator. After the following year's harvest, all of the debtors paid back their loans, which was certainly remarkable. As the cooperative was a loose community of interests without any membership obligation, it dissolved in 1848 when Raiffeisen was promoted and had to move to Flammersfeld, roughly 10 km away, where he took up office as a mayor responsible for 33 villages.[98]

There he founded, in 1849, the Flammersfeld Benefit Society for the Support of Poor Farmers [*Flammersfelder Hülfsvereins zur Unterstützung unbemittelter Landwirte*] likewise on the basis of inclusive microfinance, with 60 wealthy individuals jointly liable for the loans conferred. Loans were granted for the purchase of home and property as well as of tools, seeds, and livestock. With regard to

---
[97] For details concerning biography and approach see Faust 1977, 323–386; Kluge, 1991, 48–52; Klusak 1969; Koch 1991, 85–104; Raiffeisen 1866/1970; Schäfer 1994.
[98] With regard to early activities, see Koch 1991, 105–155.

livestock, the association at first bought livestock whose ownership would then be transferred to the farmers on credit with regular repayment of the loan, which ran for a five-year term. Because of the great effort involved, however, Raiffeisen quickly switched over to granting loans for the direct purchase of the livestock by the farmers. Thus, this cooperative can be considered as the first rural credit cooperative.

Nevertheless it was also dissolved when Raiffeisen, in 1852, assumed a position as mayor in Heddesdorf, a village 30 km away near Neuwied on the Rhine. According to the historical record, both the general population and the municipal authorities doubted the sustainability of the concept despite the successes achieved. But Raiffeisen was undeterred and founded the Heddesdorf Charitable Society [*Heddesdorfer Wohltätigkeitsverein*] in that same year. Comparable to the Aachen Association for Promoting Industriousness, Raiffeisen's approach aimed to holistically foster educational and social projects. Yet only the credit business was successful. When the loans assumed by the society exceeded 21,000 Taler,[99] the citizens became concerned about a possible loss of assets; Raiffeisen then put intensive effort into seeking solutions and allies for his business endeavors.[100]

Snapshot 34: "Agricultural Association for the Rhine Province"

Based on the "Association for Non-Profit Endeavors for Promoting Agriculture, Industriousness, Intelligence and Public Morality in the Eifel Communities" founded in 1832 by the economist and Bonn-based professor Peter Kaufmann; renamed the "Lower Rhine Agricultural Association for the Rhine Province" in 1833, and in 1840 the "Agricultural Association for the Rhine Province" [*Landwirtschaftlicher Verein für Rheinpreußen*]. In 1871 there were 18 such associations in Prussia. Operating under the patronage of the king, these associations received financial subsidies. The Agricultural Association for the Rhine Province itself received one million Marks, and thus 50% of its revenues, in the form of royal grants during the period from 1832 to 1882. The association's members were mainly large property owners, so-called "Friends of Agriculture" (such as civil servants, aldermen, teachers, and pastors) and a few farmers. The latter tended to convene in local associations that, in turn, could become affiliated with the main and central associations. The aim was to promote agriculture and to represent agricultural interests through congresses, exhibitions, and prizes for excellence in agricultural production. In 1889, 3,494 local associations consisting of 260,000 members were affiliated with the Prussian central association.[103]

---

[99] With regard to local banking structures, including credit cooperatives, see Spoo 1999; Krauss 2012, 29.
[100] *Landwirtschaftlicher Verein für Rheinpreußen*; Aldenhoff 1984, 2002, 102; Brockhaus 1908, S. 943 ff.; Erdmann 1968, 44 ff.; Trauth 2012; http://www.scholarly-societies.org/history/1833lvrp.html.

Raiffeisen successfully won over the Agricultural Association for the Rhine Province to his cause and tried to persuade the district government to establish such associations on a district level with the involvement of the municipalities. The municipalities, however, finally refused in 1862, with reference, not least of all, to the already widely established savings banks. Bitterly disappointed, Raiffeisen said,

"The paternalistic state system does not allow such a thing... All of the people must be helped, and indeed through the path of legislation" (Faust 1977).

In the same year, Raiffeisen initiated four credit cooperatives. The principles of these cooperatives were: joint liability of the members and granting of credit only to members; installment repayments of loans; no entry fee, no deposit, and no profit-sharing. Instead, the profits were to be retained in a reserve fund. At least one of the cooperatives also added the joint acquisition of seeds and tools as a further component. Loans were issued to "reliable" residents who "acted morally and aimed to acquire property through diligence and thrift, and who also were capable of giving a secure guarantee." The term of the loans could be as long as ten years. As regards administration, the volunteer boards of directors generally consisted of the mayor and the local teacher – with, here as well, a difference between the "banker" and the "banked": the public authorities on the one side and the citizens on the other, but unified by joint local interests. This also applies, at least in part, to the Schulze-Delitzsch cooperatives, some of which emerged nearby at the same time and one of which will be analyzed below as a case study (Krauss 2012).

It was no coincidence that Raiffeisen ultimately commercialized his concept, while at the same time maintaining his ethical principles. He adhered to his conviction that money alone would not eradicate societal ills. He said, "I could not part from the idea that such associations should not be based on self-interest, but rather must be founded on the ideals of Christian duty and empathy." Nevertheless in 1864, Raiffeisen reorganized the Heddesdorf Association in accordance with the Schulze-Delitzsch model: with capital shares, profit sharing, and credit terms of a maximum of five years. But he retained the commodities financing business and the humanitarian components. Apart from that, the farmers were not enthusiastic about their joint liability as members. Moreover, Raiffeisen had at first recommended to his cooperatives that they join the "Volksbank Association" (Koch 2000).

From then on, the Heddesdorf charter applied as the standard statute "for rural districts with a mixed population as well as for cities," while the credit cooperative in Anhausen was supposed to be the blueprint "for purely rural districts." At least in the early years, the assumption that Raiffeisen's efforts were confined solely to the agrarian area is false. This is also reflected in the title of the guidelines Raiffeisen published in 1866 setting forth his agenda: "The Credit Cooperatives as a

Means to Mitigate the Poverty of the Rural Population and of the Municipal Craftsmen and Workers."[101]

The decision of the Agricultural Association of the Rhine Province in 1867 to make the Raiffeisen credit cooperatives an "association matter" certainly boosted the movement. Consequently the Agricultural Association named Raiffeisen as managing director for credit cooperative issues in 1868, after he had given up his duties as mayor for health reasons in 1865 (Lukas 1972).

These developments, in turn, provoked Schulze-Delitzsch to act. He saw approaching competition that did not fit in well with his views. As a result, the Agricultural Association for the Rhine Province assumed a neutral position and allowed the privileged partnership with Raiffeisen to end. However, many local farmers' associations continued to support the Raiffeisen cooperatives. During this so-called "dispute over principles," Raiffeisen, who was not interested in confrontation, concentrated his energies on the rural local cooperatives established according to the Anhausen model.[102]

His seminal motto was: "The money of the village to the village."

The advantages of the pattern of local organizations were their homogeneous membership structure and their intimate knowledge of the local conditions, which allowed tailored credit guarantees and terms. In addition, this constellation fostered the principle of neighborly assistance and permitted administration on a voluntary basis. Even so, this structure posed a challenge in terms of liquidity management, which is why central banks emerged early on. The Cooperative Act of 1867, lent the credit cooperatives legal status and supported the spread of Raiffeisen cooperatives under the motto "…the farmer, the tradesman, the daily laborer, too, all need a banker." Consequently, Neuwied became the center of the Raiffeisen movement.[103]

7.3 Dispute over principles – Jockeying for position and an optimization process

At that time, the system conflict between the two groups had already become heated and by the end of the 1870s had spread to the highest levels of politics and legislation.[104] The conflict broke out because Schulze-Delitzsch, as noted, saw the Raiffeisen credit cooperatives as a competing system that was not acting in accor-

---

[101] Raiffeisen 1866, 12–14; Müller 2000, 17 ff.; Faust 1977, 334–337; Kluge 1991, 50 f.; Krauss 2012.
[102] See among others Westdeutsche 1984, 14, 25, 32 ff.; Koch 1991, 155 ff.
[103] Faust 1977, 339 f.; Gleber et al. 2012, 17; Kraus 1877; Krauss 2012, 26 ff.; Spoo 1999.
[104] Koch 2000, 1991 195 ff.; for a detailed comparison see Seelmann-Eggebert 1927; for the competition with savings banks see the relevant sections before and after.

dance with his aims. He cited the "golden rule of banking," in effect accusing the Raiffeisen cooperatives of breaching standard banking principles. As the most important result of this conflict, Raiffeisen had to introduce business shares and dividend payments. Raiffeisen, however, defended his public-welfare-oriented approach. The shares had only a pro forma character. So that no false incentives would be created, the dividend payments were restricted to the level of the maximum interest rate on loans. In addition, the regional clearing institutions, important liquidity instruments, had to close temporarily, as will be shown further on. In the context of a cooperative, they violated the applicable law, which was not amended until 1889. They then became newly restructured as stock corporations. The problematic liquidity situation that Schulze-Delitzsch had rightly attacked, i.e. the long-term investment of short-term funds, remained uncontested, however. In reality, this point affected the Volksbanks, too, as the following cases document. Once again, these examples reveal the crucial necessity of having a liquidity scheme as well as an effective liability scheme.[105]

The optimization and harmonization process prompted by the conflict can ultimately be considered a positive outcome; indeed, it can also be seen as an evaluation process, with the specific risks of both approaches still remaining. Thus, especially because of their differing ethical viewpoints, Raiffeisen more clearly dissociated himself from Schulze-Delitzsch and, among other things, favored competing network associations in order to keep "deviant elements" at bay. The impact of this decision is reflected in the fact that the two groups unified only in 1972 – about a century after the dispute had started (Gleber et al. 2012).

In general, it is safe to say that at the latest with the area-wide acceptance of savings deposits by the cooperatives as from the late 1870s, there was competition between the two groups of credit cooperatives and savings banks. Then as a third player the regional commercial banks also increasingly recognized the benefits of small savings. Their motivation was not primarily the inclusion of socially underprivileged people by means of financial services, but rather the realization that savings deposits represented inexpensive funding opportunities which they could exploit.

In any event, the important result of this competition was that the small savers, perhaps for the first time, were recognized as actors in the capital market who could choose between different offers – also a clear indication of a financial market that in the meantime was societally integrated. From a microfinance point of view, these developments can be viewed as thoroughly positive.

---

[105] For details see next section.

Snapshot 35: System comparison around 1870: Two approaches and one goal

Schulze-Delitzsch	Raiffeisen
Liberal approach	Christian-charitable approach
Profit-oriented	Public-welfare-oriented
Urban	Rural and urban
Larger units (> 500 members)	Smaller units (< 200 members)
Commercial members	Farmers
Short-term loans	Long-term loans
Financial business only	Commodities also handled
Share capital	Small business shares
Apex bank	No formal central bank arrangement
Self-financing	External financing

The need for organization and centralization grew apace with the dissemination and success of the cooperatives. The Volksbanks, already one step ahead, met regularly and even had a central bank in Berlin since 1865, as mentioned previously. Raiffeisen was likewise forced to adopt similar plans: in fact, a clearing house was necessary for survival. Since the associations were small, the borrowed funds and savings deposits had rather short terms, while the loans issued were mainly long-term loans and very difficult to convert into cash due to the nature of the underlying agrarian investments, such as the purchase of property or livestock. Nevertheless, joint regional establishments serving both groups, though they would have been a practical solution, had no chance because of the conflict.[106]

Instead, in 1872, the Rhineland-Westphalian Cooperative Bank was established as a stock corporation in Cologne, while in Neuwied, the Rhineland Agricultural Cooperative Bank [*Rheinische Landwirtschaftliche Genossenschaftsbank e.G.*] was founded as a cooperative with the respective local cooperatives as members. Further Raiffeisen-oriented regional central banks followed in Hesse and Westphalia in 1874. The German Agricultural General Bank [*Deutsche Landwirtschaftliche Generalbank eG zu Neuwied*] was opened the same year in Neuwied as a nationwide institution tasked with coordinating the cash balance of the regional clearing banks. In this way a three-tiered liquidity management system was formed, which Schulze-Delitzsch again disparaged polemically, and essentially falsely, as "the three-tiered monster" (Faust 1977; Westdeutsche 1984, 22).

But what was more, Raiffeisen sought to incorporate the growing demand for insurance by founding a cooperative institution which would integrate all insurance premiums into the liquidity system. Raiffeisen's inclusive vision was that: "The yearly surpluses should not be disbursed to the insured persons as dividends, but rather used to finance a pension fund" (Faust 1977, 346f.).

---

[106] Guinnane et al. 2013, 51 ff., with a differing interpretation.

Yet once again the government did not accept the scheme, although the use of the profits, as was typical for Raiffeisen's approaches, was oriented to the common good – once again, similarly to the early Aachen Association's model. Additionally, as mentioned earlier, the Raiffeisen central banks had to be reorganized during the mid-1870s, because they violated the law. Consequently, the Raiffeisen movement found itself in a crisis. What helped the movement was that, during the slower growth phase starting in the middle of the 1870s, liberal concepts lost influence, while liquidity aspects were given greater weight.[107] Already in 1876, a new central bank *[Landwirtschaftliche Central-Darlehenskasse]* arose as a non-profit stock corporation. It was supposed to build up regional branches, though this did not happen until after 1895, when Prussia established the "Central Cooperative Bank" *[Preußische Zentral-Genosenschaftskasse, Preußenkasse]* as a central banking institution for cooperatives. At first, it was criticized because of the state's involvement, which inherently violated the cooperative principles. But this new bank disregarded this criticism out of necessity and was increasingly used equally by the Volksbanks and by Raiffeisen cooperatives.[108]

Parallel to these developments, the Raiffeisen organization more or less lost its provincial character. In 1877, this led, among other things, to the establishment of an "Advocates' Federation" *[Anwaltschaftsverband ländlicher Genossenschaften]* whose aim was to provide support and represent interests in a national context. Important here in microfinance terms was the fact that the association assumed responsibility for supervising the banks, introducing an audit obligation in 1883. Thus, the association established a statistical tradition as well – long after the savings banks, as it happened. In 1888, the year of Raiffeisen's death, the association numbered 400 members. By 1901, this number had increased to almost 3,400 members with an upward trend, because its services had become indispensable in an integrated market.[109]

7.4 Wilhelm Haas and other agents of change – Salt in the soup?

As has already been implied, there were many attempts, in all German states and especially during crises, to mitigate poverty in the short term and to even out the obvious social disparities. Another prominent individual who furthered such initiatives was Wilhelm Haas (1839–1913), an educated lawyer, national liberal member of the Reichstag and civil servant in the Grand Duchy of Hesse.[110] Similarly to Schulze-Delitzsch, he sought to promote self-help. Charitable aspects played no role in his concept: "The cooperative means freedom – freedom, in par-

---

107 Rosenberg 1967; Westdeutsche 1984, 17 f.; Wehler, 2005, vol. 3.
108 Guinnane et al. 2013, 77 ff., 127 ff.; Faust 1977, 342 ff., 543–556; Pohl 1982, 342; Westdeutsche 1984, 40 ff.
109 Guinnane et al. 2013, 70 ff.; Faust 1977, 354 f., 362 ff., 370 ff.; Westdeutsche 1984, 19.
110 Guinnane et al. 2013, 73 f.; Faust 1977, 387–416; Pohl 1982, 347 f.,

ticular, under economic aspects." His greatest service was to spur the German organization process by emphasizing regional independence without any paternalistic intervention. Thus, in 1879, Haas founded a network in Hesse that spread its influence to southwest Germany within the same year and then, in 1883, throughout the country. At this point, a cooling-off phase with Raiffeisen started in parallel with a closer cooperation with Schulze-Delitzsch, whose Volksbanks found access to the rural areas. After Raiffeisen's death in 1888, the network also took up credit cooperatives. Before that, Haas had refrained from doing so out of respect for Raiffeisen. The renaming of the network in 1903 as the "National Association of German Rural Cooperatives" [*Reichsverband der deutschen ländlichen Genossenschaften*] as apex, deepened the rift in the rural cooperative movement, before a union of interests with the Raiffeisen network resulted in 1905. Up to 1913, the national association acted as a joint representation of interests. The Haas and Raiffeisen cooperatives did not take up the limited liability permitted under the Cooperative Act of 1889, which once again reflects the shared commonalities. The now permitted cooperative membership in other cooperatives was used to push the important establishment of central cooperative apex banks.[111]

Haas' own credit cooperative concept waived moral and ethical motivations as well as funds. Instead, he favored larger business shares and profit sharing. His inherent spirit of free enterprise again is reflected in the founding of a national central bank [*Landwirtschaftliche Reichsgenossenschaftsbank*] in 1902. It was explicitly intended to "free the agricultural cooperative movement from the *Preußenkasse*." From 1907 on, Haas' central bank ironically battled with latent liquidity problems and, in 1912, had to be liquidated due to excessive debt. Thus, as Faust commented, the attempt failed to give the rural cooperative scheme a head bank "based on free cooperative self-help." A year later, the Haas' Hessian Central Bank, whose business had been interwoven with that of the national institution, met the same fate. The decisive factor in this failure was the insolvency of just two big cooperatives. As it happened, Haas himself was a member of the supervisory board of both central banks. These failures illustrated the general risks as well as the predisposition of small organizations to fail, despite the liquidity mechanisms put in place in the meantime.

Even though the media relished reporting the fiasco, this negative press did not affect the Haas movement, as the historical statistics show. In mid-1914 there were 945 Schulze-Delitzsch Volksbanks with about 620,000 members and the Raiffeisen network comprised 4,400 institutions with 485,000 members, while the Haas group consisted of 1,165 cooperatives with over one million members.[112]

---

[111] Deutsche Bundesbank 1976, 65, 110; Faust 1977, 356, 375 ff., 398, 541 f.; Westdeutsche 1984, 33–39, 42 f.; see there also for the following.

[112] Guinnane et al. 2013, 47, 64 ff.; Faust 1977, 226, 316 ff., 381 ff.; 406–416; Pohl 1982, 207; 343, 350 f.; Westdeutsche 1984, 25 ff., 32–39; Deutsche Bundesbank 1976; the figures partly differ; see there also for the following.

> **Snapshot 36: Supervision and organizational design in the German Cooperative Act of 1889**
>
> *Supervision every two years in the form of an external obligatory audit by an auditor named by the District Court or through cooperative audit associations.*
>
> *Possibility of eGmbH (cooperative with limited liability) status and membership of cooperatives in other cooperatives.*
>
> It is interesting to note in this context that after the law was passed, the Prussian provincial and district governments expressly encouraged the municipal bodies, which in many places already ran savings banks, to promote the establishment of commercial cooperatives.[113]

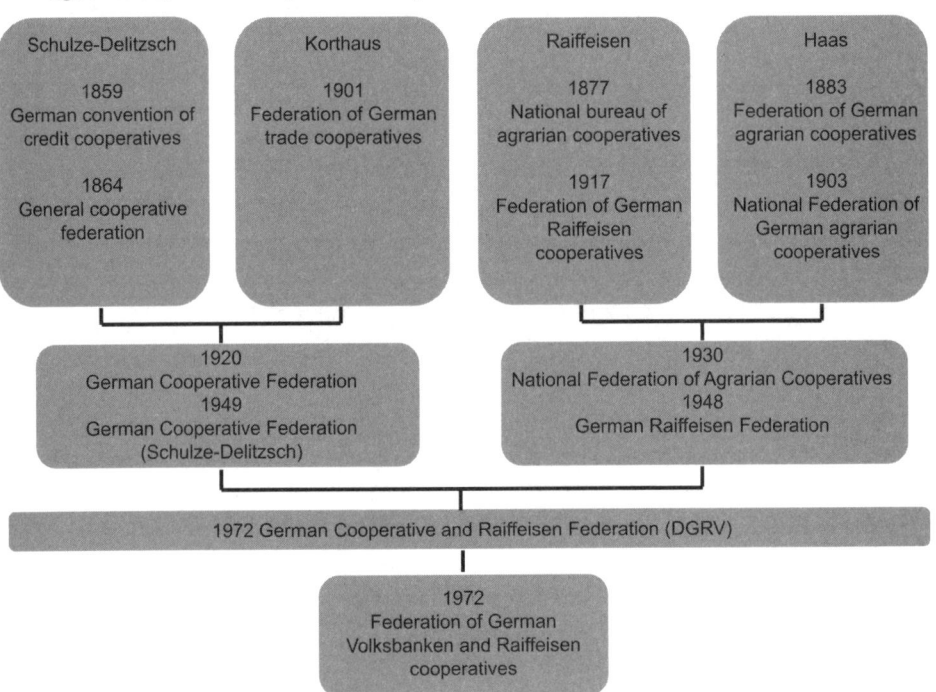

Figure 13: Cooperative networks (Gleber et al. 2012)

Schulze-Delitzsch	Korthaus	Raiffeisen	Haas
1859 German convention of credit cooperatives	1901 Federation of German trade cooperatives	1877 National bureau of agrarian cooperatives	1883 Federation of German agrarian cooperatives
1864 General cooperative federation		1917 Federation of German Raiffeisen cooperatives	1903 National Federation of German agrarian cooperatives

1920 German Cooperative Federation
1949 German Cooperative Federation (Schulze-Delitzsch)

1930 National Federation of Agrarian Cooperatives
1948 German Raiffeisen Federation

1972 German Cooperative and Raiffeisen Federation (DGRV)

1972 Federation of German Volksbanken and Raiffeisen cooperatives

It is important to point out here that there were also numerous other regional networks. They acted over a remarkable range and also helped to mitigate the divisive tendencies of the main groups. These regional groups included the Association of the Rhine-Prussian Agricultural Cooperatives and the Trier Farmers' Association, to name only two. All of these regional groups followed the grand ob-

---

113 For the law see http://de.wikisource.org/wiki/Gesetz, https://www.google.co.uk/search?hl=en&biw=1366&bih=643&site=webhp&q=betreffend+die+Erwerbs-+und+Wirtschaftsgenossenschaften&spell=1&sa=X&ved=0ahUKEwia6KvDw8nJAhXLCBoKHQZ0CVAQBQgZKAAbetreffend die Erwerbs- und Wirtschaftsgenossenschaften; Kluthe 1985; Thomes 1985a, 1988.

jective of facilitating commercial and agrarian small enterprise, but by quite different pathways.

Historical analysis documents the fact that variety and competition contributed to the sustainable prosperity of self-help movements. Therefore, legal regulation should not narrowly limit the degree of freedom for such institutions to act – as was also found with regard to the savings banks. These aspects also should not be forgotten when considering the current microfinance movement.

7.5 Case study – The Hachenburg Credit Cooperative [*Vorschussverein Hachenburg*]

Since aggregate facts are largely missing for the credit cooperatives due to the lack of a joint organization, a local example here should serve to illustrate the developments. The case in question is the credit cooperative of Hachenburg, a city in the Duchy of Nassau around 40 km northeast of Neuwied. The association was founded in 1862 under the Schulze-Delitzsch system. It encompassed the city and 53 rural villages on the periphery of the Siegerland industrial area. Quite close to Raiffeisen's nerve center, albeit in another state, this case might elicit interesting conclusions. It operates today after many mergers with neighboring cooperatives as *Westerwald Bank eG Volks- und Raiffeisenbank*.[114]

The Hachenburg cooperative can be traced back to a pharmacist with social-liberal convictions. He had inaugurated a so-called "industrial society" together with like-minded partners as early as 1841. Their dual motivation was to stimulate business and to alleviate poverty. Then, in 1862, the pharmacist initiated the cooperative modeled after an institution established in nearby Dillenburg in 1861.

To acquire operating capital, the founding group approached the State Bank of the Duchy of Nassau, negotiated with private individuals, and collected information in the banking center of Frankfurt. A wealthy local family finally loaned 1,800 Florins at an interest rate of 5% p.a. Another 3,000 Florins came from a Wiesbaden credit cooperative. The State Bank agreed to allow a credit line of 5,000 Florins, while the neighboring cooperative in Dillenburg made 2,000 Florins available; the new cooperative adopted the business forms in use at the neighboring cooperatives as well. Furthermore, by the end of 1863, 46 members had made deposits ranging from 24 Florins to 1,450 Florins, amounting to a total volume of 23,210 Florins accruing 4% interest p.a. The share capital for the members amounted to 50 Florins and could be deposited in monthly installments.

---

[114] The following is based mainly on Krauss 2012; http://de.wikipedia.org/wiki/Westerwald_Bank. For another example see https://www.volksbank-offenburg-1864.de/Chronik-Volksbank-Offenburg.pdf.

With regard to the credit business, one guarantee sufficed for loans of up to 100 Florins, and the maximum credit was 300 Florins. The balance of the first full business year showed 335 loans with a total volume of over 31,000 Florins. Seven of these loans had already been repaid by the end of the year. The terms of some of the loans amounted to only a few weeks; the credit business actually dealt with bridging liquidity shortfalls, something which had also been intended by the very first savings banks.[115] A cashier and a so-called controller, both of whom were salaried employees, as of 1864, managed the business.

The good customer acceptance is confirmed by the fact that for 1864, another 25,000 Florins needed to be acquired to finance loan disbursement. On the other hand Hachenburg lent a neighboring cooperative the sum of 1,000 Florins at 5% interest. In 1864, the Hachenburg cooperative members earned remarkable dividends of 33.33% for every full Florin deposited by December 31, 1863 – an attractive incentive for those who were still non-members and a genuine success story that certainly attracted imitators. This example well explains, too, why the business of the Raiffeisen banks, which waived dividend payments, sometimes had more difficulties.

At that time, there were around 500 Volksbanks in the German states. The demand for such banks also substantiates the success of Raiffeisen banks in the neighboring part of the Westerwald: By the end of 1865, Heddesdorf had granted loans of a total amount of 8,406 Taler[116], while Anhausen issued credit of a total volume of 23,516 Taler and another Raiffeisen cooperative disbursed credit of a total volume of 20,708 Taler. The average loan amount fluctuated from year to year between 26 and 253 Taler, with a statutory minimum of 5 Taler and a maximum of 250 Taler. The credit terms varied between three months and 10 years at interest rates ranging from 6 1/3% for ten-year loans and 8% for three-month loans, with a typical mortgage interest rate of 5%. All the associations operated at a profit from the very beginning, and there were no losses booked up to 1865. A sum of 5 Taler, the minimum credit amount, corresponded to about 10 to 15 daily wages depending on season and need, which indeed corresponds to typical microfinance loan amounts of today.

In 1866, Nassau fell to Prussia, which did not hinder the pace of business in Hachenburg. The Franco-Prussian War of 1870/71 did not have a significant impact either. In 1873, there were 820 members; the annual dividends amounted to 10%, while the capital share, with the introduction of the Mark, the new currency of the German Reich, was rounded up from the previous 30 Taler to 100 Marks.[117] The

---

115 See the earlier relevant section.
116 Two Taler were worth three Gulden (Florins).
117 One Taler was worth three Marks.

Snapshot 37: Balances of early credit cooperatives, 1862 to 1865[118]

following years were quite successful, too, as the 8–10 % dividends in the period up to 1881 illustrate, while numerous other cooperatives fell into bankruptcy.[119]

A milestone was the establishment of a savings division in 1879. This division served as "a new source for acquiring capital" and aimed "to help members invest small funds," with a maximum deposit amount of 1,000 Marks. Even though this measure followed a general trend, to the chagrin of the savings banks, they could not prevent it. The savings terms and conditions were similar to those of the savings banks. In addition, the costs of capital acquisition sank, which tended to favorably affect the credit interest rates. Meanwhile, the savings clients likewise profited from this competition between the savings banks and the cooperatives.[120] Up to that time, the private residence of the cashier had served as the business office – also an aspect of cost-effective structures in the sense of a public-welfare-oriented mission.

In 1886, Hachenburg credit cooperative had around 1,200 members and made a net profit of 10,600 Marks on total revenues of 1.1 million Marks. From 1890 on, after it joined the cooperative network, an independent auditor regularly examined the accounts. Business contacts existed with the central bank in Berlin. Occasionally the cooperative, like many savings banks, now purchased bonds from issuers outside of the region – as a precaution to ensure liquidity, but perhaps be-

---
118 Krauss 2012, 29.
119 For details see the following section.
120 For details see the comparative section which follows.

cause little administrative effort was involved as well. Reflecting the more difficult business conditions, the dividends in the 1890s were only 5%. As from 1895, the capital share amounted to 500 Marks. As before, this could be paid in installments in order to allow the inclusive participation of less wealthy individuals.

At the end of the 19th century, Hachenburg characterized itself as having developed "wholly according to banking standards," without having to forego its principles. This development allowed it "not only to satisfy the credit needs of agriculture, but also the demands of every merchant and tradesman in every regard." The range of products included installment loans secured by a guarantee or on a Lombard basis, overdrafts, discounting bills of exchange, international monetary transactions in Europe and America, currency exchange, securities trading, coupon redemption and, last but not least, the deposits and savings business. This was truly a remarkable range of services for a provincial institution and proof of successful integration in the national capital market after around 40 years of existence (Krauss 2012, 49).

The beginning of the 20th century ushered in an era of apparent opportunity. In 1901, the dividends were raised to 6%, while by 1905 the membership exceeded 1,700 members. The year 1907 represented another milestone in that Hachenburg changed its name to fit its philosophy and business field – as a bank: It was now called *Vereinsbank Hachenburg eGmuH*.[121] Again, one year later, the bank broadened its services to include the financing of tradesmen's claims. This product met with such a huge demand that the board felt obliged to inform its customers that it was not a debt collection company.

First signs of adversity loomed in 1909/1910. Rumors about solvency problems generated such unrest that in the beginning of 1911 an extraordinary general meeting was called. The board of directors dismissed any doubts by granting a dividend of 6% and by emphasizing its careful business policies, as a result of which the institution had not experienced any losses in 20 years. Moreover, the board threatened criminal prosecution for those who had started such rumors. However, there was some element of truth to these rumors, for in mid-1912 the bank had to concede a loss of over 180,000 Marks caused by six badly secured, defaulting loans. Yet two reserve funds and the pension fund just sufficed to cover these losses. In addition, the members of the board of directors and of the supervisory board undertook to pay any shortfalls out of their own assets. Moreover, the director resigned, and his pension was eliminated. Even though a dividend continued to be paid to the members, the number of members shrank by about one-third in 1912 and 1913, from 1,862 to 1,274, and deposits were also withdrawn. On the one hand, this reflected the massive loss in trust. Yet on the other, the self-seeking behavior of the members exacerbated the financial situation of the bank,

---

[121] eGmuH = registered cooperative with full liability.

since the withdrawn share capital, which may have had a value of up to 300,000 Marks, had to be liquefied.

Consequently, the whole region suffered from this adversity. The board of directors was accordingly outraged by the behavior of the members who, at the first sign of trouble, had betrayed their own principles. In 1912, the business report of the bank stated: "The cooperative spirit completely failed during its first challenge… If any risk to the cooperative bank had been possible, then this risk would have arisen only through this mindless cancellation of membership. It is obvious that the bank does not have its funds lying in the cash registers without earning interest… Upon withdrawal of large sums of money… the bank is naturally forced to likewise respond by withdrawals." As a result, many debtors were drawn "into an unfortunate state." The bank report further charged, "Those members who cancelled their membership should have thought about this, in the spirit of the cooperative motto of 'All for one and one for all'" (Krauss 2012, 54).

The argument was poignant and precise and, at the same time, revealed the weakness of the concept. In crises, the commitment to solidarity obviously was not worth the paper on which it was printed. It is a fact that isolated, local economic systems fall rapidly in a fatal downward spiral due to the domino effect of individual panicky dealings.[122] This case also clearly demonstrated the limitations of the personal liability concept and showed that institutional liability was also necessary as well as liquidity networks.

In any event, the bank learned from these negative experiences. It examined its credit portfolio, and where necessary, it demanded additional guarantees and also

---

Snapshot 38: Aachener Bank, Urban Craftsmen Credit Cooperative, 1900

The following were eligible for membership:
1. All independent craftsmen and small businessmen of majority age … residing in Aachen and Aachen Burtscheid, and women who are proprietors of an independent craftsman's workshop.
2. Other individuals, but only in numbers which do not dilute the character of the organization as a craftsmen's cooperative.

The amount of a share in the business was set at 100 Marks, the liability amount at 300 Marks.

Task of the cooperative: The economic advancement and support of its members, in particular through the acceptance of interest-bearing deposits and the provision of credit.

Credit business: The loans were issued against own and commercial bills of exchange; as a rule, the term was not to exceed three months.

---

[122] See earlier for the Haas failure in that same year.

consistently collected outstanding payments. It is interesting to note that, at this time, the overdraft limits of most customers had been fully exhausted. This prompted the board of directors to instruct the clients "to maintain a certain reserve" to be used only in the worst situations. The bank itself subsequently subjected itself to "extensive limitations," passed on larger applications for credit to large banks, and refocused its operations on the "credit needs of medium-sized businesses and of the ordinary man" (Krauss 2012, 54). As in today's financial crisis, this maxim saved the German cooperative banks from massive losses.

7.6 Volksbanks and Raiffeisen cooperatives – A remarkable success story

The balance of the credit cooperatives in 1914, on the eve of World War I, was clearly positive – despite a few setbacks, which are normal when many new ideas are enacted and when individual and institutional learning experiences span six decades. Nevertheless, success was not guaranteed. Here as well, the local economic environment and general economic developments played a decisive role. Thus, two Volksbanks, founded in the industrial district of Aachen in 1868 and 1869, failed after a few years. And only one bank, established in 1900, was sustainably successful in a positive economic environment; it is still in existence today as the *Aachener Bank*. Nonetheless, as from 1873, the crisis in the aftermath of the economic boom following the establishment of the German Empire in 1871 severely tested the mettle of the commercially-oriented Volksbanks. Many institutions had to write off big losses due to bad loans and a number of institutions went bankrupt. One spectacular failure was that of the big Düsseldorf Trades Bank [*Düsseldorfer Gewerbebank*] in 1875. It was not surprising that Schulze-Delitzsch criticized this bank for "violating, in all essential points, the principles of the cooperative movement." (Westdeutsche 1984, 13, 25). In fact, until 1879 the number of Volksbanks stagnated, because there were only few new bank establishments and a considerable number of Volksbanks converted to joint-stock banks or merged with commercial banks or savings banks. As a result of the crisis, interested circles even demanded state supervision.

Moreover, the essential issue of joint liability was intensively discussed – subsequently being changed to limited liability in the Cooperative Act of 1889 (Kluthe 1985). Thereafter, the founding of credit cooperatives boomed, starting from the mid-1890s.

Between 1896 and 1913, the number of credit cooperatives in Germany more than doubled, from around 9,400 to about 19,300 institutions. This figure represented a total of around 3 million members, or about 5 % of the population. The institutions' total assets amounted to a little over 5 billion Marks, while the credit volume came to just over 4 billion Marks. Total business assets and reserve funds ran well over 600 million Marks. Moreover, there were 46 central institutions that were indispensable for liquidity management, 31 of which were rural. These banks had total assets of around 500 million Marks, while the Prussian Bank alone had total assets of 212 million Marks. Naturally, these central banks increasingly cooperated with one another, but they also worked, for example, with the public state banks, the branches of the *Reichsbank* or commercial banks. Thus, they formed a multi-layered and effective, interwoven liquidity network, despite the inherently unavoidable problem cases.[123] The same applies for the regional associations. Besides publicity work and lobbying, they optimized the exchange of information and experience and, not least of all, the supervision system. The latter was a crucial instrument to prevent corruption and other business irregularities – the central risk factors.

Regarding the number of institutions, one has to differentiate between them based on the group, as two comparisons from the Rhine Province of Prussia show. In 1866, the province had ten "industrial" banks (Schulze-Delitzsch Volksbanks) and five rural (Raiffeisen) banks; in 1871, by contrast, the ratio was 82 to 77, which illustrates the dynamic rate of diffusion as well. The number of cooperatives, mainly operating in urban areas, peaked in the mid-1890s. Afterwards, there was a consolidation. The number of members certainly grew further, namely from ca. 526,000 to 815,000 in 1913 – an increase of over 50%. The volume of business grew even more strongly. With total assets of roughly 2.2 billion Marks, the total balance sheet volume tripled; inflation was negligible. More than 75% of the assets were loans. The remainder comprised bank assets and securities, thus investments that mainly served to secure liquidity. Of the loans issued, 85% were short-term loans, and thus, typical microfinance-type loans. The largest share in liabilities, i.e. over 90%, was accounted for by savings and current account deposits. That means that the credit linkages of the Volksbanks, among each other or with other banks, had become negligible. Share capital and reserve funds amounted to over 400 million Marks – which implied a solid foundation.

It is even more difficult to establish an assessment of the rural Raiffeisen credit cooperatives. According to statistics published by the German central bank, *Bundesbank*, the situation for around 15,800 institutions captured in the statistics for 1913 was as follows: With total assets of around 3 billion Marks, the loans outstanding added up to approximately 2.7 billion Marks. Of this amount, 1.7 billion Marks comprised long-term loans, which mainly included the traditional rural mortgage business. A few cooperatives deviated considerably from this structure. The legal framework, even in 1913, allowed sufficient leeway for business policies to be adapted to fit local conditions.

---

[123] Deutsche Bundesbank, 1976, 65f., 110, 114ff.; Pohl, 1982, 343; partly divergent and rough figures, because in 1913 around 10% of the institutes were not registered; see Westdeutsche 1984, 25–44; Guinnane et al., 2013, 137ff.

Apart from this, and like the savings banks, both groups – the Volksbanks to a greater extent and the Raiffeisen cooperatives less so – had become universal banks, in the sense of offering all financial services (though they received the legal status of banks, togther with the savings banks, only in 1934). They were nationally and to an extent even internationally linked. In this way, the financial services offered and the customers' needs could be brought into convergence very flexibly.

Thus, the conclusion to be drawn here is: Their mission was fulfilled in microfinance terms. In the credit business of rural areas, the cooperatives made a key contribution to the locally tailored standardization of banking practices that hitherto had been non-transparent as they tended to depend on personal or business relationships. In effect, the institutions complemented the activities of the savings banks. Moreover, in the cities, the domain of the cooperatives was short-term personal loans to SMEs and start-ups. Consequently, the savings banks and cooperatives quite often competed with one other; and internal competition within each group came into play around 1900 at the latest, leading to efficiency and to lower price levels that benefited the customers. Since competition inherently stimulates business, the credit sector in 1913 had greatly changed.

Low-income households were also among those who were able to obtain loans at transparent market conditions. The savings business also showed similar positive microfinance effects, even when the credit cooperatives operated the savings business mainly for commercial reasons. They promoted the inclusion of underprivileged or low-income households even in the smallest village.

Another important aspect which should again be emphasized here was the development of a liquidity system and a supervision system. And yet another is the linking of the credit and commodities business, which was standard practice for the Raiffeisen cooperatives. This aspect seems to be of interest today because, if the aim is to secure people's livelihoods and to help generate sustainable independence and income, then the procurement and distribution of production inputs and consumer goods at fair prices brings decisive advantages for low-income households.

It is not without reason that both the cooperative idea and its business model had taken root far beyond Germany and Europe by the beginning of the 20th century – and David Roodman is absolutely right here.[124] Nonetheless, in contrast to other European countries, the 20th century path of cooperative development in Germany was consistently characterized by strong, locally and regionally focused credit cooperatives, and these institutions continue to closely serve individual customers' needs today.[125]

---

[124] For Austria, see the exemplary publications of Christian Dirninger, 2005–2012.
[125] Gleber et al. 2012; Genossenschaftsverband 1996.

SWOT analysis of credit cooperatives in 1913

Strengths:

- Local/regional embedment
- Proximity to clients
- Flexibility
- Personal short-term and medium-term loans, agrarian long-term loans
- Savings in small amounts
- Nonprofit or moderately profit-oriented institutions

Weakness(es):

- Small units
- No liability network
- Liquidity risk
- Lack of solidarity among the members
- Partly exclusive business model

Opportunities:

- Competition
- Integrated financial business
- Integrated regional and national organization
- Liquidity management
- Complementary competition with savings banks
- Strengthening of social structures

Threats:

- Competition from corporate and savings banks

8 Savings banks, credit cooperatives, and commercial banks – Complementarity versus rivalry

This comparative chapter deals with the effects stemming from the simultaneous competition and complementarity among the credit cooperatives, savings banks, and commercial banks since the end of the 19th century. This dynamic constellation resulted in a quite unique three-pillar universal banking sector structure which enabled the widespread and effective provision of microfinance services in Germany.

When the credit cooperatives began to spread, starting in the 1850s, the savings banks had already been operating in the market for around 70 years; however, they operated mainly in cities and without branch networks. These deficiencies had become clear to the government authorities, perhaps for the first time, during the crisis years of 1846–1848. The state began to intensively support the founding of district savings banks, primarily in Prussia, with the aim of integrating the rural population into the financial system. The credit cooperatives were just beginning to move into these rural areas, however, and make them their own business playing field. At that time, the state had not yet defined its position towards the cooperatives because of their organization as grassroots, democratic, and self-help-oriented commercial institutions. Indeed, the founders of the cooperative movement were considered to be critical social reformers who operated outside the radius of government action during these crisis years. Against this background, the political initiatives to establish more district savings banks from the 1850s on certainly can be seen as the state's reaction to the cooperative movement.

In 1871, the Trier senior civil servant Otto Beck outlined the aim of credit cooperatives as follows: In adherence to the principles "of self-help, self-responsibility and self-administration…," these institutions would extend to "…anyone the kind of credit, for a short term and at reasonable interest rates… which the big businesses, large traders and factory owners enjoy at the large banks." As has already been shown, the savings banks also did this to a certain extent. Thus, in 1863, the Saarbrücken district administrator denied that there was any need for credit cooperatives, because the local savings bank already "granted loans to people of modest means, in order to rescue them from the clutches of the moneylenders." And more than a few savings banks in rural areas in the late 1870s had issued out the greater part of their assets in the form of small loans, in violation of their own bank charters (Thomes 1988).

Yet the cooperatives and the savings banks quite often acted as complementary institutions at that time, because many communities had accepted the savings banks not on principle and from a genuine desire to do so, but because they had

Table 11: Savings deposits of savings banks and credit cooperatives in Germany (mn Mark), 1850–1910

Year	Savings banks	Credit cooperatives
1850	212	0
1860	477	1
1870	908	44
1880	2,615	116
1890	5,134	143
1900	8,824	202
1910	16,782	338

Ashauer 1991, 117.

been ordered to. It is not surprising that even as late as the 1880s, district savings banks, when pressed by the government to expand their branch networks, often referred to the existence of the cooperatives as making such expansion unnecessary, in a division of labour approach.

The informal cooperation of the two groups worked as follows: On the credit side, the credit cooperatives handled the complicated personal loan business that the savings banks tended to avoid. However, the cooperatives used savings bank loans as a reliable source of financing for their lending activities. Thus, there was indeed a complementary division of labor and a classic win–win situation. With regard to the savings business, the situation was slightly different. In 1851, for example, the Eilenburg cooperative was already accepting small savings deposits on which it paid customers higher interest rates than those offered by the local savings bank. The Eilenburg cooperative could afford to do this because of the higher interest rates it charged its customers on loans. Accordingly, in his guidelines of 1855, Schulze-Delitzsch argued that the cooperatives "should not be stingy with interest and should instead always aim to pay a higher rate than the savings banks." Here he was not referring to the smallest of deposits. He objected to so-called "Pfennigsparkassen," (penny savings banks) due to their security risk, for a possible bankruptcy would result in the loss of children's savings: In other words, competition should not be pursued down to the last cent. Thus, for a long time, these complementary business practices allowed for a quite relaxed relationship between the savings banks and credit cooperatives, especially since there was a continually rising demand for financial services during the ensuing industrialization and the market had only just begun to be tapped.[126]

The motivation, perspective, and mission of the actors changed, however, with their growing success. Moreover, the sluggish economic growth of the 1880s tightened the market. Credit cooperatives now focused on attracting savings in order to reduce their financing costs. In addition, the Cooperative Act of 1889 accelerated the founding of credit cooperatives. On the one hand, the network of savings banks was growing denser at the same time, because the municipalities in-

---

[126] Hörstmann 1928; Kluge 1991, 209; Trende 1957, 575; Pohl 2000.

Table 12: Savings bank locations in the Prussian Rhineland province by government district as of 1912

District	Savings banks (no.)	Savings locations (no.)	Area served per agency in km²	Savings passbooks (no.)	Savings passbooks per 100 residents
Aachen	13	110	37.8	261,032	36.85
Dusseldorf	177	300	18.3	1,220,053	33.75
Cologne	31	178	22.4	438,720	33.82
Arnsberg	127	202	38.1	770,830	30.46
Munster	48	130	55.8	265,806	24.83
Prussia	1,760	6,886	50.9	13,820,000	33.30

Statistisches Jahrbuch für den Preußischen Staat [Statistical Yearbook for the Prussian State] 1914, 350f.

creasingly recognized the economic potential of these institutions and wanted to counteract any government initiatives to establish a national postal savings bank. On the other, the authorities in Prussia and elsewhere encouraged the establishment of credit cooperatives after 1889 as well. They apparently did not foresee any threat to the community savings banks.[127]

One result of this trend was that prior to World War I, both credit cooperatives and savings banks were widespread, with internal competition within each group. The following example illustrates these developments: As from 1895, the branch network of the district savings banks operating in the district of Aachen exploded from 30 locations to at least 70 in the period from 1900 to 1913. Over the same period, the number of savings bank branches in the district of Cologne grew from 61 to 159, plus 25 sales offices for savings stamps. At the same time, growing cities incorporated formerly independent communities which had had savings banks of their own; these bank offices were not closed down, however. Thus, even though the number of savings banks stagnated, the total number of branches rose significantly.[128] The processes underway all led to the same results: more bank sites and increasing competition, going hand-in-hand with closer relationships to customers and greater socioeconomic inclusion.

The intensive rivalry sometimes led to strongly competition-oriented business policies. One way in which this change was manifested was in newspaper advertising wars fought among the groups via interest rates. Likewise, though terms and conditions had formerly remained largely consistent, this was no longer the case, and each change in the interest rate immediately affected business. The situation continued to escalate. Concerning the savings banks, the government intervened to stop "abuses through newspaper advertisements, in particular" with regard to the "form, content and number" of advertisements. Starting in 1908, the savings banks of the Rhineland province had to submit their newspaper advertisements as part of auditing. Moreover, advertising in newspapers outside the area served by

---

[127] Fabry 1986; Spoo 1999; Thomes 1985a, 2008.
[128] Haas 1976; Thomes 2007; Wysocki, 1993.

the respective savings bank was prohibited. Yet none of these measures brought about any fundamental change in the situation.

In 1912, one district administrator replied to the government's warning as follows: "These [credit cooperatives] are employing all imaginable means and often advertise in a loud, sensationalist manner. They are carrying out financial transactions which far exceed the scope of the cooperative mission and in part have expanded to become large banks with branches, whose solidity is critical. In addition, the commercial banks that accept savings deposits are rising in number. The *Röchling Bank*, a private commercial bank, to name one, including its branch offices, certainly knows how to attract savings by offering a higher interest rate and to use this money to benefit the industrial enterprises among the bank's clientele" (Thomes 1985a, 246). It is no coincidence that the savings bank's board of directors wished to have the greatest possible freedom regarding the setting of interest rates, which seemed to be the only means of addressing the competition.

From the 1890s on, in fact regional banks and even the large national investment banks increasingly opened their doors to lower-income private customers and thus took the first step towards large-scale retail banking business. In turn, the savings banks and credit cooperatives increasingly exploited business opportunities with wealthy customers. Even in mid-sized cities, there was ongoing competition. Accordingly, as from the beginning of the 20th century there were conflicts about the increasing tendency of savings banks to develop along the lines of conventional commercial banks. In turn, the savings banks were mainly disturbed about cooperatives' use of the terms "savings bank" and "savings passbook." Initiatives to establish legal protection by means of registered trademarks succeeded only in the aftermath of the banking crisis of 1931.[129]

Another interesting repercussion of this new situation was a drop in the number of private bankers on the boards of savings banks and credit cooperatives. They were no longer needed, for internal expertise had grown substantially, as had the market for trained personnel, leading, along with other factors, to a fluctuation in personnel among the groups. Moreover, the number of women bank employees rose at the turn of the 20th century. Generally, these female employees were back-office staff without any customer contact, though here again there were exceptions to the rule (Pohl et al. 2005; Ashauer 1991) – the start of a long and hard emancipation process.

From a microfinance viewpoint, these developments must be seen as unequivocally positive. They were a reflection of the accelerated convergence on all levels. Especially for low-income customers, the integrated markets meant a greater degree of transparency than ever before. At the start of the 20th century, savings banks, credit cooperatives, and even commercial banks offered a wide range of savings

---

[129] Trende 1957, 576 ff.; Pohl 2001; Pohl et al. 2005; Thomes 2007.

and credit tools for low-income households and small tradespeople. There was actually a sufficient range of financial products available to allow low-income households to manage their still volatile and uncertain cash flows or to finance the small business investments of skilled craftsmen or other individuals who wanted to start an enterprise. For the first time in history, the "ordinary man" had a real choice in financial affairs: not just a choice between worst-case scenarios – between a rock and a hard place – but an opportunity to choose among various suppliers offering different, yet consistently sound and reputable products. The geographical, societal, and financial inclusion of low-income households had taken a giant step forward.

However, we must not forget two important facts: This "step" was a process that took at least three generations, lasting a whole century, and the developments took place within a largely stable political framework. In parallel, the economy remained on a stable and quasi uninterrupted growth path from the middle of the 19th century until the beginning of World War I in 1914. Today, however, even developed regions, like Europe, face rising poverty once more in the face of the current economic and demographic trends. These developments urgently require attention and action, too.[130]

Snapshot 39: Success factors identified in the History Lab

A certain amount of legal flexibility; savings and credit; competition; a holistic approach; a local focus in terms of business operations and use of profits; nonprofit structures; networks; internal and external control and supervision; a stable political and economic environment.

---

130 See for instance the German-language article *"Unilever stellt sich auf Armut in Europa ein" [Unilever prepares itself for poverty in Europe]*; http://www.t-online.dewww.t-online.de, 27 August 2012.

9 Summary, conclusions, and outlook – Are there lessons to be learned from the History Lab?

This section summarizes the historical factors for success in achieving financial inclusion of low-income households and SMEs in the framework of a responsible, locally-based banking system in the age of European industrialization.

Firstly, it should be noted once more that, because of cultural diversity and other crucial differences with regard to the decisive factors of culture, place, technology and time, the results of the historical analysis naturally are not directly applicable to current situations or challenges in developing economies.

Nevertheless, the approach put forward here broadens our scope of thought and action. In this sense, it

- generates abstract systemic knowledge about change processes and
- enhances the ability to give and to receive criticism.

Both aspects are relevant in that:
1. Foreign advisors and donors in many cases act selectively based on their own experience. The knowledge base delivered here allows them to identify and critically discuss their own attitudes, assumptions, and actions.
2. The knowledge base delivered here allows domestic agents to discover new spheres of, and latitude for, action.

The combination of both points should lead to a better understanding of the general factors leading to convergence and a higher success rate for microfinance projects.

9.1 Organizational findings

1. Savings banks and credit cooperatives were founded as innovative financial institutions and change management institutions with the aim of addressing changing needs during the socioeconomic change process from an agrarian to an industrial society.
2. Savings banks and credit cooperatives represented different competitive approaches to handling the process. Credit cooperatives were a democratic grassroots initiative, while savings banks were the result of a politically conservative top-down approach.
3. The main financial needs of low-income households during the European age of industrialization were to manage volatile and uncertain cash-flows and to

obtain financing for small-scale business investments. Therefore, the creation of savings facilities was as important as the creation of credit options.
4. The savings banks' business model highlighted savings, while the credit cooperatives' model emphasized loans. However, both types of institution offered savings and loans, a prerequisite for their impressive development into universal banks for all.
5. The government influenced developments by means of legislation. The banks developed optimally wherever the pertinent laws were flexible, leaving local agents the scope necessary for effective change management.
6. Both groups developed numerous organizational variants depending on local needs and conditions. There were both private business models and models subject to public law.
7. All institutions in both groups primarily served a local business area. Their capital was raised in the area they served, and their profits were spent or reinvested primarily in the region or area in which they had been generated, thus preventing a capital drain. In the German states in general, there was little direct exploitation or transfer of savings to the central government.
8. All business models initially depended partly on charity. The board of directors often served on a volunteer basis and the institutions did not have to finance their own premises.
9. The approaches of both groups were not based on pure profit maximization but rather followed the idea of serving the common or public welfare.
10. The savings banks were subject to multiple forms of formal oversight by the guaranteeing bodies from the beginning. The credit cooperatives were at first subject to supervision by their members, and later by cooperative networks, including auditing organizations. This supervision and monitoring shielded the institutions from corruption and fraud.
11. Regional and national group networks were an important success factor. Such networks facilitated communication and the exchange of information, supervision, auditing and controlling, continuing education, and lobbying. Regional and national banks optimized liquidity and helped to make small banks, as well as the networks, crisis resilient.
12. The institutional integration process took at least two generations, if not three.
13. This process took place within a predominantly stable setting. In other words, there was more or less steady economic growth backed by stable political and legal framework conditions.

9.2 Practical findings

1. The initial success of credit cooperatives and savings banks in Europe was based on the collection of small interest-bearing savings deposits and the issuance of small loans at transparent and moderate terms and conditions.
2. The majority of the institutions were inclusive. They were open to both high- and low-income households and to SMEs, and integrated them into their clientele.
3. There was a broad range of savings and loan products available with incentives based on social criteria. There were no significant gender-specific terms and conditions, but there were special offers for children designed to promote a habit of saving.
4. The spread in interest rates between savings and loans was around 5 % net at its maximum, normally less, generally 2–3 %. It should be noted here that high interest rates on loans do not compensate for high risk. On the contrary, disproportionately high interest rates on loans will increase the risk of default.
5. Despite the moderate margins, the majority of banks began operating at a profit soon after their founding.
6. The initial use of earnings was the accumulation of a reserve fund.
7. Once a reserve fund had been accumulated, surplus revenue was either distributed in the form of dividends to the local shareholders of the credit cooperatives – normally depositors or borrowers with the same institution – or, in case of the savings banks, invested in public welfare projects. The latter included projects in the areas of education, health, and infrastructure (e. g. water, gas, electricity, roads, streetcars, railways). Revenues were thus overwhelmingly reinvested or spent in the region in which they were generated.
8. Both of these locally-based German business models have proven crisis-resilient since the 19th century. Savings banks, in particular, quickly became safe havens in times of insecurity. This has remained the case to the present day for these institutions in Germany, which – in contrast to comparable institutions in other European countries – adhered to their original local business model. In both cases, they fared better than the investor-owned banks. They remained stable and indirectly helped to ensure employment and inclusion.[131]

F.W. Raiffeisen analyzed the relationship between saving, credit, self-help, and subsidy aid systematically and almost timelessly in his standard work *Die Darlehnskassen-Vereine*:[132] "Where people no longer have the power of self-help, the government often steps in. Aid without service in return often turns out to be

---

[131] See latest report from the ILO, *Resilience in a downturn: The power of financial cooperatives*, Birchall, Johnston, International Co-operative Alliance, March 21, 2013.
[132] Raiffeisen 1866, here 4th edition 1883, 13; also English edition 1970, in general see Ashauer 1991, 178 –188.

Figure 14: Parameters for the achievement of above-average results

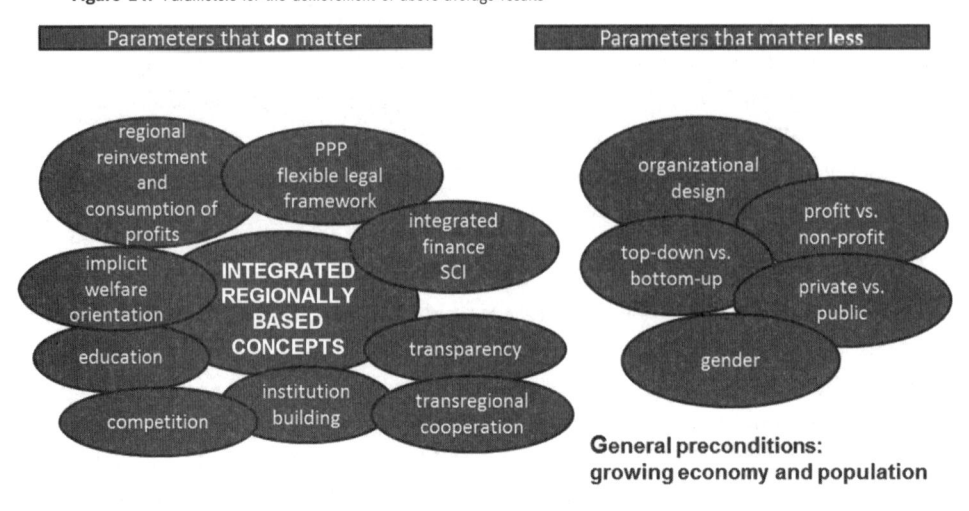

Parameters that **do** matter	Parameters that matter **less**

Parameters that do matter:
- regional reinvestment and consumption of profits
- PPP flexible legal framework
- integrated finance
- SCI
- implicit welfare orientation
- INTEGRATED REGIONALLY BASED CONCEPTS
- education
- transparency
- competition
- institution building
- transregional cooperation

Parameters that matter less:
- organizational design
- profit vs. non-profit
- top-down vs. bottom-up
- private vs. public
- gender

General preconditions: growing economy and population

Figure 15: Impact of microfinance institutions around 1900

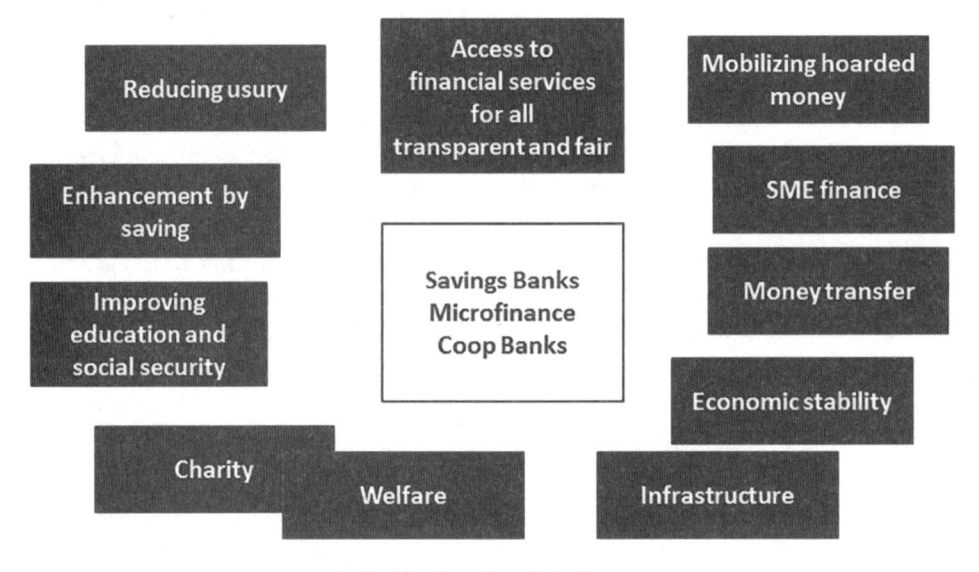

- Reducing usury
- Access to financial services for all transparent and fair
- Mobilizing hoarded money
- Enhancement by saving
- SME finance
- Improving education and social security
- **Savings Banks / Microfinance / Coop Banks**
- Money transfer
- Economic stability
- Charity
- Welfare
- Infrastructure

Individual and societal impact

harmful. What is worst, however: Favorable periods will no longer be used to save, because people begin to simply hope that they will be given aid in the event of a crisis. This is why governments must finance job-creating infrastructure projects, lower taxes and dues and foster 'public banks'."

Furthermore, Raiffeisen complained about a contemporary "social sickness" in terms of uprooting and moral decline, combined with discouragement and lethargy. Within this scenario, local savings and loans seemed to him to be appropriate instruments to influence those change processes in a positive way by enabling the establishment of flourishing businesses. Such businesses might even function as a substitute for broken social patterns (Raiffeisen 1866, 15.; Koch 1991).

In the view of many, Raiffeisen's summing-up of the social malaise of his time applies equally well to current global trends – whether in developing and emerging societies or in developed ones, which are indeed having to face similar challenges in the course of intensifying globalization.

To sum up: Our findings have shown that microfinance – i.e. institutions addressing the financial needs of low-income and underprivileged households and of small-scale entreprenuers – works in principle. However, the findings have also made clear that microfinance on its own cannot alleviate poverty. In other words: Responsible financial inclusion is only one component of several in an enablement concept, but it is a genuinely important one.

The historical analysis has identified the following key factors for success: a predominantly local focus of the business model, the avoidance of pure profit maximization as a priority business aim, and reinvestment or expenditure of earnings in the region in which they were generated. At the same time, networks and supra-local apex banks are needed to manage liquidity and supra-local investments.

Another key, if not indispensable, criterion for success in Germany was the fact that there were stable overall political and economic conditions – combined with a limited amount of governmental control which left scope for flexible development in response to emerging needs. There was a continually growing labor market, combined with better-paid jobs in all economic sectors and improving social security systems, for a period of more than 60 years from around 1850, a process of quite undisturbed growth – the era of *Hochindustrialisierung*, the peak period of industrialization.

Although financial cooperatives and savings banks emerged in response to crises, their real success story started during this era, when Germany was on the verge of surpassing Britain as the leading industrial nation and living conditions had improved significantly compared to 50 years earlier. Conversely, cooperatives and savings banks were an important part of those change processes. Financial, social, economic, and political inclusion complemented each other. Thus, what is required today, as well, is more than a purely financial approach; diversity and holistic, competitive "shared values" concepts are called for. They must include all social groups, private households and SMEs well as the state.

9.3 Connecting past and future

That leads us to the present and future. It may be somewhat surprising that it was principally only in Germany that the successful locally-based dual model of the 19th century endured. It survived two disastrous World Wars, including two periods of very high inflation followed by currency reforms, the great economic crisis of 1929 and the subsequent depression, and the liberalization movement of the 1980s; and during the last global crisis, it proved to be a remarkable pillar of stability. There is no dominant national savings bank or cooperative in Germany, operating at a great remove from its clients' needs. This mirrors, in a way, Germany's federal political structures.[133]

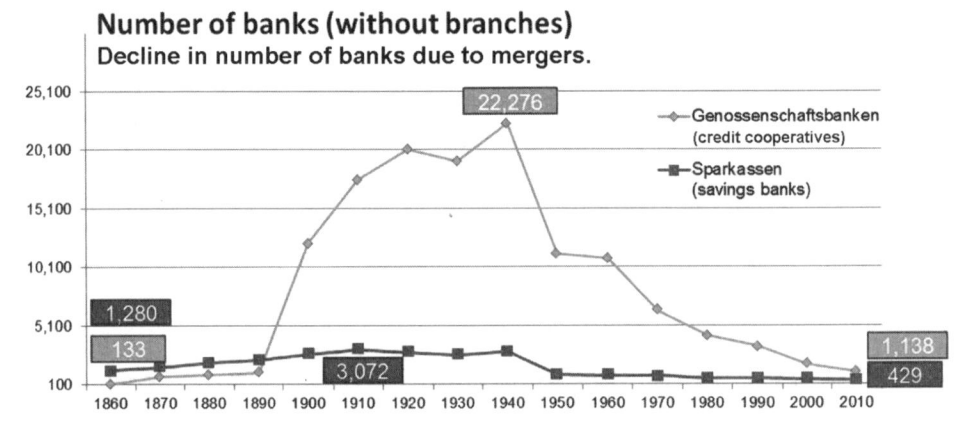

Figure 16: Number of savings banks and cooperative banks and their balance sheet volumes

Number of banks (without branches)
Decline in number of banks due to mergers.

[Chart showing Genossenschaftsbanken (credit cooperatives) and Sparkassen (savings banks) from 1860 to 2010. Key values: 1,280; 133; 22,276; 3,072; 1,138; 429]

Balance sheets (in mn EUR)

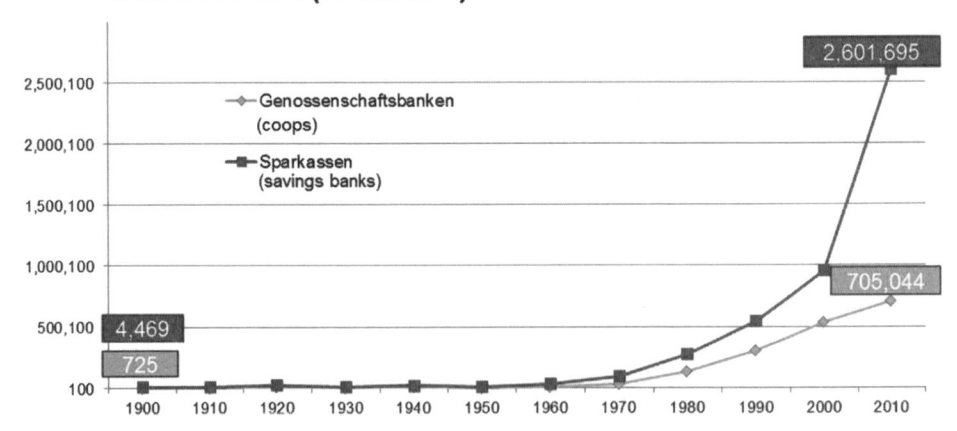

[Chart showing Genossenschaftsbanken (coops) and Sparkassen (savings banks) from 1900 to 2010. Key values: 4,469; 725; 2,601,695; 705,044]

The main factor behind this resilience of the business models is their basic local (and not regional or national) structure. It reflects diversity and a values orienta-

---

133 For a current French perspective, see www.rue89.com/2013/11/17/delevoye-vivons-moment-politiquement-tres-dangereux-247524.

Figure 17: Mobile analog banking in a digitalizing world (Source: Sparkasse Werra-Meißner)

tion, which have played a decisive role in the success and the positive image of both banking groups. They have stimulated autonomy and creativity, favoring diversity over uniform national solutions. This has enabled them to cope successfully with the challenges they have faced over their long history and are now facing today in light of globalization and digitalization.

Two examples may serve to illustrate the wide range of diversity which is characteristic of these banking groups even today. Germany's smallest savings bank is the 126-year-old city savings bank of Bad Sachsa, with a balance sheet volume of EUR 127 million and 45 employees in 2015. It has defied mergers to date and is committed to maintaining its independence in the future. It tries to maintain customer loyalty through a combination of online services and personalized customer service provided by local staff. One service which fits in well with this strategy is the so-called savings voucher, which, in accordance with an old tradition, is given to every newborn child in Bad Sachsa as a savings incentive for the parents, too.[134]

Germany's largest savings bank is located in Hamburg. The *Hamburger Sparkasse*, or *Haspa* for short, was founded in 1827 as a private institution. It has kept that status to date, organized since 2003 as a joint stock company. It holds stakes in four other savings banks in the region. It employs well over 5,000 people, operates aorund 250 branches and serves 1.5 million customers. During the last 25 years it has provided financial support for the launch of around 10,000 start-ups. It runs

---

[134] *Handelsblatt* special edition: *Deutschland, deine Sparkassen. Eine Liebeserklärung* [*Germany, your savings banks. A declaration of love*], 3.8.2012, p. 14, including an analysis of the German savings banks landscape; illustration from the same source; https://www.ssk-bad-sachsa.de/privatkunden/index.php?n=%2Fprivatkunden%2F

three non-profit foundations and donates about EUR 5 million p.a. to about 400 local cultural and social institutions. It offers a children's account which "makes money grow almost as fast as children": With a minimum deposit of only EUR 1.00 and interest of 3% p.a. up to EUR 500, the account is designed to encourage young people up to 14 years of age to save; additional incentives including small presents, a school savings service and campaigns for World Savings Day. This represents the vital savings banks' tradition at its best.[135]

The so-called "everyman account" (*Jedermann-Konto*) or "citizen's account" (*Bürgerkonto*) is a classic account perfectly in line with tradition as well. It is a basic checking account with no overdraft designed to give everyone, regardless of income or assets, access to financial services. This product was defined in 1995 as a commitment on the part of all German banks. No group implemented it with as much conviction as the savings banks, and this undertaking is codified in the savings banks' laws in most of the German states. In September 2012 all German savings banks undertook to enable every individual access to such an account. About 50% of all such accounts in Germany are operated by the savings banks.[136] Similar examples are to be found in the credit cooperative sector.

These few examples show the timeless and universal potential of a holistic, inclusive finance approach which had its earliest beginnings at the end of the 18th century and has been creatively reinterpreted ever since. At the same time, the examples demonstrate the relevance of this approach. It is no coincidence that the *Sparkassen Finanzgruppe* [Savings Banks Finance Group] and the *Genossenschaftliche FinanzGruppe* [Cooperative Financial Services Network] constitute two of the three pillars of the German banking sector model.

Last but not least, these findings show the potential of this model for developing and emerging nations. Thus, the German model, with its many variations on responsible local retail banks, at least merits serious attention, as opposed to starting from scratch again and again. There are some encouraging signs that these historical models with a modern presence are undergoing a renaissance, as the United Nations International Year of Cooperatives in 2012 and research on current developments in this book shows. To paraphrase Pope Francis, financial institutions have to serve, not to rule; savings banks and credit cooperatives have largely done so.

---

135 L.c., 13; www.haspa.de
136 DSGV, press release 97, 26.09.2012; for *Genossenschaftliche FinanzGruppe* see Gleber et al 2012; www.dsgv.de/de/presse/pressemitteilungen/120926_PM_Buergerkonto_97.html

Figure 18: Structure of the German banking market (Finanzgruppe Deutscher Sparkassen- und Giroverband, Inside the Savings Banks Finance Group, 2012, 7)

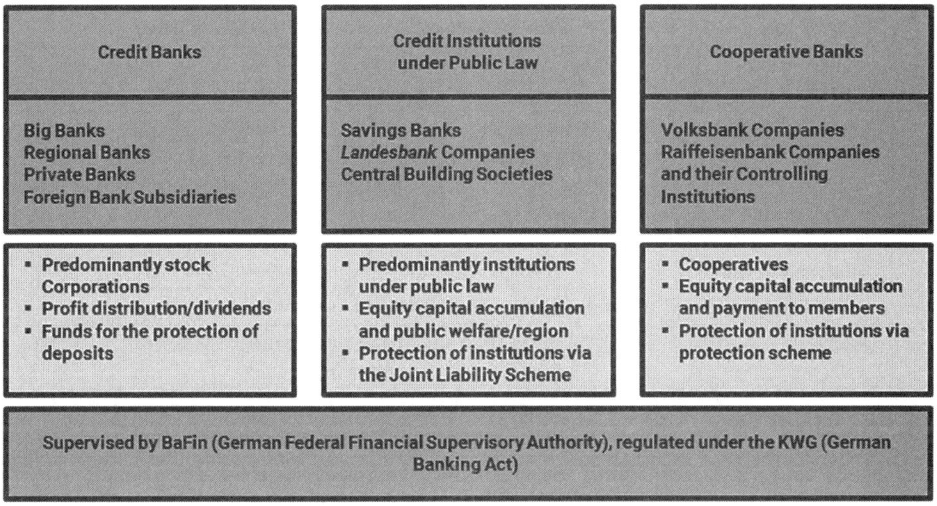

Credit Banks	Credit Institutions under Public Law	Cooperative Banks
Big Banks Regional Banks Private Banks Foreign Bank Subsidiaries	Savings Banks *Landesbank* Companies Central Building Societies	Volksbank Companies Raiffeisenbank Companies and their Controlling Institutions
• Predominantly stock Corporations • Profit distribution/dividends • Funds for the protection of deposits	• Predominantly institutions under public law • Equity capital accumulation and public welfare/region • Protection of institutions via the Joint Liability Scheme	• Cooperatives • Equity capital accumulation and payment to members • Protection of institutions via protection scheme

Supervised by BaFin (German Federal Financial Supervisory Authority), regulated under the KWG (German Banking Act)

9.4 Overview – Constitutive elements of local banking in Germany – From microfinance to inclusive banking

The following table summarizes two centuries of local banking in Germany. In the framework of the three-pillar banking system, the commitment of savings and cooperative banks to local development has had three outstanding results: The first is a virtually universal extent of financial inclusion, covering all segments of society from bottom to top, with unlimited opportunities of graduation from start-up to MSME finance. The second is a highly innovative and internationally competitive SME sector with an extraordinarily high rate of employment generation, financed, albeit not exclusively, by local banks. The third is the crisis resilience of local banks, as in the recent global financial crisis. Paradoxically, it has been their lack of profit maximization objectives which has contributed as much to profit maximization of the SMEs as to crisis resilience. There is yet another aspect of this paradox: social inclusion started with a focus on the poor, without excluding the non-poor; it is this non-discriminatory focus which has made the local banks a driver of innovation and economic growth. This historical experience, as presented in Chapter II, and the gist of the case studies in Chapter III, provide the basis for our recommendations to development agencies.

Table 13: Constitutive elements of local banking in Germany: from microfinance to inclusive universal banking

Savings banks (Sparkassen)	Financial cooperatives/cooperative banks
1. Origin and mission: inclusive financial institutions, a response to widespread poverty	
~ 1800: Municipal, and some private, local initiatives "from above"	~ 1850: Local self-help initiatives "from below" in rural and urban areas
Mission: Promoting small interest-bearing savings for emergencies, old age, consumer items and housing, and micro and small enterprise credit ~ 1900 to date: Inclusive universal banking services for all, incl. MSME finance and local municipal infrastructure finance	*Mission:* Promoting savings and credit for member enterprise development in agriculture and crafts ~ 1900 to date: Inclusive universal banking services for all, incl. MSME finance for individual and corporate members
2. Conducive framework: evolving regulation and supervision for local banks	
Adaptive legal framework since 1838; since 1934 under the Banking Act	Adaptive legal framework since 1867; since 1934 under the Banking Act
Evolving process of oversight from local control to auditing associations plus prudential supervision by financial authorities	
Local banking, "local deposits into local loans," no capital drain; profit orientation, but not maximization, aiming at the public good; crisis resilience	
3. Ownership and governance: local corporate autonomy	
Under public law, municipal trusteeship, not alienable, no classical ownership	Members are owners
Capitalization at inception by municipalities; self-reliance based on savings and retained earnings	Equity capital in the form of member-owners' deposits, capitalization of profits, self-financing through savings deposits, later through commercial banks and apex institutions as well
Supervision by supervisory boards made up of experts drawn from the public and private sectors, initially on an unpaid basis; management initially by civil servants, subsequently by professional management boards approved by the banking supervisory authorities	Supervision by elected representatives *(Vorstand)*, "one member, one vote" principle, initially self-administration, subsequently professional management by experts appointed by the members and approved by the banking supervisory authorities
Corporate autonomy and independence of decision-making from government bodies (no specialized ministry, no loan channelling, no tax privileges)	
4. Networking and safety nets: subsidiarity at its best	
Self-organized regional and national networks (associations) and apexes for representation and advocacy, external audit and supervision, offering among other things leasing, insurance, asset management, professional/academic training (complementing *dual apprenticeship training* in banks and vocational schools)	
Within the network: mutual protection and deposit guarantee scheme *(Haftungsverbund)*; mergers as a strategy to preserve the existence of single institutions of the group.	
5. Orientation toward the client and the municipality: individual clients and MSMEs first	
Inclusive local outreach of financial services; enterprise promotion, serving all segments of society, using part of the surplus for the municipality	
Serving the private sector (individual clients and MSME), the municipality and the region	At the start serving the economic interests of members; now covering the needs of broad strata of the population

Table 13: Constitutive elements of local banking in Germany: from microfinance to inclusive universal banking (continued)

Savings banks (Sparkassen)	Financial cooperatives/cooperative banks
6. Product innovations: savings first	
From inception: Interest-bearing savings, positive (real) returns, doorstep services; low or no minimum deposit requirements; spread ~2 % to 5 %	
Universal banking services for individual and corporate customers, urban and rural clients; fair and transparent terms	
Financing of infrastructure and other public projects	Financing MSME and other cooperatives
7. Impact innovations: inclusive access, growth, and development for all	
Effective non-discriminatory inclusive finance catering to all regions	
Strong institutions, independence of the individual institutions within the group, savings mobilization, and responsible lending	
Promoting economic growth within the local area by financing local clients (that might themselves be operating nationwide or internationally)	
8. Conclusion: Sustainable poverty alleviation requires local banks with a social commitment; conducive financial, social, economic and political inclusion policies; adequate regulation and supervision; effective change management creating crisis resilience; continual growth and employment.	

III.
GLOBAL DEVELOPMENT AND CURRENT STATUS OF MICROFINANCE PRACTICE

1 An overview of institutions, concepts, and approaches

Any discussion of the development and the current situation of microfinance necessarily presupposes a certain understanding of what microfinance in fact is. At least in advanced countries, most people have a conception of what the term means. In rich countries, the typical answer to the question "What is microfinance?" is: "Microfinance is what Professor Yunus has invented and what his bank in Bangladesh is doing. They give loans to poor people who use them to improve their lives." This answer has presumably been inspired by television and other media coverage of the topic, as reflected in innumerable photos and other images that aim to create a notion of microfinance that is simple, easy to remember, and plainly positive.

This answer is not wrong: What the respondents have in mind is indeed microfinance. But at the same time it is also grossly incomplete; microfinance encompasses much more, and is about much more, than could ever be conveyed by the popular notion of what the Grameen Bank does and who is supposed to benefit from microfinance:

- It is not only about getting loans but also about repaying them.
- It is not only about women using borrowed funds wisely but also about borrowers, male and female, squandering money on things they do not really need or cannot really afford.
- It is not only about credit but also about saving and managing risks.
- It is not only about foreign funds but also about local funds being lent out and later collected by people working for organizations that sometimes use questionable methods.
- It is not only about the finances of really poor people but also about those of people who belong to the middle class in their respective countries – and, indeed, people from the local middle class are typically the main users of microfinance services.
- It is also not only about clients and their situation but also about the institutions that provide microfinance and about how well they do their job and how liquid and how profitable they are.
- It is not only about the finances of poor and sometimes not-so-poor people in some exotic and "underdeveloped" country, but also about poor people's finances in places like Britain, the US, and Germany.
- And finally, it is not only about poor people's finances today, but also about the role that finance – defined very broadly – played in the lives of the poor in earlier times, and how they met their need for what would today be called "financial services."

The photos and the TV coverage, and the notions they convey, refer to one part of microfinance: finance for the poor which has been provided for about 40 years, mainly by well-intentioned people and organizations that have obtained not only their funding, but also the strategy on which their overall approach is based, and quite often the moral impetus which guides them, from Western sources. In our discussion we will call this "microfinance in the narrow sense" and use the term "modern MFIs" for those institutions, like the Grameen Bank, that have been inspired, created, and/or funded from abroad.

A number of the positive aspects that are enumerated above and which are *also* a part of microfinance are rarely shown in the media images, and they rarely come to mind when people think about microfinance. But they are a very important element of microfinance in the broader sense of "finance for the poor," "finance for ordinary people" and "inclusive finance" or "finance for all." Microfinance in the broader sense has been around for a long time and even today it is much more widespread than one would tend to think. Of course, microfinance in the narrow sense is a part – and in fact an important part – of microfinance in the broader sense, and one which is steadily growing.

As was noted in the introductory chapter, microfinance is not a well-defined concept, and therefore it is very difficult, and perhaps even impossible, to distinguish clearly between microfinance in the narrow sense and microfinance in the broader sense. But is it really important that this is difficult, and if so, then why? Difficult as it may be, the distinction is a significant one given what we want to achieve in this chapter. We must give adequate consideration both to microfinance in the broad sense and microfinance in the narrow sense, and we must also be aware not only of the differences between the two, but also of the ways in which they are related, for the following three reasons:

First of all, the emergence of institutions providing financial services for broad segments of the population is not a new phenomenon. In the preceding chapter we discussed the development of savings banks and cooperative banks in the 19th century in Germany and other countries which have in the meantime joined the ranks of the advanced economies. As was shown, given what these institutions did and how they were organized, back then they looked very much like the institutions which are part of what today constitutes microfinance in the narrow sense. But over the years they have developed in such a way that – assuming they can still be characterized as "MFIs" at all – the savings and cooperative banks in their present form, and with the present scope of their operations, can only be regarded as being part of microfinance in a very broad sense of "inclusive finance" or "finance for all."[1]

---

[1] "Finance for All?" with a question mark and the subtitle "Policies and Pitfalls in Expanding Access" is a very interesting policy research report issued as a brochure by the World Bank in 2008. The authors are Asli Demirgüç-Kunt, the Senior Research Manager of the Finance and Private Sector Division at the World Bank, Thorsten Beck and Patrick Honohan.

Secondly, microfinance in the narrow sense is also constantly changing. Some of the organizations that were once very small and exclusively oriented towards serving really poor people are now transforming themselves into institutions that provide "finance for all." But in addition, those organizations in developing countries, such as newly created microfinance banks, that might have in some way been inspired by historical lessons from 19th century Germany, are themselves no longer like the Grameen Bank in Bangladesh[2] or Financiera Calpiá in El Salvador were in their early years.[3] We do not wish to characterize the goal of expanding and transforming an MFI into a provider of "finance for all" as being intrinsically good or bad, since such an assessment would necessarily be much too sweeping. If the transformation is successful, the resulting organizations may one day be efficient providers of more and better "finance for all." But this will not necessarily be the case, and drawing the appropriate lessons from history may help to make the transition from microfinance in the narrow sense to microfinance in the broader sense easier and more successful.

The third reason is that irrespective of whether they themselves change and aspire to change, the organizations that might benefit from an understanding of the history of finance in other countries are embedded in their own country's financial and cultural systems, and therefore, when they consider redefining their strategies and business models, they must take into account how both the poor and the general population in their operating environment handle their financial affairs. Thus, the new, "transformed" versions of organizations that once provided microfinance in a narrow sense, and even those which still retain a narrow focus, must take into account what currently constitutes microfinance in a broader sense in their country.

This chapter is structured as follows: Section 2 starts with an overview of the spectrum of financial institutions that can be regarded as providers of financial services for the general population, and especially for relatively poor people and for small and very small businesses. We provide a classification of various types or forms of institutions, and a brief explanation of why we selected specific types or forms for a more detailed discussion; we then conclude with extensive case studies of the selected institutional types. Section 3 provides general information on the supply of microfinance in different parts of the world. Section 4, the

---

2   A particularly remarkable example of a transformation of an MFI is that of the most prominent one: the Grameen Bank, a paragon of micro*credit* in the 1980s and 1990s and an institution that had for many years been strongly subsidy-dependent. When Professor Muhammad Yunus and the Grameen Bank received the Nobel Peace Prize in 2006 for their achievements in microcredit to the poor, only a few observers and commentators knew of the bank's turnaround during the early 2000s to mobilizing voluntary savings. The new concept became known as "Grameen II." Within less than ten years the bank was literally swamped by (micro) savings of the poor and not-so-poor. By early 2013, it had become self-reliant and had more deposits (USD 1.62 billion, 61% mobilized from members) than loans outstanding to members (USD 1.01 billion, Jan. 2013).
3   Other examples of modern MFIs that have undergone far-reaching changes were mentioned in Chapter I, and many more will be the topic of our case studies in section 2 of this chapter.

last section of this chapter, views microfinance from the perspective of development policy makers. There we first discuss the evolution of development finance, of which microfinance is clearly a part, as an aspect of development aid policy. After briefly describing the early phases of development finance and microfinance in the narrow sense, we characterize the different ways in which MFIs can be created – with or without foreign support. Finally, we turn to more recent phases, in which the commercial and institution-building approaches gained widespread acceptance, and conclude by briefly addressing what we will call the excesses of commercial microfinance.

2 The spectrum of microfinance institutions

2.1 A typology of microfinance institutions

This section first provides a classification of the most important types of financial institutions that offer services for a broad range of customers, starting with informal finance and ending with formal and licensed banks with a certain focus on microfinance. The classification is presented in the overview below, which also indicates the types of institutions for which we will present extended case studies in the following sections.

Overview: Types of microfinance institutions

1. Informal microfinance
   (with case studies from Africa in section 2.2 of this chapter).
2. Savings-led microfinance
   (with case studies from Laos and Bali in section 2.3).
3. Cooperative financial institutions
   (with case studies from India and Vietnam in section 2.4).
4. Microcredit and microfinance NGOs.
5. Government-owned development banks.
6. Microfinance banks
   (with case studies from Uganda, Latin America, and Indonesia in section 2.5).

Broadly speaking, there are two major types of institutions that provide microfinance services: those relying predominantly on savings as a source of funds, and those relying on external funds from government and foreign donors or investors which they use for their lending operations. Contrary to widely held beliefs during the phase of poverty lending in the 1960s and 1970s, when external funding was the dominant source of onlending funds for development finance institutions that were supported by foreign-aid donors, there is mounting evidence that even relatively poor people can and do save, and have done so at all times. Therefore institutions which accept their small savings for safekeeping, and enable them to accumulate funds over time, do their clients a great favor.[4] They also do themselves a great favor by generating a growing source of loanable funds.

Based on examples from Africa, we begin our discussion of different types of MFIs with a brief look at informal finance, examining the rotating and non-

---

[4] This has been forcefully argued in an inspiring book by Rutherford et al. (2000). While historians and anthropologists have known for decades that poor people can and do save, for many years savings seemed to be "the forgotten half of development finance" (Vogel, 1984), rediscovered by the UN (1981, 1984, 1986) in three symposiums between 1980 and 1984.

rotating savings and credit associations, an extremely widespread form of basic financial intermediation, and private doorstep deposit collectors.

We then discuss the semi-formal "offspring" of informal finance, village funds or village "banks", which are organized in larger associations or networks and may have access to bank loans. In most cases village funds or village banks (which do not fall under the banking law) are community-based MFIs, although, in terms of their functions and the way they are organized, it is often difficult to draw a clear distinction between community-based and member-owned institutions. These institutions have a certain similarity to what would be called *Sparkassen* in German, *caisses d'épargne* in French, *cajas de ahorros* in Spanish or *sanadiq* in Arabic.

The third type of MFIs for which we provide case studies are mutual or cooperative – and thus clearly member-owned – institutions. As we will argue, financial cooperatives in developing countries may find it difficult to adhere to the core principles of their underlying philosophy, namely self-help and self-reliance, member ownership, and member governance. Many governments and also donors have been so enthusiastic about the cooperative philosophy that they have used cooperatives as a means of channeling credit by funding targeted lending to their members, eventually exerting growing influence on these institutions and intervening in their operations. This is reflected in case studies based on experience in India. Provided with a conducive operating environment in the Raiffeisen tradition[5], the Indian credit cooperatives got off to a great start early in the 20th century – until eventually state governments took over their operations. More recently, vast numbers of self-help groups of the rural poor, organized as savings-led informal cooperatives with credit linkages to banks, have evolved in India. But again, seemingly generous state help is now undermining self-help and self-reliance. In contrast, the People's Credit Funds (PCFs) which evolved in Vietnam in the 1990s are regulated and supervised by the central bank in a way that ensures self-reliance, growth, and good performance and keeps direct state influence at bay.

Banks with a focus on lending to micro, small, and medium-sized businesses, combined with deposit taking and payment services, for which we use the general term "microfinance banks," are the fourth type of financial institution which is discussed in detail in case studies. Those which we examine in our three case studies perform very well in terms of savings-based self-reliance, outreach, growth, and financial sustainability. No other type of institution can match the scale and performance achieved by commercial banks such as BRI in Indonesia or Centenary Bank in Uganda and the ProCredit group of banks. All three institutions have undergone processes of transformation, in the course of which the design of demand-driven financial services, careful staff selection and training, incentives,

---

5   The discussion of the origins and history of the Raiffeisen movement in the preceding chapter suggests the nature of a conducive regulatory and legal environment.

and good corporate governance have played crucial roles. Numerous other banking institutions would deserve to be included here: not only banks that are operating on a country-wide scale such as Khan Bank in Mongolia, Acleda in Cambodia, and Equity Bank in Kenya, but also large numbers of small banks serving limited local areas and operating under central bank regulation – institutions such as the rural banks in Indonesia and in the Philippines.

All of the MFIs for which we will later provide case studies are financial intermediaries, that is, they offer both savings deposit services and some form of credit, and in some cases money transfers as well.

Since we consider financial intermediation to be an extremely important – indeed indispensable – function of financial institutions over the longer term, we have decided not to include case studies of micro*credit* institutions, a category which covers agricultural and small business-oriented development banks and credit-granting NGOs.[6] This decision may seem odd given the fact that the expansion of modern microcredit in the past five decades has been driven to a considerable extent by international donors, who over the years have provided ample financial support to precisely these two types of micro*credit* institutions, and largely ignored the numerous formal and informal micro*finance* institutions that are savings-based, rely on deposits as their main source of funds and, last but not least, also provide more credit to their clients than the "microcredit-only institutions." Therefore, in the following we briefly explain why we have decided not to give space to development banks and NGOs that only provide small and very small loans – as, in our view, they are simply no longer relevant today.

The foreign support for microcredit-only institutions lasted well into the 1970s and 1980s. At first it was mainly directed to various types of government-owned development banks, which, in most cases, were large, bureaucratic, and heavily politicized institutions. However, most of them did not perform well, both in purely financial terms and also in terms of the extent to which they reached poorer client groups – even in those cases where this had been their explicitly stated objective. The generally poor performance of state-owned and foreign-funded development banks was in fact a major reason for the emergence of a broad spectrum of "credit-only NGOs", that is, private institutions with a non-profit orientation but which, like the institutions they were intended to supplant, were funded predominantly from foreign sources, or in some cases from government sources. Most of these NGOs did better than the development banks in reaching low-income people and the poor, which the development banks had largely failed

---

6 Their fundamental weaknesses were first publicly exposed in the *Spring Review* conference and publications of USAID in 1973 (Donald, 1976; Von Pischke et al., 1983; Adams et al., 1984), which set in motion a process that eventually led to closures, privatizations, a funding stop by international financial institutions, and, in a number of cases, to reforms (Seibel et al., 2005; Seibel, 2009; Yaron, 2006). For a critical assessment of the "prospects, problems and potential of credit-granting NGOs" see also Schmidt and Zeitinger (1996).

to do.[7] But otherwise they suffered from flaws similar to those which characterized the development banks, including excessive donor dependency, a lack of deposit services, interest rate subsidization, and, overall, a lack of efficiency, profitability[8] and self-reliance which restricted the breadth and depth of their outreach and tended to undermine their institutional stability.

These deficiencies were recognized in the late 1980s, and this insight led to a paradigm change, referred to as the "*microfinance* revolution" (Robinson 2001), which gathered momentum in the 1990s and sought to resolve these flaws. This paradigm shift spurred the creation of new types of MFIs – or the adoption of new policies by existing ones – focusing on cost-coverage and profitability as a prerequisite of sustainability and expanded outreach, and many of these institutions added savings facilities to the range of services they offered. Thus, at least to a certain extent, they were genuine financial intermediaries even though many of them still depended on donor resources for a considerable portion of their funding. This new orientation later became known as the commercial orientation.

The emergence of this new type of microfinance led to an enormous expansion of the market and to improved access to microfinance products, and better-quality service, for a great many members of the new institutions' target groups: poor people as well as micro and small enterprises. Initially, their more general orientation, with services no longer strictly limited to credit, was met with great enthusiasm and gave rise to high expectations, and it attracted additional donors as well as a number of private investors to MFIs. However, after this boom in commercial microfinance, the approach has recently suffered a setback for a number of reasons, which we will discuss at more length in section 4.4 below.

2.2 Informal microfinance

Informal financial institutions continue to be extremely widespread in developing and emerging economies, with some having been in existence for several centuries (as in Nigeria) or even thousands of years (as in India). They are far from being a thing of the past; even in the more advanced countries they continue to fill a gap left by the formal banking sector.[9] In the following we will discuss two types of institutions in some detail: (i) indigenous savings and credit associations; and (ii) indigenous doorstep deposit collection.

---

[7] See Levitsky (1989) on the emergence of the new breed of credit NGOs.
[8] These problems are documented in a study of the efficiency and profitability of credit-granting NGOs by Schmidt and Zeitinger (1996).
[9] "... even with increased access to formal products, the poor [*and non-poor – author's comment*] do not automatically favor formal services at the expense of their informal counterparts. ... Rather than seeing informal and formal instruments as alternatives, we should see them as complements." (CGAP, http://www.cgap.org/blog/benefits-and-costs-financial-products-poorhttp://www.cgap.org/blog/benefits-and-costs-financial-products-poor, 4 Oct 2012)

2.2.1 Informal financial intermediaries

Labor, rice, and money: The origins of informal microfinance

In much of Africa and Asia the majority of savings-based MFIs[10] are informal, indigenous, member-owned, and small, and their ubiquity is in no way threatened by the existence of formal institutions; they also exist in the MENA (Middle East and North Africa) region and in South America, but are generally less frequent there. Examples are the *hui* in China, the *chitty* or *chits* in India, the *arisan* in Indonesia, the *dhikuti* in Nepal, the *paluwagan* in the Philippines, the *djanggi* in Cameroon, the *likilemba* or *chilemba* in the Congo area and neighboring countries, the *ekub* or *iqqub* and the *edir* or *iddir* in Ethiopia, the *(e)susu* in Nigeria and other parts of West Africa; and furthermore, the *gama'iya* in Egypt and other Arab countries, the *cuchubal* in Guatemala and the *esu* or *susu* in several Caribbean countries. There is a dearth of relevant historical studies; only of Nigeria do we know that the *esusu* existed among the Yoruba during the 16th century and was carried by slaves as part of their social capital to the Caribbean, and from there by their descendants to North American cities in recent decades. Most ethnic groups have their own name for these institutions.[11]

Here is a brief account by one of the authors of his discovery of the (pre-) cooperative allocation of scarce resources, nonfinancial and financial, and eventually of informal microfinance:

In March 1967, on one of my first field trips into the interior of Liberia, I had the opportunity to observe a group of peasants among the Mano in a forest area, felling trees with their cutlasses. Before they started their work, they placed wooden hoe-shaped cult objects in a small circle, chanted words and – turned into animals: a lion, a bush hog, and so on; and as they worked on the land they continued to behave like those animals. I realized I was onto something serious, and at the end of the day, when they had put the masks into a box and changed back into humans, I started asking questions. I learned that they belonged to a group working on the fields of each one in turn and carrying out all the tasks performed by men in slash-and-burn cultivation; their wives formed a parallel group for sowing and weeding. During subsequent visits to each of the 17 ethnic groups in Liberia, I continued to ask questions. The journey began with the study of work groups; it ended with informal microfinance. (Seibel 1967, 2006)

Even in the remotest villages of Liberia people were neither too poor nor too lacking in ingenuity to establish groups in which each member contributed equal amounts of something scarce: labor, rice, money or other valuables. One participant at a time received the accumulated total: the labor of a rotating work group

---

[10] Moneylenders are not included in this study, even though they are also important providers of microfinance.
[11] See Adams and Fitchet 1992; Ardener 1964; Bascom 1952; Bouman 1977, 1994; Geertz 1962; Seibel 1970; Seibel and Massing 1974; Seibel and Damachi 1982: 59–79.

to help with the felling of trees, the rice accumulated by a rice saving group as food for a wedding party, or the total amount of money provided by a savings and credit group to serve as working capital for a microenterprise. A cycle was completed when each member had received the total once. A new cycle could then start with the same or different members. Accumulating and reallocating labor, rice or money are three seemingly different forms of economic cooperation. Yet in the eyes of a peasant interviewed in Côte d'Ivoire in 1985, all three were about financial intermediation: *"Le travail, c'est notre argent!" ("Work is our money!")*.

With the expansion of the money economy, these informal institutions have not lost their vigor; on the contrary, they have multiplied, increasing in both number and diversity. In many instances, the staff of commercial banks, and of the central bank, was found to be participating. Some banks have adopted the technologies of the informal institutions, for example doorstep deposit collection.

From labor to microfinance

Substantial changes have occurred in recent decades: a shift from labor, payment in kind or pre-monetary currency to cash; from non-financial to financial groups; from fixed rotations to sequences determined by auction; from rotating to non-rotating patterns (with a permanent loan fund); from short-lived to permanent groups; and from savings only to savings and credit. Such transitions have taken place not only in a historical perspective over a period of many years; they may also occur in the life cycle of individual groups. For example, in a first phase, a rotating work group may allocate its services to one member at a time, for a fee. In a second phase, the group may abandon the rotating pattern of distribution by keeping the fee income in a common fund for emergencies, joint activities or distribution at the end of the year. In a third phase, it may turn itself into a credit association, using the accumulated savings as a permanent fund for providing loans to members. In a fourth phase, as the financial volume increases, the lending becomes commercialized as indicated by adjustments in interest rates and insistence on collateral. In this phase, income from interest payments may be the main source of internal resource mobilization.[12]

The evolution of non-rotating ("accumulating") savings and credit institutions has been a major innovation. In Liberia, this process started with the opening of the rubber plantations of the American tire company Firestone in the late 1920s, which brought together workers with varying cultural traditions. By the mid-1960s the non-rotating institution was the predominant type of financial institution in rural areas and had reached virtually all ethnic groups (Seibel 1970; Seibel and Massing 1974; Bouman 1994). Such organizational changes have been paralleled by changes in terminology: Initial studies in the 1960s were devoted to *tradi-*

---

12 See Krahnen and Schmidt (1994: 44–51) on the economic rationale of rotating savings and credit groups.

tional organizations. During the 1970s, technical assistance agencies rediscovered an old name used by Raiffeisen (1866, 1970; see also Smiles 1859/2002): *self-help groups.* In the mid-1980s, they began using the term *informal financial institutions* and, in 1990, switched to *microfinance.*

Bridging the gap between theory and practice: upgrading vs. linking informal finance

An early policy-related proposal referring to these informal groups focused on development from below, building on indigenous foundations, and more specifically on *upgrading informal finance*. This was a rediscovery of what the German ethnologist Westermann (1935) had proposed in Togo in the early 20th century, inspired by his discovery of indigenous savings and credit groups, *sodyodyo*. Since 1967 Seibel had argued in favor of upgrading, resulting eventually in a proposal for an incentives-driven approach to mainstreaming informal finance along the following lines: (i) enhancing management skills and operational practices; (ii) transforming associations and funeral societies into financial intermediaries with a permanent loan fund; (iii) upgrading to regulated financial institutions; and (iv) entering into linkages with banks (Seibel 1970, 1985, 1991, 1997, 2001; Kropp and Osner 2017).

However, official development assistance agencies found it difficult to work with informal private entities. Discussions with the German development agency (then) GTZ and with FAO, the Food and Agriculture Organization of the United Nations, led to the adoption of a hybrid approach: *linking formal and informal finance,* or *banks and self-help groups (SHGs).* While the focus was on *linking*, the approach was based on the incorporation of two other strategies which were to play a complementary role: *upgrading* informal institutions and *downscaling* banks (see section 4.3). While the linkage model was first developed in Africa, it was first implemented on a large scale in Asia (Seibel 1985; Kropp et al. 1989; Kropp and Osner 2010, Seibel 1989a, 1991, 1992b, 1996a, 1996b, 2005, 2010b; Tankha 2012).

The Village Savings and Loan Association (VSLA) represents another widespread approach involving upgrading and, more recently, linking as well being promoted on an expanding scale, under different names, by national and international NGOs. Its focus is on people in both rural and urban areas who are beyond the direct reach of banks and MFIs. Building on the indigenous model of savings and credit associations, it was originally developed in 1991 in Niger by CARE International and has spread to 73 countries, with 10.9 million members, predominantly in Africa, as of April 2015. It is predicated on the assumption that, "While MFIs stress credit, it is savings that improve household cash-flow management and are a better fit for this clientele, which prefers to minimize risk by limiting its exposure to debt" (VSLA 2012). While the model is flexible, groups tend to have 15 to 25 members and meet weekly for transactions. Elements of upgrading introduced by promoting agencies include: formation of intergroups and higher forms of networking, training, registration with local authorities, transmission of assets to the next cycle, monitoring and oversight, access to banks and other financial service providers, and more recently, access to mobile banking and mobile money (Aeschliman et al. 2008; Allen 2006, 2007, Gash and Odell 2013; Seibel 2014; VSLA 2012).

The issue of whether the VSLAs (now more generally referred to as Savings Goups) and their members might profit from a conducive regulatory framework, developed by private and state partners working in close cooperation, is a contentious one; many of the promoting NHGOs are sceptical.

Regulating informal finance?

Informal finance fills a gap left by formal and semiformal finance; historically in the developing world there has been little desire to make informal finance subject to state regulation. This is in contrast to Europe, where, in the early years of their existence, informal financial institutions established self-regulation and self-supervision through self-initiated federations, followed by eventual integration into the formal financial sector. This has not happened in developing countries, where informal financial institutions have stagnated insofar as they have continued to operate without any form of regulation, either self-imposed or external. An exception is India, where the government felt compelled to intervene when rotating *chit* funds grew substantially in size and volume, and some of them fell prey to fraudulent operators who turned them into pyramid schemes. The government reacted by creating a legal and regulatory framework for these institutions in 1982. Minimum capital regulations, ceilings on aggregate chit amounts and procedures for dispute settlement have greatly contributed to the growth of licensed chits. At the same time, large numbers of small, unregulated chits continue to exist, particularly in southern India (Seibel 2010b).

In some cases the potential of indigenous finance to serve as a basis for credit co-operatives was examined, as in Nigeria in 1934 in the study conducted by Strickland (1922, 1934), a former registrar of cooperatives in India. Speculating that the *esusu* must have come from India, he found them "improvident" and "fraudulent" and concluded that he was "not hopeful" that they could be reformed (Strickland 1934:14). The consequences of his assessment were far-reaching: the Co-operative Societies Ordinance of 1935 prescribed rules, procedures, organizational forms, etc., which were modeled on those utilized by British-Indian cooperatives and became the blueprint for cooperatives in all of the British colonies in Africa.

The fact that so little has been done to build on indigenous foundations represents a missed opportunity in terms of financial system development. Only recently have some regulators taken cognizance of informal finance, as in Rwanda and Laos (a case which will be discussed further on). In 2008, both countries adopted new microfinance laws and both included informal financial institutions in the range of institutions covered by these laws: in Rwanda they are regarded as tier-1 institutions which are to be registered but not regulated, while in Laos they are placed in various categories depending on the volume of deposits involved.

2.2.2 Doorstep deposit collection

Daily deposit collection at doorsteps is a financial institution which two of the present authors first observed at markets in Ghana during the 1980s. It can be traced back to the Yoruba in Nigeria, where it is called *àjó* seems to have originated.[13] From there it spread throughout West and Central Africa, where millions of small traders, craftsmen and households now participate on a daily basis in doorstep deposit collection schemes.

We will describe the situation in Ghana in detail because in that country informal deposit collectors struggled in vain for 30 years to establish their own bank, persisting in their efforts until their informal financial activity eventually came under central bank supervision in the framework of microfinance legislation – a second-best option in the eyes of the *susu* collectors.[14] Moreover, Ghana is a country in which the outreach of formal banks is still limited, thus indirectly providing fertile ground for informal finance.

A deposit collector may serve several hundred clients a day; the numbers are smaller in rural areas and at smaller markets. From each client a certain amount (usually fixed, but sometimes variable) is collected and entered on printed cards, one each for the collector and the depositor. The collector deposits the day's total in a bank account. At the end of the month the client receives his or her deposits back, which may be used to replenish the client's working capital. The collector receives a fee of one daily deposit per month, equivalent to a monthly service charge of around 3%. As an additional service clients may obtain a short-term loan of up to half the monthly total. The institution is highly efficient; depositor transaction costs are virtually nil, and collector efficiency is high. For instance, a researcher who accompanied one of the collectors in Accra observed that the shortest transaction took 10 seconds, the longest 25 seconds, including walking from one stall to the next. No bank can beat this informal institution for efficiency.

The *anago susu* in Ghana are registered under the Business Act, pay taxes and are organized in regional associations. In the 1980s the Greater Accra Susu Collectors Association (GASCA), with some 300 members, maintained its accounts with the National Savings and Credit Bank. The association was hoping to establish its

---

[13] The institution's presumed origins in Nigeria are reflected in some of the names used in neighboring countries (*anago susu* in Ghana, *nago* in Côte d'Ivoire, with *anago* and *nago* meaning "Nigerian"); the Yourba term *àjó* does not seem to have been adopted by other ethnic groups.
[14] This contrasts sharply with cooperative SHGs in 19th-century Germany, which almost immediately came under the protection of the law and eventually acquired the status of banking institutions.

own bank, but this initiative was not supported by the central bank (Seibel and Marx 1987).

Subsequently the regional associations registered as cooperative societies and, in 1994, joined together in a national apex organization, the Ghana Co-operative Susu Collectors Association (GCSCA), registered under the Department of Cooperatives at the Bank of Ghana (BoG). With 11 offices throughout the country, by the end of 2014 GCSCA had over 1,000 individual and 536 corporate members, the latter employing agents and serving over 220,000 clients. The corporate members are required by law to report monthly to the association, which submits summary reports to BoG on a quarterly basis.

Susu companies had come into existence in the late 1980s. Having little experience of their own, they hired agents as collectors and promised loans to clients for amounts equivalent to twice the amount of their savings. Due to the mathematics of pyramid schemes and mismanagement, most of these companies collapsed. This led to calls for a new regulatory framework, and in 1993 to the passage of the Non-Bank Financial Institutions (NBFI) Act, which required the *susu* companies to be licensed by the BoG as savings and loan companies.

Many rural banks in Ghana have adopted the doorstep savings collection approach. Initially, they used hired agents, but their experience here was negative. However, the approach now works reasonably well as the banks either work with their own staff as collectors or with well-established *susu* collectors. For the customers this is an attractive option, as they have access to bank loans and do not have to pay a commission to the collector, who collects both deposits and repayments. By utilizing doorstep collection, the rural banks, a separate category of banks in Ghana that operate under a special regulatory regime, benefit from a higher savings retention rate, lower risk, and a substantial increase in outreach (Steel and Tornyie 2010). In December 2005 Barclays Bank Ghana also launched a program operated in cooperation with GCSCA, in which it accepted the deposits of individual *susu* collectors and also provided credit to fund onlending. Initially the program was profitable for Barclays, but in the financial crisis of 2008, the bank put its lending partnership with GCSCA on hold, while continuing its deposit mobilization with *susu* collectors.[15]

Doorstep savings collection as a financial technology is not limited to the sphere of informal finance. Daily deposit collection has been adopted by most MFIs and banks in Ghana. In Indonesia, where deposit mobilization is highly competitive, it is utilized by commercial banks, many rural banks and the LPDs on Bali, which we will discuss in section 2.3.3 below. Interestingly, it was also practiced by savings banks in Germany from 1826 up to the end of the 20th century.

---

15 Information provided in personal conversations with Paul Appiah and William Derban, Barclays Bank Ghana. See also Derban 2007.

With the growing involvement of banks and MFIs, there are signs of an increasing focus on providing credit to microenterprises and their owners via the *susu* collectors; whether this will prove to be a positive or a negative development remains to be seen.

2.2.3 Conclusions and policy implications

Informal finance continues to be widespread in developing countries, irrespective of whether, and to what extent, people have access to formal finance. In terms of convenience, cultural familiarity, and transaction costs, savings and credit associations and doorstep deposit collectors beat banks, MFIs, and credit NGOs by a wide margin as long as amounts are small and maturities short. Their appeal is strong across a broad range of groups within the population, from low-income people to bank staff to many others. However, as long as they stay informal, they tend to be short-lived, and their capacity is limited.

In a historical perspective it is remarkable that despite the flexibility and adaptability of indigenous financial institutions, there is not a single country in the developing world where such institutions have become the foundation of a modern financial system. This is in marked contrast to Europe, where associations and apex organizations made up of initially informal groups and organizations evolved from below, without donor involvement, and were able, through negotiation and engagement with the political sphere, to secure the enactment of a legal framework for their operations at an early stage of their development (the German cooperatives discussed in the preceding chapter are a prime example). Exceptions notwithstanding, it is a quite recent phenomenon that financial regulators in the developing world have begun to provide tiered regulatory frameworks, with an entry position for informal institutions and defined steps leading to higher tiers of licensing and supervision.

For some time to come we may expect formal and informal finance to occupy parallel worlds, with a continual strengthening of the formal sphere, but not necessarily a weakening of the informal sphere. So far, attempts to link informal finance and formal banks have not passed the historical test of creating long-term, sustainable connections to bridge the gaps between these two worlds of finance, perhaps because of a lack of continuity and scale in donor support, but more importantly because of a lack of national champions. The exceptions are India, a case which we will examine in section 2.4.3, and perhaps Indonesia and the Philippines, where GTZ/GIZ supported linkages on an national scale through Bank Indonesia and Landbank, respectively, until the late 1990s; here, however, current monitoring data is lacking.

2.3 Community-based microfinance, or village "banks"

2.3.1 Two case studies of savings-led and village-based institutions

Village funds, or village banks as they are also called, are a modernized and in some cases more or less regulated version of informal finance, not at the group, but rather the community level. In this section two types of community or village "banks" will be presented which bear a similarity to early German *Sparkassen*: semiformal village funds (VFs) in Laos and provincially regulated village financial institutions, Lembaga Perkreditan Desa (LPD), in Bali. Both employ the individual lending technology,[16] and both have achieved a broad, inclusive outreach. They have developed over the same time span of 20 to 30 years, but with quite different trajectories.

In Laos the institutions started out as revolving funds which were initially established and financed by international donors who believed in microcredit and ignored the local savings culture. In a second stage, development agencies familiar with local traditions and values promoted the conversion of the revolving funds into village "banks" – village-level funds which mobilize savings and rely exclusively on their own financial and human resources. They also helped establish associations of village banks which are self-financed, self-managed and self-governed – like the village "banks" which own them. The results have been impressive: More than half the villages in Laos now possess a VF, the vast majority of which are financial intermediaries that are self-financed from savings and retained earnings.

On the island of Bali, village "banks" originally came into being as a result of a regulation facilitated by the Governor of Bali which was explicitly designed to preserve the culture of Bali. The Balinese village "banks" were developed on a foundation of earlier self-help structures and drew upon strong local savings traditions. They all started as self-financed and self-managed institutions with the customary village as their owner; beyond a small start-up injection, no donor, investor or government capital has been involved. Today they are perhaps the most inclusive type of MFIs anywhere, covering virtually all villages and native adults on Bali. Operationally, both types of village "banks" are examples of the successful integration of new types of financial institutions into the local culture, based on indigenous values and community participation – a much-ignored subject in microfinance.

The key distinction that can be drawn between the two cases has to do with the role of regulation. In Bali, regulation preceded the establishment of the first village "banks," and the regulatory framework directly reflects the integration of the in-

---

[16] The term village bank is also used by the international microfinance organization FINCA and others, though with a different meaning (see www.finca.org). FINCA-style village banks are small groups of 20 to 25 members which utilize the group lending methodology.

stitutions into the local culture, including ownership and governance by the customary village. This has given the LPDs a unique strength and enabled them to provide a range of financial services whose depth and breadth are such that they can meet the requirements of a broad spectrum of the population. In Laos, the VFs were launched without the involvement of a regulator, and as there was no participatory process in which these institutions could have provided input to help shape the evolving regulatory framework for microfinance, the VFs and their associations were not covered by the regulatory regime that was established. This has kept the VFs outside the purview of regulation and supervision and undermined their effectiveness. However, a significant number of VFs have submitted to semiformal regulation by the Lao Women's Union (LWU), as reflected in the widespread use of a training manual developed by the LWU based on the pertinent regulations. As can be seen from the preceding brief discussion of the institutions in Laos and Bali, culture and regulation emerge as two central topics of relevance to the design and operation of community banking systems.

2.3.2 Village funds in Laos: Regulation gone awry[17]

The development of microfinance in Laos and the role of village funds

The history of microfinance in Laos dates back to the early 1990s when the country was evolving towards a market economy and a two-tier banking system was established. Laos had virtually no reported history of informal finance apart from credit obtained from relatives, better-off neighbors, and suppliers. Professional moneylenders are rare; rotating savings and credit groups are a recent phenomenon, mostly encountered at urban markets. The development of semiformal microfinance,[18] starting with revolving village credit funds (initially involving payment in kind in most cases), was driven by donors working in close cooperation with mass organizations, in particular the LWU. As women are the holders of the family purse strings and saving is a habit deeply engrained in the Laotian culture,[19] there has been a transition over time from earlier donor- and government-funded credit programs to savings-led VFs, which are true intermediaries providing both savings and credit services.

The outreach of microfinance, comprising regulated MFIs and semiformal VFs, has increased considerably in recent years in terms of the number of villages covered, the number of clients served, and the volumes of savings mobilized and loans disbursed. The two most significant developments have been the emergence of a formal, albeit small, microfinance sector and the transition within the semi-

---

17 This section is largely based on Kunkel and Seibel 1997; Seibel 2010c; Seibel and Rohmann 20012; a consultancy mission to Laos in 2013 for SFBIC; and other sources as indicated.
18 These institutions are recognized by the authorities and registered with the district administration.
19 In 1996, 97% of rural households were found to hold savings, averaging USD 65, mostly in kind; only 0.5% held deposits with banks and only 0.3% had deposits with informal groups. (UNDP/UNCDF 1997; Kunkel and Seibel 1997)

formal sector from revolving credit funds to self-reliant savings-based village banks. Comprehensive information on microfinance in Laos is available in surveys conducted by the National Economic Research Institute (NERI), the latest of which was published in 2012 with data for 2011 (NERI 2012; Seibel and Rohmann 2012).

Laos is a country with 6.4 million inhabitants and almost 9,000 villages. According to the NERI survey of 2012, the total formal and semiformal microfinance sector (excluding banks) comprises 4,476 institutions with almost 500,000 clients or members, of which some 421,000 have savings accounts and around 241,000 have loans outstanding. The total assets of all MFIs stand at a volume equivalent to USD 91 million, deposits at USD 58 million and loans outstanding at USD 47 million; total equity is USD 29 million (2011 data).

In 2011 the subsector of formal MFIs comprised 42 institutions with an average of 1,622 clients: nine were licensed as deposit-taking (DTMFIs), 15 as non-deposit-taking (NDTMFIs),[20] and 18 as savings and credit unions (SCUs), and the three categories of institutions had an average of 3,648 clients, 1,510 clients and 703 clients, respectively. According to NERI, the ROA for the subsector as a whole was 1.4%.

By all measures, the subsector of VFs is much larger than that of the licensed MFIs. In 2011, NERI identified 4,434 VFs (or 99% of all MFIs) with a total of 431,000 member-clients (or 86% of all microfinance clients), of whom 372,000 have savings accounts and 222,000 have loans outstanding. On average, a VF has 97 member-clients. Total assets of the VFs are USD 74 million (or 81% of the total for the microfinance sector as a whole), loans outstanding come to USD 37 million (or 80% of the total), deposits equal USD 50 million (or 86% of the total), and combined equity stands at USD 23 million (or 80% of the total for the sector). The ROA amounts to almost 10%, a stunningly high level.

Village funds are community-based and member-owned institutions which operate in accordance with the principles of self-financing, self-management, and self-governance. During the last 15 years, deposit-taking VFs (DTVF) have to a considerable extent replaced non-deposit-taking village funds (NDTVF) that rely on government and donor money. The most recent data indicate that 80% of all VFs are deposit-taking, with revolving funds accounting for only 20% of the total. DTVFs are substantially larger than NDTVFs: they have an average of 110 members, compared to 46 for the non-deposit-taking institutions. DTVFs account for 86% of the total number of members of VFs, for 83% of the funds' total number of borrowers and for 100% of their reported voluntary savers.[21]

---

20 Paradoxically, both DTMFIs and NDTMFIs mobilize deposits; the main difference between the two types of institutions, as defined by the regulator, lies in the level of minimum capital requirements to which they are subject.
21 All data reported here are based mainly on NERI 2012.

The high returns on assets – and thus also on equity – which DTVFs achieve, resulting in large dividends for savers as well as relatively high levels of compensation for committee members, are one factor explaining their attractiveness. However, the ROA figure for regulated MFIs – 1.4% – and that for VFs – 9.1% – are not directly comparable, as the two types of institutions operate according to different business models and use different accounting systems. Village funds have no regular expenses during the year, but pay dividends to savers and compensation to management committee and governing board members from their profit at the end of the accounting year.[22] This turns out to be a very flexible mechanism for allocating profits and a means of limiting the risk that would result from fixed costs.

The emergence of village fund associations

One of the more interesting developments in the nascent subsector of deposit-taking VFs has been the emergence of service associations built on the same principles as the funds themselves: self-financing, self-management, and self-governance. Starting in 2003, two institutions from neighboring Thailand, in close cooperation with the LWU, promoted the creation and operation of district-level associations, headquartered mainly in the city of Vientiane Capital, which are owned by the VFs as shareholders. Their expenses are covered by a fixed share (2%) of the profit of the VFs. Two bodies are at the core of each district network: a network committee which serves as a governing board, made up of representatives elected by the zonal committees (with delegates being sent from each zone); and an administrative center, which is housed in the offices of the district administration. The zonal committees, in turn, are elected by the VFs, with delegates from each VF participating in the elections.

The main tasks of the zonal committees are to provide guidance, monitoring, reporting, and oversight. The network furnishes a template for financial statements, comprising a balance sheet and an income statement. The associations also manage voluntary life insurance funds at district level; as of 2010, 25% of the members of VFs participated in the insurance funds. The zonal committees are responsible for inspecting the books and collecting financial data and also for reporting to the administrative center, which functions as an auditing body. The staff of the administrative center consolidate the financial data and prepare monthly, quarterly, and annual reports. They also review dividend payments undertaken by VFs. The zonal committees report problems encountered by the VFs to the district administrative center and to the network committee, which deliberates on steps to be taken. Responsibility for specific initiatives to remedy a problem situation is nor-

---

22 A widely propagated model of profit allocation recommends that 70% of the profit be paid out as dividends to savers, with 15% going to management committee members, 5% being paid to advisory committee members, 2% being allocated for network services, 4% going into a development fund and 4% being allocated to reserves.

mally delegated to the zonal committees, which in turn contact the VF committees, or, in extreme cases where the committee of a VF is not functioning, the general assembly of the VF.

The emerging associations have a crucial role to play in the development of the VFs. Several development organizations have adopted the approach of creating associations as apex service institutions for VFs. The associations require further strengthening, particularly in two areas: capacity building for zonal and district committees and the district administrative center; and strengthening of their ability to carry out core network functions such as registration of VFs within the network, guidance and monitoring, and reporting and supervision. In due course, support might also include the establishment of specialized services in the areas of training, liquidity exchange and auditing at the district, provincial and national level. Better communication among the organizations that are promoting the establishment of apex institutions may lead to a certain harmonization of bylaws, operations, and development strategies.

The regulatory framework for microfinance

Since 1992, Bank of the Lao PDR (BoL), the country's central bank, has been responsible for regulating banks and non-banks. Initiatives undertaken in the mid-1990s had already created a consensus on the need to regulate microfinance. But it was not until 2004 that a microfinance division was created at BoL; this was followed in 2005 by the announcement that large MFIs had to apply for licenses, while smaller ones merely had to be registered. In June 2008, BoL issued three microfinance regulations establishing two basic requirements: (i) any organization, group or enterprise that carries out microfinance activities – including village banks, savings groups, VFs and development funds – is required to register; and (ii) any microfinance entity with voluntary deposits exceeding LAK[23] 200 million (USD 24,000 at the exchange rate as of end-2015, or USD 23,000 at the exchange rate as of end-2008) or annual revenues exceeding LAK 1 billion (USD 120,000) is to be licensed as a prudentially regulated MFI. BoL has set a ceiling of LAK 10 million (USD 1,200) on microloans, but imposes no interest rate restrictions.

However, compliance by VFs with these basic requirements has not been enforced. Smaller ones are locally registered, but not with BoL; and larger ones with more than USD 24,000 in savings, of which there are more than 200 in Vientiane Capital alone, are not licensed. It should be noted, though, that compliance with the regulatory framework established by BoL poses a challenge for the VFs: they are all obliged to register with BoL, the smaller ones as non-deposit-taking MFIs (even though they do in fact take voluntary deposits), and the larger ones, with deposits above USD 24,000, as prudentially regulated MFIs, most likely as Savings and Credit Unions (SCUs). The obstacles to compliance are the result of a lack of

---

[23] The Laotian national currency, the Kip.

communication between BoL and the VFs and their networks regarding the design and implementation of the regulations.

An additional obstacle to compliance with the regulatory framework results from the fact that the VFs are reluctant to rigidly enforce timely loan repayment for both commercial and social reasons. Penalties on overdue loans are a major source of income. At the same time, "terminal defaults" – in the sense of an absolute and final failure to repay – are rare, as, in the local culture, this bad deed would have a negative impact on the borrower's life after reincarnation. However, persistent delays in repayment have a negative impact on cashflow and the availability of loan funds. They may also undermine efforts to promote sound business attitudes and practices among credit clients, leading to complacency among borrowers as regards cash-flow management. It may be difficult for management committees to enforce timely repayment in a tightly knit community if they are not compelled to do so by a supervisory agency.

Moreover, accounting practices among the VFs vary widely, and many are not in conformity with the requirements established by BoL. For example, each individual fund starts its financial year on its foundation date rather than on the date prescribed by the regulations; the sequencing of balance sheet items is not standardized; no share capital is reported; some income and expenditure items are reported on the balance sheet rather than the income statement; and compensation paid to management and board members, and interest payments to savers, do not appear as expenditures in the income statement. Moreover, the annual income and expenditure statement is used as the basis for calculating net income and allocating it among dividends paid out to savers, compensation paid to management and advisory committee members, reserves, special funds and network costs – a practice which inflates income and profits and would lead to substantially higher taxation if corrected; and there is no provisioning for bad and doubtful loans.

Even though BoL has put regulatory measures in place which cover VFs as member-owned institutions, six years after the publication of the microfinance regulations none of the VFs are directly registered with BoL, none of the several hundred larger ones have been licensed, and none report to BoL as required. The core problem lies in BoL's failure to effectively communicate and coordinate with the VFs and their networks and the organizations which are promoting their development. This may be typical of the situation in many countries insofar as central banks often tend to be distant and uncommunicative. In the case of the village banks in Laos, in any event, the result has been (i) that the regulations are not fully appropriate to the institutions they are designed to cover; (ii) that the operational systems of the funds are not standardized and have not been modified to bring them into line with the regulatory requirements; and (iii) that compliance has not been enforced.

There are three areas in which negotiations with the VFs, as well as adjustments to the regulatory framework for these institutions, may be required: (i) the issuance of share capital and its amount; (ii) the application of BoL's standardized provisioning rules; and (iii) the practice of treating both the interest paid to savers and the compensation provided to committee members as distributions from profits ("dividends") rather than as regular expenses. The latter is the thorniest issue, as it involves not only BoL but also the tax authorities. Annual or quarterly reporting by registered smaller funds to the central bank, and quarterly or monthly reporting by larger licensed funds, should be acceptable to the VFs, given the fact that the networks already require the submission of monthly reports by their members. However, as of early 2014 there was still no indication that BoL plans to take concrete measures to enforce compliance with its regulations, which, moreover, are undergoing revision.[24]

Conclusions

Over a 20-year period Laos has seen the emergence of some 4,500 semiformal VFs, with an active membership of over 430,000. Many government and donor agencies have been involved, but the most significant impact has been achieved by two Thai organizations working in cooperation with the LWU. Due to their insistence on self-financing through savings mobilization, 80% of the sector, which in the early 1990s, in the initial phase of its development, consisted exclusively of revolving funds, is now comprised of self-managed and self-governed deposit-taking village "banks" which are fully self-financed. With an ROA of 9.7%, they not only outperform government-funded revolving funds (ROA = 3.6%), but also licensed MFIs (ROA = 1.4%). At the same time, in their areas of operation the two Thai organizations were instrumental in establishing district associations for guidance and oversight, which are financed and managed by the village "banks" as shareholders.

BoL, the central bank, issued regulations in 2008 which could have provided a basis for the expansion of self-reliant village "banks" throughout Laos. However, given the lack of communication between BoL and the associations and other stakeholders – the central bank having made no effort to establish a dialogue with these key actors – the regulations have not been implemented. As a result, the provisions of the regulations are not fully appropriate to the situation of the VFs, their operational systems have not been standardized, and there is no external supervision of the institutions.

Establishing a stakeholder communication forum to facilitate a dialogue with BoL would have to be the first step. The first major task of the forum would be to review and revise the regulatory framework and initiate necessary modifications to the various operational systems of the funds. This might be accompanied by efforts to strengthen the district (and perhaps provincial or national) associations of

---

[24] As set forth in the Prime Minister's Decree No. 460/G on MFIs of 3 October 2012.

village "banks" and by preparations for the establishment of a system of delegated supervision (by BoL), perhaps through a national or provincial apex institution with responsibility for auditing which would be controlled and operated by an external organization, for example the LWU. Finally, the associations could – and should – play an instrumental role in the registration of VFs with BoL and the licensing of large funds. Perhaps foreign aid agencies – such as those from Germany that are already cooperating with the VF system[25] – together with the industry's national professional organization, the Microfinance Association (MFA), could take the initiative here. Such an approach might serve as a model for many countries where central banks find it difficult to provide an appropriate regulatory framework for evolving informal and semiformal financial institutions. From a longer-term perspective, these measures might perhaps lay the groundwork for a strategy of upgrading the semiformal financial sector through appropriate regulation and supervision.

The evident discrepancy between the impressive performance of the village banks, especially those that take deposits, and the weaknesses in the areas of regulation and compliance, suggest two lessons that may also be relevant for similar countries whose institutional and administrative structures are still weak: The first lesson is that self-regulation and self-administration of the VFs, implemented mainly through their local associations, may be far more important and also more conducive to the success of grassroots institutions than formal sector regulation and supervision. The second lesson is that it may be beneficial for the development of the VF system, and thus ultimately for the country's overall development, if the task of formal state regulation and supervision is allocated to the central bank and not to a ministry or other entity with closer ties to the ruling government, since this arrangement serves to protect the VFs from the inappropriate political interventions that have led to the decline of similar organizations in many other countries.

2.3.3 Lembaga Perkreditan Desa in Bali: The challenge of culture and governance

Culture and microfinance in Bali

In Bali, the local society is organized into two socio-political systems which are distinct but at the same time overlap. One is secular and is part of the overall Indonesian political system: a province headed by a governor with a structure defined by an administrative hierarchy of districts, sub-districts, administrative villages (*desa dinas*) and communities (*dusun*), each under an elected head. The other is cultural and religious: a Hindu island determined to preserve its identity in a predominantly Muslim country, headed by the same elected governor who presides over the province, but structured along customary lines of affiliation. Preservation of the society's cultural and religious identity is a key concern in Bali.

---

25 GIZ, SBFIC and DGRV.

The customary system is comprised of customary villages (*desa adat, desa pakraman*) and constituent customary communities (*banjar*). The highest authority of the village is the assembly of the customary residents (*krama*), which elects the village council and the head of the village. The *banjar* is the basic social and residential community. *Krama* are the residents of the *banjar*, and thus of the customary village (Seibel 2013; see also Geertz 1959).

The drop in the price of oil in the early 1980s led to fundamental changes in financial sector policies in Indonesia: from supply- to demand-led finance, from financial repression to a market-driven approach, from the dominance of government banking to the pre-eminence of private-sector banking. In June 1983 interest rates were fully deregulated, credit ceilings were eliminated, and the supply of credit to state-owned financial institutions was substantially reduced. This resulted in the rise of various types of savings-driven financial institutions and in a surge in savings mobilization throughout the country, spurred by competition. In this environment, the rural credit-supply units of BRI (discussed further on) were transformed into self-reliant microbanking units. In Bali indigenous informal savings and credit associations (*seka simpan pinjam*, or *pecinkreman* in Balinese) operated in every *banjar*, and were referred to as the *bank of the banjar*, but they were too small to meet the increasing demand for financial services created by a rapidly expanding economy (Seibel 2010a).

The establishment of financial institutions at the administrative district or village levels of the national political system was ruled out, as institutions created and operated within this framework would have lacked cultural roots. In terms of an appropriate operational sphere, two options remained: the customary community (*banjar*) and the customary village (*desa pakraman*). The latter was deemed more suitable as it would lead to economies of scale.

With the dual objective of strengthening Balinese culture while at the same time building viable financial institutions, the Governor of Bali took the initiative in 1984 to create a regulatory framework for a new kind of village financial institution – the Lembaga Perkreditan Desa (LPD). They function as village banks, but are not subject to regulation or oversight by the central bank.[26] Designed to function as an integral part of Balinese culture, the LPDs are owned, financed, and governed by the customary village and regulated by the Government of Bali. The explicit purpose of the LPDs is *the preservation and strengthening of the customary village and its component banjar as the communal space of Balinese economic life, culture, and religion*. Their unique character within the Indonesian financial landscape is shaped by a combination of several factors: a provincial-level regulatory framework; a system of self-management and self-governance that is integrated

---

26 Attempts to convert the LPDs into rural banks (*Bank Perkreditan Rakyat – BPRs*) were resisted. Eventually, in a letter dated 17 February, 1999, the central bank recognized LPDs as non-bank financial institutions.

into the customary village, with the management and staff of each LPD coming from its respective village; self-financing through deposit mobilization and retained earnings; and regular financial contributions to the customary village and the *banjar* from its earnings. The bond which forms the link between these various spheres and holds them together is one which transcends the world of finance and economics: the religious belief in a uniquely Balinese cultural essence which binds together past, present, and future lives and permeates all aspects of Balinese social life.

The evolution of outreach

Starting in 1985, the number of LPDs increased rapidly over a ten-year period, reaching 849 in 1995. By December 2012 the total number had reached 1,418, covering 96.5% of the 1,468 customary villages in Bali, including very small ones. Statistically, their outreach is virtually universal: On average, each of the island's 834,000 families (total population: 3.4 million) holds 1.9 savings and term deposit accounts, and every second family (50%) has a loan outstanding.

Picking up in 2007, growth of deposits and loans skyrocketed after 2008 (see Figure 19). In 2012 total assets amounted to USD 888 million, deposits came to USD 740 million and loans outstanding stood at USD 621 million. On average each LPD had deposits of USD 522,000 and loans outstanding of USD 438,000. LPDs are savings-driven, as indicated by a deposit-to-loan ratio of 119%. In 2012 term deposits averaged USD 3,310 per account, passbook savings balances averaged USD 265 and loans outstanding averaged USD 1,497. In 2012 the interest rates offered by the LPDs on savings and term deposits stood at around 0.5% and 0.9% per month, respectively; interest rates on loans ranged from 1.9% to 2.75% per month on the declining balance; and the annual inflation rate was 4.3%.

Governance of the LPDs: the power of krama and karma

The owner of the LPD is the customary village with its indigenous residents. The management team comprises up to seven members appointed by the supervisory board. Larger LPDs may have functional divisions. LPD Pecatu, one of the largest, had 39 employees in 2008, all from Pecatu (which numbered 6,819 families). It is mandatory that management and staff come from the same customary village. In some cases such positions are filled by bank retirees (particularly from BRI microbanking units) who come from the village in question.

Governance is the privilege and duty of the customary village, which elects a supervisory board from among its original residents every 3–5 years. The board is chaired by the elected head of the customary village. Reputation and competence are the main criteria for the selection of candidates for the supervisory board. The board appoints the management, defines the terms and conditions for financial services and the institution's operating procedures, and has full authority to exercise internal control functions and enforce compliance with its instructions and

> **Snapshot 40: If governance fails: the role of the board**
>
> The importance of good governance is most evident in those cases where the collaboration between board, management, and customary village has broken down, with the LPD in question encountering serious problems, and the subsequent re-establishment of their collaboration succeeds in turning the institution around. LPD Kapal Mengui in Badung district is one of the larger LPDs in Bali, serving a village of 18 banjar with 2,275 families and a population of 10,780. Established in 1990, it functioned well for several years. In 1994 it ran into various problems. Bookkeeping was done manually, which led to errors and eventually to fraud. The board did not function properly, as the institution's owner, the customary village, which was spread over a large number of banjar, lacked experience in monitoring and overseeing the operations of an LPD. By 1996 the LPD had accumulated losses of USD 31,500. In October 1997 a new board was installed, including two members with experience in finance. The new board immediately took action. It mobilized technical assistance from the district guidance agencies and contacted the administration of the village and of the banjar. Working together, they defined the responsibilities of the individual board members in addressing the problems faced by the LPD and stressed adherence to the regulations established by the Government of Bali. In the words of one of the board members: "We took a social approach, because the problem was in the community; so we addressed the krama at the banjar meetings." They succeeded in solving the delinquency problem and recapitalized the LPD through savings mobilization. By the end of 1997 the LPD had turned a profit and it has remained profitable ever since.[27]

findings. External audits are not compulsory, but all big LPDs are audited by a chartered accountant. The regional development bank (BPD) and the district guidance agencies (PLPDK) are involved in mandatory monthly reporting, but not in formal auditing.

Ultimate authority lies with the village and constituent *banjar* assemblies in their capacity as the owners of the LPD. Normally there is close communication between the board, the customary village, and the *banjar*. The board chairman regularly reports to the village council, and the heads of the *banjar*, who are members of the village council, report on the operations of the LPD to the monthly *banjar* assembly meetings. In cases of delinquency, board members communicate directly with borrowers, together with the head of the *banjar* if this is deemed necessary.

The strength of the LPD lies in its system of governance, which brings together all customary authorities in the village: the *bendesa* as head of the village and of the board, the other board members, the village administration and village council, the heads of the *banjar,* and the *banjar* assemblies. Intimate knowledge of all resident families, including their past histories and present situations, enables the

---

[27] For more examples of this type see Seibel 2013.

board to arrive at sound credit decisions and to enforce repayment. If necessary the board involves other authorities, particularly the heads of the *banjar*, to induce delinquent borrowers to repay. The strongest threat would be calling out the name of a defaulter before the *banjar* assembly – a procedure that would so greatly shame the family of the borrower that this threat is hardly ever invoked.

There is yet another, even stronger, sanctioning power, which represents the spiritual dimension of governance: *karma*. Good as well as bad deeds affect a person's spiritual essence, *karma*, in this world and beyond and, through reincarnation, in the next life. Saving money and investing one's savings or loans to the benefit of the family has a positive impact on one's *karma*; wasting one's resources and failing to settle one's debts has a negative impact. As one of the board members put it: *"If you die as a defaulter, you enter the beyond as a defaulter."* It is these two factors, social control by the *krama* and spiritual control by one's *karma*, which explain why the board is so successful in inducing delinquent borrowers to repay their loans.

In support of good governance: the need for effective supervision

The growth of the LPDs has been rapid, and their outreach is inclusive, covering virtually the entire population of Bali, with both poor and affluent members of the local society making use of their services. In 2012 their capital adequacy ratio (CAR) stood at 21%, ROA was a satisfactory 3.9% and ROE stood at 24.9%. Yet all is not well. Out of a total of 1,418 LPDs, 12% do not function properly. This is due partly to the fact that a number of small and very small LPDs are not adequately staffed, and partly to a lack of coordination between reporting, guidance, and supervision, responsibility for which is spread over various agencies. At the root of the problem lies the discrepancy between two systems: the customary system of social organization in Bali, which comprises a flat hierarchy of customary villages at the bottom and the Governor of Bali at the top, and the official administrative system of districts, to which administrative and budgetary responsibilities have been devolved in a process of decentralization. The power of self-organization at the level of the customary village has not been matched by the creation of a similar power at district level. The effectiveness of supervision, and of the enforcement of compliance, hinges upon the harmonization of these two systems in practice – a continual challenge. External supervision needs to be professionalized, perhaps in a uniquely Balinese way that has yet to be found.

Crisis resilience of savings-led microfinance institutions

Resilience in times of national crisis is a characteristic which the LPDs share with the BRI microbanking units. When the banking sector of Indonesia collapsed under a depositor and investor run during the Asian financial crisis of 1997/98, there were no significant negative effects on the LPDs (nor on the BRI units, in contrast to commercial banks in general, including BRI's corporate finance

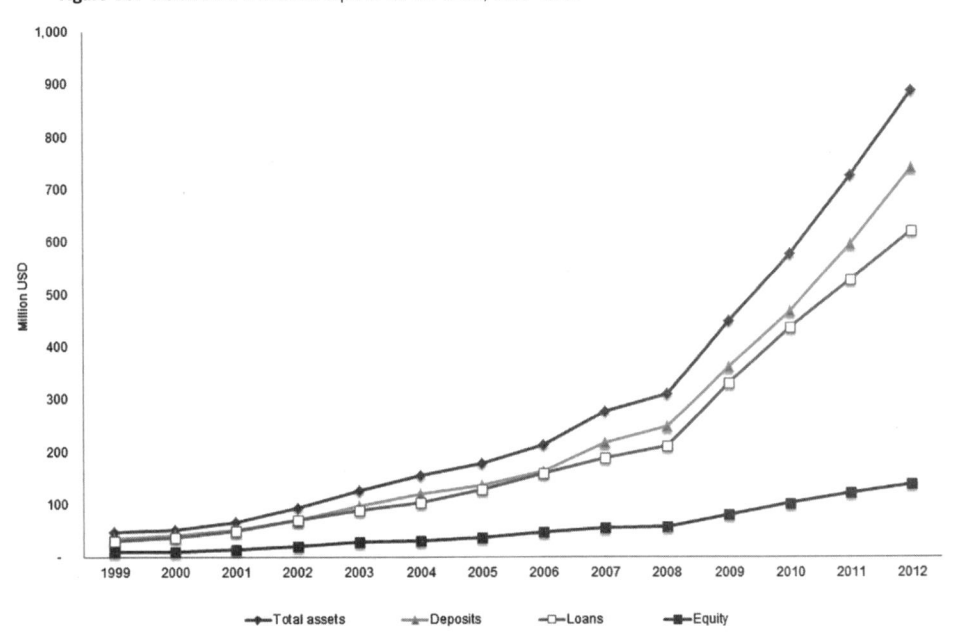

Figure 19: The evolution of financial depth in the LPD sector, 1999–2012

business). On the contrary, both emerged as trusted institutions and attracted additional savings, while at the same time continuing to meet the credit demand of their clients.[28] Indeed, both the loan classification and CAMEL rating of the LPD sector showed an improving trend over the crisis period[29] (Holloh 2000: 11).

During the global crisis which began in 2008, and led to the worst economic slowdown since the 1930s, the microfinance sector was reportedly hit hard. This may have been the case as far as donor- and investor-driven MFIs were concerned, but it was not true of most savings-based MFIs. Evidence from consolidated annual and monthly data indicates that the global crisis has had no effect on the growth of LPDs' outreach or on their performance. In fact, there has been a steady increase in the number of deposit and loan accounts and, since 2008, dramatic growth in deposits and loans outstanding, as shown in Figure 19. Moreover, the non-performing loan ratio declined from 11.6% in 2007 to 7.9% in 2012.

Over time, the Balinese LPDs have shown a remarkable resilience in the face of local, national, and global crises. The effectiveness of customary governance ar-

---

28 However, savings and credit clients of the LPDs behaved quite differently: During the three-year period 1996–99 the number of deposit accounts increased by 46% (compared with a rise of 29% during the preceding three-year period). In contrast, the number of borrowers stagnated (compared with an increase of 43% during the preceding period). Accordingly, during the financial crisis, deposits exceeded loans outstanding by a widening margin, generating a large surplus (Holloh 2000:7–8, 2001:101; see also Holloh 1998, 2001).

29 Furthermore, there is anecdotal evidence indicating that the two terrorist attacks in Bali had little or no impact on the sector: The bombing of 2002 temporarily affected some of the larger LPDs in the tourist areas, but overdue payments were subsequently recovered. The second bombing, in 2005, had no effect.

rangements in these village-level financial institutions and the Balinese culture of honoring one's obligations have played a key role. But given that, on a national scale, the experience of BRI's microbanking units has been similar, we have to conclude, at a more general level, that savings-based MFIs operating in local markets possess great strength in the face of adversity. Donors may conclude that, given the crucial importance of sustainable growth and resilience, scarce financial resources may be better invested in strengthening the capacity of local MFIs to mobilize savings in their areas of operation than in pampering them with "easy money" (cf. Seibel 2013).

Conclusions

For the Balinese, preservation of their cultural and religious identity is a key concern. Finance is one of the spheres in which that identity has been challenged. Up until the 1980s indigenous savings and credit groups were ubiquitous, forming an integral part of the customary community (*banjar*). Yet, as the economy expanded, the demand for financial services exceeded their capacity to provide such services and they were unable to compete with banks. In response, the Governor of Bali introduced a new type of financial institution, the LPD, which was regulated by provincial law, self-reliant and integrated into Balinese culture. This involved a shift in the area of operation of Balinese financial institutions – from the *banjar* to the *desa pakraman*. Within two decades the LPDs attained virtually universal and inclusive outreach, replacing the *banjar*-based groups. They owe their success to a unique system of governance, one which is integrated into Balinese culture and entails internal control through a board elected by the indigenous residents (*krama*), and, for credit clients, spiritual control by one's *karma*. This explains the success of the board in inducing delinquent borrowers to repay their loans without ever having to seize their collateral, even after periods of crisis. In fact, any LPD faces the risk that at some point it will encounter serious problems; but a motivated and dedicated board, whether newly elected or committed to pursuing a new approach, can revitalize an LPD, regain the trust of the customary village, apply a "soft" approach by effectively convincing delinquent borrowers to fully repay their overdue loans, and lead the LPD back to growth and profitability. Good governance, with owners exercising effective control over management, is crucial.

Yet, while all LPDs were closely monitored and poor performance was quickly detected by the guidance and supervision agencies, in none of the cases studied was the rapid provision of information on delinquencies followed by equally rapid remedial action. In two cases the guidance agency PLPDK played a decisive role in reviving the LPD, but only after considerable delays. In two other cases, a strong LPD in the area gave a helping hand, an approach that could be applied more systematically (Seibel 2013). Thus, once governance fails, the agencies in charge of reporting, guidance, and supervision, which are not part of the customary cultural system, have generally not been able to effectively intervene. There is no clear institutional division of labor. In the context of a national decentralization policy, resources for reporting and guidance have been created in the districts, leaving a void at the provincial level; the emphasis has been on reporting, not on supervision and enforcement of compliance. Authority for supervising the LPDs has been placed in the hands of the BPD, a bank with its own agenda and own deficiencies, and ensuring effective supervision has remained a challenge, but oversight of the LPDs is currently being strengthened. Ultimately, responsibility for supervision may have to be allocated to an autonomous financial authority in Bali unless there is a change in policy and Bali agrees to permit the central bank and the newly founded financial services authority Otoritas Jasa Keuangan (OJK) to serve as the supervisor of its LPDs.

2.4 Cooperative microfinance: What role for government?

2.4.1 Origins and expansion

Cooperative banking: An idea that originated in Germany and spread all over the world[30]

In 1846/47 Germany was hit by a famine, in an overall environment of widespread poverty in which the poor were often victims of usury and expropriation – much like the situation in Third World countries today. Many people died, indebtedness spread, peasants lost their farms to moneylenders, and small businesses went bankrupt. Interventions by governments were ineffective. Among those who took action (and whose names entered history) were Hermann Schulze from Delitzsch, a judge and later a parliamentarian, and Friedrich Wilhelm Raiffeisen, the mayor of a small village in a remote rural area. When the harvest of 1846 was about to fail, Schulze-Delitzsch formed a committee, organized collections of grain, leased a mill and a bakery and produced bread for the poor and indigent. Similarly, Raiffeisen established a charitable organization in 1847, purchasing grain from non-affected areas, which brought down the price of bread by 50%. After the famine this activity was replaced by the sale of seeds and seed potatoes (Kluge 1991).

But charity is not sustainable, and it was not an effective means of combating usury and indebtedness. This insight led to a call for self-help through joint action at the community level, the mobilization of small savings and other resources and the provision of loans secured by joint liability. Schulze-Delitzsch and Raiffeisen, the leaders of two different movements, one urban and one rural, agreed on the fundamentals: self-help, self-management, and self-governance. The years 1850 to 1851 marked the beginning of the urban, and 1864 of the rural, cooperative mi-

---

[30] For full details and a systematic and critical analysis, see chapter 7.

crofinance movement, both of which stressed the necessity of self-help and self-reliance and rejected the idea of charity. Two elements proved to be crucial: (i) starting in 1859, promotional activities and supporting services were placed in the hands of self-organized associations and central funds, with funding linkages to commercial and savings banks; and (ii) government was kept at bay, but its cooperation was gained by Schulze-Delitzsch in his role as a parliamentarian and by the associations which had pushed for enactment of a legal framework for their organizations' activities. The first Prussian cooperative law was passed in 1867, and it was expanded to cover all of Germany in 1871–73, following the Franco-Prussian War and the unification of Germany. This turned the hitherto informal associations into legally recognized financial intermediaries, and also protected them against government intrusion into their affairs. The law was revised in 1889; in its amended version it permitted the use of corporate structures based on limited liability and made auditing mandatory. These innovations significantly boosted the growth of the sector, and by 1914 there were some 19,000 credit cooperatives, which were supported by a complex institutional infrastructure. In 1934 the rural and urban cooperative financial institutions were made subject to the banking law. This helped to make them a sustainable part of the German banking sector and a major player in MSME finance – a role which the cooperative institutions are still playing today, having successfully weathered all of the political and financial crises of the last 100 years.

These are the basic tenets of cooperative banking as it evolved in Germany in the 19th and early 20th centuries in a process which we described at length in the preceding chapter. These basic tenets appeared replicable, at least in principle, in any country (albeit in a process that would have to be completed in a much shorter period than had been required in Germany): self-help and self-reliance based on savings mobilization; self-determination and self-governance, with independence from government; local area outreach and local enterprise promotion, with lasting relationships between bank and member customer; individual savings and credit accounts (rather than group credit); the use of limited liability (together with collateralized lending) rather than joint liability; a legal and regulatory framework integrating credit cooperatives into the formal financial sector; indirect (auxiliary/delegated) prudential supervision through auditing associations which cooperatives would be required to join, enabling the central bank to effectively supervise large numbers of small institutions through their apex organizations.

Once established on a firm legal basis, the credit cooperative movement that had developed in Germany soon attracted attention worldwide, leading to numerous initiatives to build similar institutions in Europe, the Americas and what were then the colonies of the European great powers. It has continued to expand ever since, with a recent report putting the total number of members as of 2012 at one billion in 100 different countries, and estimating the total number of people whose living conditions have been improved as a result of the credit cooperatives' activities at three billion.[31] However, there are vast differences in effectiveness between countries, and less research has been undertaken on this point than on purely quantitative outreach.[32]

Two contrasting roles for government

Establishing a cooperative movement through private initiatives was an approach that generally worked well in the (now mostly) developed Western countries. But can it really work in newly developing economies in a similar way? Is there a role for government, and if so, what is that role? And more specifically: are the governments of these countries able and willing to limit the extent of their influence and involvement to providing a conducive framework in which inclusive banking along the lines of the cooperative movement can thrive? Two contrasting cases will be presented below, both of which drew on the Raiffeisen model.

The first is India, discussed in section 2.4.2, where Raiffeisen-style cooperatives were set up in 1904 under the *Cooperative Credit Societies Act of India*, giving rise to what quickly became the largest credit cooperative movement worldwide. However, after this movement got off to a very promising start, the government, with the best of intentions, intervened and ultimately played a destructive role – by taking over the *operations* of the cooperatives rather than restricting itself to providing their institutions' legal, supervisory, and *operating framework*. The government is now struggling to alter and reverse this process – a task that is proving to be very difficult.

Since around 1990, an institutional innovation achieving dynamic expansion of unprecedented proportions has emerged alongside this system of conventional credit cooperatives: an SHG movement which was initially a brainchild of German development cooperation in Asia. We will examine this new movement in section 2.4.3. The SHGs function as informal savings and credit cooperatives. In many states in India they have created their own federations, many of them registered under new cooperative laws such as the *Mutually Aided Cooperative Societies (MACS) Act* in Andhra Pradesh. These registered federations are designed to free the SHGs from government interference, but they must nonetheless contend with the would-be benevolent interventions of state governments and politicians, which now threaten their autonomy and self-reliance, just as such interventions did in the case of the conventional cooperatives.

The other case is Vietnam, discussed in section 2.4.4, where the existing cooperatives collapsed together with the socialist command economy during the 1980s. In the early 1990s, the government launched a fresh initiative to establish cooperatives, this time as part of an overall policy geared to creating a market economy.

---

[31] Développement international Desjardins, 2012.
[32] Data on the global outreach of credit unions and cooperative banks is presented in section 3 of this chapter (see Birchall 2013a, 2013b for a more detailed discussion).

Operating under a new name – *People's Credit Funds (PCFs)* – and a new legal framework, these institutions have given rise to one of the most impressive credit cooperative movements to emerge in recent years. Having been defined as institutions of the formal financial sector, PCFs are prudentially regulated and effectively supervised by the State Bank of Vietnam (SBV), the central bank. SBV has also acted as a guiding agency; the PCFs have been shielded from government intervention. Most importantly, in contrast to India, the PCFs have not served as credit channels or been exploited as a tool of political favoritism; they have been free to rely instead on their own internally mobilized resources and engage in unimpeded financial intermediation.

2.4.2 How government intrusion made, and unmade, the credit cooperative system in India

A great start...

India has a long and complex history of finance and microfinance, dating back more than two thousand years. Rural finance began to spread from the 16th century onward with the introduction of taxes which, for the first time, were to be paid in cash rather than in kind. Tax-based monetization led to the emergence of a new class of usurious moneylenders and landlords and to the dispossession of peasants (Schrader 1997; Seibel 2010b). When Sir Frederick Nicholson visited continental Europe in the early 1890s to study mutualist credit institutions and assess the applicability of this model to India, he summed up the results of his mission in just two words: "Find Raiffeisen!" Ten years later, in 1904, the *CooperativeCredit Societies Act* was passed, creating a legal and regulatory framework together with cooperative banks and a supervisory structure, "replacing the moneylender with... the Raiffeisen Bank."[33]

In contrast to the beginnings of the credit cooperative movement in Germany, the impetus for the establishment of the first institutions in India came from the government and not from private initiatives. But as in Germany, the credit cooperatives were village-based; they were financed, managed, and governed by their members, not by government. They functioned as financial intermediaries, providing both savings and credit services, and unlimited liability served as a substitute for collateral. The resources mobilized were kept within the community, with no siphoning off of funds to the urban economy; in fact, there was an inflow of funds from urban areas through linkages with commercial banks. Oversight seems to have been effective, as there are reports of the closing of non-functioning cooperatives. In the words of Strickland (1922), a cooperative registrar:

"The credit movement of British India is not working with official money: about 50% of its capital consists of small shares contributed by the members and the

---

[33] Huss 1924, 83; see also Strickland 1922, 35; Bhargava 1934; Catanach 1970; Darling 1925/1928, 1930/2013.

surplus accumulated from the interest on their borrowings; another 10% consists of deposits by the members themselves, the remainder is commercial credit. The societies are not managed by Government or by officials, they are in the hands of their members, subject to an audit prescribed by law and carried out by non-officials under a decreasing official supervision."

Interest rates were in the range of 9–12% p.a. By the mid-1920s there were around 50,000 societies. Enthusiastic claims were made regarding their impact. In the words of Sir Jadunath Sarkar, a leading Indian academic at that time: "The movement of co-operative credit is tending to create a revolution… in rural India. The people have developed an extraordinary capacity for united action." (Huss 1924)

…undermined by ruinous government intervention

However, early on observers noted that the key role played by government initiative and guidance during the first two decades might have been a "birth defect" (Huss 1924); in fact, this was a prescient warning. Provisions in the Reserve Bank of India Act of 1934 regarding funding for the credit cooperatives, as well as central planning and the implementation in the mid-1950s of the concept of *state partnership* with regard to their equity, management, and governance, led to loan channeling, intrusive state patronage, bureaucracy and politicization, which supplanted the original system of self-reliance and self-governance. No autonomous networks evolved, free from government control or influence. State governments were given full authority in matters such as the appointment of chief executives, the suspension of elected boards of directors, the merger or splitting up of cooperative banks, the amendment of bylaws, the vetoing of bank decisions, the issuing of directives, supervision, and the enforcement of regulations, or indeed non-enforcement if it was deemed politically expedient. The states also held stakes in the cooperative institutions at all levels. State intervention brought the credit cooperative system to the verge of collapse. A lack of effective regulation and supervision at state and district level was the core of the problem; Reserve Bank of India (RBI), the central bank, was powerless to take remedial action.[34]

By 2006 huge losses had accumulated: more than half of the 106,000 primary agricultural credit societies (PACS) were insolvent, and more than one-quarter of the 1,112 cooperative banks reported losses. Much of the sector was kept afloat by injections of government funds, perpetual rescheduling of loans and generous accounting practices. The PACS were financing a mere 10% of their agricultural loans through deposits (NABARD 2007). "Close them or reform them" (Seibel 2000) was not a politically feasible alternative: the sector was too big to fail and too sick to heal. Implementation of a reform package has been underway since 2006. Due to

---

34 See the critical accounts in Vaidyanathan 2004 and Rangarajan 2008, 69; see also Holloh 2012; Seibel 2009a; World Bank 2007.

closures and mergers the number of PACS had shrunk by 13% as of March 2012, while of the estimated recapitalization cost of USD 3 billion, an amount of USD 2.28 billion had been spent as of that date. Of these funds, 86.6% had been contributed by government and only 13.4% by the credit cooperative sector: an arrangement which creates a perverse incentive – similar to interest and debt waivers – whereby the defaulters are rewarded.

2.4.3 Self-help group banking and cooperative self-help group federations in India: The ambivalent role of government once again

Another great start...

During the 1980s it had become clear that neither credit cooperatives nor the vast network of rural bank branches that existed in India were reaching the rural poor, a population estimated at around 300 million. A strategy of linking SHGs of the rural poor to banks, discussed at a meeting of the Asia-Pacific Rural and Agricultural Credit Association (APRACA) in 1986 and first tested in a pilot project in Indonesia, appeared promising (Kropp et al. 1989; Seibel 1991, 2006). This approach was based on a paradigm shift: from cheap credit to savings mobilization, i.e. a return to the guiding principles of the savings bank and credit cooperative movement of the 19th century.[35] Members of APRACA, including India's National Bank for Agriculture and Rural Development (NABARD), agreed to study the potential of this strategy. In Indonesia, where linkage banking was first implemented with technical assistance from GTZ/GIZ, such SHGs existed in large numbers, with ongoing savings and credit activities and an average size of close to 50 members, comprising both men and women. Under the auspices of the Indonesian central bank, existing SHGs, NGOs, and banks autonomously entered into business relationships, and banks provided financing either to NGOs or SHGs at market rates of interest, using their own funds. In India, NABARD, the supervisor of over 150,000 rural credit outlets, adopted a modified version of the approach (Nanda 1992, 1995).[36] NGOs, and subsequently state government agencies and banks, established informal groups of up to 20 women, helped them to initiate regular savings and credit activities within their groups and linked the groups di-

---

35 The new consensus had found expression in a proposition put forward by the 35th General Assembly of the UN (1980, para. 96) that developing countries "bear the main responsibility for financing their development and will adopt vigorous measures for a fuller mobilization of their domestic financial resources." The UN (1981, 1984, 1986), together with the FAO, proceeded to organize three international symposiums on the mobilization of personal savings: in 1980 (Jamaica), 1982 (Malaysia) and 1984 (Cameroon), which included deliberations on *Ways of strengthening the links between the institutional sector and the non-institutional sector* (UN 1986, 13).

36 It is worth noting that NABARD has faced tremendous obstacles in its efforts to move towards savings-based SHGs, as the government has not only continued, but in fact intensified its policy of "undermining rural finance and development with cheap credit" (Adams et al. 1984), announcing the first nationwide loan waiver in 1989. This constituted "an example of patronage that was copied by several state governments every time they wished to please the electorate" and culminated in an agricultural debt waiver in 2008–09, covering 43 million farmers and repayment obligations amounting to USD 15 billion (Mahajan and Navin, 2012, 3).

rectly to banks. The motor which was to drive the development of this new rural financing option was a so-called Micro Credit Innovation Department (MCID), established in 1998, with offices in all states, which formulated NABARD's *grand vision of one million SHGs to be credit-linked* by 2008. The fuel for the motor was a special fund to support capacity building by self-help-promoting institutions (SHPIs), with plans calling for resources to be provided to large numbers of organizations of this type. Credit resources were to be generated through the savings of SHG members, profits of the SHGs, banks' own funds, and the provision of onlending funds to the banks by NABARD. NABARD's share was meant to gradually decline as banks increasingly used their own resources. Banks were pushed to participate by the imposition of "priority sector lending rules," requiring them to earmark 40 % of their credit for socially deserving target groups including SHGs and MFIs.

SHG banking is a program that is completely in the hands of Indian organizations, and its development is driven by the active participation of the institutions involved – from the SHGs with their federations all the way up to NABARD as prime mover, the Reserve Bank of India (RBI), and the state governments. The German Agency for International Cooperation (GIZ) and the Swiss Agency for Development and Cooperation (SDC) have provided inputs, but have not been involved in the management of the program.

In terms of outreach and low transaction costs for the bank and SHGs (Seibel and Dave 2002; Seibel and Karduck 2007), NABARD's linkage banking program was an unprecedented success. The goal of one million credit-linked SHGs was achieved by 2004, with 35,294 bank branches and 3,024 SHPIs involved. Since then, the number of SHGs has continued to grow at a rapid pace. By March 31, 2011, 7.5 million rural SHGs, with some 100 million members (representing, at an average family size of five, coverage of a total of around 500 million people) had opened bank savings accounts with a total deposit balance of USD 1.5 billion; 4.8 million SHGs had bank loans outstanding with a combined volume of USD 6.8 billion, augmented by loans from internal group funds estimated by NABARD at USD 3.7 billion.[37] In addition, in recent years SHG banking has been expanding into urban areas, which is not reflected in the above figures (Seibel 2005; Tankha 2012; see also Bickel 2012; CGAP 2007; Puhazhendih 2013; Sinha et al. 2009; Srinivasan 2010, 2012).

…but the specter of government intrusion is looming once again

During the first decade of the program's existence, up until the early 2000s, increasing the volume of internal funds was a major concern of the SHGs, in addition to obtaining bank loans. However, as their numbers skyrocketed, the SHGs became a politically relevant factor in elections. In some of India's states, the gov-

---

[37] Out of total internal savings estimated at USD 5.2 billion including bank deposits (NABARD 2011b, p. iv – Status of Micro Finance in India 2010–11. Mumbai, NABARD).

ernment heavily subsidized interest rates, which led to a shift of emphasis among the SHGs from savings mobilization to cheap external credit. Autonomy, savings-based self-reliance, and the generation of credit from internal resources suffered, and the depth of financial services remained shallow. Large numbers of the poor were forced to draw upon other sources of credit, such as MFIs which were heavily dependent on funding from banks, and moneylenders, traditionally the "lender of last resort" for poor people. In 2010 irresponsible lending and the use of harsh collection methods by some aggressive MFIs led to the outbreak of the microfinance crisis in the state of Andhra Pradesh. This process was driven by the activities of SKS Microfinance, the largest and fastest-growing private, and purely profit-driven, MFI in India, headquartered in Hyderabad, Andhra Pradesh (cf. Chen et al. 2010). The extremely rapid growth of SKS and a few other institutions with a similar orientation gave rise to the Indian microfinance crisis in 2010, shortly after SKS had successfully completed an IPO and issued shares to the general public and to institutional investors. It should be noted that SKS and its peers achieved their expansion in large part by lending to SHG members, regrouping them into joint liability groups (JLGs) of five members each and pushing credit on them without regard to their repayment capacity. Many SHGs suffered. The Government of Andhra Pradesh responded by ordering a moratorium on all loan repayments to MFIs, with nationwide domino effects. Market saturation and over indebtedness came under scrutiny in many countries and were widely reported on, damaging the reputation of microfinance worldwide.

The way forward: Self-help group federations and possibly cooperative village banks?

Since the early 1990s some 165,000 SHG federations have evolved, mostly at village and district level. They were initiated and supported by NGOs, the United Nations Development Programme (UNDP), and individual Indian state governments. "Building federations as a means to ensure the sustainability of SHGs and to improve access to government programs has emerged as a key strategy of regional administrations" (GIZ 2012). "Federations ensure that economies of scale are achieved, transaction costs and default rates are reduced, value-added services such as microinsurance and input supply are provided, while increasing the outreach and simultaneously reducing the promotional costs" (APMAS 2003; see also Nair 2005; Srinivasan and Tankha 2010; Tankha 2012). With a view to turning the federation system into a genuine self-help movement, the efficacy of a new strategy – *SHG Sector Own Control* – has been tested in Andhra Pradesh through implementation of a pilot project involving self-regulation and self-supervision. The project was initiated by APMAS, a Hyderabad-based NGO, in cooperation with the IKP poverty reduction program of the Society for Elimination of Rural Poverty (SERP), a state agency, and with support from the German Cooperative and Raiffeisen Confederation (DGRV) and the German Federal Ministry for Economic Cooperation and Development (BMZ).

At the base of the federation structure are about 160,000 village organizations (VOs), all owned by SHGs. In the absence of licensed village banks, they would appear to provide an ideal institutional infrastructure for local financial intermediation as well as an appropriate repository for voluntary withdrawable personal savings. In many Indian states the VOs and higher-level federations have been organized and licensed as *MACS*, or as entities utilizing other new legal forms which are similar to that of the MACS in that they shift ownership and governance from government to members. MACS are legally authorized to act as financial intermediaries for members and SHGs. They would also be in a position to exercise control over multiple borrowings by SHG members. Once they were converted into village banks, they might help to solve the problem of over indebtedness by offering withdrawable savings accounts and small loans, with easy access at low transaction costs for depositors and borrowers. The evolving range of functions and services might include:

- Village-level financial intermediation, with appropriate deposit, credit, and other financial services for SHGs and individuals.
- Liquidity exchange between SHGs.
- Intermediation between SHGs and banks, thereby reducing banks' transaction costs.
- Monitoring, supervising, and rating SHGs as grassroots financial intermediaries.
- Monitoring multiple borrowings of SHG members, thus serving as a village credit bureau.
- Mobilizing voluntary withdrawable savings.
- Providing individual micro and small enterprise (MSE) loans to SHG members.
- Facilitating the provision of larger-sized individual bank loans to SHG members.
- Handling the sale of insurance to SHG members and serving as an intermediary between insurers and policyholders.
- Working with SHGs as collectors of deposits and payments.
- Providing financial literacy training for SHG members.

Higher-tier federations would provide a range of services to support VOs: monitoring and supervision; communication and liaison with banks, NABARD, the government's new national poverty alleviation program NRLM (2011), state governments and other stakeholders; capacity building for SHGs and SHG VOs; back-up facilitation of external lines of credit, insurance, and other services; and advocacy regarding the creation of a conducive legal and regulatory framework and smart subsidies geared to institution building. The result would be a unique system of SHG-based village banks operating under *SHG Sector Own Control*: the institutions would be owned by the SHGs, governed by elected SHG members, and supervised by specialized SHG federations under delegated authority granted by the RBI and NABARD.

So far, however, NABARD, the SHG linkage authority, has remained skeptical regarding the possible assumption of financial functions by the VOs (Srinivasan and Tankha 2010), insisting on direct linkages of SHGs to banks. Perhaps this will change in the course of ongoing deliberations over a new approach, designated "SHG-2" (NABARD 2012, Seibel 2012).

2.4.4 Credit cooperatives in Vietnam: The role of the central bank as regulator, supervisor, and guiding agency

Examining the options and designing a system

Credit cooperatives collapsed in Vietnam during the 1980s together with the command economy. The process of building a market economy started with the gradual privatization of land use rights and, in 1990, the enactment of a financial institutions law, which included credit cooperatives. As a next step, the government appointed a committee, chaired by a representative of the SBV, the country's central bank, which was tasked with preparing a strategy for the creation of a credit cooperatives sector, including a regulatory framework and an implementation structure. The committee examined the options, ruling out the idea of credit cooperatives as local agents of the Vietnam Bank for Agriculture, and visited several countries. The committee members looked at the Grameen Bank in Bangladesh, the Raiffeisen banks in Germany, and the Caisses Populaires Desjardins in Canada. While inspired by the Raiffeisen model, the committee came up with its own innovation, PCFs, which seemingly embodied a paradox, since the PCFs were meant to be autonomous cooperative self-help organizations while at the same time operating under the control of the central bank, acting on behalf of the state.

Launched in 1993, the PCFs are indeed self-managed and self-financed. Governance is in the hands of a board of three to nine directors elected by the general assembly for a five-year term. Board members are usually experienced and respected citizens who play a leading role in the funds as founding members. The board decides on capital increases, interest rates (within a range set by the SBV), recruitment, and expenditures. It also appoints the managing director, who has to be approved by the general assembly and confirmed by the local SBV branch. Internal control is placed in the hands of a supervisory committee elected by the general assembly.

Since 1995 the PCFs have been backed by a cooperative central fund (CCF), which performs liquidity exchange, funding, and monitoring functions and also serves as a representative of the PCFs in their dealings with other institutions. In 2001 the CCF also introduced retail banking for SMEs and the public. The CCF is jointly owned by the PCFs, four state banks and the government, through the SBV. In 2006, a PCF association the Vietnam Association of People's Credit Funds (VAPCF) was established which was expected to take over responsibility from the CCF for representation and advocacy, network expansion, IT development, capacity building and consultancy, and auditing; very little of this has materialized. Term deposits are insured by the Vietnam Insurance Company. In July 2013 the CCF was transformed into the Cooperative Bank of Vietnam (CoopBank), which serves as the PCFs' apex bank. In 2014 a Safety Fund was established for the rescue of PCFs in difficulty, managed by CoopBank and supervised by SBV; to capitalize the fund, CoopBank and PCFs contribute 0.08 % of the value of their annual average total loans.

Regulation, supervision, and capacity building

The SBV has been in charge of building the new system and ensuring its soundness by designing, implementing, and enforcing an appropriate regulatory framework. Prudential standards include a minimum capital requirement of VND[38] 100 million (equivalent to USD 17,000 in 1993, USD 6,000 in 2008, USD 4,400 in 2015), a risk-weighted CAR of 8 % (2015: 9 %), a fixed asset ratio of a maximum of 50 % of equity, reserve requirements of 1 % of VND deposits and 8 % of USD deposits (placed interest-free at the SBV), a single borrower limit of 15 % of equity (up from 10 % at inception), adequate maturity matching (at most, 10 % [20 % in 2015) of short-term deposits may be used for long-term loans) and observance of SBV's provisioning rules. The SBV also regulates the appraisal process, collateral requirements, loan loss provisioning, recordkeeping, and reporting.

PCFs are subject to three types of oversight involving both off-site and on-site activities: daily internal control, regular random inspections by the SBV branch, and remote supervision by the SBV Supervision Department. PCFs send their financial and credit reports to the SBV branches as well as to the CCF branches. The SBV branches forward them to the SBV's Supervision Department and to the SBV's Credit Cooperative Institutions Department. Online reporting is expanding rapidly. Based on monthly reports, an SBV branch may intervene directly in cases where irregularities have been identified or an individual PCF's performance has been poor. By closing nearly 100 PCFs at the end of the pilot period (around the year 2000), the SBV signaled that it is serious about the enforcement of standards. The SBV has also acted as a guiding and training agency, but has refrained from loan channeling and interference in the operations of the PCFs.

Savings and loans

Deposits are mobilized from members and non-members and from both individuals and organizations. PCFs offer attractive terms and conditions, combined with lower depositor transaction costs due to their proximity to their clients, and a range of services tailored to the demand of the clients including demand, term, regular and discount deposits (with prepaid interest) offering higher interest rates than are available at banks. As a result, deposits usually account for three-quarters

---

38 The Vietnamese national currency, the Dong.

or more of the volume of loans outstanding, with the ratio even reaching 90.5 % in 2011. Thus, the PCFs' deposit-taking operations provide a solid basis for self-reliance. Surplus deposits are placed with the CCF/CoopBank. Other financial services offered by the PCFs include bill payment and remittances. They may also act as trustee agencies for development programs.

Lending is restricted to members in good standing. Up to 10 % of PCFs' portfolios may consist of loans to poor non-members. About 30 % of the borrowers are women. As a rule, the portfolios of PCFs are broadly diversified, comprising loans for agricultural production and processing, crafts, trading, and other services, as well as consumer and emergency loans. The main emphasis is reportedly on agricultural production, which is the main occupation of most of the members. Loans provided to socio-economic organizations and small enterprises are used mainly to finance equipment purchases, modernization, and expansion. Except for small loans and loans to the poor, most loans are secured by land use and house ownership certificates. Many loans are granted to micro, small, and medium enterprises. Deposits are mostly short-term, for periods of up to one year.

Interest rates were liberalized in 2002, but PCF boards felt morally obligated to keep lending rates low and deposit rates high. As inflation in Vietnam rose from 6.6 % in 2006 to 22 % in 2008, the SBV once again adopted a restrictive interest rate policy, setting loan ceilings for PCFs at 21 % p.a. and deposit rates at 8–9 % (both negative in real terms). By June 2012 lending rates had fallen to a maximum of 15 %, while deposit rates stood at 9.5 %. Given an inflation rate of 7 %, this corresponded in real terms to a lending rate of 8 % and a deposit rate of 2.5 % p.a. By 2015 lending and deposit rates had dropped to a range of 8–10 % and 4–7 %, respectivly; at an inflation rate of 2 % this corresponds to 6–8 % and 2–5 % respectivly, in real terms.

Crisis resilience

It appears that the combination of local cooperative autonomy with guidance and supervision by the central bank has produced a healthy credit cooperative system. By December 2011, there were 1,095 PCFs in operation with close to four million clients, a credit portfolio of USD 1.38 billion, deposits of USD 1.25 billion and equity of USD 0.13 billion. The CAR stood at 9.7 %, and the arrears ratio was less than 1 %. The ROA for the PCFs was 1.5 % and ROE stood at 19 %. By June 2014 the number of PCFs had grown to 1,145, total assets stood at USD 3.2 billion, total loans outstanding at USD 2.4 billion, deposits at USD 2.6 billion, and equity at USD 0.17 billion; the NPL ratio was 0.97 %, ROA 1.03 % and ROE 16.02 %. Neither of the major financial crises that have occurred since the launch of the PCFs – the Asian financial crisis of 1997/98 and the global crisis in 2008 – affected the PCFs, and they also did not have a negative impact on the willingness and ability of members to repay: for example, throughout the period 2005–2010, the arrears ratio remained at 0.5 %.

Figure 20: Key balance sheet data for the PCFs, 1995–2013

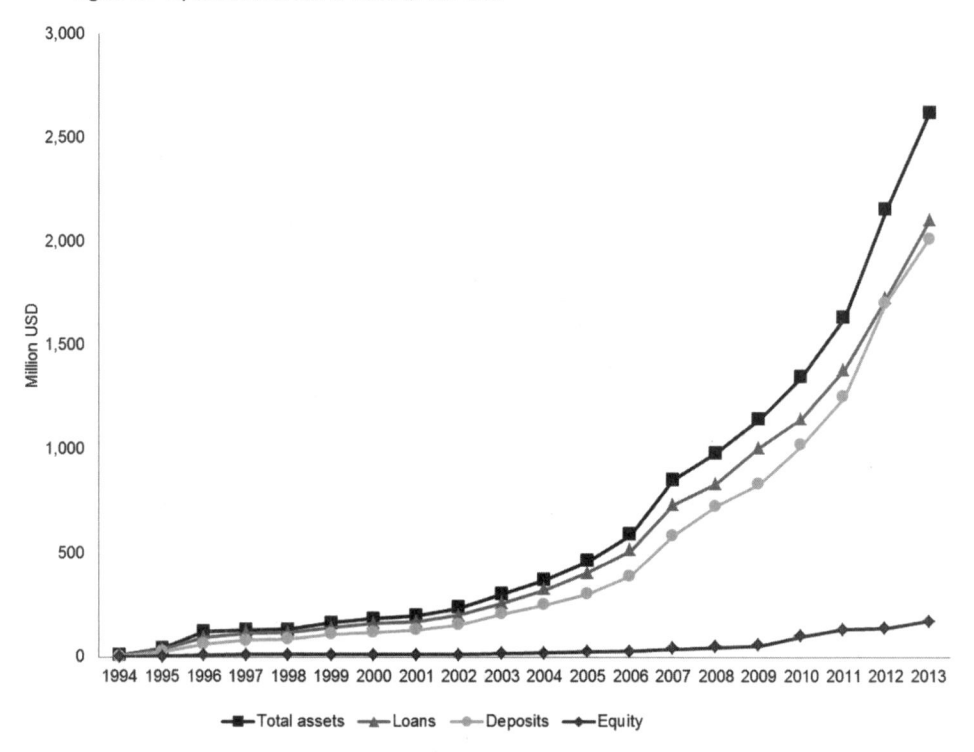

Figure 21: Key balance sheet data for CCF/CoopBank, 1995–2013

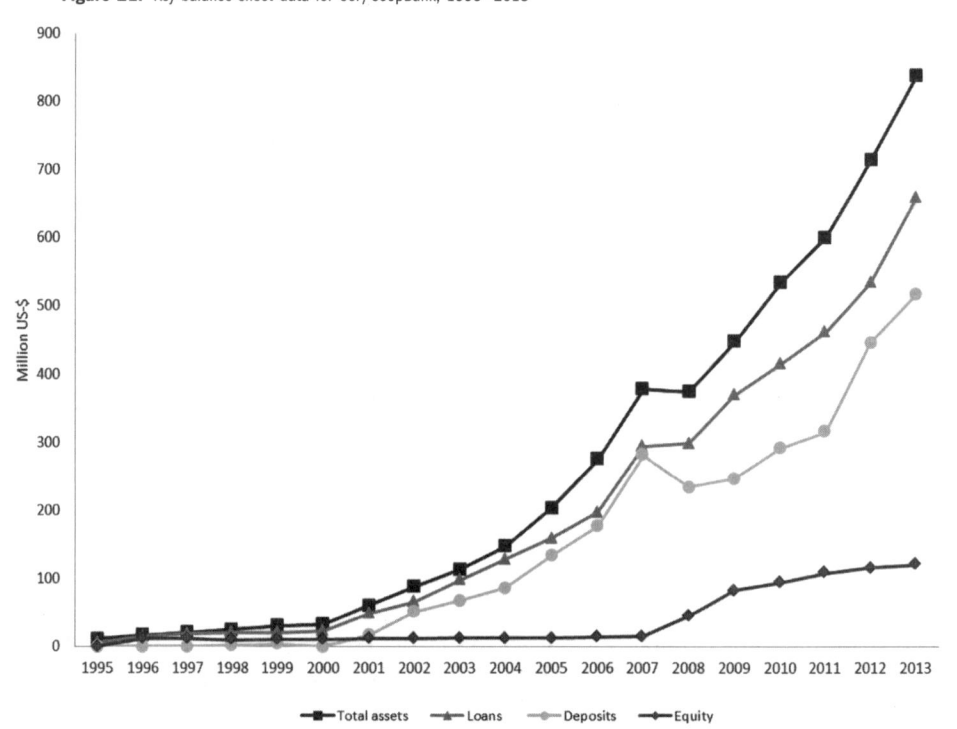

In recent years, the picture has been different, and less positive, for the central fund, whose retail business with SMEs was clearly affected by the downturn in the global economy. From 2001 to 2007 the growth pattern for CCF was overwhelmingly positive and similar to that of the PCFs. This changed abruptly in 2008. The growth of the loan portfolio, which amounted to 48.6% in 2007, stopped altogether in 2008; the growth rate for deposits fell from 58.4% to −13.8%. Loans in arrears (≥ 1 day) jumped from 1.3% to 3.1%: ROA fell only slightly, declining from 0.43% to 0.37%, but ROE decreased from 9.8% to 4.6%. Due to a large-scale investment in anticipation of the conversion of CCF into a cooperative bank, the CAR surged from 10% to 31%.

The two client groups served by CCF reacted differently to the global crisis: the PCFs deposited more in the CCF and borrowed less from it, while enterprises and individuals deposited less and borrowed more. The impact of the turmoil in 2008 on the financial performance of the CCF was pronounced, but was largely confined to that year. After 2008, growth picked up again, although the rates achieved were lower than those recorded prior to the crisis (Seibel and Tam 2010, 2012).

2.4.5 Conclusions

In summary, a comparison of the two cases, India and Vietnam, shows that the world of financial cooperatives is complex – ranging from successful self-help movements at one extreme, to failing state-supported systems at the other. Of key relevance is the role of the state – more specifically, whether it is intrusive or supportive: does the state provide a conducive operating environment, or does it take over the operation of the system? Central banks can play a crucial role, as shown by Vietnam, where the central bank acts as a regulator and supervisor, strictly enforcing compliance by cooperative institutions with regulations and standards, insisting on savings-based self-reliance and good performance, and at the same time protecting them against undue intervention by the state. In contrast, when the Reserve Bank of India Act was passed in 1934, it included provisions for funding the cooperative credit system, thus paving the way for involvement of the state in the ownership, management, and governance of credit cooperatives, which was eventually the downfall of the entire movement.

Yet the comparison is not as straightforward as it appears. Given the two countries' vastly differing histories, the settings in which credit cooperatives evolved in India and Vietnam differed markedly as well. During the first decades of the 20th century the Indian credit cooperative system got off to an excellent start, enjoying unparalleled growth and success. Later on, in the second half of the 20th century, when the states and their administrators and politicians took over the sector, they practically ruined it. It is doubtful whether the ongoing reform efforts will succeed in creating a financially sound, sustainable sector. Similarly, after SHGs got off to a great start during the 1990s, their viability as informal financial cooperatives, and that of SHG federations as emerging formal financial cooperatives, is now increasingly threatened by government intrusion into their affairs – as reflected in interest and loan waivers, or campaign promises to implement such waivers; subsidies and generous offers of funding at the expense of internal resource mobilization; and the neglect of voluntary withdrawable savings at the village level. There is little, if any, evidence that policy makers in India have drawn the appropriate lessons from the downfall of the credit cooperative movement, either as regards the reform of the cooperative sector or with respect to the SHG sector and the planning for the second 20-year phase of its existence.

One could almost say that Vietnam was fortunate insofar as it had to start anew following the collapse of both the command economy and the communist credit cooperative system in the 1980s. In the 1990s the government, the central bank, and the leaders of the credit cooperative system all seem to have learned from the experiences of both Vietnam and other countries: Savings and self-financing, self-management and self-governance matter; and so do appropriate regulation, effective supervision, and strict enforcement of standards right from the beginning, as well as the creation of effective federations and networking at the national level. With the benefit of technical assistance, Vietnam has taken the experience of the cooperative movement in Germany and put the best aspects of that experience into practice: not by blindly replicating the "German model," but by adapting it to the social, economic, and political environment in Vietnam.[39]

There are not a great many other countries in the developing world where the state has so wisely refrained from exerting undue political influence, opting instead to vest regulatory and supervisory authority over the credit cooperative system in the central bank.

2.5 Microfinance banks

2.5.1 What microfinance banks are, and why they are important

Microfinance banks are financial institutions which are licensed as banks, are regulated and supervised by the competent authorities of the country in which they operate, and also have access to the credit facilities of their country's central bank. What differentiates them from other banks is their focus on certain client groups and the range of services they offer. In contrast to most established banks, their main credit clientele does not consist of medium to large firms, well-to-do private individuals who are employed in the formal sector and self-employed people from the modern economic sector, but rather is made up of individuals and businesses that in most cases would find it difficult to obtain a loan from an established bank.

---

[39] Perhaps the time has come for the PCFs, the CCF/CoopBank, the VAPCF and the SBV to jointly establish an international visitors' program – which would, of course, operate on a self-reliant and sustainable basis, with participants paying cost-covering fees.

As regards their deposit clientele, the microfinance banks may be equally specialized or less narrowly focused, but they may also not be specialized at all. In such cases, microfinance banks mobilize deposits from all sectors and segments of the population in order to transform these funds into loans to small businesses and relatively poor people.

Unlike traditional development banks, microfinance banks are "universal banks for all" insofar as they offer their clients deposit services, credit, and domestic and international money transfers and payment services, and in some cases various additional services as well; and they are genuine financial intermediaries since they collect deposits and transform them into loans.

Some microfinance banks have a clear and exclusive focus on clients who would have problems in accessing the services of the formal financial sector if microfinance banks did not exist. Then there are other institutions which have a broader client orientation; serving relatively poor clients, and small and very small enterprises, is only one of several lines of business on which they focus. At some of these institutions, the microfinance activities are organized in a special department or division. Where this is the case, we focus in our discussion exclusively on this microfinance department or division, in effect dealing with it as though it were a separate microfinance bank, as we have done with BRI's micro-banking units in Indonesia. Centenary Bank in Uganda, on the other hand, which changed its name several times, started exclusively with microfinance and only later diversified its clientele, adding SME finance. Other banks for which microlending is only a small segment of their activities are disregarded in our presentation. Deciding whether a given bank is really a microfinance bank or not is often a matter of judgment; in many cases the situation is not clear-cut.

Three case studies of microfinance banks are presented in this section. All three banks are the product of institutional transformation processes. Centenary Bank in Uganda began operating in 1985 as a "trust fund" with a limited banking license. It did well in savings mobilization, but its performance in lending was disastrous, and it almost collapsed. The ProCredit Banks, now operating in 20 countries in Eastern Europe, Africa, and Latin America, began operating in the 1990s, relying essentially on capital from donors and investors, and generally performed well from the outset. As a way of ensuring that investors would not be in a position to exert undue influence over their business policies, and in response to calls by their MSE borrowers, the ProCredit Banks boosted and diversified their deposit portfolio in the early 2000s, creating a rapidly growing source of loanable funds. They are now self-reliant financial intermediaries whose expansions are not fueled primarily by either their deposit growth or the increase in their loan portfolios, but are driven more or less equally by the growth of both sides of their business. In 1969 BRI began establishing a network of units for the disbursement of subsidized agricultural credit, which was funded from the state budget. As their numbers increased, their performance declined sharply. By 1983 the deterioration had progressed to the point that BRI was faced with the choice of either closing or reforming them.

Technical assistance played a crucial role in all three cases. In 1993, Centenary's owner, the Catholic Church in Uganda, decided to convert the institution into a commercial bank, but this change alone did not improve its performance. The truly substantive changes that were required, and which ultimately proved successful in turning the institution around, were undertaken with assistance from the German Savings Banks Foundation for International Cooperation (SBFIC), together with IPC, a Frankfurt-based consulting firm. IPC provided a highly effective individual lending methodology and management information system (MIS) combined with powerful incentives for both staff and borrowers.

The ProCredit Banks are the brainchild of IPC, which gained its initial experience in the redesign and reorientation of MFIs in Latin America and Africa. IPC has trained large numbers of management and operating staff over the past 20 years; not only did many of them subsequently fill key positions at the ProCredit Banks, but a considerable number eventually went on to establish, restructure or run similar microfinance and microbanking institutions in other settings.

The impetus for the transformation of the BRI village units into commercially viable microbanking units was provided by the Harvard Institute for International Development (HIID), which helped BRI to design two highly successful financial products, both based on commercial rates of interest. One was a savings product with positive real returns, unlimited withdrawals, and a highly attractive lottery component with prizes offered in monthly public drawings. The other was a truly inclusive, non-targeted, and simple credit product, open to all and available for any purpose, with loan amounts initially ranging from USD 3 to USD 5,000. These two products have made the microbanking units the largest and most successful national microfinance network in the developing world. In 1997/98, at the time of the Asian financial crisis, when the Indonesian banking sector – including the other parts of BRI – collapsed, it was the microbanking units which saved BRI, thanks to their focus on inclusive deposit and lending operations. Today, as of 2016, BRI is the best-performing and second-largest bank.

All three institutions employ the individual lending technology; that is, they do not use the group lending methodology made famous by Grameen Bank and copied in numerous new microlending institutions. Moreover, they offer their business clients the opportunity to "graduate" from micro to small and medium enterprise loans. All three institutions are genuinely inclusive; they exclude neither women nor men and do not discriminate against either the poor or the non-poor.

We believe that the three cases are indicative of the future of sustainable microfinance in developing and emerging markets. In fact, in our view, they point the way to a promising new stage of institutional development which could have an impact similar to that of the transition in Germany from informal and semiformal beginnings in the 19th century to modern commercial savings and cooperative banks whose outreach is comprehensive and truly inclusive.

2.5.2 Centenary Bank, Uganda: Converting a trust fund into a microfinance bank

Origins and transformation

Centenary Bank in Uganda, an outstanding provider of microsavings services and MSME finance, was transformed from a trust fund into a commercial bank in three stages. First it was converted from a loss-making fund with a limited banking license into a fully licensed commercial bank operating as a provider of MSE finance; next, the bank diversified its portfolio by adding agricultural finance to its product range; and finally, in order to increase its outreach and sustainability, it evolved into an MSME bank, adding meso-finance products aimed at SMEs, financial products for corporate clients, and consumer finance products. Centenary's success has been attributable to an innovation: the introduction of cashflow-based lending at a savings-led financial institution, supported by technical assistance during the 1990s in the framework of a partnership program between German and African savings banks, with further support being provided later on in the form of an institutional strengthening project sponsored by the German development agency GTZ (now GIZ) and implemented by IPC. Centenary has served as a model which has been copied in many parts of the developing world, as it has demonstrated

- the feasibility of mobilizing small savings in rural and peri-urban areas
- the feasibility of transforming a rural financial institution into a bank
- the compatibility of institutional sustainability with outreach to low-income people
- the feasibility of cashflow-based MSME lending, and
- the feasibility of agricultural finance.

From an inefficient trust fund to an efficient commercial microfinance bank

In 1983 the Uganda National Council of the Lay Apostolate, a Catholic organization, established an MFI called Centenary Rural Development Trust, with a limited banking license. Its mission was "to provide appropriate financial services, especially microfinance, to all people in Uganda, particularly in rural areas" – or, putting it in modern terms, to provide inclusive finance. Operations started in 1985. Centenary was successful at collecting savings, but borrowers mistakenly considered its lending to be a form of charity, with dramatic results: "[The institution] was suffering massive losses in its current operations, its loan portfolio was for the most part worthless, its personnel did not have much technical expertise, it was poorly organized, and it was chronically overstaffed." By 1993 the central bank would have closed Centenary had it not been for the commitment given by German technical assistance organizations to provide support to address the institution's problems (Schmidt 1998).

Generating the political will to implement far-reaching reforms requires a champion within the institution. And in 1989/90 one of the founding members succeeded in convincing a board of nonprofessionals with a religious commitment to Centenary's mission to convert the trust into a full-service commercial bank, while at the same time seeking assistance from the German Savings Banks Foundation for International Cooperation (SBFIC), which brought in the Frankfurt-based consulting firm IPC to provide technical assistance.

As a first step, in December 1992, the credit trust received its new license under the name of Centenary Rural Development Bank. Within five years, with German technical assistance and equity investments from several sources to strengthen its eroded capital base, the bank was transformed into a sustainable provider of inclusive banking services.

The second step focused on organizational restructuring and the lending technology. A new chief executive came in; board members were retired; branch managers and loan officers were replaced; additional loan officers were hired; and all personnel were systematically trained, with intensive retraining measures being implemented for existing staff.

Centenary had always been quite successful at savings mobilization, but initially its lending operations had not been based on a coherent system of any kind, and the loss rate was horrendous. The management, together with IPC, put into place a new lending system based on the provision of individual MSE loans, guided by five principles:

- *Business lending to individual enterprises*, not groups.
- *Cash-flow lending* based on an analysis of the household and its existing (rather than expected) repayment capacity.
- *Acceptance of various unconventional forms of collateral where available*, for example land without a title, livestock, household items, business equipment, and personal guarantors.
- *"Graduation" of borrowers with good repayment performance*, enabling them to obtain better credit terms and larger loan amounts.
- *Computerized loan monitoring and control*, crucial for follow-up with borrowers, staff performance analysis, incentives, and provisioning.

A major emphasis was placed on *incentives*, with a focus on:

- Converting branches into profit centers.

- Rating individual staff members' performance, based mainly on repayment rates within their portfolios (weighted at 75% of the score), with incentive payments constituting up to 45% of total remuneration for lending staff.
- Grading customers on a scale of 1 to 5 and rewarding good customers with repeat loans of increasing size and increasingly long maturity periods, at substantially reduced interest rates.

Arrears management and loan loss prevention are crucial factors in lending. The single most effective element in Centenary's financial technology has been a system of loan tracking and immediate initiation of recovery action involving the borrower, the loan officer, the branch, and the head office. Operational elements include:

- Daily loan tracking based on an online MIS that provides real-time daily results.
- A zero-tolerance policy and immediate recovery action.
- Branch-level performance monitoring, with the head loan officer receiving the data generated by the MIS and submitting it to the branch manager, who checks the performance of each loan officer.
- Submission of figures to the head office the next morning, with data being furnished to all responsible managers up to and including the chief executive.
- Immediate communication, with direct telephone lines between branches and head office.
- Incentives for lending personnel, with their remuneration increasing if loans in arrears for more than one day do not exceed 5% of portfolio volume.
- Customer incentives and penalties.

The results of the measures implemented at Centenary were impressive: following implementation of the donor-supported reforms, it became a self-sustaining and profitable financial intermediary, and has remained so ever since, thereby demonstrating that rural bank reform is feasible in Africa. In 1998, after the end of the cooperation with SBFIC and IPC, the formerly loss-making institution achieved a stunning ROA of 4% and an ROE of 49%.[40] By 31 December 2000 Centenary's loan portfolio had risen to USD 10 million, with a borrower outreach of 18,411; micro and small borrowers accounted for 99% of this total. Small business loans continued to be the bank's main credit product, making up 85.5% of the portfolio.

Vigorous savings mobilization remained the bank's hallmark. As of 31 December 2000 it had 236,812 savings clients; at USD 28.8 million, its deposit balance had doubled since 1998, when it stood at USD 14.6 million. Withdrawable deposits enable a household to accumulate financial assets, self-finance investments, and

---

40 The extremely high ROE was in a sense an anomaly reflecting the extremely low level of equity that had been brought about by the losses of earlier years. Since equity grew rapidly thereafter, this ROE level was not reached again in subsequent years. Much later, in 2012, insufficient equity was no longer a problem for the bank, as Centenary reported a CAR, based on risk-weighted assets, of 25%.

protect itself against the adverse effects of uneven income streams, and it is these advantages which create the substantial demand that exists for such deposit facilities. Centenary had responded to that demand by offering three products: passbook savings, which accounted for two thirds of all deposits, current accounts, and fixed term deposits.

Sustainability and outreach in agricultural finance

The introduction of agricultural lending was the first step which Centenary took to expand its portfolio after the project with SBFIC had ended, while IPC continued to provide technical assistance. In July 1998 Centenary opened a new branch in Mbale to serve as its "experimental field station" to test the feasibility of agricultural lending. Two years later, in June 2001, the branch was already serving 13,853 depositors and 2,646 borrowers. Deposits amounted to USD 9.7 million and loans outstanding stood at USD 11.6 million, for a loans-to-deposit ratio (LDR) of 120%. This made Mbale unique among the branches insofar as it was a *deposit deficit unit*. In terms of repayment, the Mbale branch was among the best-performing units in the entire Centenary network. Its arrears ratio was 1.5%, with an even lower figure for its agricultural portfolio. By February 1999, Mbale had reached the break-even point and has been profitable ever since, with the staff earning the maximum performance bonuses. Like all branches, it is audited three times a year by internal auditors, twice a year by the branch operations supervisors and the head office credit supervisors, and once a year by external auditors and central bank examiners.[41]

Mbale's success showed that Centenary's (and IPC's) methodology (comprising prudent staff selection and thorough training, focusing on agricultural lending; holistic loan appraisal taking into account the entire family's cash-flow and repayment capacity; strict enforcement of repayment through immediate recovery action, supported by a computerized system providing instant repayment information; and powerful staff and customer incentives) also worked in agricultural credit. By 2011 Centenary had built up an agricultural portfolio of USD 26.5 million, accounting for 12.3% of its total outstanding loan volume.[42]

---

41 The intensity and frequency of Centenary's auditing activities is a consequence of a string of earlier fraud cases that had involved a number of branches. These cases were uncovered by one of the IPC consultants working at Centenary at that time, a native of Mali and a graduate of a German university. If the team of advisors had not included an individual with this unusual background, it is highly unlikely that the irregularities would have been detected. He later went on to work at the World Bank and now owns and manages a thriving development finance consultancy in Washington – just one example of the numerous IPC-trained staff who later went on to develop successful careers in the field of microfinance, as noted earlier.

42 For details see Seibel and Almeyda 2002 and 2003b, Centenary Bank 2012 and Nsibambi 2011 and 2012.

Overcoming the quality vs. productivity dilemma: from micro to medium-sized finance

The initial years after the end of the cooperation project with SBFIC coincided with a challenging period for the entire banking sector in Uganda. Centenary's loan portfolio grew only marginally; the bank's lending operations were able to absorb only a fraction of its steadily increasing liquidity, with the LDR falling from 57% to 36%. There were two reasons for this: Internally, the process of institutional redesign and reorientation had focused on portfolio quality, not quantity. Externally, Uganda was hit by high inflation and a general banking crisis, which led to the closure of several banks and forced the remaining ones to restrict their lending, while continuing to mobilize deposits. In an effort to fight inflation, the central bank absorbed the excess liquidity in the market by offering treasury bills at rates of up to 31%, with real returns in 2001 of up to 25%. This made it more lucrative for banks to invest in treasury bills than in loans.

The situation changed abruptly at the turn of 2002 when treasury bill returns briefly slumped to 3–5%, while record harvests led to the collapse of agricultural prices. As a new CEO came in, Centenary was ready for a shift from a one-sided emphasis on quality to a policy geared to boosting productivity while maintaining loan quality, i.e. a focus on portfolio growth while continuing to rigorously enforce repayment. This could not be achieved with microloans only; it required diversification, which meant adding small and medium enterprise loans, which generate greater growth and more employment. The early 2000s thus marked the beginning of another stage in the institution's transformation process: the conversion of a microenterprise bank to an MSME bank.

During the first half of 2002 Centenary modified its lending strategy. First, it changed its incentive formula by giving more weight to productivity, measured in terms of loan volume per loan officer and branch manager. Second, three new loan products were introduced, and the amounts involved were all many times greater than the average loan size of USD 600 in 2000 and 2001: home improvement loans averaging USD 1,600, salary loans averaging USD 2,100, and SME loans for amounts of at least USD 8,000.

Centenary's SME lending raises the issue of micro vs. meso finance and related differences in interest rates and productivity. Centenary had noted over its 20-year history that a number of its borrowers – the entrepreneurial poor – eventually grew their businesses into SMEs with a demand for larger loans, accompanied, as posited by microeconomic theory, by a decline in marginal productivity. Accordingly, most SMEs that applied for, or might have applied for, loans were not able to afford effective interest rates of 48% p.a. for initial loans and 30% p.a. for follow-up automatic loans. Centenary therefore introduced a new category: commercial loans at interest rates no higher than 22% (tied in 2002 to a prime rate of 16%).

The immediate result, within less than a year, was stunning and quite different from what those who fear mission drift would have expected: The business loan portfolio now included a few hundred commercial SME loans. In a very difficult year when most banks in Uganda suffered, this helped Centenary to maintain its profitability. Far from creating a sustainability–vs.–outreach dilemma, it enabled the bank to continue growing during 2002 at an unprecedented rate of 44 % in terms of borrower outreach and 63 % in terms of portfolio volume. Yet there was no mission drift: even though a substantial number of borrowers had moved out of the micro bracket and were now receiving larger loans, given the very sizeable increase in the total number of borrowers served by the institution, 99 % of its credit customers continued to be in the micro bracket.

Centenary has continued to diversify its portfolio. As of 2011, MSME loans accounted for 45.2 % of the portfolio volume, comprising microloans (15.6 %) and commercial, or SME, loans (29.6 %). Salary-backed loans contributed 27.4 %, agricultural loans 12.3 %, and home improvement loans 9.4 %. Loan sizes varied from USD 40 to USD 600,000. On its website[43] Centenary divides its credit products into three major categories: business loans (with eight products), consumer loans (seven products), and special loan schemes (six products). The bank manages its portfolio well: the NPL ratio is currently 2.4 % and the loss ratio stands at 1.1 %. All major loan products have NPL ratios (≥1 day) of between 2.0 % (for home improvement loans) and 2.9 % (for microloans), a relatively narrow range. The fact that, with an NPL ratio of 2.7 %, agricultural loans also fall in this range is a strong indication that Centenary's individual lending technology can be successfully applied to a sector which is considered by many to be too risky to be served by banks on a sustainable, commercially viable basis (Centenary Bank 2012).

Over its 30-year history Centenary has developed into a well-performing bank with a diversified portfolio which has had a strong social commitment from the very beginning and whose main outreach focus is on microfinance in rural areas. With 58 branches, 130 ATMs and over 1,300,000 customers as of the end of 2012, Centenary calls itself "Uganda's leading Microfinance Commercial Bank," with total assets of USD 417.9 million, net loans outstanding of USD 207.4 million, deposits of USD 304.7 million and equity of USD 76.1 million. With a cost-to-income ratio of 71 % and a loss ratio of 1.1 %, Centenary is highly profitable: After-tax ROE stands at 30.3 %, ROA at 5.3 %, and CAR (Tier 2) at 26.9 % (2012).[44] Deposits and equity are the backbone of its self-reliance, accounting for 90.1 % of the balance sheet total in 2012. Centenary continues to be a deposit-driven bank which caters primarily to small savers, with passbook savings accounts representing 52 % of total liabilities and shareholders' equity, current accounts 14 % and time deposits 8 %. Centenary does not receive any funding from

---

43 Annual Report 2011, http://www.centenarybank.co.ug.
44 Annual Report 2012, http://www.centenarybank.co.ug.

other banks or international development finance institutions – sources of funds which play a major role for many MFIs.

Between 2000 and 2011 Centenary was able to substantially reduce the gap between deposits and loans outstanding by continually expanding its credit outreach. Expressed in US dollars at the respective current exchange rates, deposits grew tenfold, while loans outstanding increased more than twentyfold. As a consequence, the LDR more than doubled, rising from 36% to 74%. Centenary uses a portion of its profits to support social projects in health, education, and environmental protection as part of its commitment to corporate social responsibility.

Conclusions

Centenary provides deposit, credit, and money transfer services on a non-discriminatory basis to both men and women, mostly in lower-income segments of the population. By insisting on loan recovery and cost coverage, it has been able to build a sustainable banking business and reach more customers in rural areas than any other institution in Uganda. With minimum deposits of USD 5 and minimum loan amounts of USD 40, access barriers are low. About three-quarters of its deposits and loans are in rural areas. Established as a trust fund in 1983, it proved to be good at savings mobilization but performed poorly as a lending institution. In 1990, a consensus emerged among the members of its board that fundamental reforms had to be undertaken, resulting in the implementation of measures which led to the transformation of the trust fund into a commercial bank in December 1992. In the framework of a partnership program between German and African savings banks, the newly transformed bank introduced a lending technology based on an analysis of total household income and activities, an incentives-driven repeat loan system, comprehensive but flexible loan security requirements, immediate recovery action backed by an MIS providing computerized daily loan tracking, and powerful staff and client performance incentives. The same approach was also applied to agricultural finance, and its successful implementation and consistent application throughout the institution made Centenary an *African flagship of rural and agricultural banking reform* (Seibel 2003b), combining sustainability with outreach to rural and peri-urban low-income people. During this phase the bank's main focus was on MSE finance.

The early 2000s marked the beginning of another period of institutional reorientation: the conversion of an MSE bank into an MSME bank, with loans for medium enterprises being added to the product range. During the 1990s, in an effort to solve its loan delinquency problem, the bank had introduced a staff performance incentive system which rewarded portfolio quality (i.e. high repayment rates) rather than productivity (i.e. portfolio growth). This led to excellent repayment performance, but resulted at the same time in unsatisfactory expansion of borrower outreach and a steadily increasing volume of surplus liquidity, generated through very effective savings mobilization drives. The bank responded to this challenge by changing its incentive strategy so as to resolve its quality vs. productivity dilemma – by striking the right balance between incentives to maintain high repayment rates and incentives to increase disbursements.

The results of the reforms undertaken by Centenary have been impressive. They have shown that the conversion of an MFI into a commercial bank, and its subsequent restructuring and reorientation, are feasible in Africa, without mission drift. Through its successful evolution and transformation, Centenary Bank has thus demonstrated the feasibility of self-reliance through savings mobilization and the compatibility of MSE finance with medium-enterprise finance, and even incipient corporate finance.

An increasing number of banks and deposit-taking MFIs in Africa and elsewhere are finding themselves in a situation similar to that which Centenary faced. Rapid growth in depositor and borrower outreach, in deposits and loans outstanding, is likely to cause many of them to reach a point where they are undercapitalized, as capital tends to grow more slowly than deposits. Here is where donors can help: with investments in equity or quasi-equity, rather than by providing funds in the form of credit lines which the local MFIs are then expected to use to grant loans.

2.5.3 The microbanking units of Bank Rakyat Indonesia: A miracle or simply good microfinance practice?

This case study deals with the microbanking units of the century-old Bank Rakyat Indonesia (BRI). They were created in 1969 as conduits for the distribution of subsidized state-funded credit and converted in 1984 into commercial financial intermediaries – 16 years before the restructuring of BRI in 2000, which was undertaken to address the serious problems the bank faced as a result of the Asian financial crisis. In a broader context, the conversion of the units must be seen as part of the variegated history of the reform of state-owned agricultural development banks in Indonesia, and of the transformation of BRI into a commercial bank, which, at a later stage (2003), was partially privatized. The following discussion endeavors to explain precisely what the conversion of the microbanking units involved and what has accounted for their stunning success. It also seeks to shed light on the key factors which enabled the units to perform so well as savings-led commercial microfinance providers, and thus to successfully weather first the Asian financial crisis and the concomitant meltdown of BRI in 1998, and then the global crisis of 2008/09.

Bank Rakyat Indonesia: a history of crisis and reform

The impetus for the creation of the people's (*rakyat*) credit system in Indonesia was provided by globalization, poverty, and crisis. In the last decades of the 19th century, there were a number of factors which had a sustained adverse effect on the rural population, leading over time to its impoverishment: coercive recruitment of plantation labor until 1870; the opening up of the rural sector to European and Chinese capital by the Dutch colonial administration after the adoption of the Agrarian Law of 1870, which exposed the sector to the fluctuations of global markets; a land shortage caused by an expanding plantation economy; a global commodity crisis in 1884 which led to the collapse of Indonesia's agricultural investment banking sector; and a growing level of indebtedness on the part of the indigenous rural population vis-à-vis Chinese and Arab moneylenders. As in various European countries during the 19th century, usury and the widespread indebtedness to which it gave rise were seen as a major cause of impoverishment – and were thus regarded as a social as well as a political problem which threatened the stability of the Dutch colonial system. In the first decades of the 20th century, creation of a popular credit system – dedicated to providing what would today be called "inclusive finance" – appeared to be a panacea, and the question of how best to achieve this objective was hotly debated, with attention centering on a discussion of issues such as social vs. commercial banking, centralized vs. decentralized institutions, subsidized vs. commercial credit, and government dependence vs. self-reliance.

This is the historical background for the emergence of BRI, which occupied a central place in these policy debates. BRI owes its origins to Raden Bei Aria Wirjaatmadja, who was Vice-Regent of Bayumas in central Java in the late 19th century. In 1894 he made a loan out of his own pocket to a teacher to pay back a usurious loan, and in 1895 he founded *De Poerwokertosche Hulp en Spaarbank,* a loan and savings bank – the first cooperative financial institution in Indonesia – which was licensed in 1897 as a member-owned *Volksbank (bank rakyat).* The founding date, December 16, 1895, was later recognized as the date of establishment of PT BRI. Providing savings products and credit in cash or kind to both Indonesians and Europeans, it served as a model for a decentralized popular credit system of microbanking institutions which was created in the early 20th century and by 1913 comprised 75 district banks, 12,424 "paddy banks" *(lumbung desa)* and 1,336 "money banks" *(bank desa).* In 1934 a central apex institution for the system – the *Algemeene Volkscredietbank* – was established. After many transformations and changes of name, this system eventually evolved into BRI, which was reestablished in 1968 as a commercial bank whose mandate also included lending in support of national policies to promote the agricultural sector and rural development. In line with the dual economy concept[45] of the colonial period, BRI was given a dual function: commercial *general* lending to SMEs in accordance with standard banking criteria for credit extension and concessionary *special* loan programs for small farmers and microentrepreneurs. After 1968, heavily subsidized credit programs designed by government and donor agencies increasingly dominated BRI's agenda.[46]

---

45 In the colonial-era concept of the *dual economy,* a modern, export-oriented economic sector coexisted alongside a more traditional, often agriculturally based sector serving local needs.
46 For more details, see BRI 1995; Patten and Rosengard 1991; Schmit 1994; Seibel 1989, 2009: 27–31; Robinson 2001.

The reform and reorientation of the BRI units: from subsidized credit to savings-based self-reliance

In 1969 BRI was designated as the sole implementing bank for a program of subsidized agricultural credit with the objective of assuring the country's self-sufficiency in rice production. Liquidity was made available by the central bank, with credit insurance being provided by a state insurance company. As the delivery channel, BRI established a network of village units (*unit desa*). Their number grew rapidly, rising from 18 in 1969 to 537 in 1970, 2,131 in 1973 and 3,617 in 1982. For the borrowers, the actual benefits of obtaining subsidized credit were extremely limited due to several factors: a shift of transaction costs from lender to borrower; burdensome procedures; restriction of loan purposes to targeted agricultural production; frequent delays in disbursement; and illegal extra charges demanded by loan officers, which in turn prevented them from enforcing repayment. In the absence of incentives to repay, the default rate surged to above 50%, resulting in heavy losses (Kuiper 2004; Robinson 2004).

The decline in the price of oil in 1982 led to a reorientation in Indonesia's rural finance policy. The government responded to the loss of revenues from oil exports by initiating an era of deregulation and a shift from a supply-driven to a demand-oriented approach in rural finance. Policy measures enacted in 1983 included full interest rate deregulation, the elimination of credit ceilings and a reduction in the provision of central bank liquidity. This led to the termination of disbursements by the BRI units, putting the future of Indonesia's largest rural credit delivery network – which employed 45% of BRI's staff – at risk. BRI was given two options: closing or reforming the units.

In August 1983 BRI was placed under new management, which opted for the latter course, encouraged by the Minister of Finance. With technical assistance from the HIID, a new system was designed, turning the village units into commercial microbanking units which were to be operational as of February 1984.

Under the new system the units were detached from the branches and placed within a new, separate administrative structure. The units were designed to remain small, with the standard staff size set at four, expandable up to 11. They were turned into self-sustaining profit centers with substantial profit-sharing incentives for their staff members, but it was stipulated that if arrears exceeded 5%, unit managers would lose their lending authority as well as their career prospects. Units were moved from rice planting areas to centers of commercial activity, and were in most cases located at BRI's sub-district (*kecamatan*) centers, providing financial services to both the farming and the non-farming population; unprofitable units would be closed or downgraded to service posts. Training and retraining measures were organized on a large scale at regional centers. The units were no longer involved in any way with government- or donor-supported programs; such lending activities were handled exclusively by the branches.

At the market segment level, the units moved away from the previous commodity-oriented approach with its emphasis on farmers, crop agriculture, and seasonal loans. Under the new system, loans were extended to any creditworthy person and for any income-generating activity such as petty trade, trade in agricultural inputs, production, services, smallholder agriculture, horticulture, small plantations and livestock, and consumer credit was also provided. The units began taking a proactive approach to the market: Anyone able to save and repay his or her loans was a potential customer, with no compulsory savings requirement and no targeted lending.

At the product level, the credit bias of the units was replaced by an equal emphasis on innovations in both savings and credit. Later on, money transfer, check clearing, and bill payment services were added, and unlimited withdrawals of savings were permitted at any unit throughout the country. In emergencies and other situations where customers urgently needed funds, this enabled them to draw upon their savings instead of going into debt. Based on calculations of the transaction costs entailed in microsavings and microcredit, two new commercial products were designed and implemented, both with rates of interest in line with current market rates. One was a rural savings product called "Simpedes," which offered unlimited withdrawals and a lottery component with prizes awarded in monthly public events and complemented demand and time deposits and other savings products. Of the gross interest rate of 13%, savers received 11.5%, while 1.5% was put into the prize fund. Except during the Asian financial crisis, inflation rates in Indonesia were single-digit, and thus returns were positive in real terms. Simpedes turned out to be immensely popular and was a very effective instrument of resource mobilization.

The other innovation was a non-targeted general credit product called "Kupedes," open to all and available for any purpose. Thus, from the bank's point of view, better loan portfolio diversification could now be achieved through a single product. Loan sizes initially started at levels as low as USD 3,[47] with amounts ranging up to a maximum of USD 5,000. The features of the Kupedes loan included simple procedures, short maturities, regular monthly installments, flexible collateral requirements, incentives for timely repayment, provision of repeat loans contingent upon timely and complete repayment of previous loans, and market rates of interest. The loan interest rate was 44% p.a., minus 11% for timely repayment. The net effective interest rate for the overwhelming majority of borrowers (i.e. the 95–99% who paid on time) was thus 33%, which was sufficient to cover all costs and risks. With increasing scale and efficiency, interest rates have come down over time. By 2008 terms and conditions had become more flexible; taking into account the discount for timely repayment, the effective annual interest rate ranged between 16.5% and 24.75% p.a. in nominal terms, or between 7% and

---

[47] In 2004 Robinson (2004, 12) reported a minimum loan size of USD 25. Loans below USD 100 are rare nowadays.

15 % p. a. in real terms, depending on the loan size. The discount turned out to be a powerful incentive to repay on time. The arrears rate (≥1 day), which stood at 5.4 % in 1984, fell to just over 1 %, a level at which it has remained since 2005. The number of loan accounts has grown steadily every year except during the Asian financial crisis, and in 2012 it reached 5.5 million, with the total outstanding portfolio amounting to USD 11.04 billion.[48]

Mandatory loan protection life insurance coverage has been included in all Kupedes loans from the very beginning, with the unpaid balance being covered in case of death. Following a successful pilot program in 2009 to test the feasibility of providing health insurance, BRI also began offering health insurance coverage to all Kupedes borrowers with a loan above IDR 10 million (approx. USD 1,000) and to their dependents. There is a one-time premium of IDR 50,000 (USD 5) for each person so insured, payable at the time of loan disbursement.[49]

Three sources of funds were available to the BRI units at the time of their conversion into commercial providers of microbanking services: (i) an injection of USD 196 million in 1984 by the government as start-up liquidity, which had been used in full by 1986; (ii) a World Bank loan of USD 102 million (USD 5 million for technical assistance in 1987 and USD 97 million for onlending in 1989, which, however, was reallocated due to surplus liquidity at the units); and (iii) savings deposits. By 1986 the units were already turning a profit, and in 1988 and 1989 they accounted for 30 % of BRI's total net income. At the same time an impact study showed that the units were having a significant positive impact on access to credit, also by women, and with regard to poverty alleviation (Yaron, 1992).

In 1989, the units broke even in terms of the ratio between savings mobilized and loans outstanding and began generating surplus liquidity. Ever since, the unit network has been self-reliant and viable insofar as it has mobilized the resources on its own that it needs to fund lending operations and has consistently generated profits. Surplus liquidity continued to grow, reaching a volume of around USD 2 billion every year between 2007 ans 2012. The total surplus mobilized (and transferred to the branches) between 1989 and 2012 came to USD 32.5 billion,[50] which is more an indicator of the remarkable degree of success achieved by the units in savings mobilization than a reflection of limitations in lending outreach.

Savings balances passed the USD 1 billion mark in 1991 and rose to over USD 2 billion in 1993, fell briefly below that level during the Asian financial crisis and subsequently began rising again, reaching USD 13.1 billion in 2012. The net profit achieved by the units amounted to USD 564 million in 2008 and to around USD

---

[48] The average outstanding loan balance grew from USD 197 in 1985 to USD 389 in 1990, rose further to USD 611 in 1995, fell after the 1998 devaluation of the Indonesian rupiah (IDR) to USD 300 in 2000, climbed back to USD 700 in 2005 and reached USD 2,005 in 2012.
[49] 40 % of all borrowers were enrolled in this program as of April 2010.
[50] Calculated using the respective year-end exchange rates.

Snapshot 41: Internal control and supervision of the units

The line management control system includes passive oversight through reporting and active oversight in the form of on-site inspections and audits. It comprises five organizational levels of oversight:

- Internal control within the unit:
  - Separation of functions to mitigate risks: cash transactions (recording, custody of cash, authorization); loan processing (registration, credit analysis, authorization); and non-cash transactions (execution, checking, signing).
  - Daily on-site controls by unit managers.
  - Rotation of unit managers every two years to prevent collusion.
- Branch, supervising 10–35 units:
  - One internal controller (selected from among former unit managers) for every four units: spends four days every month on-site at each of the units for which responsible.
  - Microbusiness manager or assistant manager: carries out on-site controls three to four times per month at each unit supervised by the branch; conducts monthly off-site controls based on reports.
  - Branch manager: conducts on-site controls once a year at each unit supervised by the branch and carries out off-site controls at regular intervals.
- Regional office: monthly off-site controls are carried out for each unit in the region and on-site controls are conducted annually for a sample of units.
- Regional internal audit office: on-site audits are carried out at each unit in the region once every 18 months or more often if necessary.
- Head-office Microbanking Division: On-site controls are carried out at individual units on a case-by-case basis, as needed; monthly off-site controls are conducted for all units.

Source: Based on a presentation by the BRI International Visitors Program, December 2008

900 million in 2012. Self-reliance in terms of resource mobilization and profitability has created the material basis for the units' financial autonomy and freedom from the political interference which had such a deleterious effect on the rest of the Indonesian banking system during the crisis of 1997/98.[51]

The microbanking units of BRI have achieved sound growth on a scale that has enabled them to become the developing world's largest self sustaining micro banking network, comprising 7,128 outlets spread throughout the vast territory of Indonesia: 5,000 units, 1,778 sub-units, and 350 mobile units (figures as of 2012). The units have matured to the point that BRI recently decided it was time to introduce a number of innovations: customized products tailored to the demand observed in a given area; flexible loan periods with maturities of up to six years in-

---

[51] For more details see BRI 1995; BRI reports 1990–2012; Kuiper 2004; Patten and Rosengard 1991; Robinson 2001, 2004; Schmit 1991, 1994/1999; Seibel 2009, Seibel and Rachmadi 2010; and Yaron 1992, 2000.

stead of the maximum of one year which was previously in effect; an increase in the maximum loan amount to USD 10,000, and a growing emphasis on banking services in addition to savings and loans; IT-based services to complement the customer service provided in person by staff (all units are now fully online); electronic data capture (EDC) via palmtops, enabling loan officers to accept cash payments in the field; and a line management system of internal control and supervision (see snapshot 41) (BRI 1990–2012 and Seibel 2009).

The microbanking units during the Asian financial crisis

During the crisis of 1997/98 the Indonesian currency collapsed, and so did the country's commercial banking sector. BRI was one of the insolvent banks, and it was brought down primarily by the failure of its large corporate loan portfolio. From December 1996 to December 1998, total assets in USD terms (after a drastic devaluation) fell from USD 14.44 billion to USD 4.25 billion, and gross loans outstanding from USD 11.23 billion to USD 5.41 billion. Deposits were not as strongly affected, falling only from USD 8.10 billion to USD 5.34 billion. However, total equity was wiped out completely, and indeed, as of December 1998 the bank had negative equity in the amount of -USD 3.08 billion, down from USD 0.76 billion two years earlier; income (before tax) dropped from USD 0.14 billion to -USD 3.31 billion (Seibel 2009).

In December 1996, on the eve of the crisis, the 4,000 microbanking units had 2.5 million loan accounts and a loan portfolio of USD 1.7 billion, with funding provided by 16 million deposit accounts with a total balance of USD 3.0 billion (including USD 1.3 billion in surplus liquidity). Thus, the microbanking units accounted for 15% of the bank's overall loan portfolio and 37% of its deposit balance. More importantly, ROA for the units was 5.7%, compared with 0.7% for the bank as a whole. The combination of extensive outreach and solid financial performance achieved by the units had earned the bank a worldwide reputation of excellence; in fact, the units were so well-known, and so widely acclaimed, that many people believed that the bank *was* its microbanking network. The units' reputation may have been a crucial factor in the government's decision to rescue the institution as a whole, recommitting it to its original mission as an MSME bank.

The monetary crisis did affect the microbanking units, but overall in a positive way. The number of deposit accounts (guaranteed by the government) continued to grow, rising from 16.1 million in 1996 to 18.1 million in 1997, to 21.7 million in 1998, and to 24.2 million in 1999. During the three-month peak crisis period – June and August 1998 – when Indonesia was badly hit by the effects of both a drought and the financial crisis, 1.3 million new deposit accounts were opened in the units, and an additional USD 354 million was deposited. During the crisis, deposits exceeded loans outstanding by a wider margin than ever. Many donors were willing to provide additional funds for lending to the poor, but in contrast to what they had expected, the number of borrowers with loans outstanding from the units fell from 2.6 million in 1997 to 2.5 million in 1998 and 1999 – not because of a shortage of funds, but rather due to the uncertainty about the future which many clients felt.

The crisis had only a moderate effect on repayment, testifying to the effectiveness of the incentives employed by the microbanking units as well as the resilience of the borrowers. There were delays in repayment, as indicated by an increase of the NPL ratio (≥1 day) from 3.7% in 1996 to 5.7% in 1998, but the contrast to BRI as a whole is striking: for the institution overall, the NPL ratio surged from 10.6% in 1996 to 53.0% in 1998. It is interesting to note, and is revealing in terms of what it says about the psychology of the micro borrowers served by the units, that there was *a rush to repay* in August 1998, right after the peak of the crisis, leading to an unprecedented negative one-month arrears ratio of -0.21%, as more was repaid than was actually due. Given the severely distressed economy, borrowers worried that they might not be able to repay in the future. BRI's microbanking division remained profitable throughout the crisis. ROA hardly budged, declining from 5.7% in 1996 to 4.7% in 1997, but recovering to 4.9% in 1998 at the height of the crisis (Seibel 2009, Seibel and Rachmadi 2010).

The restructuring of BRI, and how the microbanking units saved the bank

In sharp contrast to the units, which continued to thrive during the crisis of 1997/98, BRI as a universal bank collapsed. The bank's ROA declined from 0.7% in 1996 to 0.1% in 1997 and turned sharply negative in 1998, when it fell to -77.8%. As a result, the bank had negative equity capital of -USD 3.08 billion in 1998 and -USD 3.70 billion in 1999. BRI was technically insolvent.

Like most banks in Indonesia, whether state-owned or private, BRI could have been closed down or merged. The institution would probably not have survived if it had not been for the microbanking units, or if the government had indeed decided to spin the units off into a new microfinance bank, which was one of the options discussed. Before, during and after the Asian financial crisis, the units cross-subsidized the bank's other operations in two ways: through the continual transfer of profits from the units to the bank, and by transferring surplus savings mobilized at village and sub-district level to the district-level branches. Over the 14-year period from 1990 to 2003, the year when BRI went public, the cumulative net profits of the units totaled USD 1.6 billion, and their cumulative surplus liquidity amounted to USD 15.9 billion. Thus, it was the units which ultimately saved BRI: they provided the basis for the restructuring of BRI in 1999/2000 and thus indirectly for its IPO in 2003. The microbanking network has been lauded as "the most advanced example of the microfinance revolution" (Robinson, 2001) and "a flagship of rural microfinance in Asia" (Seibel, 2005), and the success of the units – as shown by their consistently excellent performance since 1984, their vast outreach and large

large number of well-trained staff, and reflected in their outstanding international reputation – presumably played a key role in the decision to recapitalize BRI.

In August 1998, the government decided to restructure BRI, and in 1999, in cooperation with the IMF, it prepared a complex operational restructuring plan (ORP) for the institution, placing major emphasis on "good corporate governance." The plan included a return to BRI's historic mission of MSME lending, with a primary focus on microfinance and small business lending, while limiting its corporate lending to 20% of the overall portfolio volume. In July 2000, a new board of directors and a new board of commissioners were installed, with specific performance targets and time frames being established for the implementation of the various components of the ORP by the end of 2003. Immediately after the installation of the new boards, BRI was recapitalized with an injection of USD 3.0 billion in government bonds. By the end of 2000 the bank had brought its NPL ratio down to 5%; ROA had turned positive again, reaching its pre-crisis level of 0.7%; and all other indicators met the prudential requirements of Bank Indonesia, the country's central bank.

In November 2003 BRI was partially privatized and listed on the Indonesian Stock Exchange, with the government holding 59.50% of the share capital.[52] Since then the institution has become the most profitable bank in Indonesia, with the largest loan portfolio in the country, and, with 9,052 outlets and 42 million customer accounts, the most extensive outreach as well. Thus, BRI in its present form can be regarded as an outstanding example of the successful restructuring of a state bank. By the end of 2012 its customer deposits amounted to USD 45.1 billion, gross loans outstanding stood at USD 36.0 billion, and it had equity of USD 6.7 billion; the government recapitalization bonds provided in 2000 had been almost fully paid back. Gross NPL stood at 1.78%, net NPL at 0.34%, CAR at 17.0%, ROA before tax at 5.15% and ROE at 38.7%. The bank attributes its excellent performance to the "consistent implementation of the principles of Good Corporate Governance, alongside with operational efficiency" (BRI 2013a), points which are discussed in detail in every annual report (e.g. BRI 2013:214-298).

MSME banking: inclusive access to finance

BRI owes its survival after the crisis of 1997/98 to the performance of the microbanking units as its most profitable business segment, and its overall success during the past decade to its emphasis on MSME banking in urban and rural areas, combined with a thorough restructuring and a substantial reduction of its corporate business. As an MSME bank, BRI offers its clients virtually unlimited opportunities to access the increasing credit amounts and the broader range of financial services they need as their businesses grow over time.

---

52 The shares offered in the IPO were oversubscribed by 15.4 times. Since 2010 the government's equity holding has been stable at 56.75%; four-fifths of the public holding is foreign-owned, one-fifth domestic.

The restructuring carried out between 1999 and 2003 substantially changed BRI's portfolio composition. Lending to the corporate sector was cut by more than half during this period, while micro and small salary-backed or (in the case of small businesses) revenue-backed lending grew from 18.4% to 54.4%. By 2012 these two business segments accounted for almost half of BRI's loan portfolio – with an excellent on-time repayment performance, as shown by NPL ratios (≤1 day) of 1.09% and 1.60%, respectively. Although BRI has struggled with its larger SME loans, it has achieved a substantial consolidation in this segment, as reflected in the reduction in the share of small commercial loans (up to USD 500,000) in the portfolio from 42.9% in 1998 to 21.7% in 2012 and the decline in the NPL ratio in this category to 3.75% in 2012. With an NPL ratio of 5.1%, medium-scale loans (up to USD 5 million) are now the most challenging segment. Amazingly, loans to state-owned enterprises (SOEs), comprising 14.3% of the portfolio, show no arrears, indicating the absence of undue government interference. At the same time, the NPL ratio for private corporate loans, comprising 11% of the portfolio, has come down to 1.0% – in other words, this segment has gone from being the worst performer in terms of NPL to being the top performer by this measure (see Table 14).

The microbanking units during the global crisis

2008/09 marked the 25th anniversary of the reform and reorientation of the units. This also happened to be the time when the global crisis hit Indonesia. It is thus worth examining how the units have coped since then. As of December 2009, BRI's microbanking units managed a total of 21.2 million deposit accounts, down from 32.2 million in 2005. The decline in numbers was due to the closing of inactive accounts, but deposit volumes continued to grow, from USD 3.7 billion in 2005 to USD 8.0 billion in 2008 and USD 13.1 billion as of 2012.[53]

Table 14: BRI's loan portfolio and non-performing loan ratios (≥1 day) by business segment, Dec. 2012

Business segment	Maximum loan size in USD*	Loan portfolio		NPL ratio in %
		in billion USD**	in %	
Micro	5,000	11.0	30.7	1.09
Consumer	20,000	6.4	17.7	1.60
Small commercial	500,000	7.8	21.7	3.75
Medium	5 million	1.7	4.7	5.09
State-owned enterprises		5.1	14.3	0.00
Corporate	> 5 million	3.9	10.9	1.00
Total BRI		36.0	100.0	1.78

* Calculated at a rate of IDR 10,000/USD 1
** Calculated at an exchange rate of IDR 9,670/USD 1 as per 31 Dec. 2012
Source: Based on BRI Financial Update FY 2012

---

53 The value of the Indonesian rupiah (IDR) against the USD fell from IDR 9,419 at the end of 2007 to IDR 10,950 at the end of 2008 and had recovered to IDR 9,400 by the end of 2009; as of 2012 the the exchange rate to the USD stood at IDR 9,670.

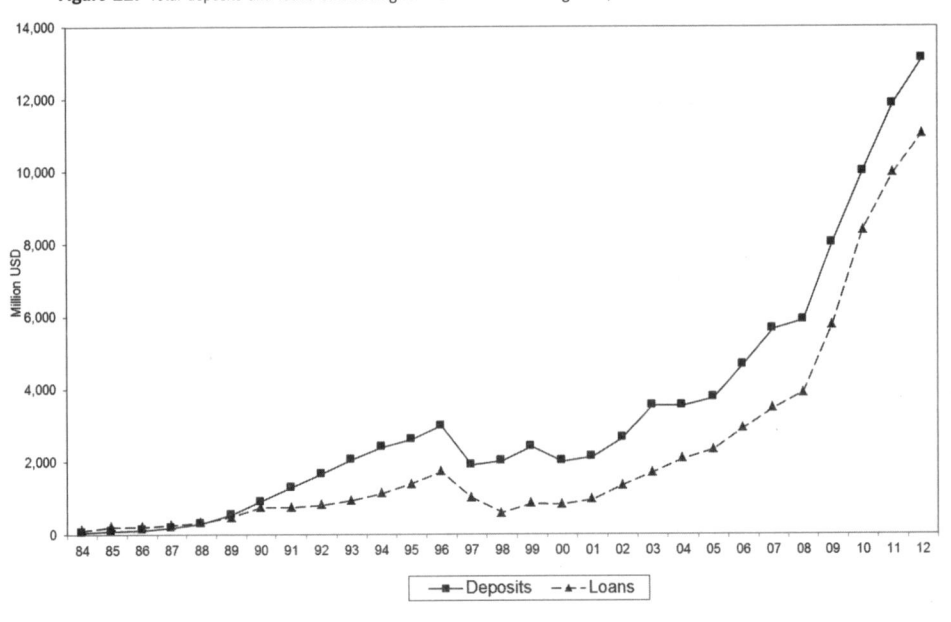

Figure 22: Total deposits and loans outstanding for the BRI microbanking units, 1984–2012

Between December 2005 and December 2009 the number of loan accounts grew from 3.3 million to 4.7 million and the volume of loans outstanding rose from USD 2.3 billion to USD 5.7 billion, in both cases without any change in the direction of the trend over the entire period, and with a surge in the number of accounts in 2008 and in the volume of loans outstanding in 2009; growth thereafter was steady, with the number of borrowers reaching 5.5 million and the loan portfolio volume standing at USD 11.0 billion as of December 2012. As Figure 22 shows, neither the growth of deposits nor that of the outstanding loan volume was in any way impeded by the global financial crisis.

Annual net profits surged from USD 250.2 million in 2005 to USD 524.3 million in 2007 and continued to grow throughout the crisis, reaching USD 787 million in 2009; in the following years they increased still further, rising to USD 904 million in 2012. ROA continued to increase every year, climbing from 7.0% in 2005 to 9.8% in 2008 and to an all-time high of 10.2% in 2009,[54] and thus was apparently not adversely affected in any way by the crisis.

Conclusions

The microbanking units of BRI are a heavyweight in commercial microfinance. With a savings-to-loan ratio of 119% as of 2012, they are obviously savings-led. At relatively moderate and historically declining interest rates, they have achieved an ROA of around 10% in recent years. Crises have played a crucial role in the microbanking units' evolution. Just as BRI, the bank of which they are a part,

---

54 ROA for 2010–12 is not available.

owes its origin to the process of globalization in the late 19th century and the crises to which it gave rise, the impetus for the thoroughgoing reform of the units almost 100 years later was also provided by a crisis. They were created in 1969 as a policy instrument for channeling subsidized agricultural credit, following the dominant paradigm of the time. When the oil price fell in 1982, the resulting decline in revenues meant that the government was no longer able to absorb the losses incurred by the units. Confronted with the choice between closing or reforming them, the government appointed a new management which opted for restructuring and reform. Local autonomy coupled with effective regulation and supervision of the network as an integral part of BRI, powerful incentives for customers and staff, savings-based self-reliance, commercial interest rates, profitability, and inclusive national outreach were the core principles which guided the design and operation of the reformed units. Within a few years they were achieving ever-increasing saver and borrower outreach, and also generating profits and liquidity surpluses.

When the Asian financial crisis hit and the Indonesian banking sector collapsed, the micro-banking units proved to be resilient. Secure deposits with positive real returns, withdrawable anywhere and at any time, and easy access to repeat loans for any purpose at competitive interest rates had made them the most trusted local financial intermediaries in Indonesia. While other institutions failed due to bank runs and mounting defaults, the units succeeded in collecting loan repayments as well as vast amounts of additional deposits. As the savers turned out to be the most effective "supervisors" of the units (using deposits and withdrawals as instruments of control), with further discipline being provided by a complex system of internal control and external supervision, profitability remained high. BRI was one of the insolvent banks, having been pulled down by the dead weight of its corporate portfolio. The government's decision to restructure BRI, rather than merging it with other defunct state banks, was to a considerable extent attributable to the outstanding performance of the unit system and its international reputation. At no other time were the strength and resilience of the BRI microbanking units more apparent than during the Asian financial crisis.

The experience of the units was one of the driving forces behind the successful restructuring and reform of BRI after the crisis of 1998. Ever since 1984 BRI has effectively applied the principles of good corporate governance, efficient resource mobilization, and sound risk management in microbanking; and since 2000, by applying those same principles across its entire lending business, it has also become a model provider of commercial finance to small and medium enterprises as well as the corporate sector (Seibel 2009).

2.5.4 The ProCredit Banks

The ProCredit Group, which is based in Germany, is an interesting example of a complex microfinance organization. At the time of writing, this group consists of

20 banks in as many countries – both developing and transition economies – as well as their parent company, ProCredit Holding AG & Co. KGaA (PCH), in Frankfurt; a subsidiary called Quipu which provides IT services for the group and is also based in Frankfurt; and ProCredit Bank AG, which was recently licensed as a universal bank in Germany and offers banking services within Germany as well as in some of the countries where local ProCredit Banks operate. The consulting firm Internationale Projekt Consult (IPC), which founded PCH and is also its largest single shareholder, remains closely associated with the ProCredit Banks and the group as a whole. In fact, the history of ProCredit, as it evolved over the years to become the international banking group that it is today, is closely intertwined with that of IPC and the specific approach to development finance which IPC originated and continuously refined in the implementation of financial-sector projects in developing and transition countries.

The ProCredit Group has a dual character. On the one hand, it is a group made up of local banks that serve micro,[55] small and medium-sized firms and the general local population, plus some additional institutions which carry out coordination and support functions. The group used to call the affiliated banks "microfinance banks," but now refers to them as "banks for ordinary people" or "neighborhood banks."

On the other hand, if one focuses more on the group's center or "hub," the holding company seems more like a microfinance support institution similar to organizations such as ACCION. The difference, however, is that PCH not only supports its affiliated banks; it also owns the majority of the shares in all of the banks that belong to the group, and in some cases indeed holds 100% of the equity. Therefore, in a strict legal sense it is also the central coordinating entity with authority over, and responsibility for, a group of companies.[56]

PCH, which was founded as a corporation in 1998, had grown out of the activities of IPC, which had been established almost 20 years earlier. Over the years IPC had become one of the leading consulting firms in development finance with a specialization in the creation or transformation of financial institutions, among them Centenary Bank in Uganda, which was presented as a case study earlier, and a reputation for being a fervent advocate of the institution building approach. IPC and PCH and their key actors and core staff are convinced that stable and well-organized institutions are an essential element of financial, economic, and social development.

---

55 However, the provision of credit to really small firms has recently been discontinued; see the end of this subsection.
56 According to German corporation law, the ProCredit Group is a group of companies under common direction and control (*Konzern*) and PCH, as the controlling entity within this group, is responsible for joint, group-wide reporting and group-wide financial and risk management in accordance with the provisions of German corporation law. As the subordinated companies within this group are banks, the "controlling entity", i.e. PCH, has also been responsible, since 2012, for ensuring compliance by the group as a whole with German banking regulation and all risk-related reporting requirements.

Both perspectives – that which focuses on ProCredit as a group of local banks, and that which emphasizes the role of the core institution at the center in guiding and directing the operations of the group – have their merits: the IPC–PCH complex is indeed one of the world's largest and most successful groups of banks for "ordinary people," and at the same time it is also an organization that continuously refines its approach. Since IPC and PCH as organizations, and their roles as innovative forces for change in development finance, evolved in parallel with the concepts of social banking and institution building, their history can help us understand how modern microfinance initially emerged and also matured over the years. The series of transformations that took place at the banks in the group, as well as in the organizations at the group's core, i.e. IPC and PCH, reflect an attempt to reconcile the requirements of running a financially viable, stable, and also profitable business with the often conflicting requirements entailed in achieving the developmental, social, and political goals defined by the group's founders and key staff members – a conflict which is typical of socially-oriented financial institutions. In this sense, the case of IPC–ProCredit is paradigmatic.[57]

The early history of IPC and its first social banking projects

IPC was founded as a consulting firm in 1981. The decision to create such a firm took shape in the course of a tour of three countries – Nicaragua, Colombia, and Ecuador – by a group of experts who had been sent by the German Federal Ministry for Economic Cooperation and Development (BMZ) to investigate what the "developmental effects of the German support to [national] development banks" might be. What the team found and later documented in its report was a shocking combination of incompetence, irresponsibility, and waste. For one member of the team, Dr. Claus-Peter Zeitinger, the experience provided the answer to the question of what he wanted to do with his life, namely: getting seriously and professionally involved in development finance and doing "the same thing [we] were observing [that is, development finance and related aid activities], but doing it right." This became the mission of IPC, and Zeitinger became its undisputed leader. He was also its principal owner for many years, with his wife Gabriele Heber also holding a share of the company's equity.

About two years later, IPC began implementing a consulting project in Peru which was funded directly by the German Association of Savings Banks (DSGV) and indirectly by the German government. Its aim was to create a savings bank in Piura, a mid-sized town in northern Peru, and, if it were deemed to be feasible, to set up a network of savings banks covering several areas of the country outside the Lima metropolitan area. The advice and political support provided by the German

---

[57] This section draws heavily on the experience of one of the present authors, who was involved in the development of IPC and many of its early projects as an advisor and later served for five years as the first chairman of the supervisory board of PCH. For an account of the early years, see Schmidt (2005).

Association of Savings Banks and its then president, Helmut Geiger, proved to be essential for the success of the project.

The savings banks in Peru were modeled on, and drew upon the historical tradition of, Germany's savings banks. They were municipal institutions, called municipal savings and credit banks (*cajas municipales de ahorro y crédito*, or CMAC), and were organized, operated and governed under a public law regime. From the very beginning, the *cajas* focused on savings mobilization, which was particularly difficult at that time since government-imposed interest rate ceilings in Peru were almost always below the high and very erratic inflation rates. Lending at first took the form of pawn loans, with gold (jewelry and other items) being pledged to serve as collateral. Only after some time did the *cajas* also begin making loans to small and very small businesses which did not have access to loans from other banks.

The initial phase of the institutions' development was successful. It proved possible to attract deposits even in a high-inflation environment, to channel loans to those who were meant to receive them, and to have borrowers pay back what they owed with almost no loan losses. In a short time, other cities also created their own *cajas* based on the model of the *Caja Municipal* in Piura. An association of *cajas*, a central training institution and a central auditing unit were created. The consultants even drafted a savings banks law which the Peruvian government later issued as a "*decreto supremo*," and with German-funded advisory assistance provided by IPC, the country's banking supervisory authority created a special division responsible for *cajas municipales*. As a result of all of these initiatives, a new and ambitious concept of financial institution building was "invented" and its potential was made visible to the community of aid experts.

The only serious problem faced by the *cajas* was their small size and the resulting high unit costs of granting loans. In an effort to solve this problem, the IPC consultants procured external funding from the Inter-American Development Bank (IDB). This did help to increase the size of the banks and to lower their costs. But it also led to conflicts within the *caja* system and to even more serious disagreements between its protagonists at IPC and the German Association of Savings Banks on the one side, and the German development agency GTZ, which had by that time become IPC's official German contract partner, on the other.

As a consequence of this conflict, GTZ terminated its contract with IPC. There were various reasons for this rupture, but it was clearly not attributable to a failure of the project to achieve its objectives or to poor performance by the *cajas municipales*.[58] In view of the purpose of this study, it may be worth mentioning that

---

58 Most of the *cajas municipales* have continued to perform very well in both financial and developmental terms right up to the present day. This is true in particular of the larger *cajas*, especially the one in Arequipa, which is regularly counted among Latin America's most successful MFIs. The public law regime under which the banks at first operated was abandoned sometime after IPC left the project, but the shares of the *caja* corporations that are now in existence are held exclusively by the respective municipalities.

among the reasons given by GTZ for terminating the contract was that the similarity between the underlying concept on which the Peruvian *cajas municipales* were based and that which provided the foundation for the German savings banks was too pronounced and, more specifically, that the "ownership" of the institutions by the respective municipalities and the public law regime were "a birth defect" that had burdened the *cajas* from the very beginning – this according to one influential GTZ staff member.[59]

For IPC the project in Peru was more than anything else a learning opportunity. In this setting the firm developed its specific lending methodology for very small businesses operating in the informal sector. Most MFIs that were in operation in Latin America in the 1980s and 1990s employed a group lending methodology which was inspired by the example of the Grameen Bank. In contrast, the *cajas* and all of the other banks that were later founded or supported by IPC issued individual loans, with good results. In addition, the success of the project created confidence, on the part of both the IPC staff and many of its business partners in the development aid community, that the firm was indeed very good at building sustainable financial institutions with a good chance of relatively quickly reaching a point where they could grant a large number of small loans and also cover their costs.

Even though one may question the diagnosis of a "birth defect," it is fair to admit that the *caja* system, with its network of decentralized and jointly operated and utilized support institutions and its ties to various donors, external funders, and local government agencies, was indeed complex and perhaps overly complex. However, the basic principles behind the institutional design of the *caja* system were sound and very carefully conceived, and recognition of this fact generated further interest in IPC's work among donor institutions.[60] While the *caja* project was still underway, IPC was given contracts for two other projects geared to building strong target group-oriented financial institutions in Latin America. One of the resulting institutions eventually became Caja Los Andes in Bolivia, and the other formed the basis of what was later to become Financiera Calpiá in El Salvador. Originally, these institutions were founded as NGOs, but from the outset their founders intended to convert them as soon as possible into licensed and supervised target group-oriented financial institutions.

Both of these MFIs have become stable organizations that play a leading role in their respective countries' financial sectors. Today, both are formal banks and are

---

59 It must be noted here that, similarly to the situation of German savings banks, under the public law regime the municipalities were not "owners" – as the individual we quoted erroneously assumed – but rather trustees with a legal position that was only to a certain extent equivalent to that of the owner of a corporation. Only once the legal status of the *cajas* was altered (see the preceding footnote) did the municipalities become owners in a strict sense.
60 That this complexity was a very good example of what he calls "systemic intelligence," resulting from the cleverly devised interaction between various parties, is explained in detail in an analysis of the *caja* system by Manfred Nitsch, one of the academics involved in the design of the system as a consultant; see Nitsch 1997. For details of the project and the development of the *cajas* also see Lepp (1996). Anja Lepp served as IPC's on-site project manager in Peru for several years.

members of the ProCredit Group, as is clearly reflected in their current names, Banco Los Andes ProCredit Bolivia and Banco ProCredit El Salvador. The institutional structure implemented in Bolivia and El Salvador was less complex than that used in Peru, but it retained the focus on achieving a balance between commercial and developmental goals, as well as a clear allocation of responsibilities and the establishment of mechanisms which ensured that leaders remained committed to the organizations' dual objectives.

With the three organizations in Peru, Bolivia, and El Salvador having almost achieved the status of model MFIs, IPC had established a solid reputation for itself, creating what amounted to a brand, and it had certainly also created a general awareness of what was becoming known as the financial institution building approach to microfinance. One factor may have played a particularly important role in the success of IPC and its projects: By the mid-1990s, the firm's managers had correctly diagnosed that very high costs were the key problem facing microfinance and that interest rates high enough to cover all costs would be the main impediment to outreach and developmental impact. IPC decided that the solution – lowering costs substantially and making MFIs' operations more efficient – could only be achieved through the utilization of information technology on a substantial scale. Therefore, IPC proceeded to create a special software system for MFIs which for quite some time was the only effective IT system of its kind in use anywhere in the world. Being able to have information available that is reliable and easy to store and can be retrieved at any moment by the bank staff, including the responsible loan officers, greatly helped implementing the individual lending technology on a large scale. In a certain sense, IPC's innovative IT system served as a substitute for the information gathering process that takes place within the groups in the competing credit technology of the group lending approach. However, for the ProCredit banks it has the advantage that the information is collected by the finance institution – and is not only available within the groups – and can therefore be used for rating clients on the basis of their past repayment performance and "rewarding" those who properly repaid earlier loans by offering them better terms on repeat loans. This pricing policy strengthens the incentives for the clients to make payments of interest and principal on time when they are due. Moreover, having information at any time about clients that are in arrears helps to keep delinquency at a low level, since loan officers can start their working day by checking which borrowers are falling into arrears and call on them immediately. Finally and possibly most importantly, having such an IT system contributes greatly to reducing the formerly very high cost of lending to small and very small businesses.

Downscaling, going east, and the expansion of IPC

Even though the work of IPC and a few other development consulting firms in Latin America led to the emergence of a few very good MFIs, generated important insights, know-how and reputational capital for the consultants, and created benefits for the clients who obtained loans from the newly created institutions, these efforts had clear limitations: At that time, the outreach of even the best MFIs was limited, and the costs of setting up a viable MFI seemed very high to those who were supposed to bear them, i.e. the international development institutions. In Latin America, the most important such institution was the IDB.

IDB was the first international financier and donor to provide funding for the search for a new approach to organizing the provision of microfinance in Latin America. IDB awarded a contract to IPC in which the firm was requested to develop and try out a new approach, which was later called "downscaling." A downscaling program involves, first of all, identifying a number of banks in a given country that are prepared to create their own internal microfinance divisions and to subsequently allow these divisions to operate largely in the same way as independent MFIs would, and secondly providing support to the banks in setting up and running such divisions.[61]

IPC's first IDB-funded downscaling projects worked well. But they were not the kind of "success stories" that would have greatly inspired donors or development experts, not to mention the general public. Creating free-standing MFIs or converting credit-granting NGOs into institutions of this type simply seemed to be more attractive.

However, only a little later, downscaling became truly important for IPC, with a new opportunity arising halfway around the world: in Russia and other parts of the former Soviet Union. A new manager had been given responsibility for microfinance in Russia at the London-based European Bank for Reconstruction and Development (EBRD). She learned about the downscaling programs in Latin America and ended up hiring IPC as a consulting firm to run one of the largest financial-sector projects ever implemented by the EBRD: the "Russia Small Business Fund." At its peak, this project involved almost 100 local banks and large numbers of consultants who were selected, hired, and trained by IPC and whose work in Russia, and later also in similar programs carried out in neighboring countries, was coordinated and monitored by IPC's staff. Much like its early projects in Latin America, IPC's downscaling projects in the east – in Russia and other parts of the former Soviet Union – were successful for all parties involved. The responsible managers at the EBRD, and subsequently those at various other donors organizations as well, were happy to see their institutions' developmental mandate being fulfilled efficiently, and most participating banks were happy to increase the range of services they were able to offer. A considerable number of clients did indeed gain access to bank loans for the first time ever, and one can assume that they were also happy to be served well. Lending volumes reached im-

---

[61] See also section 4, where downscaling is described in more detail.

pressive dimensions in a short time. The Russian financial crisis of 1998 led to a sudden cessation of almost all financial sector-related EBRD projects and programs. The only one that survived the crisis was the Russia Small Business Fund.

For IPC as a firm, "going east" was also a successful strategy: For the first time since its founding, IPC became a profitable enterprise, and the process of recruiting, training, and managing the large number of bank advisors working in these downscaling projects offered the firm an unprecedented opportunity to get to know literally hundreds of young consultants. The best among them were soon identified internally as candidates for long-term careers with IPC, and the opportunity to offer such careers to promising young staff members proved to be just around the corner, in the form of a revival of the older tradition of creating new free-standing MFIs.

The creation and rapid expansion of ProCredit Holding

The Dayton Accord of 1995, which ended the war between Serbia and Bosnia, contained a clause stipulating that the international community would create a microfinance bank in war-torn Bosnia. IPC was selected to design this bank and provide training and other advisory services to support its operations. One of the individuals involved in planning the bank on behalf of the project sponsors had a background as an investment banker. He was convinced that all consultants are fundamentally lazy and, when things don't work out as planned, invariably attempt to hide their own failures by claiming that the lack of success is due to adverse circumstances beyond their control. Accordingly, he argued that, in this case – where the circumstances were bound to be very adverse – strong incentives were needed to ensure that the interests of the consultant were aligned with those of the project sponsors. He thus recommended that the consulting firm, IPC, should be required to be a co-investor in the equity of the new bank.

This specific incentive was not really necessary for IPC because, by taking on this challenging institution building project, IPC was putting its professional reputation on the line, which was much more valuable than the moderate sum the company was expected to invest. But Dr. Zeitinger was pleased that IPC would become a co-owner in addition to being the consulting firm tasked with designing the institution and supporting the initiation of its operations, because being a co-owner would facilitate the creation of what IPC considered to be really good MFIs.

The bank in Bosnia was set up, began operations and achieved financial sustainability faster than had been anticipated. Most of those who had at first been reluctant to make a consultant participate in the undertaking as a co-investor agreed that what had worked in Bosnia should be replicated in other countries in Southeastern Europe, for example Georgia, Albania, and Kosovo, where IPC was either already working, or was about to start working, as the consulting firm on projects similar to the one in Bosnia. But IPC simply did not have the necessary funds to acquire additional equity stakes. Therefore, it created the investment or equity participation company which today is known as ProCredit Holding, or PCH for short.[62]

PCH was founded in Frankfurt in 1998 with equity of only about half a million euros and almost no staff. During a very brief initial period, the only shareholders of PCH were private-sector entities, essentially only IPC and a Dutch foundation. All of the administrative work involved in running the company was handled by IPC staff, during the first few years without any financial compensation being paid to IPC and with no clear institutional separation between IPC and PCH. But already after only a few months, PCH began to expand dramatically. New investments were undertaken in banks that still only existed on paper and which IPC was supposed to design, set up, and manage on behalf of the international donor community, and also in the Latin American institutions that IPC had created several years previously and in which some of the original investors had had to sell their stakes after reaching predetermined internal time limits for their equity investments. In only four years, by the end of 2002, PCH had become a large organization operating 16 banks in as many countries. At the end of that year, the number of staff employed by the banks stood at 4,700, the number of branches had risen to 224, and the aggregated loan portfolio had grown to EUR 347 million.

The new banks created in transition countries in Southeastern Europe typically had six shareholders, each holding an equal percentage of the equity. PCH was one of shareholders, and the others were international financial institutions (IFIs) such as the IFC (the World Bank's private sector investment arm), Germany's KfW, the Dutch organization FMO, and the EBRD, and also Commerzbank, a large German private-sector bank. Initial funding, including technical assistance grants and loans to provide onlending funds, was made available by the IFIs.

As it was undertaking equity investments on a substantial scale, PCH also had to increase its own capital. Since the joint management of IPC and PCH regarded the use of borrowed funds for this purpose as too risky, it encouraged those major IFIs that regularly utilized IPC's consultancy services in financial institution building projects, and also regularly joined it in contributing equity to the new banks, to also become shareholders in PCH. IFC, KfW, and FMO accepted the invitation; only EBRD did not. This changed the ownership structure of PCH, but the dominance of private sector entities was maintained because the combined equity share held by such entities always remained slightly above a 50% threshold.

With the IFIs being shareholders both in the new banks and in PCH, and also having seats on all relevant supervisory boards, and in addition serving as the pro-

---

[62] The newly founded investment company was initially called "Internationale Micro Investitionen AG," a name which was replaced by "ProCredit Holding AG" in 2003.

viders of start-up subsidies and initial funding through their loans to the new banks, they had sufficient control over how IPC and PCH operated. Since new banks were being set up in rapid succession, the IFIs could have easily sanctioned deficient performance on the part of IPC, if this had been necessary, by simply declining to co-finance the creation of the next new bank. This would have put a halt to the expansion of PCH. While this set-up was a sound internal governance regime for the ProCredit Group, it could only function properly if the scale of the group as a whole was small enough to ensure that the public-sector investors, the IFIs, could remain well informed.

For IPC and PCH, the rapid pace at which new MFIs were being created also had advantages. It made it possible to transfer staff who were experienced in setting up banks from one institution to the next. Moreover, bank supervisors who had to grant a license for a new bank of a new type in their country could be shown how their peers in other countries had dealt with the relevant regulatory and supervisory issues and how well the banks in these countries were doing.

In the beginning, some of the IFIs had little confidence in the financial value of their investments in PCH, but they were proud to be involved in an undertaking which clearly had considerable developmental value; they saw their investments as being relevant primarily in terms of public relations. Some of them even charged their investments in PCH directly to their PR budgets. But this was soon to change, i.e. when they recognized that PCH was becoming a profitable business enterprise.[63]

The consolidation of the ProCredit Group and the plan to undertake an IPO

Shortly after the turn of the century the size of the ProCredit Group and the scope of its activities had increased considerably. This created the danger that the IFIs might no longer be sufficiently well informed regarding the development of the member institutions and their operations. In addition, the financial exposure of the IFIs to the group had also grown, and in some cases had reached an internally imposed limit. Finally, some of the international investors had begun to realize that ProCredit was not only a viable and sustainable undertaking that was making a valuable contribution to development in its countries of operation, but that it had also become a profitable business enterprise. In other words, they now saw that ProCredit could be regarded as an attractive asset not only by their PR heads but also by their treasurers. For its part, PCH was becoming increasingly aware of the potentially problematic consequences of these developments. Then, in the early 2000s, a Russian bank that had been created by IPC and operated like many

---

63 The reputation of IPC and its projects and of ProCredit was acknowledged by Elisabeth Rhyne, a key member of ACCION, in her book "Microfinance for Bankers and Investors": As she writes, "investors trusted ProCredit's growth, profitability and track record. ProCredit is part of the 'cream of the cream' of microfinance; there are few other possibilities [for investors] that match its scale and quality" (Rhyne 2009: 89).

other IPC-inspired microfinance banks, but which was not a part of the ProCredit Group, was sold to private investors for a stunningly high price. Some of the representatives of IFI shareholders on the supervisory board of PCH requested that PCH give serious consideration to selling some of its most valuable banks and distributing the resulting profits to the shareholders.

This request was perceived as an outright attack on the principles that had so far always guided the development of PCH and on its successful business model. The management of PCH and a majority of the shareholders rejected the request, arguing that breaking up the group would take away its core strength, endanger the entire venture, and undermine its developmental mission. Thus, there was suddenly a need to make the ProCredit Group much less reliant on a continuing flow of donor financing, and at the very least to make sure that it would not be dependent on an increase in funding from this source.

This had three far-reaching strategic consequences. The first and most immediate one was that the expansion of the network of banks was slowed down substantially. The pace at which new banks were founded and new investments were undertaken slacked off abruptly. At the same time, however, the banks that were already part of the group continued to grow, and the existing institutions, which had formerly had different names based on historical coincidence, were renamed "ProCredit Bank" in order to clearly identify them as members of the ProCredit Group. They also adopted a more uniform branding as ProCredit institutions, standardizing the appearance of their business premises, marketing materials, etc. as far as possible. Over time, PCH acquired several stakes in individual banks from the IFIs in exchange for additional IFI investments in the holding company. When this process was completed, PCH had become the largest – and indeed in some cases the only – shareholder in the individual banks that belonged to the group. Thus, the first consequence of the changed situation outlined above was a drastic shift from expansion to consolidation.

The second consequence was that the entire group launched a vigorous campaign to mobilize deposits. The ProCredit Banks had always taken deposits, because poor clients want and need deposit facilities. But traditionally deposits had not really been regarded as an important funding source, and customer deposits had rarely covered more than one third of the banks' loan portfolios. However, after a few years of intensive efforts to boost deposit collection, the deposit-to-loan ratio for the group as a whole rose to almost 100%.

The third consequence involved changes of an even more fundamental nature. Or rather, it would have involved very far-reaching changes had it materialized. Relatively early on, leading figures in the IPC-PCH complex had contemplated undertaking an IPO, that is, issuing shares and having the company's shares listed on a stock exchange. PCH's record of increasing profitability up to the time when the financial crisis broke out in 2007 would have made this a realistic plan. Indeed, three investment banks that had been asked to assess this option signaled their approval. One purpose of the IPO would have been to offer attractive exit opportunities for IFIs – and possibly also other investors – who wished to terminate their investments, or who were compelled to do so because of some pertinent internal rule or directive. Moreover, an IPO and a listing of PCH shares would have provided an opportunity to raise new equity from investors, in turn enabling the holding company to meet the increasing need for equity on the part of the local ProCredit banks, which at that time were continuing to grow rapidly and had to comply with local equity requirements.

However, there was a strong argument against undertaking an IPO – one which was advanced even during the period prior to the financial crisis, when it appeared that such a move would have been feasible. Many members of PCH's top management feared that with publicly traded shares, the majority of the voting rights might end up in the hands of new owners who would not feel committed to the social and developmental mission that had always been so important for IPC and PCH and their staff members, as well as IPC's owners and most of PCH's existing shareholders. What later happened with Compartamos and SKS – the two well-known and highly problematic examples of MFIs which chose to go public – shows that this concern was justified.[64]

It was indeed the concern that an IPO might mean the end of the social and developmental mission of PCH which kept the holding company's management and most of its owners from pushing ahead with the plan to go public. However, around 2005 there was a surprising new development. Two important international institutional investors from the US, a foundation and a very large pension fund, showed an interest in acquiring shares in PCH. These organizations were considering a significant investment and sent a large team of experts to carry out a thorough due diligence assessment. Once it was completed, the organizations' representatives declared that they were now convinced that it would indeed make sense to invest in PCH and that they definitely wished to do so. PCH's reception was decidedly cool; the management indicated that, while they appreciated the organizations' interest, they did not wish to lose control over their company and feared that these large institutional investors would not be able to commit to the social and developmental mission which was highly important to PCH. Much to the surprise of the PCH leadership, the American organizations responded that they agreed that what the company was doing was extremely impressive, that they respected and shared PCH's desire to promote social and developmental goals, and that they would therefore be willing to acquire non-voting shares. And that is what happened: The two institutions made their investments on the planned scale, but with 90 % of their funds being used to purchase shares without voting rights.

---

64 For details regarding the Compartamos IPO, see Rosenberg (2007), and regarding that of SKS, see Chen et al. (2010). We will discuss these two cases in some detail in section 4.4.

Snapshot 42: Facts and figures about ProCredit Holding

PCH was founded in 1998 (under the name Internationale Micro Investitionen) with an equity of DM 1 million (approx. EUR 0.5 million). During the initial phase of its activities it undertook investments in banks in Bosnia, Georgia, Albania, Kosovo, and other countries and regions; in some cases it provided equity for the establishment of new banks, while in others, such as in Bolivia and El Salvador, funds were used to acquire participations in existing MFIs that had been built up by IPC in its capacity as a consulting firm.

The founding shareholders were IPC, IPC Invest (a company that held shares on behalf of IPC and ProCredit Bank staff), and the Dutch Foundation DOEN. Shortly thereafter, they were joined by a group of national and international financial institutions including Germany's Kreditanstalt für Wiederaufbau (KfW), its Dutch counterpart FMO, and International Finance Corporation (IFC), the private sector arm of the World Bank Group. Currently, the group of shareholders is comprised of 15 organizations, with the original investors holding the largest portion of the shares which, under the legal form of a KGaA (partnership limited by shares) adopted by PCH in 2011, confer special voting rights. The holders of these shares have the final say in all important decisions.

Table 15 provides quantitative information on the ProCredit Group of banks for selected years. All figures are taken from the respective annual reports of ProCredit Holding AG & Co. KGaA (formerly ProCredit Holding AG), which are available on PCH's website.

Table 15: Data on the ProCredit Group

Year	2003	2006	2009	2012
Number of banks (and countries)	16	18	22	22
Number of banking outlets	224	472	831	687
Total staff	4,689	12,585	19,616	14,675
Total loans outstanding (mn EUR)	585	2,111	3,229	4,191
No. of loans outstanding ('000)	288	735	921	930
Total client deposits (mn EUR)	548	1,814	2,998	3,627
No. of deposit accounts ('000)	473	1,924	3,777	3,704
Total assets (mn EUR)	966	3,107	4,949	5,760
Total shareholder equity (mn EUR)	122	340	388	503
Profit before tax (mn EUR)	14.4	36.0	41.7	46.3

For the leadership of PCH, this was a development that opened up new options. The PCH managers went back to the investment banks to ask their advice, and they were told that issuing non-voting shares would be a definite possibility, but of course one which would generate a substantially lower price than issuing shares with voting rights. Thus the idea of undertaking an IPO was revived, but subject to the condition that only non-voting shares would be issued and listed.

This was the state of affairs in the middle of the last decade. Then two things happened which caused PCH to put its plans for an IPO on hold: the IPO of the Mexican MFI Compartamos in 2006, which caused an uproar of criticism among development finance experts, and, in 2007, the outbreak of the financial crisis, which led to a complete cessation of IPO activity all over the world. In this environment, it would have been impossible for PCH to carry out an IPO. But as one can see from certain remarks made in PCH's annual report for 2012, and in the information presented on the website of the newly created ProCredit Bank Germany, the idea is by no means dead and might be taken up again in the course of the next two or three years.

The financial crisis and the change in client focus

Today the ProCredit banking group's main, but not exclusive, geographical focus is on Southeastern Europe. This region was seriously affected by the global financial crisis that began in 2007 and lasted until 2009, and then again by the Eurozone crisis which emerged in May 2010. Some of the countries in this region in which PCH operates banks were particularly hard hit, most notably Ukraine, Romania, and Bulgaria. One of the reasons why the situation was particularly difficult in this region is that in these countries, as in many others, the problem of multiple borrowing from microfinance banks and other lenders was revealed to be much more widespread than experts had believed prior to the crisis. During the crisis it also became evident that, once there are many competing providers of small-scale credit in a given market, it is almost impossible to make a clear distinction between small loans that finance income-generating projects and outright consumer lending.

Although PCH was also seriously affected by the financial crisis, it survived the ensuing turbulence and global economic downturn without posting a loss for the group as a whole in any single year.[65] Individual ProCredit banks, however, reported substantial losses for some of the crisis years. Today, profitability is once again at pre-crisis levels, and this may be one reason why the idea of an IPO is being revived, or at least kept alive.

Asked why the group was able to get through the crisis relatively unscathed, people at PCH invariably point to two factors: one is their very cautious approach to

---

65 For details, see the annual reports that are available on PCH's website.

granting loans, and the other is the liquidity buffers which the banks had built up by mobilizing deposits on a substantial scale well before the crisis broke out.

That said, there were important lessons to be drawn from the crisis experience, and those lessons were taken very seriously at PCH and the individual ProCredit Banks. Like many other microfinance providers, ProCredit had been quite naïve in the pre-crisis years, lending too much money to really poor individuals who simply could not handle the resulting debt burdens. As a consequence, people at PCH no longer regard it as responsible business behavior if their institutions grant loans which can easily be used and abused to finance (unnecessary) consumption expenditures. Thus, the ProCredit Banks have substantially raised their minimum loan size and have even ceased using the term "microfinance" to describe what they do because, as they see it, this entire concept has been discredited by the events of the last seven years, including those related to the two IPOs of MFIs described in section 4 of this chapter. The ProCredit Banks now see themselves as small business-oriented "banks for ordinary people" and lenders to small and medium-sized firms – and describe themselves accordingly.

In spite of these changes, the ProCredit Banks still have more of a microfinance "flavor," even today, than most other banks in the countries in which they operate. This change in nomenclature is only a symptom, albeit an important one, of something much larger and more significant. It reflects a conviction which has grown in the course of the recent financial crisis and the resulting global economic downturn, namely that microfinance of the kind that was practiced, and was indeed very valuable, only ten years ago may not be feasible, or valuable, or even necessary any longer in most countries in the second decade of the new millennium. Accordingly, instead of micro-scale businesses, many of which operate in the informal sector, the ProCredit Banks are now targeting small and medium-sized firms in their lending activities. These borrowers are more stable, they are less likely to succumb to the temptations of readily available consumer loans and the concomitant overindebtedness, and they are also able to generate employment and income. But what is even more important is that even today, businesses in this size category are rarely able to obtain loans from other, more conventional banks.[66]

PCH has not only raised the minimum size of the loans its banks grant, and thus turned away from what used to be called microlending to focus now instead on

---

[66] See Chapter IV. Suffice to say here that the nature and the business activities of the microcredit clients who used to account for the overwhelming majority of the ProCredit Banks' borrowers have changed; that the purposes for which they wish to obtain loans have changed; and that the "supply situation" in the microcredit sector has also changed, indeed dramatically: In most countries a large number of MFIs have been established and as a consequence, microcredit is no longer in short supply. But paradoxically, this has made microlending more difficult, since lenders can no longer exert pressure on borrowers to repay their loans by threatening to refuse future loan requests if they willfully default, given that clients who have defaulted on a loan from a given provider often find it easy to simply turn to other lenders.

lending to small and mid-sized businesses; it also recently sold its entire microloan portfolios in El Salvador and Georgia and even its entire banks in Mozambique, Ghana, and Honduras, banks which it felt would not be able to effectively complete the shift from operating predominantly as micro-lenders to operating as lenders to local small and medium-sized firms. As a consequence, the number of banks in the group and the number of loans outstanding have shrunk considerably. Most importantly perhaps, the number of total staff has also been greatly reduced. Concomitant with a substantial increase in the average loan size, the total volume of outstanding loans has so far been maintained.

It might seem that PCH was unnecessarily radical in the way that it reacted to the effects of the crisis on its banks, specifically as regards the change in minimum loan amounts, and thus also in the types of activities supported by ProCredit's loans. However, in view of the changes that have occurred in recent years in the structure of the economy in many of the countries in which the group used to operate, one can also assess the change of strategy differently and more positively. The verdict is still open on whether this was the right move to make; only time will tell.[67] In Southeastern Europe, the character of local business is indeed radically changing. Individuals who used to be independent and to some extent even informal traders and owners of small artisan shops in the early years after the transformation are now, in many cases, employees of larger firms, be they local small and medium-sized firms or local subsidiaries of large international groups. This structural change is a fact that the management of a group of banks must take into account if it wants to act in a responsible way. However, whether the same strategic move makes sense in other parts of the world, i.e. in Africa and Latin America, is a different question, and one may indeed wonder why PCH has undertaken it.

A new supervisory regime for the ProCredit Group

A final development worth noting in this context has to do with the supervisory regime to which PCH and the ProCredit Banks are subject. The issues which were involved here, and the way in which they were addressed by PCH, also gave rise to far-reaching changes for the entire group. With one exception, all of the institutions in the group were fully licensed banks that are subject to regulation and supervision by the banking authorities of the countries in which they operate; the exception, the group's institution in Moldova, was licensed as a finance company and as such was also allowed to take deposits from the general public. The holding company, by contrast, is not a bank and thus, while it is duly registered as a corporation in Germany and operates in compliance with all of the applicable legal regulations and requirements, it is not regulated and supervised by the German banking authorities. This caused the following problem: PCH had created microfinance banks in Bulgaria and Romania years before these two countries became

---

[67] For details see the annual report for 2013.

members of the European Union. But once they became EU member states, the EU's banking laws applied to them. The relevant EU-wide regulation requires that if one or more banks belonging to a banking group operate within the EU, then the supervisory authority of one member state in which a bank belonging to that group operates shall be responsible for supervision of the entire banking group, irrespective of where the individual banks are located, operate, or are licensed. In the case of ProCredit, the implication was that either the Bulgarian or the Romanian supervisory authority would suddenly have a mandate to supervise all ProCredit banks, many of them located in Latin America and Africa. Obviously, this was not an attractive option for any of the parties concerned.

In response to this challenge, the PCH management consulted BaFin,[68] the German banking supervisory authority, for advice as to what they should do in order to comply with the EU rules and, even more importantly, to ensure that BaFin would be responsible for supervision of the group – the optimal regulatory arrangement from PCH's point of view. BaFin suggested in response that PCH should do two things more or less in parallel: (i) establish a German subsidiary operating as a bank under a banking license issued by BaFin, which could subsequently become the central institution for purposes of group-wide supervision by BaFin; and (ii) modify all structures and processes in all of the banks belonging to the ProCredit Group so as to bring them into compliance with the requirements set forth in German banking laws and regulations. Completion of this second step would be a prerequisite for securing BaFin's agreement to assume supervisory responsibility for the group as a whole.

PCH was firmly committed to carrying out the measures recommended by BaFin, but both processes proved difficult to manage. The requirements of German banking law are not easily reconciled with the specific challenges involved in financing small – and in some cases very small – businesses in developing and transition countries. Implementing the necessary modifications at the banks was a process that took two years to complete, after which BaFin carried out a comprehensive review to check whether its requirements had been met. It determined that PCH had modified the relevant structures and processes to its satisfaction and then indicated that it would be prepared to grant a license to a ProCredit Bank in Germany. But the supervisory authority noted that before doing so, it would have to sign memoranda of understanding with the banking supervisory authorities in all of the countries in which ProCredit institutions operate in order to ensure that they were willing and able to cooperate fully with BaFin. Completion of this additional step took another two years and required a large commitment of PCH staff resources. Finally, in late 2012, the German ProCredit Bank received its license. It began operating soon thereafter, and BaFin has designated

---

68 The abbreviation BaFin stands for *Bundesanstalt für Finanzdienstleistungsaufsicht*, the official name of the German federal financial supervisory authority.

PCH as the "super-ordinated" entity within the group which is responsible for group-wide reporting and risk management.

Several years ago, PCH had already understood the enormous importance of staff quality, and accordingly, the need to organize consistent staff training to ensure ongoing business success and a lasting developmental impact. Training has taken on an important role in the group: A two-tiered system of training institutions, called ProCredit Academies, was created, one tier consisting of regional academies that mainly train middle management staff, and the other of a central academy in Germany at which highly qualified staff members from the local banks are given the comprehensive training that is deemed necessary for them as future leaders in the local banks. This training system is an additional component in the strategy of ensuring that the different group banks all operate in a similar way and that all of the group's managers truly understand and embrace the importance of pursuing the dual objective of operating commercially strong banks and making an impact in social and developmental terms.

In retrospect, one can assess the far-reaching recent changes in the structure and the strategy of the entire ProCredit Group as being largely successful. It has prepared the group for a new step in its ongoing development. At least this is how insiders at PCH tend to see it. There are a number of factors that have worked together in shaping the new structure and strategy: one is the desire to create and maintain a high degree of similarity among the banks that belong to the group, a feature that has proved to be very important over the years, as it permits learning and an easy transfer of newly gained knowledge. Another is the response to the lessons of the financial crisis years and the mistakes of the go-go years of microfinance in the years preceding the crisis. Then there is the effect of the influx of many more MFIs into the formerly neglected markets of most host countries, which has reduced the urgency of providing genuinemicroloans. Finally, one cannot overlook the role of regulation – in this case, European and German banking regulation – in reshaping the business and making it more homogeneous across the group's countries of operation.

3 Sources of data on access to finance

Since the 1990s, major efforts have been made to collect data on access to finance, initially mainly to microfinance, and in recent years to finance in general, by all population groups, aspiring to provide a quantitative description of "financial landscapes."[69] Historically, non-supervised financial institutions have reported to their respective national networks, formal institutions to their central bank or other supervisory authority. Global data is collected on the basis of either national data or the self-selected reporting of individual institutions. This section presents eight major data sets, some of which are available to the public for analysis. They fall into three categories:

1. Self-selected reporting by individual institutions: compiled by the Microfinance Information eXchange (MIX), an affiliate of CGAP, and the Microcredit Summit Campaign.
2. Reporting by global networks: covering savings and postal banks, credit unions and cooperative banks, and VSLAs.
3. Global surveys: the Financial Access Survey (FAS) of the IMF, the World Bank's Global Financial Inclusion (Global Findex) survey, and the IFC's study of access to finance for formal and informal MSMEs.

The data sets presented[70] vary widely in terms of completeness. This is obvious in the case of self-selected reporting, but pertains to the reporting of national and global networks and to the IMF's FAS as well. Not only small and recently established institutions refrain from reporting, but also well-established institutions and national banks. In one spectacular case, this even led to the discontinuation of data collection by the UN's FAO. It had been covering 75 agricultural development banks which are major providers of rural microfinance. But many of them were reluctant to report, and as a result data collection was stopped in 2000.[71]

---

[69] The term "financial landscapes" was made popular among microfinance experts by Bouman and Hospes (1994) from the University of Wageningen in the Netherlands. However, in contrast to the approach taken in this section, Bouman and Hospes describe financial landscapes by providing empirical and case-based analysis that is mainly qualitative in nature.
[70] See also Nielson 2014, http://www.cgap.org/about/people/karina-broens-nielsen; http://www.cgap.org/blog/10-useful-data-sources-measuring-financial-inclusion, which appeared after this section was completed.
[71] Forty-four banks reported data on a total of 24 million loan accounts and 87 million deposit accounts. See Seibel, Giehler and Karduck, 2005: 17–31, 58–59.

3.1 Self-reporting by individual institutions

Microfinance Information Exchange (MIX)[72]

All microfinance reporting systems, at least the earlier ones, are biased one way or the other. MIX is perhaps the one with the highest reputation. It basically comprises self-identified MFIs, its main implicit selection criterion being a high standard of reporting quality including certified audits of outreach, cost, and financial performance. Many microfinance investment vehicles (MIVs) and donors who support MFIs request them to report to the MIX; MFIs without such backing may not be able or willing to annually submit to that standard. As of 2011, this had resulted in a non-random reporting sample of 1,334 MFIs, including banks, financial cooperatives, non-profits, and others (out of about 2,000 which have reported to MIX), with total assets of USD 115.8 billion, or USD 86.8 million per MFI on average (Table 16).

Particularly because the MIX data is so widely used, we find it important to emphasize its incompleteness. For instance, MIX's sample of Indonesian institutions for 2011 comprises 75 MFIs; this includes only 36 rural banks (BPRs, regulated by the central bank) out of a total of 1,669. The number of BPRs alone exceeds the total number of MFIs in the MIX database. The sample also includes only 15 village banks (LPDs) on Bali out of a total of 1,418 LPDs (many in fact very small),

Table 16: MIX market microfinance data by region, 2011

Region	MFIs	Billion USD			Millions of clients		Avg. MFI (in mn USD)	
		Assets	Deposits	Loans	Borrowers	Depositors	Loans	Deposits
Africa	264	11.0	7.6	7.7	5.8	18.9	29.3	28.6
East Asia & Pacific	222	46.8	30.8	31.7	15.0	14.8	143.0	138.7
Eastern Europe & Central Asia	201	13.5	6.9	10.0	2.5	2.9	49.8	34.1
Latin America	378	34.8	18.3	28.0	18.3	16.6	74.1	48.3
Middle East & North Africa	57	1.9	0.2	1.3	1.9	0.1	23.6	4.3
South Asia	212	7.7	1.7	7.3	42.2	17.2	34.2	8.0
Total	**1,334**	**115.8**	**65.4**	**86.1**	**85.7**	**70.3**	**64.5**	**49.0**

---

72 http://www.mixmarket.org.

and out of some 40,000 financial cooperatives (many non-performing[73]), only three are included. The sample does, however, include BRI's huge network of microbanking units discussed above.

In Laos, with an emerging microfinance sector, the MIX sample for 2011 comprises 20 out of a total of 42 licensed MFIs, many of them new; and it includes none of the nearly 5,000 village banks which are registered with local authorities, but not licensed by the central bank, as reported above. It does include ACLEDA, a bank newly established by a parent corporation in Cambodia, with a loan portfolio of USD 35.8 million, accounting for 83% of the total portfolio reported for Laos; however, it excludes Nayoby Bank, a large state-owned policy bank.

In a number of countries data is heavily skewed by the preponderance of a single large institution (like BRI in Indonesia) and a general absence of data from small, homegrown institutions. Javoy and Rozas (2013) noted similar discrepancies in their comparison of the Global Findex and the MIX data. Thailand, for instance, "which has a high penetration rate [on Findex], has no microfinance activity reported to the MIX."

Despite its limitations, the general MIX database is widely used in econometric dissertations on microfinance and frequently treated as if representative of the microfinance sector, and also seems to inform numerous statements made by policy makers and other public speakers. While the MIX does serve as an important and reliable source of information on a variety of licensed institutions, some knowledge of these institutions is required before valid conclusions can be drawn.

Perhaps in view of the problem of the incompleteness of its main database, the MIX has established a separate and much more detailed dataset on sub-Saharan Africa, called Mapping Africa Financial Inclusion.[74] This dataset does not rely solely on self-reporting. It covers 23,000 institutions in 45 countries, including commercial, savings and postal banks, regulated MFIs, mostly unregulated financial cooperatives (as reported by the World Council of Credit Unions (WOCCU)) and informal savings and credit groups (as reported by the Savings Groups Information Exchange (SAVIX)). According to this dataset, total outreach is 71 million accounts, including 20 million loan accounts, mostly with banks and regulated MFIs, and 44 million savings accounts: 18 million with financial cooperatives and 4 to 6 million each with savings, commercial and postal savings banks, regulated MFIs and savings groups (Figure 23). Mobile banking, concentrated in a few flagship markets, reaches more than 18 million individuals. However, here as well,

---

[73] In a mapping survey in the province of Aceh in 2006, GTZ/GIZ found that out of 1,502 financial cooperatives reported by the cooperative authority, 708 could be traced, 85 were found to be active, and only a few performed satisfactorily (Seibel 2008).

[74] http://www.themix.org/publications/mix-microfinance-world/2011/09/mapping-africa-financial-inclusion-overview.

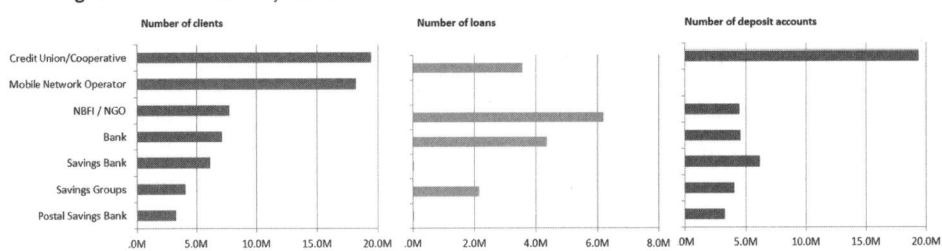

Figure 23: Financial access by data source for sub-Saharan Africa

Source: http://www.themix.org/publications/mix-microfinance-world/2011/09/africa-financial-inclusion/results; also in Ardic et al. 2012: 14.

vast numbers of informal providers outside the reporting networks are not included.[75]

Since 2013 the MIX has been expanding its focus through ongoing geospatial mapping efforts (http://finclusionlab.org/) designed to aggregate and visualize data for financial service providers including and beyond MFIs, enriching the supply-side data landscape (Nielsen 2014).

Microcredit Summit Campaign[76]

The Microcredit Summit Campaign is an American non-profit organization managed by the public relations and advocacy firm RESULTS. Since 1997, the organization has been holding annual so-called Microcredit Summits in locations around the world, attended by thousands of practitioners and others. The Microcredit Summit Campaign set itself the aims of (1) reaching 175 million poorest families with microcredit for self-employment and other services by 2013, and (2) helping 100 million families lift themselves out of extreme poverty, rising above the USD 1.25 income a day threshold (adjusted for purchasing power parity), between 1990 and 2015. The results, published in Microcredit Summit Campaign Reports, are based on self-reported action plans of a wide variety of MFIs and other institutions, including banks and international organizations.[77]

The Microcredit Summit Campaign reports that in the period from 1997 to 2010, 3,652 MFIs reporting to the Campaign had reached 205.3 million clients. Of these, 137.5 million were among the poorest when they took out their first loan, and 40% of them were reported on by NABARD's SHG-Bank linkage program (NABARD 2007–2013).

---

[75] Mapping Africa Financial Inclusion achieves much broader coverage of this region than the IMF's FAS. The correlation coefficients of MIX data and FAS data for sub-Saharan Africa for 2010 were 0.22 for number of providers, 0.50 for loans per 1,000 adults and 0.25 for deposits per 1,000 adults.
[76] http://www.microcreditsummit.org.
[77] Among them is NABARD in India. NABARD is in charge of supervising and providing funding to rural financial institutions, and does not itself offer any retail services. In 2012 it reported to the Campaign on 67.9 million clients, including 54.3 million poorest, 54.3 million women and 43.5 million poorest women. These are members of the SHGs in NABARD's bank-SHG linkage program described above. Beyond such special cases, it is surprising that all reporting institutions, including banks, provide data on the number of women and the poorest as requested, even though banks do not normally distinguish between the accounts of men and women, poorest, poor and non-poor.

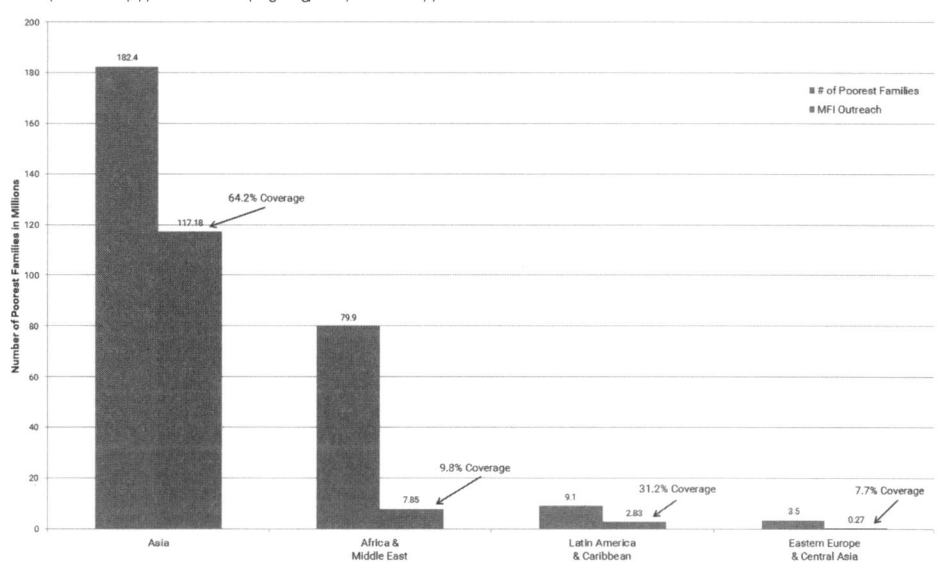

Figure 24: Data of the Microcredit Summit Campaign on MFI outreach compared with World Bank data on poverty, by region, 2010 (Source: http://stateofthecampaign.org/data/2011-data/)

Reporting cumulative outreach data is a misleading practice. Current figures submitted to the Campaign in 2011 by 609 MFIs differ considerably from the cumulative figures as of that date, and cover only 78 million poorest. The Campaign was able to verify the data of 328 MFIs, with microloans outstanding to 72 million poorest families.[78] Unreliable as they may be, these figures do not amount to even half the target of 175 million by 2015 that the Microcredit Summit Campaign has been proclaiming for more than ten years.

The second target mentioned above, i.e. ensuring that 100 million families rise above the extreme poverty threshold between 1990 and 2015, will hardly be reached, according to the Microcredit Summit Campaign Report 2012 (p. 4).

3.2 Global reporting by networks of financial institutions

The World Savings Banks Institute (WSBI) in Brussels reports on savings and postal banks in 88 countries: 33 institutions in Europe and the US, and 57 in developing countries – 30 in Africa, 16 in Asia, and 11 in Latin America. Japan, the country whose postal savings bank is one of the world's largest savings banks, is not included. The WSBI data includes national banks as well as networks of independent savings banks such as the German Savings Banks Association (DSGV) in Germany, with 426 retail savings banks, and Independent Community Bankers of America (ICBA) in the US, with 6,922 independent member community banks

---

[78] About 90% of the poorest are served by the 85 largest reporting institutions.

reporting aggregated data. In developing countries, large numbers of clients of savings banks are low-income clients.[79]

The quality of the information on developing countries is impaired by very uneven reporting on the various parameters, particularly in Africa. Two outreach indicators are reported: outlets and clients. Of the total number of outlets worldwide (184,315) as of 2011, 42% are in developing countries, the majority in Asia (64,723), followed by Africa (8,399) and Latin America (5,151). Of the total number of clients, which comprise 751 million individuals and business entities, 62% are in developing countries, with a similar regional distribution.

Reported total assets worldwide as of 2011 amount to USD 16.8 trillion, with 21% (USD 3.6 trillion) accounted for by developing countries, most of that in Asia (USD 3.2 trillion), followed by Latin America (USD 368 billion) and Africa (USD 42 billion). WSBI divides data on loans and deposits into interbank transactions and non-bank financial intermediation with clients; the following data pertains only to the latter. Total loans outstanding amount to USD 9.5 trillion, 23% of that amount in developing countries: USD 1.2 trillion in Asia, USD 0.9 trillion in Latin America and only USD 7 billion in Africa. Total deposits are reported at USD 8.2

Table 17: WSBI retail savings bank data, 2011, Clients in millions, amounts in billion USD

Region	Outlets	Clients	Assets (inter-bank + retail)	Retail loans	Retail deposits	Deposit-loan ratio
Europe	75,803 (41%)	212.9 (28%)	10,650 (64%)	5,848 (61%)	4,963 (61%)	0.85
of which Germany	20,470 (11%)	50.0 (7%)	3,572 (21%)	1,708 (18%)	1,636 (20%)	0.97
USA (ICBA + Wells Fargo)	30,239 (16%)	70.0 (9%)	2,514 (15%)	1,500 (16%)	1,000 (12%)	0.67
Africa	8,399 (5%)	15.5 (2%)	42 (0%)	7 (0%)	28 (0%)	4.03
Asia	64,723 (35%)	363.4 (48%)	3,192 (19%)	1,242 (13%)	1,986 (24%)	1.60
Latin America	5,151 (3%)	89.4 (12%)	368 (2%)	928 (10%)	192 (2%)	0.21
Total developing countries	78,273 (42%)	468.2 (62%)	3,602 (21%)	2,177 (23%)	2,206 (27%)	1.01
Global total	184,315 (100%)	751.1 (100%)	16,766 (100%)	9,526 (100%)	8,168 (100%)	0.86

Sources: WSBI 2011 (data for 2010 is used where none for 2011 is reported; data on ICBA member institutions is taken from the ICBA website), WOCCU and European Association of CooperativeBanks (EACB).

---

79 In a special study of savings banks in India, Mexico, Tanzania, and Thailand, WSBI (2008) found that they are large providers of financial services, with significant outreach among the poorest households. Cf. http://www.savings-banks.com/SiteCollectionDocuments/Perspectives%2056.pdf.

trillion, 27% of that amount in developing countries: USD 2.0 trillion in Asia, USD 192 billion in Latin America and USD 28 billion in Africa.

In Europe loans outstanding slightly exceed deposits. In developing countries, loans and deposits are balanced overall, but there are marked differences between continents: The institutions in Latin America are credit-led, lending almost five times the amount of deposits. In contrast, in Asia deposits exceed loans outstanding by a factor of 1.6, and in Africa even by a factor of 4.0, indicating that overall, African savings banks – most of which are national institutions, and not local or municipal – mainly finance their respective states or governments, rather than local individuals and MSMEs, with the savings that they mobilize.

The WOCCU and the European Association of Cooperative Banks (EACB) report on cooperative financial institutions. Terminology is not standardized and definitions overlap: there are credit unions, savings and credit cooperatives, financial cooperatives and cooperative banks, and tiered systems of cooperatives. Rural and urban credit cooperatives tend to be traceable back to origins in Germany, with an equal emphasis on savings and credit. Credit unions, a terminological variant of credit cooperatives, tend to have their origins in the Anglophone world, where they were established for the support of factory workers and other company employees, with an emphasis on "saving for a rainy day."

In terms of reporting, there are two main spheres of cooperative finance: credit unions, on which WOCCU reports, and cooperative banks in Europe, on which EACB reports. Credit unions serve only members, while most cooperative banks may serve both members and non-members. In addition, there are two non-reporting realms of cooperative finance: credit unions and cooperative banks which do not belong or report to either of these two networks (among them building societies); and independent local cooperatives, informal cooperatives including indigenous ROSCAs and VSLAs, semiformal pre-cooperatives and other member-owned financial institutions. This section is limited to reporting institutions, with the implication being that actual numbers exceed those reported by a wide margin. Indonesia, for example, contributes only 930 credit unions with 1.8 million members to the WOCCU figures (2010), while official figures for savings and credit cooperatives (including credit unions), most of doubtful standing, exceeded 40,000, with 11 million members in 2000.[80] India contributes 1,645 credit unions with 20 million members to the WOCCU data, while official NABARD figures report 95,000 PACS for India with 126 million members as of 2010. China, which has vast numbers of credit cooperatives, is also not included. Thus, one can safely conclude that the number of registered, non-credit union financial cooperatives exceeds that of credit unions by far.

---

80 These figures refer to 2000; see ADB Rural Microfinance Indonesia (TA No. 3810-INO), March 2003, Annex 4.

Table 18: Financial cooperatives: credit unions (2011) and cooperative banks (2010)

	Credit unions worldwide	European cooperative banks
Number	51,013 (100 countries)	3,874 banks (20 countries)
Members	196.5 million	50 million
Assets	USD 1,563.5 billion	EUR 5,647 billion
Deposits	USD 1,222.6 billion	EUR 3,107 billion
Loans	USD 1,016.2 billion	EUR 3,305 billion

Source: Birchall 2013a:13, based on WOCCU 2012 and EACB 2011.

A few countries report to both WOCCU and EACB. In the case of the European cooperative banks, it should be noted that in addition to some 50 million member clients, they also serve 130 million non-member clients, together accounting for market shares of 21% of deposits and 19% of loans.

Credit unions globally have a market penetration (not share!) of 7.8% as reported by WOCCU, defined as the ratio of the number of members to the total economically active population between 18 and 64 years of age. Credit unions are reported to exist and operate in 14 developed countries (USA, Canada, and 12 European countries), with some 11,000 institutions and more than 100 million members. The US is the global market leader, with 7,351 credit unions, 94 million members and a market penetration of 45%. More information on credit unions in different parts of the world is provided in Table 19.

Table 19: Credit unions by market penetration of region

Region	Countries	Market penetration in %	Number of credit unions	Members (in millions)
North America	2	45.0	8,164	104.5
Oceania	5	23.6	326	5.1
Caribbean	19	17.5	433	2.9
Africa	24	7.2	18,221	18.0
Latin America	15	5.7	1,750	18.1
Europe	12	3.5	2,321	8.1
Asia	22	2.7	19,798	39.7
World	100	7.8	51,013	196.5
Developing countries	86		40,528	83.9
Developed countries	14		10,485	112.6

Source: Adapted from Birchall 2013a:17 and Birchall 2013b:46 based on WOCCU 2012.

Snapshot 43: How financial cooperatives performed before and after the global crisis

Some recent studies that compare cooperative and investor-owned banks in Europe before the crisis, in the two-year period from 2005 to 2007, found better loan quality, higher cost efficiency, higher returns on equity, and markedly higher stability among the cooperative banks; their assets increased by 23%. They went into the crisis with a strong capital base which they subsequently strengthened. With limited exposure to sub-prime mortgages and fewer investment activities, their losses were lower than those of investor-owned banks. After the crisis they continued to be stable and more efficient; they had lower write-downs, and their losses remained lower than those of investor-owned banks, though some of their central organizations took a beating. 2008 was a difficult year, but overall, between 2007 and 2010, assets grew by nearly 10%, customer numbers by 14%. In general, cooperative banks in Europe have survived the crisis very well. Seven of them are ranked among the top 50 safest banks in the world. At an average of about 9% across Europe, they exceed the minimum capital requirement set at 8% (Birchall 2013).

Similarly, growth and resilience have been observed among WOCCU credit unions before and after the crisis. During the two-year period 2005–2007, savings deposits increased by 29%, loans by 39%, reserves by 26%, assets by 32%, and membership by 13%; market penetration grew from 6.65% to 7.5%. Again, 2008 was a difficult year; but over the three-year period, savings deposits increased by 24%, loans by 13%, and reserves by 14%. The most impressive growth rates for savings and loans were found in the Caribbean, at 50% and 57%, respectively, and in Oceania, both at 49%. In Latin America savings grew by 48%, while loans experienced a slight decrease. In sub-Saharan Africa, savings deposits grew by 34% and loans by 37% (Birchall 2013).

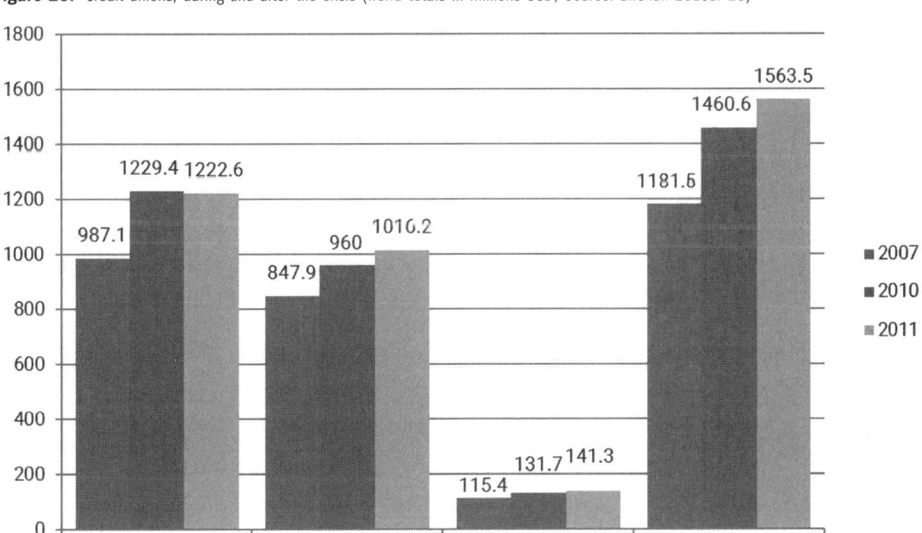

Figure 25: Credit unions, during and after the crisis (world totals in millions USD, Source: Birchall 2013a: 28)

	Savings	Loans	Reserves	Assets
2007	987.1	847.9	115.4	1181.6
2010	1229.4	960	131.7	1460.6
2011	1222.6	1016.2	141.3	1563.5

Birchall (2013a) concludes that financial cooperatives "are not just weathering the financial downturn but taking a lot of business from the investor-owned banks... There must be something about the customer-owned business model that makes it so resilient in a downturn." The main explanatory factor is that "financial cooperatives are not just about financial deepening. Like other types of cooperatives, they are 'people-centered' businesses, owned by the people they serve."

Savings Groups Information Exchange (SAVIX)[81]

The SAVIX, together with VSL Associates,[82] reports on financial SHGs facilitated by NGOs and organized in national networks. The initiative was first taken by CARE International in Niger in 1991, which experimented with upscaling the ubiquitous indigenous model of rotating and non-rotating savings and credit groups. In rural areas beyond the reach of banks and MFIs, CARE promoted what came to be known as VSLAs, or simply savings groups (SGs). These groups tend to have 15 to 25 members and usually meet weekly for savings and credit transactions. An increasing number of groups are linked to banks to obtain access to deposit facilities and to onlending funds. Promoted by numerous NGOs, the model has spread rapidly, reaching 400,000 facilitated groups with close to 9 million members in 70 countries by the end of 2013 (see Table 20), plus about the same number replicated spontaneously. SAVIX also tracks the long-term performance of a randomized sample of 332 independent SGs established by 33 projects in Asia and Africa. The Bill & Melinda Gates Foundation and the MasterCard Foundation support the movement.

Table 20: VSLA membership in facilitated groups (as of October 2013)

Region	Countries	Members	Percent
Asia	15	612,427	7.1
Middle East	2	1,056	0.0
Latin America	13	288,771	3.3
South Pacific	2	1,966	0.0
Africa	38	7,761,447	89.6
Total	**70**	**8,665,667**	**100.0**

Source: Allen Hugh on behalf of www.vsla.net, October 2013. The data provided by vsla.net exceeds the number of institutions reported by SAVIX by a wide margin.

3.3 Global data sets

At its June 2004 meeting the Group of Eight (G8) endorsed CGAP's *Key Principles of Microfinance*, which were formulated in the context of CGAP's newly declared *inclusive financial systems* approach. Referring explicitly to "the integration of mi-

---

[81] http://www.thesavix.org/home.
[82] http://savingsgroups.com/; http://www.vsla.net; cf. http://www.cgap.org/blog/savings-groups; cf. Seibel 2014.

crofinance into formal financial systems to ensure permanent access to financial services by significant numbers of poor people" (CGAP 2004), this shifted attention from predominantly unregulated providers of microcredit and microfinance to the formal financial sector as the ultimate provider.

At the Pittsburgh Summit in 2009, the G20 leaders made an even stronger commitment to "improving access to financial services for the poor... building on the example of micro finance... [to] scale up the successful models of small and medium-sized enterprise (SME) financing... [and] to launch a *G20 SME Finance Challenge,*" together with CGAP, IFC, and others.[83] This commitment to financial inclusion was reiterated at every subsequent meeting.

At the 2010 summit, the Global Partnership for Financial Inclusion (GPFI) was established "to institutionalize and implement the G20 Financial Action Plan." One of its three subgroups was tasked with "identifying the existing financial inclusion data landscape, assessing data gaps, and developing key performance indicators." First results were presented by Ardic, Chen, and Latortue (2012) in a study prepared on behalf of CGAP and IFC. They report that "interest in financial inclusion is at an all-time high. Policy makers and standard-setters, ranging from local central banks to global standard-setting bodies, increasingly view stability and inclusion as complementary, mutually reinforcing goals." They confirm access to formal finance as the objective of inclusion: "Financial inclusion refers to a state in which all working-age adults have effective access to credit, savings, payments, and insurance from formal service providers."

Measurement is to be guided by a set of seven principles (Ardic et al.):

- Build country-level data capacity.
- Use harmonized definitions and standardized methodologies.
- Proactively seek data from a range of providers, beyond commercial banks.
- Use unique financial identity of users more systematically.
- Collect more detailed data on customer segments.
- Include more enterprise data, especially that of MSMEs.
- Promote open access to data.

Financial inclusion is at the center of two global data sets: the FAS database of the IMF, with time series of basic access and usage indicators collected from regulators, and the World Bank's Global Financial Inclusion (Global Findex) database covering over 150,000 people in 148 economies. In this context, the Alliance for Financial Inclusion (AFI) was founded in 2008 with the objective of developing policy measures to provide millions of people in developing countries with access to bank accounts and financial services. AFI is a global knowledge-sharing network for financial inclusion policy makers, comprising at present more than 100

---

[83] The G20 Pittsburgh Summit 2009, September 24–25, 2009, Leaders' Statement.

institutions (mostly central banks) from 87 developing countries (www.afi-global.org; cf. AFI 2013).

The IMF's FAS is the only available global supply-side source of comparable geographic and demographic data on access to and usage of basic consumer financial services by households and enterprises across the world. Launched in October 2009, the results of its fourth annual survey among regulators worldwide went online for public use in September 2012.[84] FAS compiles annual data and metadata on 187 economies, reported by regulated financial institutions to their respective financial authority.[85] The dataset as of mid-2013 covers an eight-year time span, 2004–2011. The enhanced 2012 survey, conducted in collaboration with CGAP and IFC, added time series on access indicators from financial cooperatives and MFIs and includes data on SMEs, households, life insurance, and non-life insurance. FAS data shows a positive trend in financial inclusion since 2005, indicated by increasing numbers of deposit and loan accounts with commercial banks, though with very little growth in 2009 and 2010 due to the global financial crisis, which impacted borrowing slightly more than saving.

Ardic et al. (2013) note that, in addition to commercial banks, "nonbank financial institutions (NBFIs) contribute significantly to reaching unserved and underserved clients in many markets. Indeed, deposit-taking NBFIs are playing a more important role in deposit and loan penetration, and NBFI loan penetration increased relative to that of commercial banks everywhere in the [developing] world." At the same time, NBFIs "are transforming into commercial banks, and local commercial banks are showing new interest in reaching the base of the pyramid" (Ardic et al. 2013). Overall, the financial landscape has become more complex, and regulators are making efforts to also cover NBFIs in their reporting (Latortue and Ardic, 2013).

The World Bank's Global Financial Inclusion survey (Global Findex) is a nationally representative poll measuring how people around the world save, borrow, make payments, and manage risk, using regulated, unregulated, and informal institutions, It also includes information on the percentage of adults with an account at, and at least one loan outstanding from, a regulated financial institution – two of the G20 basic financial inclusion indicators (endorsed in June 2012). Launched in 2011 it was replicated in 2014 in partnership with the Gallup Organization and funded by the Bill & Melinda Gates Foundation, covering around 150,000 people in more than 140 economies. The two surveys went online in 2012 and 2015, respectively, and are the largest source of demand-side data. Their headline result is that half the world, about 2.5 billion adults (age 15+) out of

---

84 It can be accessed under http://fas.imf.org.
85 Fifteen countries did not report the number of commercial banks; a few others did not report any data on the commercial banks apart from their number. Twenty-four countries reported no financial cooperatives; 40 countries reported having no MFIs.

5 billion, were unbanked in 2011 and that, within a time span of three years to 2014, that number had dropped by 20% to 2 billion out of 5.2 billion. Globally, 62% of adults (up from 50% in 2011) have an account at a bank or another type of financial institution, such as a credit union, cooperative or microfinance institution, or with a mobile money provider, up from 51% in 2011.[86]

The gaps in account penetration are considerable: 94% of adults in high-income OECD economies have an account at a formal financial institution (up from 89% in 2011), compared to 54% in developing economies (up from 41% in 2011). As shown in Figure 26 and Table 21, in 2014 86% of adults in the Middle East and North Africa (2011: 82%) and 71% in sub-Saharan Africa (2011: 76%) lack a formal account, compared to 6% in high-income economies (2011: 11%). The share of the unbanked is 55% in South Asia (2011: 67%), 49% in Latin America and the Caribbean (2011: 61%), 49% in Eastern Europe and Central Asia (2011: 55%) and 31% in East Asia and the Pacific (2011: 45%).

The percentage of the population (age 15+) with an account at a formal financial institution in 2014, the converse of Figure 26, is given in Table 21 together with the percentage of account holders in 2011. The table also includes data on accounts held and loans taken out by formal SMEs at formal financial institutions.

Figure 26: Global Findex (2014): Adults (age 15+) who do not have an account with a formal financial institution (Source of data: Demirgüç-Kunt et al. 2015: 4; map: Savings Bank Foundation for International Cooperation)

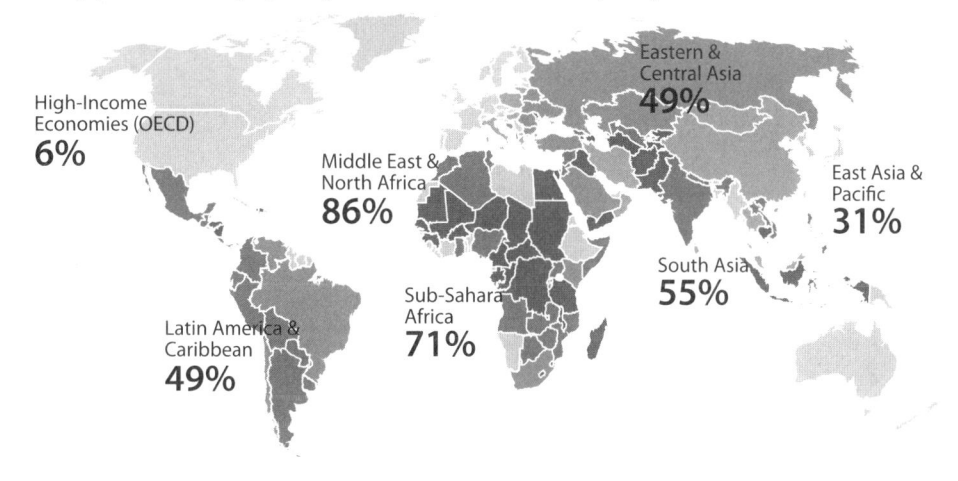

High-Income Economies (OECD) 6%
Eastern & Central Asia 49%
Middle East & North Africa 86%
East Asia & Pacific 31%
South Asia 55%
Sub-Sahara Africa 71%
Latin America & Caribbean 49%

---

[86] This section is heavily based, partly verbatim, on Demirgüç-Kunt and Klapper 2012 and Demirgüç-Kunt et al. 2015.

Table 21: Access to formal financial institutions (in %)

	Account holders in % of population (age 15+)		% of formal SMEs (5-99 employees)	
	2011	2014	Account	Loan
World	50	62	82	37
High-income OECD	89	94	84	47
East Asia and Pacific	55	69	88	36
Eastern Europe and Central Asia	45	51	88	42
Latin America and Caribbean	39	51	93	46
Middle East and North Africa	18	14	36	6
South Asia	33	45	80	28
Sub-Saharan Africa	24	29	87	21

Sources: For population data, Global Findex, 148 economies in 2011 and 143 economies in 2014; for SME data, World Bank enterprise surveys, 128 economies, 2011 or later (Demirgüç-Kunt and Klapper 2012; CGAP 2013; Demirgüç-Kunt et al. 2015)

With the expansion of formal finance and the growth of access in developing economies, informal financial institutions have not lost their vigor; to the contrary, they have multiplied in number and diversity (Seibel 2014). Demirgüç-Kunt and Klapper (2012) and Demirgüç-Kunt et al. (2015) confirm that large numbers of people save and borrow informally, using the services of rotating and non-rotating savings and credit associations, community-based institutions, friends and family, rather than commercial banks; this is most pronounced in Sub-Saharan Africa.

With the advent of mobile money financial inclusion may enter into a new era not only of access to, but also actual use of, formal financial services. Starting from South Africa in 2004 and Kenya since 2007 where it first became common, mobile money has spread rapidly in Africa and elsewhere. Only 2% of adults worldwide have a mobile money account as of 2014; in Sub-Saharan Africa, however, 12% do. All 13 countries around the world where the share of adults with a mobile money account is 10% or more are in Sub-Saharan Africa. Digitizing payments can play an important part in financial inclusion, argue Demirgüç-Kunt et al. (2015: 2-3): "Shifting payments such as wages or government transfers from cash into accounts can increase the number of adults with an account. And digitizing payments such as those for school fees or utility bills allows people who already have an account to benefit more fully from financial inclusion–by enabling them to make the payments in a way that is easier, more affordable, and more secure."

Access to finance for SMEs, and not only for individuals, in developing countries has been one of the major concerns of the G20. Given the importance of SMEs for economic growth and employment creation, the GPFI has focused on SMEs as one of its four priority topics. The year 2012 was the first that the IMF included data on SME lending in its Financial Access Survey, contributed by 37 out of 187 countries. SME lending as a percentage of GDP varies from a low of close to 0 % in Kenya, Zambia, and Madagascar, to 7 % in India, 10 % in Bangladesh, 15 % in China, and 18 % in Malaysia and El Salvador, to highs of 33 % in Thailand and 39 % in Korea.

In a recent study, the IFC reached largely similar conclusions concerning access to finance for the 25 to 50 million formal and informal MSMEs[87] in developing countries, based on data from enterprise surveys of the World Bank. The large majority of SMEs (with 5–99 employees) have an account at a formal financial institution, but the percentage of SMEs with a loan is much lower, ranging from 6 % in the MENA region to 46 % in Latin America and the Caribbean. Thus, there still seems to be a credit gap, which is estimated to be around USD 1 trillion.

We sum up our overview of the available data on microfinance worldwide and in different parts of the world, as well as the sources of data and their reliability, as follows:

1. As far as the availability of data on microfinance supply and use is concerned, the situation has clearly improved in recent years. However, since most data is available only for short time periods and only covers recent years, it does not allow a sound assessment of how much the provision of microfinance services has really changed over time.[88]
2. The two oldest data sources, the databases of the MIX and The Campaign, are more comprehensive as far as the number of years covered is concerned. However, for various methodological reasons, they are also less reliable than the newer databases, and therefore their data is also not suited for an in-depth comparison over time.
3. Despite providing some indications of a trend towards a general improvement, these databases, as well as those of a more recent vintage, consistently suggest that today there are still huge gaps in the supply of microfinance, and thus limits in the extent to which financial services are accessible for relatively poor segments of the general population and for MSMEs in most developing countries.
4. Thus, the problem that microfinance aspires to solve, or at least mitigate, remains a challenge, and most probably one that deserves high priority.
5. Of course, there can be no doubt that the situation differs greatly between regions and countries and even between different areas within a single country.

---

[87] The study defines MSMEs as micro (1–4 employees), very small (5–9 employees), small (10–49 employees) and medium (50–250 employees) enterprises.

[88] In a recent paper Rozas and Erice (2014) have pointed out another shortcoming of statistics referring to the availability and use of savings facilities: The large numbers of savings accounts that are reported in several sources tend to overstate the true extent of savings activity, since at least 50 % of the accounts are dormant, i.e. permanently unused, or empty most of the time. Accordingly, reporting on average saving volumes per savings account tends to be substantially downward-biased.

6. Looking at all available data, one might be inclined to assume that, generally speaking, at least the supply situation has changed, and the supply side in fact expanded, in many countries. However, whether this is a positive development or not is an open question – and this open question is the starting point for the deliberations in the next section.

3.4 Market saturation

Improving access to financial services for the poor is a widely accepted policy goal, but too much credit can be a bad thing. Obviously, credit granted by a lender is a debt for the borrower, since it implies the legal and possibly also moral obligation to repay the borrowed funds plus fees and interest. The repayment obligation is more of a burden if the volume of the loans contracted is high and, even more importantly, if the use of the borrowed funds does not improve the borrower's income and repayment capacity. Not all credit-financed ventures necessarily bear fruit, and not all small loans are used for income-generating purposes.

Thus, loans may be risky for the borrower even if they are for income-generating purposes, and all the more so if they are used for consumption purposes. While consumption loans can be extremely valuable for the clients if they permit them to bridge a temporary gap in income, for instance after a poor harvest or during temporary unemployment, there are also consumption loans of a questionable value: loans to finance expenditures that can be deemed unnecessary or even luxurious by local standards and that surpass the borrower's permanent income. Their main lasting effect for a borrower is simply a higher debt burden and the possibility of him or her defaulting on the loan or even on several loans taken out from various lenders. There is a real danger of "overborrowing" and "multiple borrowing."

Markets are called saturated if there is not enough demand compared to the available supply. In the case of microfinance, market saturation can be the result of a decline of "good," that is, revenue or income-backed, loan demand or an increase in loan supply facing a given "good" demand for loans. The latter case is more relevant in practice. In most countries the supply of small and very small loans has greatly expanded in recent years, and this has often happened without due consideration of the limited loan demand for purposes that would benefit borrowers and not ultimately harm them. A considerable number of new loan providers have entered the market, attracted by the good fortune of MFIs that they had observed during the early years of the new millennium, and most existing providers have expanded the scale of their operations.

Of course, entering a market and increasing supply can in retrospect easily be qualified as a mistake if the "good" demand is limited. But given the uncertainty of the future, such mistakes can happen. They are all the more likely if the relevant decision is not based on careful and cautious considerations but rather on political or bureaucratic reasoning – as in the case of many aid-funded MFIs – or on excessive optimism and the hope of gaining a share in a growing and attractive market – as in the case of market entry by established banks which suddenly realize that granting microloans may be a very lucrative line of business.

If the market for loans used for income-generating purposes is saturated, providers of microloans tend to fight for business and market share by relaxing their lending standards and granting consumption loans of questionable value. In both cases the danger of borrowers defaulting is higher than it was in the microfinance markets of a few years ago, in which the "good" demand for microloans regularly exceeded supply and in which savvy microlenders could expect to find a sufficient number of "good," creditworthy borrowers.[89]

The danger for clients of lenders lowering their lending standards is obvious: It may induce them to take out loans which are too burdensome for them and which they would not even have asked for if lenders had at least tried to find out for what income-generating purpose the loan will be used.[90] But it also constitutes a challenge for the lenders: the likelihood of borrowers defaulting is higher, and higher default rates may destabilize a lending institution. Lower interest rates also pose a challenge: they lead to lower revenues and possibly also lower profits, and this can also undermine the stability of a microcredit institution. These two effects are evident, but there are more dangers of increasing competition: If many lenders are competing for clients, it is easier for individual borrowers to get a loan from more than one lender at the same time. This increases his or her debt burden, reduces his or her ability to repay his or her loans properly and makes him or her less dependent on any single lender – since he or she can easily switch lenders – and thereby greatly reduces the incentive to make sure he or she can repay a loan or even several loans.

There are a number of countries in which the influx of new lenders and the expansion of the activities of those already in the market have led to serious repayment problems, to "overborrowing" and "multiple borrowing," high default rates and even debtors' rebellions against microlenders which tried to collect outstanding claims from borrowers. The list of countries that have experienced this phenomenon includes Bosnia Herzegovina, Morocco, Nicaragua, and not least of all India, specifically in the state of Andhra Pradesh (Roodman 2012). In several of these countries market entries were funded by international donors and commercial investors, and in a number of them political powers soon took the side of frustrated borrowers and encouraged them to simply refuse to repay their loans.

---

89 The wording is intended to remind the reader that finding creditworthy borrowers has never been easy for the providers of microloans. But it may indeed have been easier under earlier market conditions.
90 It is important not to overlook the fact that it is difficult to find out the purpose for which a loan is really being used, since money is fungible.

One notorious example is Nicaragua with its "no pago" movement; the other is the state of Andhra Pradesh in India (Oliver 2010). Reporting on such events may be anecdotal evidence of local microfinance crises, with limited scientific value. However, they indirectly support the assumption that there was also market saturation and even oversupply in these countries. But in some cases, for instance Bosnia-Herzegovina and the Indian state of Andhra Pradesh, a look at the details of the respective crisis reveals that there was not only market saturation, but also an oversupply of small and very small loans for which there was not enough "good" demand.

The discussion of market saturation and oversupply of microloans as a causal factor for a local microfinance crisis does not have to rely exclusively on anecdotal evidence and case studies of affected countries. There is also statistical evidence concerning the possible extent of market saturation. In their broadly conceived study of market saturation Javoy and Rozas (2013) rightly state that "[k]nowing where the upper limit [of supply] lies is critical for microfinance practitioners."

Using the Global Findex database, Javoy and Rozas have calculated market penetration rates for all 148 countries in the World Bank's Findex sample; this includes 109 poorer countries with a human development index below 80, for which they have also compiled supplementary MIX data.[91] On this basis they constructed what they call a credit market penetration scorecard, assigning countries a score from 1 to 5. Category 1, comprising 26% of poorer countries, denotes a country where retail credit appears to be substantially below its potential demand. Categories 2 and 3, comprising 29% and 27% of countries, respectively, are regarded as having "normally functioning markets," differentiated by their capacity for growth. Countries in category 4 are at, or above, the saturation level; a detailed analysis of market stability factors, including over-indebtedness, is suggested. Countries in category 5 have credit utilization rates at least double the value predicted by three analytical variables and are likely to be at or above their long-term sustainable credit-carrying capacity.

There are 20 countries with a high probability of market saturation and correspondingly high risks of credit failure. Seven are in category 5: Bangladesh, Bolivia, Cambodia, Cyprus, the Kyrgyz Republic, Laos, and Mongolia; and 13 are in category 4: Armenia, Azerbaijan, Belarus, Guatemala, Iran, Malawi, Montenegro, Paraguay, Peru, Sri Lanka, Thailand, Uruguay, and Vietnam.[92] For these countries the authors recommend focusing on preventing over-indebtedness and ensuring that external financial inflows do not push markets over the edge.

---

91 The complete market penetration file is available for further use: MIMOSA v1 0 XL file Planet Rating 2013-03, available upon request from Daniel Rozas <daniel@rozas.com> (cf. Javoy and Rozas 2013).

92 Interestingly, the more recent list of "problem countries" in the study by Javoy and Rozas does not overlap with the list in Roodman's 2012 book. This might be an indication that the set of countries suffering from the interrelated problems of market saturation, oversupply, and crisis may be quite large.

4 Microfinance as a field of international aid and cooperation

In the course of the past 40 years microfinance has been widely recognized as being a very sensible form of finance in those countries where much of (modern) microfinance takes place. It has also become a centerpiece of international aid or, to use a more modern and more politically correct term, international development cooperation.[93]

> **Snapshot 44: Some facts and figures about funding sources of microfinance institutions**
>
> Since the 1950s, large amounts of donor money from foreign – national and international – public sources have been provided for all kinds of development finance projects. Formerly, most of these funds were given to the large national development banks of the recipient countries, which were rarely concerned with financing small and very small businesses and poor people. With the development banks losing favor with the international donor community since the 1970s, the fraction of foreign funding from public sources that is meant to support microfinance has constantly increased. Some of this funding – the lion's share – came in the form of loans, often loans on very "soft" terms; some were provided via outright grants; and some also came in the form of equity investments for the creation or expansion of MFIs – the newest funding option.
>
> While in the past MFIs obtained funding almost exclusively from public, government-related sources, recent trends[92] indicate that the funding landscape for microfinance has changed greatly in several respects. First of all, in purely quantitative terms, it has increased enormously. In less than one decade, it has grown from USD 2 billion (in 2002) to more than USD 12 billion (Lützenkirchen 2012). Also, private foreign lenders and investors have greatly gained in importance, contributing almost half of the total. However, the most significant change concerns the role of deposits and thus of national funding sources. More than half of the funds of all MFIs covered by the relevant data sources are by now locally raised deposits. According to a study published by CGAP (2011), for all types of MFIs, the share of borrowings (mainly from abroad) in total funding is slightly below 30% for the years 2007 to 2010; that of equity is close to 20%, and that of deposits approaches 50%. Of course, the role of deposits is much more pronounced in the case of licensed microfinance banks, and much smaller for microfinance in the form of NGOs or non-bank financial institutions.

---

93 Unfortunately, relevant hard data for earlier decades is not available, and all recent publications use the same data provided by the MIX, a quite incomplete data source, as we have discussed in section 3. MIX data only cover the years since the turn of the century.

This section looks at microfinance as a field of development aid or cooperation and thus it views its subject matter largely from the perspective of decision makers in international organizations or advanced countries that are responsible for what can broadly be characterized as development finance. Returning to some of the topics discussed in the first chapter, we look at the evolution of development finance – and microfinance in particular – as a field of international aid and then focus on the various forms that aid projects in this area take. The section concludes by taking another look at recent events and debates that have raised doubts as to the ability of microfinance to play its intended role as an instrument of development policy.

4.1 Early forms of development finance and the emergence of microfinance[94]

Development finance in general and financial sector development in particular have consistently played an important role in development policy. However, in spite of this continuity, there have been dramatic changes over the years as policy makers have considered the issues of (1) how much weight development finance should be given in the overall context of development aid or development cooperation; (2) how much weight financial sector development should be given in comparison to other aspects of development finance; (3) what constitutes a good financial sector and what foreign aid can and should do to support financial development; and finally (4) what the vague term "finance" should even be understood to mean. The changing answers to these questions over time eventually led to changes in development finance-related policies, and ultimately to the emergence of modern microfinance.

Development finance as large-scale capital transfers

The modern origins of development policy date back to the first decade after World War II. At that time international aid consisted essentially of American support for the reconstruction of the economies and societies of the war-torn countries of Western Europe. The main instrument was the so-called Marshall Plan. The support provided by the US came primarily in the form of substantial quantities of physical capital goods that were transferred to European countries so that they could rebuild their economies. A complementary activity was the creation of specialized financial institutions that at first were charged with channeling the funds generated by the sale of these capital goods to public and private organizations that were deemed capable of using them for large investment projects. The implementation of such projects would in turn kick-start a broad-based process of growth and development (Abelshauser 2005).

---

[94] This section is based on Chapter II of Krahnen and Schmidt (1994).

This policy was very successful, and its success inspired several Western countries to use the Marshall Plan as a template for their aid policies vis-à-vis the so-called Third World countries during what we shall call the first phase of development finance. It lasted for more than 20 years, from the mid-1950s to the late 1970s. In essence, the approach taken during this period consisted of channeling substantial sums of capital to newly created specialized financial institutions in the recipient countries which took the form of government-owned development banks. Since these funds were mainly earmarked for buying investment goods, such as machinery and transportation equipment, from the industrialized countries, the economic substance of this form of donor support was equivalent to the direct transfer of physical or real capital, as opposed to the provision of financial capital.

This policy was based on the idea that foreign-funded large-scale projects would give a great push to development, setting processes in motion that would, in a positive way, "infect" the rest of the recipient countries' economies.[95] Investment and growth were supposed to "trickle down" more or less evenly over the entire economy. Not least for this reason, the financing was mainly provided on favorable terms, which usually meant loans at subsidized interest rates or merely access to large amounts of long-term funds and also foreign currency loans, both of which would otherwise have been impossible to obtain in most poor countries at that time.

After a few years, what had started as narrowly targeted support for large industrial and infrastructure projects financed with foreign funds and executed with the help of industrial development banks was expanded and implemented on a broader, more comprehensive basis. Other types of development banks were founded and they also received substantial financial support from Western governments and international organizations such as the World Bank and so-called regional development banks. Agricultural development banks were one example of the new kinds of institutions that were set up. These specialized banks mainly provided financing for large-scale agriculture and modern agricultural businesses, and most of them implemented large-scale, heavily subsidized and tightly supervised lending schemes that were meant to modernize agriculture and boost agricultural productivity and exports. Other new kinds of development banks established during this period included housing banks, typically with one being set up to serve higher-income people and another being created to finance social housing, as well as small business development banks for what were, however, in most cases not really small businesses. Even though the focus during this first phase was clearly on the transfer of large volumes of capital, some financial sector development occurred as a by-product.

In a few cases the activities carried out during this first phase of development finance were successful, but generally speaking the measures based on this approach were not. The underlying policy failed in both an economic and a political

---

[95] One of the most influential authors who advocated the underlying concept of "unbalanced growth" was Albert O. Hirschman; see, for example, Hirschman (1958).

sense.[96] The expected growth rarely materialized, and instead economic dualism became a problem: A few people benefited from the projects that were implemented while large parts of the population suffered as a result of their economic impacts. To take one typical example, consider a foreign-financed shoe factory which, with its huge advantages in terms of costs and efficiency, put hundreds of artisan shoemakers out of work. Moreover, many large-scale projects never came to fruition. As rigorous studies later showed,[97] the policy also led to a massive redistribution of income and wealth from the poor to the rich part of the population. Even more importantly, most development banks were notorious loss-makers and eventually failed, but in many cases were reopened with the same staff, and often in the same premises, only to pursue the same unsound policy again with fresh money from the same international sources. Support for this approach among donors and development institutions waned eventually, but it was never completely abandoned.

Development finance as capital transfers to the poor

In politically difficult times in the recipient countries, this state of affairs was not acceptable, especially given that the focus on large-scale capital transfers had begun to be seen as an important factor in the widening inequality that was at the root of much of the political unrest and instability. Therefore, a major reorientation was initiated in the policies of the donor countries and institutions around the middle of the 1970s, ushering in the second phase of development finance. As before, aid-supported development finance consisted of measures to channel foreign donor money to developing countries – but no longer to those who exercised control over presumed catalysts of growth; rather, funds were now to be provided directly to poor people in local societies who, it was hoped, would then experience, and learn to appreciate, the benefits of a well-functioning capitalist market economy.

However, actually reaching poor people and identifying suitable channels to provide credit for their business activities was not an easy task. Banks were not interested in serving as conduits for foreign funds for various reasons, most importantly because local regulations rarely allowed them to charge interest rates that would have been high enough to cover the presumed high costs of achieving the outreach necessary to actually serve poor borrowers. And then there was the strongly held belief that poor people create high risks and transaction costs. The banks simply did not know how to lend to poor borrowers in an efficient way. Finally, social prejudices made bank managers and staff reluctant to serve lower-class clients.

---

96 See footnote 24 in Chapter I.
97 An extensive investigation of the effects and the effectiveness of a major part of this policy is documented in the 21 volumes of the so-called Spring Review of Small Farmer Credit sponsored by USAID (1973). For a summary, see Donald (1976). Through the work of a group of researchers at Ohio State University, the highly critical findings of the Spring Review became one of the starting points for the new thinking about finance and development that strongly influenced the emergence of modern microfinance. See for example Adams et al. (1984).

If banks could not be involved, new channels for the distribution of donor funds were needed. And they quickly appeared in substantial numbers. Church-related and other philanthropic NGOs assumed this role, at least for a time.[98] The people working in these NGOs were compassionate, well-meaning, and politically motivated. Many of them were development volunteers with a background as social scientists and in some cases even as theologians. They wanted to help the poor, but they knew nothing about banking or how banks operate. Moreover, given their own social and cultural backgrounds and life experiences, they also did not have the necessary ability to understand and empathize with the members of the most important target group of this new form of development finance: local small-business people. The vast majority of these people were struggling to survive and keep their businesses afloat in a difficult and often hostile environment instead of planning a revolution, as some of the young foreigners may have wished.

Many of the new foreign-funded credit-granting organizations disappeared again after a very short time. They ran out of funds or staff, or both, and had to close down.[99] Good intentions are not enough to ensure that an organization will have an impact and also be able to survive.

A different type of NGO seemed to offer better prospects. For the new version of development finance – what was now called microenterprise lending – some business experience and an understanding of the situation of the presumed borrowers was indispensable. The NGOs staffed by foreign volunteers were soon replaced by local NGOs created and funded by established local business people – people who understood how important it is to prevent societies from losing their inner cohesion under the pressure of growing inequality and who also, because of their own backgrounds, understood what the owners of microenterprises need, how they think and feel and what motivates their behavior. The idea behind this shift was absolutely correct, and it was in harmony with the ideological trends of the period, as exemplified by the political philosophies of Ronald Reagan and Margaret Thatcher: These NGOs were sufficiently independent of their local governments and also seemingly supportive of private enterprise, and the combination of "microentrepreneurs," as borrowers were now called, and business-backed private NGOs became the new dream team in the development policy arena.[100]

---

[98] A number of relevant cases are very well documented in the so-called PISCES Studies (Farbman 1981) and later, similar studies that were initiated and funded by USAID.

[99] One of these institutions was the Grameen Bank, but it is almost the only one of its kind that managed to survive and grow, thanks to the charismatic leadership of its founder, Muhammad Yunus, and his prodigious fundraising skills. But like most of its peers, Grameen also absorbed huge amounts of donor money for many years; see Morduch (1992, 1999).

[100] Two of the present book's authors attended a large-scale conference held in Washington D.C. in 1989 entitled the "First World Microenterprise Conference," which contributed greatly to making the newly discovered "dream team" popular among development finance experts. The conference proceedings, which are truly interesting, are documented in Levitsky 1989, cf. Seibel 1989a. A similarly enthusiastic endorsement of certain types of NGOs as "Alchemists for the Poor" was published by ACCION at about the same time (Drake and Otero 1991).

A number of IFIs jumped on the bandwagon and started to promote the new type of business-based and business-oriented NGOs. One such institution, the IDB, set up a program to support local credit-granting NGOs. The support consisted of giving money to NGOs that claimed to make loans to local microbusinesses: they received USD 500,000 as a loan on extremely soft terms, or in other words, as a de facto grant, and an outright technical assistance grant of USD 50,000. Money was rapidly disbursed to selected NGOs, and its use and the impact of the lending funded by these disbursements were not monitored.

After some time the IDB began to question whether this was indeed the right way of supporting microcredit and microenterprises, and it commissioned a study to find out how effective and how efficient the recipient NGOs really were. This proved to be a difficult question to answer because many of the NGOs which were funded by the IDB – and also selected by it for inclusion in the study – declined to take part in the research, and almost none of the 15 that agreed to participate had an accounting system or other internal records that could produce the required information.

Nevertheless, the IDB decided to go ahead with the project and the study was executed as it had originally been conceived. Its findings were devastating for those who had at first been so enthusiastic about credit-granting NGOs (Schmidt and Zeitinger 1996b). With one exception, a foundation in Ecuador whose annualized interest rate reached a stunning 160% after inflation adjustment, none of the participating IDB-supported NGOs included in the study even came close to achieving cost coverage. This was also true of a subset of six NGOs which had explicitly committed themselves to pursuing a business policy that would at least make it feasible for them to cover their costs.

The study found that the loan portfolios were very small, rarely surpassing USD 1 million. What was more surprising was the level of costs. Expressed as a percentage of the NGOs' average outstanding loan portfolios, the combined costs of administration and loan losses p.a., excluding funding costs, were on average more than 50%. For full cost coverage, interest rates would have had to be about twice as high as those the NGOs were charging their clients.[101] This was not good news for the IDB, which decided to discontinue its program.

It was clear that microfinance could never have any appreciable impact as long as its costs were so high and the efficiency of the providers of microfinance so low. Only if costs could be brought down to much lower levels would it be economically justifiable, and also socially acceptable, to charge clients the full costs of credit provision, and thus feasible to achieve financial sustainability and still create value for the clients. But this would scarcely be possible with MFIs which were extremely small and operating under governance structures like those typically found in

---

[101] Only one NGO had sufficient revenue to cover its full costs – and its realized revenue after inflation adjustment was a stunning 200% of its loan portfolio.

NGOs, suggesting that in order to be truly viable and perform their intended function on a long-term basis, MFIs would have to become much more efficient and to adopt at least some features of conventional banks.

This was also during the period when so-called Grameen replication had begun to spread to many countries, including the Philippines. The term "Grameen replicators" designates institutions modeled after the Grameen Bank in terms of strategy, organization, and lending methods. Grameen replication was generously funded by several donors and implemented in numerous countries beginning in the 1980s. In 1993, the Agricultural Credit Policy Council (ACPC) of the Philippines, a government institution, examined its experience as a program executing agency with 27 Grameen replicators. Its findings were similar to those of the IDB-sponsored study. The Grameen replicators had a negligible outreach, and the entire replicator program was found to be donor-driven; internal resource mobilization was minimal; interest rates were inadequate; and costs, shared about equally between government and the replicators, were exorbitant. Some replicators heeded the advice to change their strategy, among them the Philippine institution known as CARD MRI.[102] Its core unit was licensed as a rural bank in 1997, and it has achieved stunningly positive results ever since.[103]

Development finance as financial sector deregulation

Almost in parallel to the second phase, another important trend in the field of development finance began to take shape. Although this trend emerged while the second phase was still underway, the shift in thinking which it embodied, and the approach to which it gave rise, represented enough of a departure from the prevailing wisdom that it was seen as marking the beginning of a third phase. This one was not about channeling funds to developing countries, but rather about changing the character of their financial systems and sectors. Based on two publications by Shaw and McKinnon in the early 1970s and clearly reflecting the dominant ideological currents of the time,[104] policy makers came to the conclusion that the old policy of financial repression was a big mistake and that the best thing one could do in order to make finance accessible for business people of all kinds and all wealth levels, and even for the relatively poor people who constituted the majority of the population in developing countries, was to liberalize and radically deregulate the financial sector as fully as possible. In practice this meant abolishing interest rate ceilings for loans and deposits, eliminating minimum reserve requirements for banks, doing away with entry barriers to banking, granting banks the freedom to engage in all types of financial business which they wished to conduct and to do so in whatever way they chose, and privatizing state-owned banks.

---

102 The institution undertook the reorientation with technical assistance from SBFIC and others.
103 http://cardbankph.com/?page_id=1411.
104 See Shaw (1973) and McKinnon (1973). These two influential studies were written independently of each other and came to largely similar conclusions. The ideological spirit of that time, and the policy assumptions to which it gave rise, later came to be known as the Washington Consensus. For a summary and assessment see Williams (1993).

If all of this were done, it was thought that large volumes of deposits would flow into the banks, and, no less importantly, that banks would find it attractive to lend to micro and small businesses at cost-covering interest rates – which would also solve the problem that microfinance was trying to address.

The advice was heeded, especially by US policy makers and development agencies, and the measures outlined above were implemented in most of Latin America, most radically in the so-called Southern Cone countries. The immediate impact was in line with what the deregulation advocates had predicted: Banking business boomed. But this only lasted for a short time. Quite soon the boom was followed by a bust. The bankers had used their new freedom to undertake extremely risky operations which could not be sustainable. As a consequence, the banking systems of Argentina, Chile, and Uruguay collapsed almost simultaneously. Many banks went under, and a few big banks had to be rescued through nationalization. The economist Carlos Diaz-Alejandro (1985) describes this episode very well in an article aptly entitled "Good-Bye Financial Repression, Hello Financial Crash."

The boom-to-bust cycle repeated itself in Indonesia. After the decline in oil prices in 1982 and the resulting loss of income from oil exports, Indonesia initiated an era of liberalization, shifting from a supply-driven to a demand-led financial system approach; market forces replaced the government as the prime mover of development. Interest rates were fully deregulated (1983); the establishment of private banks was made easier (1988); and 32 out of 36 major subsidized credit programs were phased out (1990). Inflation fell; between 1982 and 1990, financial depth (M_2/GDP) rose from 16% to 43%; GDP growth rates averaged 7% p.a. during the period 1979–1996; and according to World Bank (1999) data, the poverty rate fell from 60% in 1970 to 11.5% in 1996. In 1990–91 Bank Indonesia, the central bank, announced the introduction of prudential standards for the country's banks, but was unable to enforce them due to fierce opposition on the part of the corporate sector, which had a vested interest in maintaining the status quo, and by the advocates of rapid and unbridled liberalization; by this point the banking sector was practically out of control. The Asian financial crisis of 1997–98 revealed the downside of the liberalization policy and ushered in its demise. The collapse of the Indonesian banking system was both a cause and a consequence of this crisis.

The key lesson drawn from the experience of this period was that radical liberalization without concomitant prudential regulation was also not a panacea for solving the problem of poor people's lack of access to finance. As Joseph E. Stiglitz,[105] and various other economists with whom he has co-written numerous papers down through the years, have argued convincingly, financial markets do not

---

[105] Stiglitz was a member of President Clinton's Council of Economic Advisors, served as the Chief Economist of the World Bank between 1997 and 2000 and received the Nobel Prize in economics in 2001. Main topics of his very broad research agenda are how well financial markets function, or fail to function, and how this is related to economic development.

function like the markets for chairs or cement.[106] One of the practical implications of the critique of the former regime of financial repression, the presumed necessity of closing down many development banks in a number of countries, may even have made the access problems worse.[107] However, at least one element of the liberalization policy remained in place and proved decisive for the further development of microfinance: the phasing out of interest rate ceilings. The reason for this is quite simple: only if banks are able to freely determine the interest rates they charge on their loans to difficult-to-service client groups, and to pay interest rates on deposits that will in fact attract a sufficient deposit volume to fund their lending operations, will they be inclined to grant loans to such clients. And only if bank lending rates are deregulated will MFIs be able to opt for the legal and institutional form of a bank, instead of having to remain NGOs, which in most countries are not allowed to take deposits.

Taken together, the first three phases of development finance provide important lessons. One is that financial services must indeed be offered directly to those who are supposed to benefit from them. The trickle-down effect, which policymakers in the era of large-scale capital transfers expected to materialize as a result of those transfers, is an illusion; finance must be "finance for all." The second important lesson was that merely relying on good intentions and making use of institutional forms which, while seeming particularly well suited to the task of delivering credit to local target groups, will simply never be able to perform that task efficiently, is a dead end. Finally, the experience gained during the third phase showed that it would be naïve to have too much confidence in the ability of free markets for financial services to eliminate the problems and constraints which had emerged during the first two phases. At any rate, complete freedom does not make viable, sustainable providers of microfinance suddenly sprout up like mushrooms; liberalization must be combined with regulation and supervision. However, some freedom is indispensable if microfinance is to become efficient and have the desired impact.

---

106 See Stiglitz and Weiss (1981) and Hellmann, Murdock and Stiglitz (1997), among many other papers.
107 Dissatisfaction with development banks, including agricultural and rural development banks, was clearly justified. Many of them were indeed extremely inefficient, overly politicized and corrupt. The excessive political influence to which they were subject often tended to encourage corruption, primarily in the form of favoritism towards certain "preferred" target groups and individual borrowers. This phenomenon was mainly an outgrowth of the old government or central bank policy of putting a cap on the permissible interest rates on loans and deposits. However, in many countries the agricultural development bank was the only financial institution with a large branch network in many regions, and it thus also had considerable outreach. This was a strength that could have been preserved if these banks had been thoroughly reformed instead of being closed. In some Asian countries, for example Indonesia (see the case study of BRI above), Thailand, and Mongolia, where institutions of this type were reformed, the effects were clearly positive. For details see Seibel (2009a) and Seibel, Giehler and Karduck (2005).

4.2 The turn towards modern microfinance

Conflicting views

Like any other financial institution, an MFI must be commercially viable, but at the same time it must also have a social or developmental mission. Ensuring that both of these goals are met and striking the right balance between them are the challenges that began to guide the evolution of development finance after the end of the third phase. In this fourth phase, which started around 1990 and is still ongoing, the focus has been on giving microfinance an increasingly commercial orientation and on institution building to create the structures it needs to achieve its dual goals on a sustainable basis (cf. Krahnen and Schmidt 1994; Seibel 1996).

The lessons to be drawn from the history of development finance in the preceding years, i.e. during the first three phases, were recognized and understood by an increasing number of experts. Some of them worked in national and international development aid institutions such as the World Bank, the IDB, the EBRD, the UK development agency DFID and the German development bank KfW, others in the academic world, and still others at local MFIs in developing countries; and the consensus began to spread among consultants and staff members of microfinance support organizations such as CGAP and ACCION as well. They all shared the view that if microfinance really did possess the enormous potential that it was widely assumed to have, there should be many MFIs, they must be large institutions which reach large numbers of clients, and they should also be able and willing to serve them on a lasting basis and in an efficient way. This would require that, apart from receiving a certain amount of start-up assistance, MFIs should be capable of operating without continuous subsidies because the resources of those in a position to provide grants and soft loans are limited. For the advocates of this view, the Grameen Bank, which at that time was heavily subsidy-dependent and consistently incurred substantial losses, was not the model of a good MFI; rather, they took their inspiration from other providers such as BancoSol or BRI's microbanking units.[108]

Of course, in all of these organizations and institutions there were also experts who remained attached to the older notion that microfinance is an instrument for the furtherance of social policy objectives on a worldwide scale. In their eyes, it was thus in essence a form of public welfare, and as such it was, almost by definition, an activity that could never be financially self-sufficient and had to be subsidized permanently by the better-off countries and their citizens. For them, the Grameen Bank remained the model of a really good and valuable MFI. One quite

---

[108] Yaron developed a Subsidy Dependence Index (SDI), which he applied to numerous development finance institutions in Asia; see for example Yaron 1992. BRI achieves a very low score, indicating a very low level of reliance on subsidies, while at that time the Grameen Bank had a high dependence score.

influential group of authors have called these advocates of the older approach, including themselves, the "welfarists" and the adherents of the opposing camp the "institutionalists."[109]

The second group of experts, i.e. the "institutionalists," would have subscribed to the commercial approach if that term had already been invented at that time. And they would also have agreed that if one wishes to have a commercially viable, subsidy-independent institution, the basis must be a sound and carefully elaborated concept for the design, establishment, and operation of such an institution. In other words, they would also have subscribed to the financial institution building approach. However, these two names or labels – "commercial approach" and "institution building approach" – were not coined and popularized until later in the 1990s, when they were invented to characterize the strategies that had emerged in the course of the debate between the two camps described above.[110] For the "institutionalists," creating stable institutions that offer financing for small and very small businesses, and opening up access to formal finance to new segments of society, make much more sense as strategic objectives of microfinance than what their opponents, the "welfarists," believed – namely, that the main, or at least the most important, target group of microfinance should be defined as people who are really poor by local standards, and that the overriding goal of microfinance is to lift these people out of poverty. From the point of view of the "institutionalists," these two "welfarist" dogmas are much too ambitious, and adopting them can only lead to disillusionment later on.

The commercial approach

In order to understand the essential characteristics of development finance in this fourth phase, it is necessary, first of all, to recall what the core concepts mean. "Commercial approach" simply means creating and managing MFIs in such a way that they are able to cover their full operating costs from the revenue they earn. This point should be reached after an initial period, hopefully a short one, in which the institution is set up, is provided with the necessary resources, launches its operations and establishes itself in its market.

---

109 See Hulme and Mosley (1996) and Woller et al. (1999). In the 1990s all of these authors also served as co-editors of highly respected journals in the field of development finance: Hulme and Mosley at the *Journal of International Development*, and Woller and his co-authors at the *Journal of Microfinance*.

110 The terms were coined by members of two organizations that competed for the honor of being the conceptual leaders in the development of modern microfinance, namely ACCION and IPC. And they were competing not only on a conceptual and intellectual level, but also in very practical terms for funding for their projects, for staff and, to a certain extent, for revenue as well. Nevertheless, as far as the overarching debate between the "welfarists," i.e. the advocates of the Grameen Bank's approach, and the "institutionalists" was concerned, they were clearly allies – and they were always aware of how much they had in common. From our current perspective, the once hotly debated question of which of the two strategies – the "commercial approach" or the "institution building approach" – is superior, is largely a matter of historical interest; in substantive terms, it is no longer really relevant.

"Full costs" can be defined in different ways: either only the costs of administration plus the amount required to cover loan losses; or, more broadly, these costs plus the effective cost of funds obtained from donors; or, in the broadest definition, these three categories of costs plus the cost of equity.[111]

There can be no doubt that achieving full cost coverage and earning a positive ROE with an MFI is not an easy task. It requires a great effort to keep operating costs, the cost of risk, and funding costs low. To achieve this goal, a commercially oriented MFI will restrict the range of services it offers its clients, prefer borrowers who are less risky and less costly to serve, and aspire to grow to the point that it can spread its largely fixed overhead costs over a substantial volume of loans and possibly also deposits. And it must attempt to increase its revenue. The simplest way to do this is to raise prices, that is, to charge high interest rates on loans and pay a low rate on deposits.

But there are limits to how far a financial institution of any type can go in its efforts to keep its costs low and its revenue high. It must take into account that its customers may no longer exhibit a demand for its services if its prices are too high and it must be aware of what competitors are offering their clients. For an MFI, an additional constraint comes into play: Prices and product or service quality must meet the standards implicitly defined by the social and developmental goals to which the institution is committed in addition to commercial viability. Products that are too simple to truly meet clients' needs, and interest rates that are too high to be truly affordable, are ruled out.

Therefore, the latitude available to an MFI is quite limited. What it can in fact do is make internal processes as efficient as possible and, in addition, be very strict with respect to the repayment discipline of its credit clients and quite demanding in terms of the performance standards it sets for its staff. As a consequence, some commercially oriented institutions may not always seem to be particularly nice or "understanding" when dealing with borrowers who try to avoid repaying their loans or with staff members who do not wish to work as hard as they know they should. But if such an attitude is necessary in order to ensure that an MFI remains viable and can offer its services on a lasting basis, this may be a price worth paying.

The institution building approach

Pursuing a financial institution building approach means designing an MFI in a way which enables it to do two things at the same time: first, serve a designated, hitherto disadvantaged target population with no previous access to formal sector loans, not only for a short time, but on a long-term basis; and second, become and remain a stable institution that is also growing and that provides good service to its clients. In the first chapter we have already described what is necessary in order

---

[111] In practice, the cost of debt can be assumed to be in the range of 4 to 7%, and that of equity between 10 and 15% plus, possibly, a country risk premium.

for this to be feasible: the creation of a coherent, internally consistent set of incentives and rules of behavior for all of the people who, as clients, as staff members, as managers, or as owners, are expected to contribute in their respective capacities to the healthy development of the institution. Once an institution is up and running, it is of course also necessary that it be managed in a commercially oriented way.

The basic idea underlying the institution building approach is an ambitious one, and this raises the question of whether it is in fact feasible to implement this approach in practice. However, the experience of the early 1990s had already indicated that it might indeed be feasible. The experience of early institution building projects had shown that, with this approach, it required *less time,* and also *less money* from donors, to build an MFI which was stable and profitable and could grant *a large number* of *small and very small* loans to *relatively poor clients* at *acceptable costs* for the clients, and to do this in a way that enabled the institution to begin *covering its full costs* after a *short* start-up period. Indeed, a few experienced institution builders seemed able to create such an institution in almost any developing country at *limited costs* for the international donor community, which clearly seemed willing to pay for this service.[112]

The advocates of the institution building approach claimed that it was possible to create MFIs that met these requirements in many countries. It was a bold claim and possibly also a rather optimistic one, as it was based on experience in only a few countries in which, at that time, the competition between MFIs was not yet intense and the microloan market was not yet saturated. But subsequent experience gained in more difficult environments showed that it was not overly optimistic.

Only a few years later, around the year 2000, the battle was largely over between, on the one side, those who believed that development finance – and in particular, microfinance in developing countries – could not, and also should not, aspire to be cost-covering (and certainly not profitable, even if only marginally so), and that it must therefore rely on worldwide support, mainly from Western countries, as a moral and political obligation on the part of the rich countries and their citizens; and, on the other side, those who regarded a commercial orientation, financial self-sufficiency and the creation of stable MFIs as something worth pursuing and as a promising strategy in developmental terms. The "institutionalists" had scored a clear victory over the "welfarists," although perhaps more among development finance experts than among the members of the general public, in the eyes of the media, and among certain policy makers.[113] This outcome raises a

---

[112] See Schmidt and Zeitinger (1998) for specific quantitative data that can be filled in to replace the very imprecise terms set in italics in the text above.

[113] In Schmidt (2010) the assertion that there had been a victory of the "institutionalist" position over that of the "welfarists" among development finance practitioners and other experts in this field is backed up with specific numbers and a simple measure of impact that serve to demonstrate the economic and also ethical superiority of the new approach over the old one.

somewhat technical, but very important question: How can institutions which are sustainable, and at the same time relevant in both social and developmental terms, be created?

4.3 Strategies for creating efficient and sustainable microfinance institutions

In the transition from financial repression to increasingly inclusive financial systems over the last 40 years, the creation of access to finance for all segments of the population – including, or even focusing exclusively on, the poor and the owners of small and very small businesses – has become an overwhelming concern. And after a long learning process it has become abundantly clear that only commercially viable institutions which employ sound operating procedures and business practices, and which mobilize their own resources and cover their full costs, can respond to the rapidly increasing demand for savings, credit, and other financial services on a sustainable basis. Thus, financial institution building is at the heart of financial sector-related development policy.

The available options

Early on it was recognized that a wide variety of existing institutions could potentially serve as microfinance providers, but it was also understood that they would all have to undergo significant modifications to enable them to play their intended role as financial intermediaries for low-income people and MSMEs effectively. The range of existing institutions covered commercial and development banks; formal local banks; regulated MFIs; semiformal financial institutions under private, cooperative, community or local government ownership; credit NGOs; and informal financial institutions. And of course there was also the option of creating new institutions, but these would have to be designed and operated in such a way that they could perform their assigned functions both efficiently and in a commercially viable manner. Since the late 1980s, a number of new approaches to financial institution building[114] with broad fields of application have been devised and implemented. In this process, a classification of strategies of institutional modification and transformation has emerged which distinguishes between four basic approaches, and the terminology employed in this classification scheme has been widely adopted by development finance experts. These are the four strategies and the terms used to designate them:

---

114 The term institution building is much older, but its meaning has changed over time. Formerly it was used for a relatively unimportant component of a financial development project, such as the funding of advisory assistance or the donation of a vehicle that went along with what mattered more, namely the transfer of funds. New-style institution building, in contrast, aims to devise a comprehensive approach to designing an institution as a whole.

- *Upgrading* is the term for a strategy that aims at transforming an informal or semi-formal institution, most often an NGO, into a formal and regulated microbank or a commercial bank. The "up" refers to an assumed hierarchy of degrees of formalization. Therefore, one can also use the term in a more general sense and apply it to all development measures that seek to enable an institution to operate at a higher level of formalization.
- *Downscaling* is the term for projects that aim at enabling an existing institution that has not so far served poorer people and really small and informal businesses to start serving these clients. The "down" refers to an implicit ranking of clients according to their economic status. In other words, the goal is to enable the institution to "move down market" and begin catering to more "downscale" target groups. Thus, a "downscaled" institution is one that has begun to actively seek the business of lower-income clients; it is not one that has itself in any way been "downscaled" in the sense of being reduced in size.
- *Linking* is the term for projects that aim at establishing links between formal and non-formal financial institutions, or between poor clients and different types of formal, semi-formal, and informal institutions.
- *Starting from scratch* or, as it is also called, "*greenfielding*," is the term for the creation of new socially-oriented formal financial institutions where none had previously existed (cf. Seibel 1985, 1997).

These classifications and the corresponding terminological distinctions have grown out of development aid practice. They therefore reflect the perspective of donors and consultants and the challenges and choices that they faced at various times and in various institutional, social, and political environments. More specifically, they reflect the perspective of experts who have for a long time focused merely on two types of financial institutions: NGOs (in the form of associations or foundations) and formal banks.[115] In the following, we mainly adopt this narrower perspective, but to round out the picture we also refer to cases involving other types of institutions to which these terms can usefully be applied.

Upgrading existing microfinance institutions

In the first half of the 1990s, when the enthusiasm regarding credit-granting NGOs had begun to wane, several development finance experts came to the conclusion that, at least in the long term, it would make sense to also take advantage of the technical and operational benefits offered by the institutional form of a bank[116] in the context of microfinance. According to this new view, the preferred

---

[115] A great deal of the practical experience that inspired the terminology was gained in projects in Latin America, where NGOs had for a long time been the most important players in microfinance and the most important recipients of donor support. The debate of the 1990s was strongly influenced by people at ACCION, the IDB, CGAP, IPC, and Ohio State University, most of whom had mainly worked in Latin America.

[116] By this time, the state-mandated interest rate ceilings, which previously would have made the issuance of small and very small loans by a bank impossible for all practical purposes, had been eliminated almost everywhere.

long-term objective in the area of institutional development was the conversion of at least some MFIs, i. e. the really good ones, into banks. They would need to have a banking license, which would allow them to offer a wider range of services and to take deposits; they would have to be supervised by the appropriate national authorities; and they would have to operate on a commercial basis and at the same time be target group-oriented. Deposits are necessary in order to enable a rapid expansion of a financial institution's credit business, and in most countries only institutions which have an appropriate license and are subject to supervision by the local banking authorities are permitted to engage in deposit-taking. At the same time, most of the representatives of the development aid organizations were still largely convinced of the advantages of working with local NGOs and their founders and existing managers. To a certain extent, this was a matter of political correctness; but it also reflected a genuine conviction that local leaders would have a better understanding of local circumstances and possibly also of the clients' needs. Thus, the upgrading strategy seemed to be an almost ideal way to achieve the long-term goal of creating a bank while maintaining close relationships with the preferred project partners at the local level.

An upgrading project consists of two phases, and it can only begin after a suitable organization, usually a credit-granting NGO, has been identified as a project partner. The organization's representative(s) and spokesperson(s) have to be genuinely committed to serving the designated target group and also sufficiently open to the idea of adopting a commercial orientation, and they must also be – or at least appear to be – willing to carry out far-reaching institutional changes. Typically, such an NGO will be small at the outset and not very successful, and will therefore only have limited outreach and developmental impact.

Given that this is the initial situation, it is not surprising that the first phase of an upgrading project typically consists of making the existing institution, often an NGO, larger and more efficient through the provision of consultancy services, necessary equipment and, last but not least, a substantial volume of funds for onlending. Once the process of institutional strengthening has been completed, the second phase can begin, with the now solidly performing NGO being converted into a formal bank.

Both the strengthening of the institution in the first phase and its formalization in the second require a large-scale deployment of competent advisors experienced in institution building, which, as a rule, must be financed by one or more development aid organizations which also provide the necessary loan funds.

There were some cases of successful upgrading, but far fewer than one might imagine, given the high expectations which its supporters had for this new type of project.[117]

---

[117] Using the most recent data available at the time at which they did their research, Nair and Von Pischke (2007) provide an overview of the number of successful upgrading projects and also emphasize that this number is clearly lower than had once been expected.

One reason for this is that there were relatively few NGOs that would be suitable for conversion into a bank and whose founders, top managers or leaders would opt for the institutional transformation. Another reason is that the two-phase project design fails to create appropriate incentives, and may even create perverse ones. To illustrate this point, imagine the hypothetical case of an NGO which is relatively small and unsuccessful, but has high ambitions in ethical and development policy terms. It was founded – or is led, managed, or represented – by a local individual who typically also has high personal ambitions and aspires to achieve a higher social status, not least through the success of the organization. This NGO leader is likely to accept the invitation to be a partner in the project because this could be expected to strengthen his or her organization and, indirectly at least, also benefit its existing clients, who would be better served, and also those additional clients which the NGO would be able to serve after completion of the first phase.[118]

Once the first part of the upgrading process, the institutional strengthening, has been completed successfully, the second phase is launched: the institutional transformation. At this stage, bank supervisors and possibly also donors and consultants are likely to tell the local leader that managing a formal bank is a much more demanding role than leading an NGO and that he or she might simply lack the qualifications required by the relevant national authorities. This would cause the local leader to reconsider the commitment given to also support the formalization of "his" or "her" NGO, because a change in the legal form might imply that he or she would lose control over the organization – and with it lose the prestige that had been conferred by the success of the institutional strengthening phase. He or she might be inclined to work "behind the scenes" to delay or otherwise impede the implementation of phase two, or even to openly boycott the institutional transformation process. There is a good chance that his or her efforts would be successful, resulting in the termination of the project. For the staff of donor institutions, the attitude of the individual who has traditionally been in charge of the NGO and guided its development is an important factor. Simply ignoring the concerns of the person who has been closely associated in the public perception with the past improvements in the NGO's outreach and performance is difficult for the staff of development agencies, and efforts to bypass this individual can quickly lead to conflicts that seriously undermine the feasibility of the entire undertaking. By the same token, an overly accommodating approach to dealing with his or her wishes or criticisms can also make it difficult or impossible to carry out the far-reaching institutional changes that are needed. Thus, if it turns out that the person who has traditionally served as the NGO's leader does not fully support the institutional transformation with all of its ramifications; an upgrading project can come to a premature end – as has frequently been the case in practice.

---

118 Based on a specific real-life case, this scenario is described in detail in Schmidt (2005).

Even if this does not happen and the former leader of the NGO remains more or less in charge of the upgraded institution, he or she may become a burden for the newly created microfinance bank if, as is also frequently the case in practice, he or she is too closely identified with the old ways of doing things in the NGO. Moreover, practitioners report that the value of the former NGO leader's familiarity with the local environment has often been vastly overestimated.

Who benefits and who is harmed when an upgrading project is terminated under the circumstances described here, i.e. after completion of the first phase? The beneficiaries of the first phase are the existing customers of the larger, stronger NGO; the new customers attracted during this project phase; and the NGO's leader and other local managers. Those who are adversely affected by the failure to carry out the second phase are the large group of people who would have become customers in the course of the further expansion that would have been feasible following the conversion of the institution into a bank, and those who would have constituted the additional staff employed in a larger MFI in the form of a licensed bank.

Upgrading projects imply an additional challenge of a structural nature: The transformation of an NGO and its formalization as a licensed bank require that the NGO first be converted into a corporation, or that a new corporation be founded. In most cases in which phase two of an upgrading project has been successfully implemented, further shareholders have been required for this strengthening of the institution's equity base through the formation of a corporation – investors in addition to the original NGO, which often becomes an important shareholder. Together, the shareholders are then the owners of an institution which was created primarily with development aid funds and which will also remain strongly dependent on its donors for a fairly long period of time. Given its purpose, the new MFI should of course be a successful undertaking in commercial terms because otherwise it cannot become a stable, growing institution. However, its task is ultimately to contribute to the country's economic development and to serve the less prosperous members of its society. That gives rise to the question of who has, or should have, control over the MFI created in this manner, and how – and by whom – the ownership rights should be distributed.

The first case of a successful upgrading of an NGO to create a formal bank was BancoSol in Bolivia, which was founded in 1992 and evolved out of the NGO Prodem.[119] For a number of years Prodem had been strongly supported by ACCION, a private US-based non-profit microfinance support organization. Thanks to the rapid success of the institution launched by this bold and innovative step, ACCION soon became the main protagonist of the upgrading strategy. It also became an important shareholder of BancoSol, alongside Prodem, and later, when

---

119 See Drake and Rhyne (2002), and Otero and Rhyne (1994).

BancoSol's continued development was threatened, possibly because of the kind of problems described above, ACCION played an important and constructive role in keeping the bank on track.

A number of other former credit-granting NGOs in Latin America followed the same path; some had also been affiliated with ACCION[120] prior to the institutional transformation and had been converted into banks under its guidance, while others had been created as NGOs by IPC, acting as a consultant.[121] There are by now numerous other examples of microcredit NGOs that have been successfully upgraded to rural or commercial banks, among them CARD Rural Bank/MRI in the Philippines, Equity Bank in Kenya, and ACLEDA in Cambodia.

In our collection of case studies in section 2, we have included several cases which can be classified as examples of upgrading, at least in the broader sense of this term. VSLAs are an upgraded version of indigenous rotating and non-rotating savings and credit associations. The evolution of the system of doorstep deposit collectors in Ghana is another example of upgrading in a broader sense. The deposit collectors' proposal to establish their own bank was repeatedly rejected by the BoG; instead, reflecting changes in the country's banking legislation, BoG recently created a regulatory framework for microfinance and established a direct licensing procedure for companies formed by deposit collectors as well as a licensing process for individual deposit collectors which is being implemented via their national association.

In Laos, a long-term process has taken place of upgrading a local network of credit funds to create a system of formal financial intermediaries. Most VFs now operate as locally registered village "banks" which mobilize their own onlending resources from savings and retained earnings.

Perhaps the most impressive story of upgrading among our case studies is that of Centenary Bank in Uganda. It had been started as a "trust fund," a kind of NGO, to help the poor through the provision of financial services. With funding from various sources, including the German SBFIC, and the advisory support of IPC, Centenary was transformed into a very successful microenterprise (and later MSME) bank.

---

[120] ACCION is probably the best known, most widely acclaimed and most successful microfinance support organization worldwide. For information about the large network of MFIs that are affiliated in one form or another with ACCION, see its website.

[121] The institutions whose transformation was guided by IPC are Calpiá in El Salvador and Caja Los Andes in Bolivia. The latter case is particularly interesting as it involved a process of "pseudo upgrading": Caja Los Andes was created as an association by a group of highly respected Bolivian citizens who had been brought together for this purpose by the consultants. It was agreed with the founders right from the start that the institution's status as an NGO should only be temporary and that the conversion into a bank should be initiated as soon as possible. The temporary NGO status was considered necessary in order to obtain the start-up funding and the start-up subsidies that were customarily provided by foreign donor institutions, because at that time it would have been unthinkable for these institutions to support an MFI operating in any other legal form than that of an NGO (Schmidt 2005). By contrast, Prodem, the institution from which BancoSol evolved, had originally been a "true NGO."

Downscaling existing banks

Downscaling consists of first convincing an existing bank that providing small and very small loans to small and very small enterprises can be a worthwhile new line of business, and then using development aid funds to support this bank in the creation of a small business division that operates essentially like an independent MFI.

In virtually every developing country there are commercial and development banks which have the potential to undertake the institutional adjustments that would be needed to enable them to provide the banking services required by microentrepreneurs and the poor. However, tapping this vast potential is a major challenge. The key prerequisite is interest rate deregulation; banks must be permitted to offer attractive interest rates to savers and to charge adequate interest rates on loans. The institutional modifications required to enable banks to serve the microfinance market can include: the adoption of a corporate culture combining commercial and social objectives, a performance-related governance and incentive system, a decentralized and specialized delivery structure, and simplified procedures; the introduction of demand-led savings, credit, and other products with appropriate terms and conditions; a shift to risk management focused more on arrears prevention and incentives for timely repayment than on formal collateral; the creation of opportunities for borrowers to "graduate" from micro to small and medium loans; and increased emphasis on the recruitment and training of staff with appropriate communication and social skills. Downscaling may also include linkages with SHGs which serve as grassroots financial intermediaries, as well as with specialized MFIs and NGOs as service providers. With respect to virtually all of these aspects of the process of institutional adaptation, BRI, the subject of one of our case studies, can serve as a model: this is a bank that was saved in the Asian financial crisis by the success of its "downscaled" microbanking units.

Within the microfinance community, downscaling – like upgrading – was generally seen as a project type which emerged in Latin America, and the term "downscaling" was even more closely associated with project experience in that region. Donors, especially the IDB, were frustrated with the slow process of "upgrading" microcredit NGOs. The IDB was looking for another, more efficient way of creating a supply of loans for relatively poor people, and based on the insight that banks have certain advantages over NGOs, and given that an appropriate lending methodology for micro and small businesses had already been sufficiently tested in the early 1990s, the downscaling strategy appeared to be a promising one.

A downscaling project typically involves a (foreign) donor agency, a consultant with expertise in microlending and institution building, and a set of local partner banks. It functions as follows: The donor agency commissions the consultant to identify existing banks that are both willing and able to develop the institutional capacity needed to engage in small and micro business lending. The consultant then trains the banks' staff, showing them how to grant very small, small and medium-sized loans successfully, and helps the banks to set up small business departments. In addition, and as an incentive to participate, the development agency offers attractive lines of credit to the participating banks to finance their small business lending, thus enabling them to adopt and test the new lending methodology with only a limited risk exposure and a limited investment of their own funds.

The first downscaling projects – in the sense of projects that were explicitly described as such – were implemented in Paraguay and Costa Rica with funding from the IDB. Subsequently the approach was also implemented in Russia, after which it was applied in other former Soviet republics in Central Asia and Eastern Europe. Many of the downscaling projects in these countries were surprisingly successful.[122] The EBRD's Russia Small Business Fund, probably the largest downscaling project which was ever undertaken – and also officially called a downscaling project – even survived the Russian financial crisis of 1998 and is still ongoing.

However, this project type also has certain characteristic weaknesses. One challenge it faces is that the new clients, the owners of small businesses, will never have been regarded as a particularly important target group by the top management of the banks that participate in a downscaling project. Moreover, many top managers of banks find it extremely difficult to accept the idea that there should be a division within their bank that requires, and indeed has, considerable autonomy and is expected to follow rules and procedures which differ from those applicable in the rest of the bank. As a result, in a number of cases the micro and small business units created as a part of downscaling projects have not been given the full support by top management that they would have needed to perform optimally, and that they might receive in a specialized MFI. Finally, it is a common weakness of downscaling projects that they are exclusively focused on lending operations, while deposit-taking from the target group is neglected.[123] The BRI microbanking units are a notable exception.

Linking clients, self-help groups, and banks

Linkage banking was developed in the early 1980s and was intended to be an intermediate, transitional institution building strategy combining elements of both upgrading and downscaling. The thinking behind the concept proceeded from an analysis of three factors: the poor performance of development banks and credit NGOs, the widespread existence of savings-based SHGs, and the rediscovery of

---

[122] See the interesting accounts in Holtmann, Rühle and Winkler (2000) and Terberger and Lepp (2004).
[123] This argument applies to most downscaling projects that have been implemented in the past. However, it should be noted here that an important initiative, supported by the Bill & Melinda Gates Foundation, aims at remedying this weakness, as it focuses on savings mobilization and supports existing banks in their efforts to offer better deposit facilities to formerly neglected target groups.

personal savings as a key element of self-reliance in the lives of small farmers and microentrepreneurs. That thinking was based on the premise that the first of these factors represented a problem which could be addressed by exploiting the potential of the other two.

The initial discussions regarding the implementation of linkage projects focused on Asian countries, and two types of institutional links were proposed at this stage:

- *Indirect linkages,* i.e. establishing a relationship between banks, NGOs, SHGs, and these groups' members; this was an approach which could be taken in a situation where banks lacked confidence in informal SHGs as potential business partners.
- *Direct linkages,* i.e. creating a relationship between banks, SHGs and SHG members, with NGOs involved merely as capacity-builders.

In a linkage project SHGs were expected to deposit savings mobilized from their members in banks as partial collateral for loans, and in return they could expect to obtain progressively larger repeat loans over time, i.e. at increasing "loan-to-deposit" ratios. The SHGs would lend to their members on their own terms. All partners involved would cover their costs from the interest rate margin and generate a surplus, making the arrangement sustainable. Bank resources were to be the main source of loanable funds, complemented by the savings deposited by the SHGs.

Linkage banking was not designed to be a permanent feature of an emerging financial system. As noted, it was meant to be an intermediate, transitional stage of development, leading over time either to direct access by individuals or households to banks, or access to banking services as provided by their own SHGs; this latter option presupposed that these organizations would at some point be upgraded and converted into licensed local financial institutions such as rural banks or financial cooperatives owned by their members.

The concept of linkage banking represented a compromise between academic advisors who advocated the upgrading of informal financial SHGs, comparable to the transformation of Raiffeisen's village credit associations first into credit cooperatives and finally into cooperative banks, and bilateral and multilateral organizations (GTZ, FAO) which, for various reasons, would only work with governmental partners. The result was a hybrid model operating under the umbrella of central banks and state-owned banks: the *linking* of formal and informal financial institutions. While the focus was on *linking* existing institutions, as part of the underlying compromise the approach also included two complementary strategies which, over time, were intended to facilitate the development of new institutional structures: *upgrading* measures for informal institutions and *downscaling* measures for formal financial institutions.

GTZ first presented the linkage strategy at a workshop organized in Nanjing, China in 1986 by APRACA, an association of agricultural and central banks in Asia and the Pacific. It was to include the following elements: building on the existing formal and non-formal financial infrastructure; mobilization of savings by financial SHGs and the granting of loans by SHGs to individual members; and approval by the regulatory authorities for informal groups to set up savings and credit accounts at banks. In the model of savings-based credit linkages between SHGs and banks, NGOs – which were also called SHPIs in this context – played a role as facilitators and initially also as financial intermediaries or guarantors.

This was a rather flexible model of collaboration between SHGs, NGOs, and banks as autonomous business partners, each with its own interest rate margin to cover transaction costs. APRACA initiated a program on the basis of this model in 1986; it was the focus of the association's development activities and was supported by a GTZ sector project over a ten-year period. Starting in 1988, GTZ also supported bilateral projects in Indonesia, the Philippines, Thailand, and Nepal and subsequently in Africa as well. In Indonesia, where SHGs were widespread, linkages took off in 1988, with activities being carried out in collaboration with BRI and Bina Swadaya, an NGO, and with the central bank as a partner. The program benefited from a conducive policy environment, particularly interest rate deregulation in 1983, and the introduction, in 1988, of a legal framework for small local banks, which became the main linkage partners for SHGs. What was lacking was an appropriate legal framework for SHGs, which had proved impossible to secure due to the opposition of the state-dominated cooperative sector. By 1998 some 800 rural banks and 16,000 SHGs were involved in linkages.

Early on, linkage banking attracted attention in development policy circles. In the foreword to the World Development Report 1989, the then president of the World Bank stated: "Informal financial institutions have proved able to serve the household, agricultural, and microenterprise sectors on a sustained basis. Measures that link informal institutions to the formal financial system will improve that service and ensure a competitive environment" (World Bank 1989).

India's NABARD had first become acquainted with the linkage banking model through its participation in the APRACA conference in 1986; this, together with the international attention which the new approach had attracted as well as exposure visits to the pilot project in Indonesia, inspired NABARD, in collaboration with RBI, the Indian central bank, to examine the potential of linkage banking to provide access to basic financial services to some 250–300 million rural poor who had been impoverished by centuries of exploitation and dispossession. In our case study on India in section 2.4.3, we described how linkage banking in India developed – at first very positively and then, as government intervention increased and seemed likely to become excessive, much less so (cf. Seibel 1985, 1989a, 1991, 2001, 2006, 2010b, 2012).

Starting from scratch or "greenfielding"

As a technical term, "greenfielding" described a strategy for building new regulated and viable financial institutions as an alternative to the inefficient, unsustainable agricultural development banks and credit NGOs which were widespread at the time. The authors who first used this term (Krahnen and Schmidt, 1994) had been inspired by their collaboration with IPC, the German consulting firm which had been founded in 1981, and which had gained its initial experience in financial institution building in projects geared to overhauling and transforming loss-making institutions in Peru, Uganda, and other countries. The strategy of starting from scratch was in essence developed and tested by IPC, and later applied on an increasing scale by PCH, a company founded by IPC and a group of partners in 1998 to set up and operate target group-oriented financial institutions (see section 2.5.3). Since then, the approach has been adopted by a number of other development consulting firms and microfinance support organizations[124] from various industrialized countries and implemented in many developing countries – and in a number of former communist countries as well, which is a particularly important point in this context.

A brief review of the prior experience of a small group of consultants and microfinance support organizations which led to the development of the "greenfield" strategy and its widespread adoption is important if one wishes to understand the essence of this strategy. The first two elements of that experience were clearly positive: First, lending to people with limited means who had formerly not had access to formal sector loans is feasible, without incurring continuous losses, if – but only if – it is done properly. This was a lesson that had already emerged in the late 1980s. And second, creating viable, financially self-sustaining MFIs that do not require any subsidies from donors beyond those needed during the start-up phase and that soon become cost-covering, and even marginally profitable, is also feasible; this was a lesson of the next decade.

The negative elements of that prior experience had to do with the types of projects that were most prevalent at that time, mainly because they were the kinds of projects that donors wanted to see implemented. The first negative element concerned upgrading: It was seen as taking too long and entailing too many conflicts with incumbent NGO leaders, who were reluctant to commit to, and support, the thoroughgoing institutional transformation required to create truly efficient and inclusive microfinance banks. The second negative aspect was the disappointing performance of certain downscaling projects: Only rarely was the top management of the participating banks sufficiently committed to the institutions' microfinance activities, and they were not really prepared to grant their newly created

---

124 Among those that adopted the "greenfield strategy" is the German consulting firm LFS Financial Systems, which created AccessBank in Azerbaijan.

microfinance departments the degree of autonomy that seemed necessary to enable these units to achieve the goals defined for them.

In retrospect it appears that the process of bringing development aid resources to bear in order to improve access by "ordinary people" to financial services could have been greatly simplified. The entire undertaking would have achieved greater success if it had been recognized early on that there were also direct ways of creating formal microfinance banks. This can be done by simply establishing a new formal bank which is geared from the start to offering reasonably priced loans and other financial services for the owners of small and very small businesses and other "ordinary people" on a cost-covering basis, and by creating the new bank on a "greenfield" basis. This would have been a viable alternative wherever institutions were lacking that would be candidates for upgrading or downscaling and would also make suitable project partners.

The end of the East-West divide after 1989 offered development institutions the opportunity to begin carrying out "greenfield" projects, because in the former communist countries there were simply no credit-granting NGOs that appeared suitable for upgrading. This situation made it easy for donors to recognize that the option of creating microfinance banks "from scratch" deserved serious consideration. Early endeavors of this kind in Eastern Europe, involving donor institutions as investors as well as providers of credit lines and start-up subsidies, were successful, and convinced donors of the merit of the new strategy.

But naturally, important questions arise in connection with this strategy as well, and while they are in effect the same ones that must be answered for an upgrading project, with "greenfielding" they become even more urgent: Who pays for the creation of the new banks? Who should be the investors that provide the required equity capital? Who manages and controls the new banks? Who is responsible for seeing to it that they are successful in commercial terms and also in social and developmental terms? How can their commitment to their original target group be ensured, and what prevents them from charging their borrowers excessively high interest rates in order to boost profits? The established international financial institutions, i.e. the members of the donor community, were the best candidates for several of these roles, and they did indeed perform them, providing equity capital, loanable funds to kick-start lending before sufficient deposits were mobilized, and also some technical assistance funding, i.e. subsidies.

The most important question is: Who should be the "strategic owner" of a microfinance bank that has been created on a "greenfield" basis? "Strategic owners" must meet many requirements: They must be investors who are reasonably well-funded; they must be prepared to follow a business strategy that seeks to reach profitability relatively soon and at the same time refrain from profit maximization; they must have a long-term commitment to creating a supply of credit and other financial services for "ordinary people" which will have a positive social impact and promote economic development; they must understand the reasoning behind the business policy which a microfinance bank will typically adopt and the financial needs of an institution of this type; and they must recognize that it may take a considerable amount of time before they can enjoy the financial fruits of their investment. Do competent, patient, and socially committed investors of this kind even exist? On the face of it, the answer to this question might seem to be "No," but soon after it was first posed, when the "greenfielding" approach began to be discussed seriously as a practical institution building option, it proved possible to overcome this obstacle as well.

Working in close cooperation with a group of public- and private-sector partners, PCH repeatedly assumed the role of strategic owner in projects to set up new banks in Eastern Europe and later on in various countries in Latin America and Africa as well. Most of these partners invested in the equity of PCH and, at the same time, in parallel with the investment in PCH, they invested in the equity of new banks that IPC set up on their behalf.[125] In the case of PCH, and of several other organizations which emerged later and adopted the same institutional model, such as AccessHolding[126], what was established are genuine public-private partnerships (PPPs) (Schmidt and Moisa 2005).

4.4 Commercial microfinance and its challenges

Why the commercial approach seems to be superior

As we have already described, in the late 1990s a conflict over the allegedly weak ethical foundations and the shaky economic foundations of the commercial approach split the microfinance community into two camps. For the opponents of commercialized microfinance, the "welfarists," even suggesting that "the poor" should bear the full cost of lending to them was naïve in economic terms and questionable from a business perspective, to say nothing of its ethical implications. The advocates of the commercial approach, or, as they were called by their opponents, the "institutionalists," rejected this critique as unfair and also as simply wrong. They could point to the successes of MFIs that were based on a commercial model and whose operations did not jeopardize their social and developmental mission. Indeed, these institutions were successful in both commercial and developmental terms. The reason they were able to achieve success according to both sets of criteria was that, for them, the relationship between financial and social or developmental success was one of complementarity and not of conflict.

---

[125] Employing a strategy that was largely similar, but implementing it in a way that differed in many respects from the course followed by PCH, ACCION made similar moves and started to become an important – and possibly also a "strategic" – investor in a number of MFIs. Other organizations that had their origins in consulting firms or donor institutions, such as LFS/AccessHolding, followed the IPC/PCH model even more closely and also adopted an organizational structure similar to that of the IPC/PCH group.

[126] http://www.accessholding.com.

The greater success of the commercially oriented MFIs in business terms enabled them to raise funds much more easily and on a much larger scale, and therefore also to grant many more small loans to the target population which the advocates of both approaches – the "welfarists" and the "institutionalists" – wished to serve. And conversely, having larger loan portfolios, a measure of developmental success, allowed them to operate with lower unit costs and thus contributed to their success as business establishments.

The commercial approach clearly came out as the winner in the controversy of the 1990s. That the banks involved in downscaling projects adhered to the commercial approach can be regarded as self-evident. But the microfinance banks that had been created in the course of upgrading projects or as "greenfield" projects also adhered to this approach. In the case of these institutions, resolving the ownership issue was one of the principal challenges facing those who established them: Who should be the owners of institutions whose main financial backing, including equity capital, was provided by donor agencies? Were these agencies the "natural born owners," as Schmidt and Zeitinger (1998) had argued in one paper? Or should the poor people and the owners of small and very small businesses – those whom these institutions were ultimately meant to serve – be considered as their owners?

Who should be the "owner" of a commercially oriented microfinance institution?

This is not an easy question to answer. Of course, the donors, most of which are large IFIs with a development mandate, could be owners of the MFIs they were so instrumental in creating, and in many cases they have indeed become shareholders and co-owners, retaining this role for a long period. But being the "strategic owners," who take responsibility for the ongoing success, in both commercial and developmental terms, of the institutions they have helped to establish, would go beyond their mandate and place demands on them that would exceed their resources. The idea that helpful donors could assume the role of strategic owners, with all that this entails, was naïve. The idea that "the target groups" would be able to serve as the strategic owners of MFIs that had adopted the legal form of a corporation would also have been naïve because the clients would constitute a very heterogeneous group; by its very nature, this group would tend to consist of an unorganized collection of individuals, giving rise to the "free rider" problem and possibly leading to a situation in which some people assumed the role of leaders without any true accountability. Making the clients the owners might possibly work in the case of a microfinance provider organized as a cooperative, but this would only be feasible if the institution were fairly small and had only a limited outreach. Theoretically, there are others who could also assume the role of a principal or strategic owner – namely, private investors. But this does not seem like a particularly good idea either, at least if such private owners were interested primarily in achieving maximum profits for the institution and for themselves. Purely profit-driven strategic owners might turn MFIs into "normal" banks like those that have always discriminated against poor people and small enterprises, charged excessive interest rates when lending to these target groups, or found other ways of exploiting those whom microfinance is actually intended to help. As we will see, this is a very real danger.

Despite the difficulty involved in determining at a more or less theoretical level who should be the strategic owner of an MFI, in practice it has proved possible to find viable solutions to this problem: Since the late 1990s, groups of microfinance providers organized as companies have been formed, with ties of varying closeness between the institutions within each group that have taken on the role of strategic owners. Most of these groups have grown out of consulting firms or microfinance support organizations. They are international groups, which gives them the advantage of geographical diversification and opportunities for the transfer of know-how between countries, and they are, to a greater or lesser extent, driven by the desire to promote and practice microfinance or "finance for all" or "inclusive finance" largely in accordance with the vision that had originally inspired the emergence of modern microfinance. In a certain sense, they tend to regard themselves as trustees acting in the best interests of the target population, but, to a certain degree, they also see their role as that of trustees who have a responsibility and an obligation to act in accordance with the interests of those who have provided a large part of the funding that made it possible to create the MFIs in the first place.

Acting as trustees for an institution that has the overarching and long-term objective of serving its clients, and thus as trustees for the clients as well, has also traditionally been the role that public authorities play – or in any case, claim to play – in public banks, including public savings banks. Public ownership of some kind is of course also an option for MFIs. However, it presupposes that these trustees will be willing and able to strike a sound balance between the business objective of making the MFI become and remain a strong and stable enterprise and the development objective of ensuring that it serves those whom it is supposed to benefit. This requires the expertise needed to make wise decisions and at the same time the restraint that is required to prevent abuses of the power which owners exercise – two features that one would not expect to find in all public authorities in the countries in which microfinance is particularly important.[127]

Thus, there are in principle three possible solutions to the problem of how key ownership rights in MFIs which follow a commercial approach can be defined and to whom they might be allocated. One solution is private ownership, possibly with public co-owners, but in any case with a private owner in the role of being

---

[127] The recent conflict between the government of Bangladesh and Muhammad Yunus is a well-known illustration of the problematic role of governments in their capacity as owners of public banks.

the strategic owner. The second solution is one based on elements of cooperative governance, with clients as owners. This option may be appropriate for small institutions; once they are embedded in larger networks, a more sophisticated governance structure incorporating additional elements must be created. The third solution builds on public ownership and has a certain resemblance to the governance and ownership structure of German public savings banks.

In Chapter IV, the concluding chapter of the book, we will discuss the latter two solutions in more detail. Before doing so, however, we will first look at some of the risks and limitations entailed in the first solution, that of mainly private ownership.

The risks of excessive commercialization

There is no direct correlation between the orientation of an MFI, its legal form and its ownership structure. In other words, utilization of the commercial approach is not necessarily connected with having the legal form of a corporation, even though this is usually the case, and there is much that speaks in favor of this legal form. But NGOs with the legal form of a foundation or an association can also follow the commercial approach, and currently many such organizations do so. The legal form of a corporation allows private ownership, but this does not imply that all owners are necessarily private individuals or private-sector institutions. In fact, many MFIs are PPPs in the legal form of a corporation, with private and public owners involved on an equal footing and working side by side (Schmidt and Moisa, 2005). Typically, a private shareholder is also the "strategic investor."

The standard logic of a PPP (assumed to consist of just one public and one private partner) is as follows: Private ownership and a strong role for the private partner allows the undertaking to benefit from the private partner's presumed competence, flexibility, initiative and creativity, and possibly also its strong motivation to make sure that the enterprise becomes and remains profitable. The role of the public partner in a typical PPP is to monitor the quality of the service provided by the institution and ensure that it is maintained at the required level; in the case of MFIs, this means making sure that they retain their original target group orientation, that their prices remain affordable for their clients, and that they continue to adhere to the institution's guiding principles with regard to other, similar issues.[128] The more the private partner is also committed to maintaining a social and developmental orientation, as is indeed often the case in the area of development finance, the less important will be the role of the public partner in shaping the institution's business policy, and its job will be more one of monitoring the performance of the strategic owner and the management in the fulfillment of their respective tasks and supporting them in their roles.

---

[128] This is how Otero and Chu (2002) see the role of development-oriented institutions like ACCION in their capacity as shareholders of commercial MFIs.

However, the dynamics of organizations are more complex than this brief sketch of a PPP in microfinance might suggest. There are cases in which the private owners' interest in achieving truly high profits is not effectively counterbalanced by public co-ownership or by a sufficiently strong "ethical" orientation and motivation on the part of the private owners. In such a case the model of private "strategic" ownership may not function well and there is the danger of clients being exploited, of public funds involved either as subsidies or equity or loans being misused and, generally speaking, of the aims of microfinance being perverted. One cannot simply rely on private owners' self-restraint; and self-restraint is all the less likely if the prospects of benefiting from conduct that greatly increases owners' wealth are good, even if it hurts clients' interests. In such cases one can say that the commercial orientation of an MFI has become too strong, i.e. that commercialization is "excessive." It is impossible to say in general terms how widespread the problem might be, but clear examples of excessive commercialization have emerged in recent years and they have done great harm to the formerly excellent reputation of microfinance. Two cases are particularly noteworthy.

The IPOs of two microfinance institutions

In 2007, the Mexican MFI Compartamos went public. 30% of the outstanding shares were sold to American and Mexican investors, and the Compartamos shares were listed on the Mexican stock exchange. In the course of this IPO, no new shares were issued and no new capital was raised for Compartamos. Most of the shares that were sold had been held by the founders and managers of the institution and by two important development-oriented institutions, the World Bank's private sector arm IFC and ACCION, the world's largest and most highly regarded microfinance support organization.

The IPO of Compartamos was very successful in financial terms. The offering price of the shares was very high. Valuing all of its shares at this price gave Compartamos a market value of approximately USD 1.5 billion. Some observers, and especially the founding shareholders of Compartamos, hailed the IPO as an important step showing that microfinance had finally arrived in the "real financial market" and had clearly passed its test there (ACCION 2007).

Others saw it differently and supported their critical assessment by pointing out that the high offering price could only be a reflection of the enormous profitability of Compartamos as an enterprise during the preceding six years, i.e. since the conversion of the former NGO into a corporation, and of shareholders' expectations that it would maintain its profitability in the foreseeable future (Rosenberg 2007). What had made Compartamos so extremely profitable in the years prior to the IPO, and what the buyers of the shares most probably expected to continue, was a policy of charging exorbitant interest rates: rates approaching 100% p.a. *after* inflation adjustment. A feature of the IPO that seemed particularly worrying was that a large portion of the shares were sold to American hedge funds, the kind of investors whose inclusion in the corporation's group of shareholders provided little reason to expect that Compartamos would discontinue its high-interest-rate policy; and so far it appears that the institution has stuck to this policy.

In 2010 SKS, the largest and fastest-growing MFI in India, also undertook an IPO with similarly spectacular financial success. In this case, it was not exorbitant interest rates but extremely high growth rates which seem to have induced investors to pay a very high price for the shares. The issue price was indeed so high that it could only be explained by an assumption on the part of investors that the extraordinary growth achieved by SKS would continue for an extended period of time. In this case as well, the shares were purchased by purely profit-oriented investors, mainly private equity companies, and top managers used the opportunity offered by the share issue to pocket substantial profits for themselves.[129]

The highly problematic aspect of this IPO is that SKS and a handful of other large Indian MFIs seem to have pursued policies regarding the granting of loans and the enforcement of repayment obligations that have nothing in common with responsible microlending. As is well known, a number of borrowers who were unable to repay the excessive loans that they had obtained from SKS and its peers committed suicide. As is equally well known, this led to a general microfinance crisis in the state of Andhra Pradesh.

These two cases are not only important in themselves and for those who have been directly affected by the consequences of the conduct of these two MFIs. They also point to a general danger inherent in, and a general drawback of, the idea of letting private individuals and institutions become the "strategic owners" of MFIs. It appears that the influence exerted on MFIs by "the stock market" and, more generally, by the profit motive of private shareholders, can prove to be so strong that any other intentions or convictions that individual persons within the institutions – or even certain shareholders – may have are insufficient to prevent the institutions from adopting policies that are essentially detrimental to the interests of their clients.

At any rate, in the spectacular cases of Compartamos and SKS this was what happened: The pressure of the capital market and of the private profit motive was so strong that it led Compartamos to adopt an exploitative pricing policy, and SKS to use credit-granting procedures and loan recovery methods that violate all of the rules of sound microfinance. The crucial question is: is this the inevitable consequence of private ownership? It is conceivable that the answer to this question might turn out to be "Yes"; and if this were indeed the case, then the prospects for commercial microfinance using the legal form of a corporation might simply not be very good. However, one can also make a good case for answering this question

---

[129] For details, see Chen et al. (2010). Schmidt and Noth (2013) provide an economic valuation of these two MFIs at the respective times at which they went public.

with a cautious "No," given the scope that exists for private owners to enter into binding commitments that make it possible for them to tap the capital market in order to raise the equity capital needed for expansion, while at the same time keeping the pressure to achieve high profits sufficiently at bay to enable them to continue pursuing social and developmental aims.[130]

4.5 Why microfinance is losing its clout

Microfinance has changed in recent years. To be more precise, the reality of microfinance – which has always been somewhat at odds with its public image – has changed quite significantly, and it now no longer has much in common at all with what was traditionally thought of as "microfinance." Moreover, the general tone of the debate about microfinance has changed, perhaps even more profoundly. Taken together, these two changes have gravely affected the image of microfinance among both experts and the general public, making it more difficult to generate support for microfinance among political decision makers as well as private investors, be they purely profit-seeking investors or so-called social investors, who expect to get an emotional as well as a financial dividend from investing in microfinance. The remainder of this subsection looks at how the reality of microfinance has changed and expands on some of the ideas that were briefly introduced in the first chapter of this book.

Relevant changes in the reality of microfinance

The most high-profile events that did serious damage to the reputation of microfinance were the IPOs of Compartamos and SKS, two large and well-known MFIs. Since these organizations' IPOs and their implications have already been discussed, they do not require further elaboration at this point.

Unfortunately, these were not the only events that caused a loss of reputation for microfinance on a worldwide scale. Another problematic development was the aggressive entry by a number of purely commercial banks into what they called the microfinance market, as from 2005. But instead of granting loans that were in some way related to income-generating activities undertaken by their clients, they pushed outright consumer lending, often with little regard for people's actual repayment capacity, thereby causing serious problems for their clients. In addition, in a number of countries the supply of very small loans available to poor clients from microfinance providers expanded at a very rapid pace, leading to over-indebtedness on the part of borrowers and rising default rates for lenders.

Last but not least, there was a controversy surrounding the activities of the individual who had represented the positive side of microfinance like no one else,

---

[130] Schmidt (2010) describes in detail how such a commitment can be implemented.

Nobel Laureate Muhammad Yunus. The operations of his bank, and of other firms in the Grameen Group of enterprises, were the subject of a number of critical reports and comments in the media casting doubt on the ethical and developmental merits of the group's ever-growing range of business activities and highlighting what was portrayed as a remarkably close collaboration between Grameen and large multinational firms. Possibly due in part to these accusations, but perhaps more as a result of moves by political actors to gain power, in 2011 the government of Bangladesh forced Yunus to relinquish his position as the CEO of Grameen Bank and claimed the right to choose the future CEO of the bank. Even though the accusations leveled against Yunus turned out to be ill-founded, the fact that a shadow had been cast over the single most highly respected representative of microfinance also affected the reputation of microfinance in general. This has had two implications in terms of the way microfinance is perceived by investors, policy makers, and observers in general. For one thing, it gives rise to the suspicion that, in spite of all the information that was made available by Yunus's defenders to exonerate him, there may be something behind these accusations after all, fostering a general sense of mistrust toward microfinance. The other implication is that there are reasons to fear that other governments might follow the example of the Bangladeshi government, and that the risk of harmful political interference is therefore greater than was believed for a long time. Both of these perceptions can have a negative effect on the willingness of individuals and institutions to support microfinance.[131]

Relevant changes in the discourse about microfinance

While the Compartamos IPO and its problematic aspects were not widely reported in the press, the events surrounding the SKS IPO (Chen et al. 2010) and the ensuing Indian microfinance crisis, as well as the emergence of purely commercial lenders who aggressively pushed consumer lending under the misleading name of "microfinance," made headlines. A widely read American business magazine published several articles about the "dark side of micro-lending"; the highly respected German newspaper *Frankfurter Allgemeine Zeitung* bluntly declared that the microfinance model had failed; and others even asserted that microfinance was as good as dead, at least as far as its ethical appeal was concerned.[132]

Even more important was the change in attitudes as expressed in the more specialized microfinance-related literature. For the sake of brevity, we will only brief-

---

[131] It should be noted at least in passing that another aspect of microfinance has also changed for the worse, namely its attractiveness for retail investors. Until the middle of the past decade, microfinance was considered to be particularly attractive for such investors because the profitability of MFIs and of MIVs was largely uncorrelated with general economic and stock market developments. Therefore, investments in this asset class were considered as valuable instruments for portfolio diversification (see Krauss and Walter 2009). In recent years, though, microfinance has become much more closely linked to the general financial system. As a consequence, the financial returns on microfinance investments began to be highly correlated with general market developments and thus lost an important part of their appeal for investors. For empirical evidence, see Wagner (2012).

[132] The sources for these harsh statements are, respectively, Business Week (2005), *Frankfurter Allgemeine Zeitung* (2011) and the Financial Times of India (2012).

ly comment on three recent books on microfinance which were widely read and discussed and exemplify this shift (but see also Dichter and Harper 2007).

The first is *Confessions of a Microfinance Heretic* by Hugh Sinclair (2012). As the title suggests, this book is provocative in its tone and content. The author recounts his negative experiences with several MFIs and microfinance support organizations for which he had worked. He provides what he sees as extensive evidence to demonstrate that these institutions and organizations and the people who determine their policies and run them are irresponsible, motivated by a desire for profit and power, and not in the least interested in furthering social and developmental goals, and, moreover, that the organizations which invest in these MFIs seem to tolerate this. Of course, there are institutions and individual people in the microfinance business that deserve the kind of criticism that Sinclair expresses in his book and has repeated in related publications and public appearances. The "microfinance hype" that was so much in evidence some years ago may indeed have encouraged some shady characters to enter the microfinance "industry." Sinclair refrains from explicitly generalizing what he documents for individual cases. Therefore, one could perhaps conclude that he simply had the bad luck to run into black sheep several times in his career as a consultant. But despite his caution regarding generalizations and the resulting absence of any sweeping statements about the overall state of microfinance, his book conveys the impression that what he reports is generally characteristic of microfinance today and that there are many black sheep. In this sense he provides substantial support for the current tendency to disparage microfinance.

The second book is more important and richer in substance. In *Why Doesn't Microfinance Work?* Milford Bateman (2010) attacks what he considers to be the central weakness of the relatively new breed of MFIs. The subtitle, *The Destructive Rise of Local Neoliberalism*, suggests how his book will answer the question posed in the title. Criticizing microfinance in perhaps even stronger terms than does Sinclair, Bateman attacks aid-supported microfinance providers and donor support for these "new-style microfinance institutions" because, in his view, microfinance actually serves to perpetuate underdevelopment and poverty instead of fostering development and making a contribution to poverty alleviation – in contrast to what has again and again been claimed by thousands of microfinance enthusiasts. He concludes that it would be best to simply discontinue the policy of supporting microfinance with assistance from the advanced countries.

Bateman presents two main arguments in his book. The first is that modern microfinance is a manifestation of a neoliberal political philosophy which grossly underestimates the role that government interventions can – and perhaps should – play in economic development. Much of modern microfinance is indeed inspired by anti-big government and pro-private sector thinking. However, if he had been more versed in the history of development finance and development aid policy, Bateman would most probably have also noticed how problematic the kind of government interventions, that he so strongly advocates, have been in practice.[133] In other words, one can accept his diagnosis on this point and still disagree with his conclusions and recommendations.

His second main argument relates to the kind of economic activity that many "new-style MFIs" seek to support with small loans. As he argues, the economic activities of the very poor do not generate sufficient income to warrant the application of development aid funds. Development would be strengthened, and thus the economic situation of large segments of the population would also be improved more if funding were directed to small and medium-sized firms with some growth potential instead of informal businesses and other microenterprise activity. Bateman is not alone among microfinance experts in making this second argument, and, based on similar ideas, some important players in microfinance have already modified their strategies to reflect the insight that more development impact can be generated by providing credit to small firms than through lending to support informal and micro-scale economic activity, to say nothing of pure consumer lending.[134] Moreover, a large share of the commercially oriented MFIs have not even claimed to be interested in bettering the situation of poor people, or, at best, have only half-heartedly adopted the poverty alleviation rhetoric of Yunus and his followers. It is therefore difficult to understand why Bateman arrives at the sweeping conclusion that "microfinance does not work."

The third and by far the most important recent book is David Roodman's *Due Diligence*, published in 2012. The subtitle, *An Impertinent Inquiry into Microfinance*, might lead one to expect that this is one more book containing a full-blown attack on microfinance. Fortunately, however, this expectation proves unwarranted. The book offers a very serious and thoughtful, indeed "diligent," account of modern microfinance and a careful assessment of its merits. The standard against which microfinance is assessed is that established by the claims which are frequently made about what microfinance can achieve. And measured by this standard, Roodman concludes that the performance of microfinance has been disappointing. One claim, and probably the one that has gained the greatest popularity, is that microfinance is an ideal instrument for the alleviation, or perhaps even the eradication, of poverty. Roodman looks at the facts and at recent econometric studies that appear to support the poverty alleviation claim and comes to the conclusion that there is in fact no evidence that being clients of an MFI actually helps people rise out of poverty. This finding should, however, be taken with a large grain of salt. What both Roodman and the researchers whose work he analyses[135] have examined are immediate

---

133 What Bateman recommends is in many ways stunningly similar to the policy that is forcefully criticized in a book by Adams et al. (1984) and in other publications by members of the same group of authors from the 1980s.

134 See the references in Chapter I, footnote 6, and also the Annual Report of PCH for 2012.

135 The leading researchers who have applied the method of randomized control trials (RCTs), known from pharmaceutical research, to microfinance in order to investigate in a methodologically sound way whether microfinance helps people get out of poverty, and to whose work Roodman refers extensively, include Abhijit Banerjee, Esther Duflo and Dean Karlan.

and very short-term effects. If such effects cannot be found, this by no means implies that microfinance does nothing to increase the welfare of large segments of the population, including the poor and the very poor. If one looks, for example, at the impact which the German savings banks and cooperative banks have had over time, since their creation in the 19th century, one can hardly question that they have had a very positive effect. But this effect took decades to materialize, and the mechanisms through which these financial institutions opened up access to finance for groups in society which had formerly been excluded from such access are more complex than what the recent econometric studies can capture.[136]

The second claim investigated by Roodman is that microfinance creates empowerment. Here his assessment is similarly skeptical. No immediate empowerment effect can be identified in serious econometric studies. However, as in the case of poverty reduction, the argument advanced by the author is relatively weak in so far as the pertinent studies can only capture short-term and readily observable effects.

Based on the discussion so far, one could say that both the thrust of developments in the "real world" of microfinance and the popular and academic debate about microfinance appear to point in the same direction: Microfinance does not, and cannot, keep its promises and therefore has lost a great deal of its appeal. However, this assessment would disregard the fact that Roodman also considers a third claim. It is the claim of those who advocate financial institution building and financial sector development as a means of creating a more inclusive financial system. On this point, the ability of these strategies to make finance more inclusive, his assessment is unambiguously positive. Unfortunately, though, he does not examine in any detail the question of the extent to which the positive developments in what he calls "microfinance as industry building" also have a positive impact on large parts of the economically active population in developing and transition countries in a longer-term perspective. But the general literature on the finance-and-growth nexus provides ample reason to take a much more positive view of microfinance as a factor in the overall promotion of economic development, including its welfare effects for broad segments of the population (e.g. Levine 2005).

Thus we can conclude our final look at the current reality of microfinance, and the way it is perceived and assessed both in the media and in the ongoing academic discourse, by highlighting a lesson from the preceding discussion which we consider encouraging for our undertaking in this study: It certainly makes sense – not least for a fair assessment of microfinance, "finance for all" or "inclusive finance" – to take a close look at the history of what has come to be known as "microfinance," as we have done in Chapter II of this book.

---

[136] Additional arguments which suggest that the findings of these studies should be taken with a rather large grain of salt are presented in Terberger (2012), although Terberger does concur with the assessment that the poverty-reducing effects of microfinance have been vastly overestimated in the past.

IV.
LOCAL FINANCIAL INSTITUTIONS – LEARNING FROM THE HISTORY OF SAVINGS BANKS AND COOPERATIVE BANKS FOR DEVELOPMENT POLICY TODAY

1 Summing up the historical survey

Savings banks and cooperative banks in Europe evolved as local financial institutions in order to cope with far-reaching socioeconomic changes during the industrialization process some 150 to 200 years ago. Even though they were structured differently, they both followed a largely similar business model. Credit cooperatives started as a democratic "bottom-up" movement, focusing initially more on loans, while savings banks followed a more conservative approach emphasizing savings. However, both types of institution offered both savings and loans from the very beginning, and they were thus able to develop quickly into genuine financial intermediaries and eventually into commercially operating universal banks. During the industrialization process, lower-class households in European countries had to cope with uncertain and volatile cash flows – a situation which, beyond all cultural differences and historical variation, is comparable to that currently faced by households in developing economies. In this environment, loans, and to an even greater extent savings, played a vital role in smoothing consumption. The savings and cooperative banks were the first institutions to offer transparent access to credit and other financial services at fair terms and conditions to low-income people – precisely what we would call "microfinance" today – and they ultimately expanded that access to the general public – "inclusive finance" in today's terminology.

Readers familiar with banking in developing countries may be surprised by this positive assessment, since in many countries savings banks and cooperative banks are government-dominated national institutions which collect the savings of the general populace and channel them into wasteful government bureaucracies, rather than making them available for local investment and development. Therefore, it has to be made clear from the start that the German savings and cooperative banks have consistently been local banks serving local depositors, borrowers, and investors: institutions for the people and by the people, not for the state and by the state as in the English and French traditions.

To sum up the success factors discussed in detail in Chapter II: The German savings banks and cooperative banks of the 19th century were locally controlled. They paid market standard interest rates on savings with positive real returns and extended loans at fair and transparent terms and conditions. Even though interest margins were small, institutions of both types were able to cover their costs and to begin operating profitably soon after their foundation. Moderate interest rates consistent with the borrowers' ability to pay also helped to keep credit risk low, since high interest rates would have tended to trigger business failures, which in turn would have had a negative impact on the lending institutions as well. Achieving profitability at an early stage was also due to favorable cost structures: Many savings banks and cooperative banks were able to draw on infrastructure free of charge and, during their early years, staff who worked on a volunteer basis.

In addition, in some cases capital donations by charitable individuals and organizations reduced the cost of funds. A large share of profits was reinvested, helping the institutions to stabilize and to grow. The rest was consumed locally. In accordance with their mission of promoting the common welfare and supporting their member-clients' business activities rather than maximizing their own profit, their earnings were used to create reserve funds that could be (in the case of cooperative banks) or had to be (in the case of savings banks) used for the benefit of the local economy and to make the institutions crisis-resilient.

Another precondition for the lasting success of the two groups of institutions has been their focus on business activities in the very regions in which they were founded. Locally focused institutions benefit from knowing their customers, and by definition have to refrain from pursuing large-scale and seemingly profitable, but unfamiliar and thus inherently risky business opportunities. Most of the locally mobilized savings and the profits of the local savings and cooperative banks flow back into the region, contributing to overall economic development. In the institutions' early years, a strong regional focus was inevitable in view of the limited means of transport and communication of the time. Later, a rule of adhering to a local area focus, the so-called "regional principle," was formally introduced through laws and statutes.[1] The rule implied that, as a matter of principle, savings and cooperative banks from one region are not expected to do business in the area covered by a sister organization of the same type. This regional principle was meant to prevent the local banks from getting involved in business dealings with clients whom they did not really know and who would therefore be too risky for them. At the same time it also restricted competition within the respective groups, thereby offering a certain degree of protection for the individual local banks. And finally, it strengthened the role of the institutions' national and regional associations, which have been in existence since the middle of the 19th century, and that of the groups' own regional clearing banks,[2] because it caused the individual local banks belonging to one group to view one another as partners and not as competitors. The associations and clearing banks enabled both groups to realize economies of scale by facilitating the exchange of information, and thus collective institutionalized learning; the cost-effective organization of training and lobbying at political institutions; and last but not least the organization of internal and external audits. Moreover, they made it possible to retain funds within the groups. Through these emerging networks of affiliated institutions, the individual local institutions have been able to achieve decisive savings on costs without compromising on quality. The creation of regional clearing banks with the original role of pooling the liquidity of the individual local institutions made the latter much

---

1 For the concept of the regional principle (*Regionalprinzip*) see Schepers (2003).
2 These clearing banks were later called *Landesbanken* (or state regional banks) and as such had acquired an additional function of serving the governments of Germany's federal states as "house banks."

more robust and able to withstand economic fluctuations. When the regional clearing banks began to offer additional products and services, they helped the individual local institutions to realize further economies of scale and scope. There was, of course, competition between the local savings banks and the local cooperative banks, which provided an important impetus to further develop their business models to best meet clients' needs.

Another central, if not indispensable factor of success was the prevalence of relatively stable overall political conditions throughout most of the 19th century – combined with a certain amount of regulatory control and oversight over the small local banks. State authorities in most German states supervised the emergence of small, decentralized financial institutions in a supportive and constructive manner. They created a favorable legal and institutional environment for the local banks and at the same time largely refrained from interventions, thus giving the local management of the savings and cooperative banks the scope to manage their banking business as they saw fit. With only a few exceptions, savings were not captured by the state authorities. In addition, savings banks underwent control and monitoring by public authorities (and later on by their own associations as well), and cooperative banks have been subject from an early stage not only to control by their members, but also by their respective associations and their auditing federations. This elaborate system of control and monitoring substantially limited the incidence of fraud and corruption and also kept the bank officials under pressure to perform their functions according to expectations. Taken together, these factors allowed the savings and cooperative banks to become stable and sustainable financial institutions.

Both savings and cooperative banks were most successful at the end of the 19th century, when Germany was about to overtake Britain as the leading industrial nation and when living conditions in Germany had improved significantly compared to 50 years earlier. Savings banks and cooperative banks had played an important part in this transformation and catching-up process. Financial, social, economic, and political inclusion accompanied and accelerated industrialization – and vice-versa. There can be no doubt that these two groups of banks had a substantial impact, even though this impact took a long time to materialize and would therefore have been almost imperceptible over very short spans of time.[3]

Today the savings and cooperative banking groups make up almost one half of the German banking industry.[4] Both groups survived two World Wars and a number

---

[3] The recent impact studies using the RCT methodology quoted above try to measure the poverty-alleviating effects of microfinance over a time span of not more than two or three years and their skeptical results can therefore hardly be regarded as conclusive.

[4] This is inclusive of their respective second-tier financial institutions, which are the regional banks (*Landesbanken*) in the case of the savings banks and the two central financial institutions DZ-Bank AG and WGZ Bank AG in the case of the cooperative banks. Without the central institutions, the combined share of the local savings and cooperative banks in total bank assets is about 25% and their combined market shares in retail loans and deposits are close to 50%.

of economic and political crises, including a period of hyperinflation and several currency reforms. One reason for this remarkable resilience is the federal structure of Germany, which makes national solutions and heavy-handed interventions much more difficult than in other countries. Another reason is the locally focused business model of both these groups of banks: They are able to tailor their services to the needs of their local clients.

2 The general relevance of the historical survey for the design of development projects

One overarching question from a development policy perspective has motivated our study: Are there conclusions or insights that can be derived from the history of German savings and cooperative banks that might inform financial-sector-related policies, in particular development aid, and if so, what are these lessons to be learned?

Three general remarks are in order before we turn to details:

1. Any lesson that one might want to derive from history must be interpreted with great caution. Naturally, it is impossible to present the history of German institutions as a blueprint that developing countries could simply replicate. Wherever a simple approach of replication has been undertaken, it has typically failed. Therefore, any lessons derived can at best serve as an input informing the deliberations of responsible decision makers. But in this limited sense, our study of the history of local and "popular" banking in Germany might indeed be useful, making it possible to identify important parameters of success and failure.
2. Our study not only analyzes the history of German savings and cooperative banks and tries to draw some cautious conclusions from it, but also looks at a number of financial institutions in developing countries, at their history, at their successes and failures and at the factors which may have caused success or failure, and in our inquiry we found a number of surprising similarities. Some of the successful financial institutions in the developing countries of today are savings banks or cooperative financial institutions in a strict, formal sense, or they have many of the features of such institutions, notably those of being locally owned, locally focused, and locally managed. Some of them owe their existence to development aid, while others do not. Any lessons to be drawn are necessarily derived from carefully combining the history of socially-oriented financial institutions in Germany and from our knowledge of financial institutions in developing countries.
3. To the extent that lessons derived from history or any other empirical material may be perceived as cautious recommendations, it is important to have a clear idea of who the persons or the institutions are for whom the recommendations are intended and of the decisions that they have to make and the problems that they have to solve. The (policy) question "Should the competent authorities in industrialized country X support the creation of savings or cooperative banks in a given developing or transition country Y?" is just one possible policy question. Others might be "Given that developing or transition country Y already has savings banks or cooperative banks or is set to create such institutions, in what sense could and should industrialized country X support these undertak-

ings?" But by far the most relevant policy question from our point of view is this: "Given that there is an institution that caters specifically to small businesses and to the general public, or that the creation of such an institution is being considered, what features of the German savings and cooperative banks might be taken into consideration for its design?"

Here are eight general policy-relevant conclusions that are supported by a close look at history:

1. The first and by far the most important conclusion is clearly positive: It is indeed possible to create financial institutions that achieve the dual goal of being relevant from a social and developmental perspective and of being financially and economically sound, difficult though this undertaking may appear. German savings and cooperative banks, throughout their history and today, as well as several of the financial institutions in developing countries described in detail in Chapter III have demonstrated that this is indeed possible.

2. Even though there is a danger that one of the two objectives – long-term impact or value for the clients on the one hand, and financial and organizational success as an institution on the other – may come to be neglected, it is possible to maintain a certain balance over time, though it requires adapting to changing conditions. Not only have savings and cooperative banks mastered far-reaching changes over time; successful microfinance and small business banks have also undertaken similar steps in recent years. Otherwise, they would hardly still be in existence today.

3. Both in our historical survey and in our case studies of successful MFIs and small-business-oriented banks, one factor emerges as being of great importance: Sustainable institutions must place utmost emphasis on mobilizing savings, so that they function as intermediaries in the narrow sense of institutions transforming (local) savings into (local) loans. This is important for several reasons: (i) Clients, and especially those with limited means, need deposit facilities as a banking service; (ii) At least under certain conditions, clients' deposits can serve as a source of low-cost funds for the financial institutions that mobilize them, even if they pay normal market rates of interest on deposits; (iii) Mobilizing and using savings strengthens and stabilizes institutions and makes them independent of external funding, which may prove unreliable and, to the extent available, often goes hand-in-hand with undue interference; (iv) There is a certain synergy between the lending and the deposit-taking operations of a financial institution, for instance insofar as the information gained in one line of business can be used in the other; and (v) Deposit taking by a financial institution strengthens the willingness of borrowers to repay their loans and/or that of their neighbors and peers to exert social pressure on them to repay loans. The latter lesson can also be stated in the negative sense: "Credit-only" or "deposit-only" institutions are more likely to fail, whether as a business undertaking, or in developmental terms, or both.

4. The enduring success of the savings and cooperative banks in Germany and some other European countries seems to be due to a combination of the following factors:[5]
   - The primary institutions were firmly rooted in their local environment; central institutions were created later and did not "grab power" at the expense of their local member institutions.
   - From early on, they have been "socially relevant universal banks," that is, they focus on mobilizing local savings and granting small loans to creditworthy individuals of limited means. In other words, they did not restrict their operations to either deposit taking or lending.
   - They pursued what would today be called a "commercial approach to microfinance," that is, they aspired to operate in a financially responsible manner (covering their costs and making a moderate profit), while at the same time acting in a socially responsible manner (offering access to formal finance, serving relatively poor people) and fostering social cohesion and local economic development. Their institutional and governance regimes were designed in such a way as to support this dual-bottom-line orientation. Profits stayed where they had been generated. There was no "plundering of the poor" and no capital drain.
   - They benefited from the support of the "civil society": In the beginning, well-intentioned and better educated members of the respective local communities, including private bankers, took over various important functions, including that of monitoring the institutions' management, on a volunteer basis.
   - They benefited from a conducive political environment in a dual sense: Firstly, there was a legal framework in place that allowed the institutions and their managers to carry out socially relevant banking in the manner they found appropriate, and secondly, there were few attempts by politicians or other influential individuals to use or misuse these institutions for their personal financial and political aims.
   - After some time, the German savings and cooperative banks began to create supra-local institutions, namely the associations and the central clearing banks. These supra-local institutions are still in existence today and play an important role as networks (*Verbünde*) which also include service subsidiaries and, most importantly, institutional mutual protection and deposit guarantee schemes. An approximate description in English of what the German term "*Verbünde*" implies in this context might be: "networks of independent, yet closely related and cooperating financial and non-financial institutions." These *Verbünde* enable the local banks to achieve economies of scale in certain operations, disseminate information and knowledge among their member banks, and allow better management of risks, and they contribute in an

---

[5] For details see the conclusion of Chapter II of this book.

essential way to the monitoring of the local institutions and of those who manage them.

5. It is precisely the combination of these features that enabled savings and cooperative banks to thrive as socially-oriented local banks in Europe. In Germany, it has allowed them to survive to the present day in what is essentially their original form. In most other European countries, savings banks and/or cooperative banks have either undergone fundamental changes in their features and policies or have disappeared entirely. To the extent that disappearance was due to institutional failures, the failures may be attributable to the fact that some of the core features of savings and cooperative banks set forth above – such as the regional principle or the dual bottom line mandate – were abolished.[6] In developing countries as well, a number of attempts have been made to create savings banks and cooperative banks, and many of them did not fulfill the expectations that their creators may once have had. In most individual cases, it is possible to pinpoint the lack of one or more of the essential features described above as the reason for failure or poor performance.

6. It is easy to state the last finding in generalized terms: Any institution can be described as a set of features that includes contracts, incentives, and constraints, as the new institutional economics points out.[7] It is of utmost importance for the lasting success of an institution that these features complement each other – that is, that they fit together well and that they mutually support each other in their strengths and mutually mitigate their respective weaknesses. But this is not enough; such a complex of features must also be compatible with the objective and the purpose of the institution and the environment in which it operates. Therefore, the enduring success of the savings and cooperative banks in Germany can, on a more abstract level, be explained by saying that they have, in their respective ways, been well-adjusted systems of institutional features.[8]

Table 13, at the end of Chapter II, gives a comprehensive summary of the constitutive features of German savings banks and cooperative banks and, at the same time, of the long-term development of local banking in Germany. It demonstrates that both institutional forms are internally consistent, and shows the similarities and differences between savings banks on the one hand and cooperative banks on the other.

7. In Germany the commitment of savings and cooperative banks to local development has had three important effects: The first is the achievement of virtual-

---

[6] For details see Bülbül et al. (2013).
[7] See Chapter I, section 3.3.
[8] Understanding the role of complementarity between the various features of an institution is not only important for explaining or understanding why institutions succeed or fail, it is also a general rule of how institutions should be designed. This rule can, and indeed must, be applied in any undertaking of creating, reshaping, and supporting a financial institution that serves to foster social and economic development and financial inclusion irrespective of whether this financial institution calls itself a savings bank or a cooperative bank or a small business bank.

ly universal financial inclusion, encompassing all segments of society from bottom to top, and offering businesses unlimited opportunities for graduation from start-up to micro, small, and medium enterprise finance. The second is a highly innovative and internationally competitive small and medium enterprise (SME) sector with an extraordinarily high rate of employment generation, financed – albeit not exclusively – by the two groups of local banks. The third is the crisis resilience of the local banks, as revealed in the recent global financial crisis. Paradoxically, it has been the lack of profit maximization objectives among these two groups of banks which has contributed both to the profitability of the SME sector and to the institutions' own crisis resilience. There is yet another aspect of this paradox: social inclusion started with a focus on the poor, without excluding the non-poor. It is this non-discriminatory focus which has made the local banks a driver of innovation and economic growth. This historical experience, as presented in Chapter II, and the gist of the case studies in Chapter III provide the basis for our recommendations to development agencies summarized at the end of this chapter.

8. We believe that it can, and indeed should, be a valuable role of development aid to ensure that these aspects of institutional design receive the appropriate attention in the creation, redesign, and support – and even the ongoing management – of the financial institutions they aim to support.

3 The direct relevance of the historical survey for the design of development projects

While it is no trivial task to understand and explain what makes socially-oriented local banks strong, and to draw general conclusions from history and from our observation of successful microfinance providers of today, that task appears almost an easy one compared to the further step of deriving, on the basis of this analysis, practical implications that can serve as recommendations. However, the general thrust of these practical lessons is also straightforward and can be summarized as follows:

> It would appear to be highly desirable to have institutions with the features of the early German savings and cooperative banks and even to adopt similar legal and institutional forms for these institutions, *provided* that all or at least most of the core features are present or can be created.
>
> However, it is important to be aware of the possibility that in many countries the conditions under which genuine savings and cooperative banks can function properly, and remain in existence for a long time, simply will not be in place. This is why simply replicating the German models does not appear to be good development (aid) policy.

But it is unlikely that anyone would really think of using a historical survey as a blueprint for replication. At least for some decision makers, the question may instead be whether it makes sense to support or create banks that are public institutions, under municipal trusteeship, as is the case for the German savings banks, or under outright public ownership; or member-owned financial institutions like the (German) cooperative banks. Our analysis also suggests an answer to this question: Mere public ownership or member ownership alone – in the absence of at least some of the other features listed above – is unlikely to lead to viable financial institutions that benefit the general population, work against financial exclusion, and foster economic growth and social development.[9]

The reason why we are skeptical of public banks is that in many countries the traditional power structures are such that government (or state or even municipal) ownership or trusteeship implies almost irresistible temptations for those in power to use their power for their own political and personal aims. Ensuring "good governance" can indeed be a challenge. Undue political interference or interference by other power brokers comes in many forms, ranging from loan forgiveness programs, to political pressure to lend to cronies of those in power, to

---

9 This is also the general thrust of most of the articles contained in a recent book edited by Butzbach and von Mettenheim (2013). Public savings banks and cooperative banks are the most important classes of what the editors of this volume call "alternative banks."

outright corruption and even to theft. Drawing up firewalls against such abuses is possible, but difficult, given that those who might benefit from the abuses typically have a strong say in how the firewalls should be built – and they tend to prefer firewalls that are permeable.[10]

A major challenge for the cooperative banking model, on the other hand, lies in the problem of organizing control in such banks. There are many examples which show that the inherently weak governance role of cooperative members, which is enshrined in the rule of one-person-one-vote, can lead to a failure to effectively monitor those in power. Insufficient member control can rarely be compensated for by the ethics of those who wield power in a financial cooperative, even though there are also many examples of a benign use of power. The risk that some people will achieve too much power and can avoid undergoing any serious monitoring will be even greater if a cooperative banking system obtains external funding, whether from abroad or from the national government. The requirement that in order to keep costs low, cooperative organizations must have a certain minimum size, implies that financial cooperatives are rarely isolated small entities that could operate successfully merely according to "democratic principles." In our view, cooperative financial institutions and their networks, much like local savings banks, only have a chance of being successful if effective control and monitoring functions are organized within and by the network, for example through an audit function based in the respective association (as is the case with the German auditing associations), and if the institutions, taken as a group, are financially self-sufficient.

None of this should be taken to imply that it is impossible to create viable and at the same time socially relevant financial institutions in developing and transition countries that entail elements of savings banks or cooperative banks. There are positive examples of both, and we have described some of them in the Chapter III.[11]

The historical exercise contained in Chapter II is even more encouraging in this respect. Savings and cooperative banks have evolved as two types of institutions that:

- adopted and largely retained the dual objective of striving for financial viability and, at the same time, social and developmental impact.
- were able to develop corporate governance regimes that have been by and large conducive to their dual bottom line orientation.

---

10 The World Bank recently (2012) published the 2013 edition of its "Global Financial Development Report." Two features of this report, which is entitled "Rethinking the Role of the State in Finance," are particularly surprising: (1) It does not even mention savings banks at all; and (2) it does not contain a single word about the challenges mentioned here in the text, with which every practitioner is familiar.

11 See in particular the sections on the government-majority-owned BRI, the village banks (LPD) in Bali and the financial cooperatives in Vietnam.

- developed into universal banks for the general public and were able to make a lasting difference.
- benefited from judicious social and political support and a favorable legal framework, which constituted a defense against attempts to exploit socially-oriented financial institutions and their clients.
- have been embedded in networks that strengthen the decentralized local financial institutions.
- have had a tremendous positive impact in supporting the small businesses of their time, opened up access to financial services for the general public, and succeeded in becoming powerful and stable financial institutions.

If such institutions could be created in the past, there is a chance to do it again in the 21st century in ways that take current conditions and today's technological and economic opportunities, such as mobile banking and the extensive use of IT, into account. The possible positive impact that such an attempt could have makes it worth undertaking. After all, in spite of the considerable progress of the new microfinance in the past decade, there is still an urgent need to improve and strengthen the financial systems of many countries and to make them more inclusive, and the elements of what makes a successful MFI or, more generally, a truly inclusive finance institution are by now quite well understood.

In our view, it would thus be a serious mistake to stop providing foreign support for socially and developmentally oriented banking as a part of international development cooperation, as Milford Bateman (2012), for instance, has recently pleaded.[12] Many of those who are in a position to make relevant decisions seem to see the need for, and the potential of, socially and developmentally relevant inclusive finance as much as we do. But the crucial question remains: Through what institutional and legal forms should this be accomplished?

Policy decisions must be based on a precise view of the objectives that are to be achieved and the set of alternatives available as a means of working towards these objectives. If, for whatever reason, policy makers consider creating or supporting just one type of institution in developing countries that is meant to be locally focused and to serve the general public, and in particular small and very small businesses and relatively poor people, they have three strategic options: (1) public banks or, in a broad sense, public savings banks; (2) cooperative or member-owned banks; and (3) shareholder-owned private banks with the legal form of a corporation. Is one of these alternatives preferable, and if so, which one? Looking back over the last decade helps us to find answers to these questions.

About ten years ago modern microfinance was advancing rapidly, it was beginning to have an impact, and it enjoyed a growing reputation among experts, poli-

---

12 See also our discussion of Bateman's book 'Why doesn't microfinance work?' (2010) in section 4.5 of the last chapter.

cy makers, and the general public. MFIs were widely regarded as powerful instruments to fight poverty and to advance equitable social and economic development and even began to be regarded as an attractive investment opportunity for private investors.[13] At that time, it was easy to get the impression that there was only one successful model for how to organize and manage microfinance successfully, namely that of a corporation owned by private and public institutions and private persons as investors. These owners or investors included international and foreign national development organizations, socially minded private investors and also local and foreign private investors with a predominant or even exclusive financial interest. With notable exceptions – among them BRI in Indonesia, Khan Bank in Mongolia, BAAC in Thailand, Cooperative Bank in Vietnam and Banco del Estado in Chile – public banks and cooperatives were rarely considered good models for microfinance, and in much of the general discussion about microfinance or "finance for all," these legal forms were hardly mentioned at all as alternatives seriously worth considering.

At that time the private microfinance corporation was indeed the institutional form or model that showed the greatest potential for achieving the generally accepted aims of development finance,[14] and a great deal of this potential was in fact realized over the course of the past decade. Given the track record of the three basic institutional models, as it was generally perceived at that time, it is not all that surprising that most international microfinance support organizations and most donor institutions largely favored the concepts of private microfinance or of microfinance in the form of a public-private partnership. For some observers, the more private-capital-dominated it was, the more attractive microfinance seemed to be. And there is of course one strong argument that speaks for the private capital model: Private firms have genuine owners with a strong interest in seeing to it that their corporation is run in an efficient manner and remains a stable and viable institution, and with better means at their disposal of imposing this efficiency requirement on the management of an MFI. The managers can therefore be assumed to be under more pressure to ensure that the institution operates in an efficient manner and conducts itself accordingly; and this governance advantage may ultimately also be in the interest of the clients of the institutions.

However, at that time it would also have been easy to overlook the negative side of a microfinance model based mainly or exclusively on private investment. The experience of the private and purely pro-profit MFI SKS and its peers in India and in a number of other countries illustrates the downside of the private model. If private capital plays the dominant role in an MFI, there is always the risk that the commercial orientation will gain the upper hand and that the developmental and

---

[13] The attractiveness of microfinance for private profit-seeking investors is highlighted in Dieckmann (2007) and Reille and Foster (2008).
[14] Among the numerous publications that argue to this effect, see the particularly cogent exposition by Michael Chu (2007), who for a long time served as president and CEO of ACCION International.

social aspirations which were meant to be the hallmark of microfinance lose their importance and are replaced by pure profit-seeking. One of the consequences of a one-sided and excessive profit orientation is the expansion of consumer finance that has taken place in the recent past. In a number of MFIs, consumer lending has started to largely replace the former focus on lending to small and micro-scale businesses. Of course, consumer lending cannot be considered negative in general, since it may be extremely valuable for those who borrow to bridge a temporary gap between current income and current expenditure needs. But all too often, consumer loans are granted for purposes that can justly be criticized and that ultimately only burden people with repayment obligations that they cannot fulfill. Over-lending and over-borrowing are related socially undesirable phenomena, and they harm those whom microfinance was originally intended to benefit. Even though it would obviously be unfair to state that all private MFIs are prone to indulge in irresponsible lending, it is important to be aware of this potential downside of private MFIs, and this downside may partially negate the evident advantage that the private capital model has as far as the incentives to strive for efficiency are concerned.

As the "dark side of (private and for-profit) microfinance"[15] has increasingly been revealed, a number of microfinance organizations or banks which aspire to provide "finance for all" (World Bank 2007) and are not organized as corporations have learned their lessons. They have adopted a number of the positive features that had first been implemented in the private institutions that constituted what was once called "The New World of Microenterprise Finance" (Otero and Rhyne 1994), especially those like BancoSol that were organized as corporations and relied largely on foreign equity capital. Many financial institutions that provide services to the general population and that are not shareholder-owned corporations have in the meantime reshaped and modernized their policies and processes and have become more professional, more efficient, and more effective.[16] This applies at least to some public or semi-public banks which resemble savings banks or are former national development banks, to cooperative banks, and even to a number of NGOs. Recent econometric studies show that neither in terms of financial stability nor in terms of outreach can MFIs with the legal form of a corporation with predominantly foreign shareholders today be regarded as being generally superior to MFIs with other legal and institutional forms or to corporations with mainly local shareholders.[17] According to a recent study by Martins and Winkler (2013), the only factor by which it is possible to distinguish between successful and unsuccessful MFIs in a strict statistical sense is whether, and to what extent, they

---

15 Business Week (2005). It should be added here that the exact title of this article is "The Dark Side of Micro*credit*," not micro*finance*.
16 Several chapters in the book edited by Butzbach and von Mettenheim (2013), notably the editors' introduction, highlight the considerable advances that these types of banks have made in recent years and their substantial contributions to financial inclusion.
17 See among others Hatarska and Nadolnyak (2007), Mersland and Strom (2009) and Martins and Winkler (2013).

mobilize local deposits. This finding would appear to confirm the results of our historical analysis.

Taken together, these two developments of the last decade cast doubt on what only a few years ago was almost a dogma in the debate about (modern) microfinance: The dichotomy of "modern" and efficient new-style MFIs with the legal form of a private corporation on the one side, and the remaining, apparently old-fashioned, inefficient and ineffective institutional forms on the other, is no longer appropriate today. In a picture that once appeared to be black and white, we now see many nuances.

What does this state of ambiguity suggest for policy? The future is always difficult to predict, in microfinance just as much as in any other area. Examining the long history of the German savings and cooperative banks starting in the late 18th century, as we have done in Chapter II of this study; informal finance and selected MFIs that are rarely discussed at any length in the literature on microfinance, as we have done in Chapter III; and finally, the most recent developments in the field, as discussed in this section, is instructive in terms of deriving implications for policy. Taken together, our empirical material suggests that one cannot claim, as some people seem to be trying to do, that only one institutional and legal form of microfinance, namely that of a private corporation, is superior to all others in the long run and under all possible circumstances. We have to acknowledge that we do not know and cannot seriously claim to know what legal and institutional form will ultimately prove to be best. Moreover, the legal and institutional form alone is too general a criterion for determining the potential of an MFI. Too much depends on the details of how a given institution of whatever legal and institutional form is designed, governed, and managed, on the identity of the owners or other top decision makers, and of course on the specifics of time and place.

If this rather agnostic assessment is correct, it suggests that it would be best not to place all bets on one horse – in other words, that it would be best not to discard the savings bank and cooperative bank models as generally unsuited for achieving inclusive finance, in spite of any weaknesses these legal and institutional forms may have, especially with regard to their governance features. One should not overlook the fact that they also have considerable strengths. We therefore recommend that endeavors to support savings banks and cooperative banks in the context of international development cooperation be continued. This will make it possible to further test their potential and to determine how their strengths can be further enhanced and their weaknesses limited. Of course, this requires that foreign partners in their capacities as donors and supporters are aware of the possible limitations of public and cooperative banks in developing countries as described above, and it implies the need for a rigorous and demanding partner who insists that certain conditions be fulfilled, if it is going to make sense to support these models as a strategy for establishing financial institutionswhich benefit the general population.

4 A concluding comparative remark and a plea for diversity of banking structures

In support of our recommendation to continue efforts to strengthen savings banks and cooperative banks – alongside other types of banks – in developing countries, we would like to draw a last parallel to the situation in our home country of Germany and in other European countries and to put these considerations in the context of the international political and academic debate about saving banks and cooperative banks.

Germany has a three-pillar banking system comprising private shareholder-owned banks, public savings banks, and member-owned cooperative banks.[18] For decades all three groups of banks have been strong elements of the German banking system and have served the German economy well. It also seems plausible to assume that this system of three pillars is one of the reasons for Germany's economic strength and the ability it has shown to overcome the recent financial crisis faster and more effectively than most of its neighboring countries. Over the last 20 years prior to the start of the great financial crisis, the performance of the German savings and cooperative banks has been impressive by almost any standard. Measured by ROA and ROE, they have been no less efficient, and on average even more efficient, than comparable large shareholder-owned banks, that is, those that also have large branch networks. The savings and cooperative banks are equally well capitalized and their cost-income ratios have been lower. They have continuously expanded their lending and deposit-taking business and have consistently enjoyed a very positive reputation with their clients. Even more importantly, all performance indicators and levels of lending activities have remained much more stable than those of the large private banks.

The differences in performance became even more pronounced during the crisis years. It is fair to say that as a group, the German cooperative banks have come through the crisis better than all other groups of banks; and if it had not been for their multifaceted relationships with the large regional banks, the *Landesbanken*, some of which were seriously and negatively affected by the crisis, the same would apply to the German savings banks as well. Speaking only of the local savings banks, they can be said to have fared as well as the cooperative banks – and much better than the large shareholder-owned banks. The stability of the savings and cooperative banks and their reliable supply of loans to large parts of the German economy is one of the main reasons why Germany has been able to overcome the general economic crisis of the past years better than most comparable countries.

---

18 Calling the German banking system a three-pillar system is not entirely correct given that there are other banks which together form a fourth group with substantial aggregate assets. This fourth group is quite heterogeneous, and it comprises, among others, state-owned promotional banks (or development banks) such as the large Kreditanstalt für Wiederaufbau (KfW). Nevertheless, the customary label used for the German banking system is that of a three-pillar system.

All of this clearly constitutes a strong endorsement of these two types of "unconventional banks" as important elements of the German three-pillar banking system. More generally, it also seems to speak in favor of having a diversified banking structure – the kind of diversity that we think it would also be good to have in developing countries' microfinance systems.

While Germany has retained its three-pillar banking system for decades and seems to have benefited from having this system, the recent evolution of the banking structures in most other European countries differs greatly from that in Germany. Only 20 years ago, the banking systems of most other countries on the European continent largely resembled that of Germany, that is, they all had a three-pillar system of shareholder-owned private banks, decentralized public (savings) banks, and local cooperative banks. But this is no longer the case, and now shareholder-oriented banks have started to dominate most national banking systems by a wide margin. Savings banks have been privatized or merged or even completely abolished, and cooperative banks have been consolidated and centralized or have ceased to be member-owned. Where savings and cooperative banks have survived in a modified form, essential aspects of their earlier core strengths, such as the regional principle or the mandate to serve the local community, have been eliminated.

Not least for development policy considerations, it is important to understand why this happened at all and what the basis for the recent changes in most other European countries has been. The answer is that there were strong political and intellectual forces behind these reforms, and they were underpinned by a view that was widely held in the last two decades of the 20th century. This view deserves a closer look. Its essence is that banks with other governance and ownership features – notably public banks, including public savings banks, and also, though to a lesser extent, cooperative banks – are in some sense inferior to large, shareholder-owned, and purely profit-oriented listed banks.

This view has had strong advocates and a long history.[19] At first, in the 1980s, it was inspired by a political doctrine known as the Washington Consensus. Then, in the 1990s, it was largely adopted by the IMF as the conceptual basis of its financial sector work, and until the advent of the great financial crisis it seems to have also influenced the financial sector policy of the EU Commission.

Moreover, around the turn of the century it also received strong academic backing in the form of the findings of a group of four researchers from top American universities, professors La Porta, Lopez de Silanes, Shleifer, and Vishny.[20] Their

---

[19] For an extended account of the political debate about savings banks and its history, see Schmidt (2009).
[20] See La Porta, Lopez-de-Silanes, Shleifer and Vishny (1998) for the first and programmatic of these publications and La Porta, Lopez-de-Silanes and Shleifer (2002) with regard to government-owned banks.

work was empirically based and published in all leading economic journals; it therefore appeared credible and it became widely known. Based on their empirical findings, these researchers came to a devastating verdict on public banks, a verdict that had a great influence on policy makers at a time in which the concept of shareholder value maximization dominated the debate in finance, economics, and corporate governance.

However, the empirical data that this group of authors used is quite limited in scope and quality, and therefore the policy relevance of their findings is limited as well. Their data mainly related to large centralized public banks, and the performance figures they used mainly cover the 1980s and 1990s. For the banks surveyed, the authors' negative assessment may indeed be valid, but this does not justify extending their assessment to the decentralized and locally focused public banks in which we see considerable merit and potential.

The view described above was indeed influential, and for that reason it needs to be taken seriously. But as our study should have made clear, we do not share it, and in particular we neither agree with the generalizations it implies, nor with the conclusions derived from them. Of course, we also abstain from any general statement to the effect that banks that are not shareholder-owned and not purely profit-oriented would be generally preferable. As our historical survey in the second chapter and our case studies in the third chapter of this book clearly show, any serious assessment depends on the specifics of time and place and on the institutional and organizational design of banks of all legal forms, meaning that any attempt at a positive or negative generalization would be futile.

The experience of the crisis years, at the latest, casts a doubt on this earlier negative assessment of all public banks and the reforms induced by it. Moreover, these reforms have had a negative impact on relatively poor people and small businesses in particular, as their access to financial services has deteriorated as a result. And as it turns out, the reforms have also reduced the stability of the respective national financial systems.[21]

Since the end of the last decade and under the influence of the financial crisis, which created widespread skepticism regarding big and purely profit-oriented banks, the general negative attitude towards "unconventional" banks has to a certain extent given way to a more positive assessment of savings banks and cooperative banks among policy makers and international institutions that had formerly been utterly skeptical about the merits of such banks. In some countries in Europe, there is even a debate now underway as to whether it would be desirable and feasible to recreate institutional forms of banking that have features of savings banks along German lines. But this may only be a temporary change of attitude, and there are reasons to fear that the former reservations and the preference for

---

21 For details and additional sources to support these assessments see Schmidt et al. (2013).

just one form of banking firms may once again start to dominate the political debate. If this fear turns out to be justified, the prospects for a diversified institutional structure of banking – both in Europe and in developing countries – are not all that good.

Especially for those who think that large shareholder-owned and purely profit-oriented banks are the optimal model of how banking should be organized, we want to offer one more argument – possibly an even stronger one – as to why diversity of banking structures may be valuable.[22] This argument is inspired by the ongoing debate among experts in life sciences about preserving biodiversity: Most of these experts argue strongly for preserving all species, including those whose function for the ecosystems does not seem obvious at present. Their main argument is that we do not know today, and in fact cannot know, what plant or animal may one day play a crucial role in the cure for some disease which may not even be known at present. Once a species is extinct, it can no longer play this possibly beneficial role in the future – regardless of how valuable its contribution may then have been.

A similar argument applies to institutions in general, and thus also to different institutional forms of organizing banking in both developed and developing countries. It goes like this: Even though banks in the form of a corporation with only private shareholders, or with a mix of private and public shareholders, may currently appear to be in some sense "better" than public and cooperative banks (a view that we ourselves do not share), the possibility cannot be ruled out that for some reason of which we may not be aware today, even those individuals who are *now* skeptical towards savings and cooperative banks might at some time in the future see things differently and would *then* prefer to have institutions resembling public savings banks, or some form of cooperative banks, or banking systems with a mixture of different bank types. Being able to switch to other bank types or to a different mixture of banks within a national banking system would *then* be highly desirable, but it would hardly be feasible if savings banks (in the form of public banks) or cooperative banks no longer existed and if, as a consequence, the valuable expertise as to how to organize and manage these types of banks were also to be "extinct" and possibly lost for good.

This is the real danger of an "institutional monoculture" of only shareholder-owned banks, because the knowledge of what a savings bank or a cooperative bank is and how these institutions can be made to function in the interest of the general population is a part of a country's social capital – and no trivial part at that. After all, a sound balance between financial and social objectives is difficult to maintain over the long term, and it is equally difficult to create and maintain the network structures that are so important for the competitive strengths of these

---

22 This argument was first presented in Ayadi et al. (2009).

types of banks. Therefore it seems unlikely that this know-how could simply be reinvented once it appears valuable to have it again. And for this reason, we should not simply follow what has for a long time been a prevailing trend in political circles outside of Germany and may again become the predominant view; we should instead now take measures to keep various types of banks "alive" – much like endangered species.

Apart from the actual benefits that savings and cooperative banks can offer the people they are to serve, supporting different forms or types of banks now in a way that allows them to thrive, to develop, and to adapt to changing circumstances, and thus to remain competitive, is a strategy of protecting countries and their inhabitants from the risk of being stuck with a banking model that may one day be judged as less attractive than it currently seems to be. In the light of this consideration, preserving institutional diversity in banking is simply rational, and it is also a strong argument for supporting various forms of MFIs in developing countries now.

5 Summing up: Insights and recommendations for national and international decision makers based on 200 years of inclusive microfinance and local banking history

Most people must allocate their time carefully. This is why they often only read the first and last sections of books, or at least start with these sections when they first pick up a book. As academics, we perfectly understand that this is rational; after all, we often do it ourselves. Therefore we have decided to conclude this book with a summary of what we regard as the 18 most important insights of our study for donors and other decision makers. For those with extremely little time, the essentials of each insight are in boldface.

Strategic insights

- **Local banking can work.** Provided that it is implemented in a sound and effective way local banking has an enormous potential that can and should be utilized and furthered, and the development and the proper functioning of local banking should be supported by an appropriate legal and regulatory framework for local banking as well as by international aid.
- **Finance can contribute greatly to the creation of value in a broad sense.** It fosters economic growth, employment, and social development at large. But it also creates risk and can have negative effects on the distribution of wealth and income and on social cohesion.
- History and current good practice hold an important positive lesson: microfinance or inclusive finance or "finance for all" can work. But success is not assured and good intentions are not enough.
- **Sound and effective local financial institutions can be characterized by the following salient features:** They are inclusive, responsible, sustainable and profitable, locally focused, resilient, value based, reliable, fair to their clients, transparent, and customer- and community-oriented, have a consistent institutional design, and are embedded in networks of related institutions.
- **A patient approach to supporting inclusive finance makes sense in economic and political terms,** because the processes involved take a great deal of time. Therefore it is important to avoid creating expectations – especially any expectations of fast results – that cannot be fulfilled.
- **Local as well as international policy should aspire to foster inclusive finance** in terms of the clients that are served and the financial products that are offered. But serving small and very small businesses and poor or near-poor peo-

ple should rank high on the agenda of inclusive financial institutions. The time for targeted policies and institutions aimed exclusively at poverty alleviation or any other single objective is over.

Insights concerning financial institution building and governance

- **Financial institution building is of paramount importance.** It consists of creating and supporting locally-based financial institutions. Good local financial institutions must be effective, stable, and financially viable over the long term if they are to have a positive impact. Sound governance and management are the basis of any stable and developmentally valuable financial institution.
- **Good microfinance or inclusive finance institutions must follow a moderate and responsible commercial approach** in the sense of aspiring to strike a sound balance between being profitable, as a precondition of their survival and growth as institutions, and having a social and developmental impact. But this is a complicated mandate and there is always the danger that an institution will end up pursuing only one of these two objectives.
- **The success of financial institution building depends on the design features of an institution and the details of people, place, and project.** Institutional design shapes incentives, and incentives determine how an institution functions and how successful it can be. A core issue of institutional design is the allocation of decision and ownership rights. In many institutions, critical design features have not been properly coordinated, and therefore they cannot become stable institutions and will not achieve their well-intentioned mission, whatever it might be.
- **Fostering networks of related and cooperating institutions is an important element of financial institution building** since such networks make it possible to combine the benefits of proximity to clients with those of scale, scope, and ongoing learning. This is a lesson that can be derived from the history of German savings and cooperative banks as well as from studying successful MFIs of today.

Insights concerning development policy approaches

- **Development aid to support microfinance or inclusive finance is sound development policy.** But it risks being excessively interventionist and undermining local initiatives, and it might even do more harm than good if it follows the wrong model – one based, for example, on current fads and fashions in expert circles and the assumed preferences of the electorate in the donor countries.

- Development aid policy should set priorities but should not promulgate one governance and ownership model for a development finance institution. Different governance and ownership regimes should be supported as long as they are consistent with development objectives and local conditions. Fostering diversity of governance and ownership regimes can make sense as a process of testing and learning. Therefore development policy should be prepared to support various institutional forms ranging from (public) savings banks to cooperative financial institutions to various forms of PPPs as well as to purely private MFIs. Each of them has its strengths and weaknesses. Naturally, however, arguing for diversity does not imply that "anything goes." There will be cases in which the weaknesses of a given institutional form will clearly outweigh its strengths.
- The same applies to different development strategies. In principle, it is recommendable to continue experimenting with different types of development projects ranging from upgrading to downscaling to linking and to "greenfielding" (or creating a new institution ex nihilo). All of them have their merits and their drawbacks, and the choice of project type must be made on a case-by-case basis.
- Donors and international decision makers must realize that finance is about money, wealth, and power. Therefore, helping local inclusive financial institutions to withstand undue political interference and abuse by those who wield power can be very important. Donors are not always aware of the fact that they are a part of the governance regime of the institutions in foreign countries that they help to create or support.
- Donors and international public and private investors must be prepared to support local financial institutions over a long period of time with debt, equity, and expertise. But in doing so, they should take into account the fact that the role of external support is limited and that flooding local institutions with money can undermine the incentives to mobilize savings as the basis of self-reliance and autonomy and to safeguard institutional stability.
- Donors and other international decision makers must also accept responsibility for the way in which local financial institutions that they support interact with their clients, i.e. for ensuring that clients are treated fairly and respectfully, that they are not exploited by excessive interest rates and that they are not induced to take out more loans than they can repay.
- International donors and supporters are expected to ensure that their local partner institutions adhere to the dual objective of being profitable and stable on the one hand, and aspiring to and achieving a social and developmental impact on the other.
- Finally, The international donors must furthermore ensure that the local partner institutions are properly regulated and supervised by competent national authorities.

References

Aachener Bank, ed. (1974): *75 Jahre Aachener Bank*, Aachen

Aachener Verein zur Beförderung der Arbeitsamkeit [The Aachen Association for Promoting Industriousness], ed. (1884): *Der Aachener Verein zur Beförderung der Arbeitsamkeit, sein Werden, Wirken und Wollen von seinen Anfängen bis zur Gegenwart*, Aachen: Festschrift zur Feier des 50jährigen Bestehens am 21. Juni 1884

Abel, W. (1986): *Agricultural Fluctuations in Europe: From the Thirteenth to the Twentieth Centuries*, London and New York: Routledge/http://en.wikipedia.org/wiki/Taylor_and_FrancisTaylor & Francis

-- (1978): *Geschichte der deutschen Landwirtschaft vom frühen Mittelalter bis zum 19. Jahrhundert*, 3rd ed., Stuttgart: Ulmer

Abelshauser, W. (2005): *Deutsche Wirtschaftsgeschichte seit 1945*, Bonn: Lizenzausgabe für die Bundeszentrale für politische Bildung

ACCION (2007): *The Banco Compartamos Initial Public Offering*, ACCION InSight No. 23

Adams, D.W., and D.A. Fitchet, eds. (1992): *Informal Finance in Low-Income Countries*, Boulder, CO: Westview Press

Adams, D.W., D.H. Graham and J.D. Von Pischke, eds. (1984): *Undermining Rural Development with Cheap Credit*, Boulder, CO: Westview Press

Adeyeye, S.O. (1981): *The Place of the 'Esusu-Clubs' in the Development of the Co-operative Movement in Nigeria*, Amsterdam: IUAES Inter-Congress

Aeschliman, C., F. Murekezi and J.-P. Ndoshoboye (2008): Extending the outreach of Rwandan Peoples' Banks to the rural poor through village savings and credit associations, in: M. Pagura, ed., *Expanding the Frontier in Rural Finance*, Bourton on Dunsmore: Practical Action Publishing, 201-216

AFI – Alliance for Financial Inclusion (2013): *Measuring Financial Inclusion: Core Set of Financial Indicators*, Bangkok, http://www.afi-global.org

AFYB (2011): *Agricultural Finance Yearbook 2010*, Kampala: Bank of Uganda, Plan for Modernisation of Agriculture Secretariat and GIZ

-- (2012): *Agricultural Finance Yearbook 2011*, Kampala: Bank of Uganda, Plan for Modernisation of Agriculture Secretariat and GIZ

Alchian, A.A. (1950): Uncertainty, Evolution and Economic Theory, in *Journal of Political Economy*, vol. 55, 211-221

Aldenhoff, R. (1984): Schulze-Delitzsch, *Ein Beitrag zur Geschichte des Liberalismus zwischen Revolution und Reichsgründung*, Baden-Baden: Nomos

Allen, H. (2006): Village Savings and Loan Associations – sustainable and cost-effective rural finance. *Small Enterprise Development*, vol. 17 (1), 61-68

Allen, H. (2007): *Village Savings and Loan Associations: A Practical Guide*. Bourton on Dunsmore: Practical Action Publishing

APMAS (2007): *SHG Federations in India*, Hyderabad: APMAS

-- (2009): *Status of SHG Federations in Andhra Pradesh*, Hyderabad: APMAS

-- (2011): *Member-Control and Self Reliance: Concept and Implementation of the Pilot Project Sector Own Control (SOC)*, Hyderabad: APMAS

APRACA – Asia-Pacific Rural and Agricultural Credit Association (1997): *Linkage Banking in Asia*, 2 vols., Bangkok: APRACA-GTZ Publications

Ardener, S. (1964): The Comparative Study of Rotating Credit Associations. *The Journal of the Royal Anthropological Institute*, vol. 94 (2), 202-229

Ardic, O.P., G. Chen and A. Latortue (2012): *Financial Access 2011: An Overview of the Supply-Side Data Landscape*, Washington, DC: CGAP and IFC

Ardic, O.P., K. Imboden and A. Latortue (2013): *Financial Access 2012: Getting to a More Comprehensive Picture*, Washington, DC: CGAP and IFC, http://www.cgap.org/publications/financial-access-2012

Arnold, W., and F.H. Lamparter (1985): *Friedrich Wilhelm Raiffeisen. Einer für alle – alle für einen*, Neuhausen and Stuttgart: Hänssler

Arunachalam, R.S. (2011): *The Journey of Indian Micro-Finance: Lessons for the Future*, Chennai: Rawat Publications

Aschoff, G., and E. Hennigsen (1995): *Das deutsche Genossenschaftswesen, Entwicklung,*

Struktur, wirtschaftliches Potential, Veröffentlichungen der DG Bank, Deutscher Genossenschaftsbank, 2nd ed., Frankfurt: Knapp

Ashauer, G. (1991): Von der Ersparungscasse zur Sparkassen-Finanzgruppe. *Die deutsche Sparkassenorganisation in Geschichte und Gegenwart*, Stuttgart: Deutscher Sparkassenverlag

-- (2005): *Sparkassen und Banken im Wettbewerb. Strukturwandel im deutschen Kreditgewerbe*, Stuttgart: Deutscher Sparkassenverlag

Ayadi, R., S. Carbo-Valverde and R. H. Schmidt (2009): *Investigating Diversity in the Banking Sector in Europe: The Performance and Role of Savings Banks*, Brussels: Centre for European Policy Studies (CEPS)

Ayadi, R., D. Llewellyn, R. H. Schmidt, E. Arbak and W. P. de Groen (2010): *Investigating Diversity in the Banking Sector in Europe: Key Developments, Performance and Role of Cooperative Banks*, Brussels: Centre for European Policy Studies (CEPS)

Badischer Genossenschaftsverband, ed. (1992): *1867-1992 Tradition, Leistung, Aufbau. 125 Jahre genossenschaftliche Selbsthilfe in Baden*, Karlsruhe

Banerjee, A., E. Duflo and C. Kinnan (2015): The Miracle of Microfinance? Evidence from a Randomized Evaluation, *American Economic Journal: Applied Economics*, vol. 7(1), 22-53

Banken, R. (2003): *Die Industrialisierung der Saarregion*, vol. 2, Stuttgart: Steiner

Baron, J. N., and D. M. Kreps (1999): *Strategic Human Resources: Frameworks for General Managers*, New York: Wiley

Bascom, W. (1952): The Esusu: A Credit Institution of the Yoruba. *Journal of the Royal Anthropological Institute*, vol. 82 (1), 63-69

Bass, H. H. (1991): Hungerkrisen in Preußen während der ersten Hälfte des 19. Jahrhunderts, in: *Studien zur Wirtschafts- und Sozialgeschichte*, vol. 8, St. Katharinen: Scipta Mercaturae

Bateman, M. (2010): *Why Doesn't Microfinance Work? The Destructive Rise of Local Neoliberalism*, London: Zed Books

-- (2011): *Confronting Microfinance: Undermining Sustainable Development*, West Hartford, CT: Kumarian Press

-- (2011): *Over-indebtedness and Market Forces*, CGAP Microfinance Blog

-- (2013): *The age of microfinance: Destroying Latin American economies from the bottom up*, Vienna: Austrian Research Foundation for International Development

-- (2014): Microfinance. Failed, so what do we do now? *The Global Analyst*, January 2014, 20-23

Bayerischer Sparkassen- und Giroverband, ed. (1987-1995): *Zeitschrift für bayerische Sparkassengeschichte*, vol. 1-9, Munich

Beaudoin, S. M. (2007): *Poverty in World History*, London and New York: Taylor & Francis

Beck, O. (1868-1871): *Beschreibung des Regierungsbezirks Trier*, Trier

Berndt, H., H. Forndran and G. A. Schmidt (1994): *Leistungen der Sparkassenorganisation in den neuen Bundesländern: eine Gesamtbilanz*, Bonn, Sparkasse: Manager-Magazin für die Sparkassen-Finanzgruppe

Bhargava, B. (1934): *Indigenous Banking in Ancient and Medieval India*, Bombay: D. B. Taraporevala and Sons

Bickel, J. (2012): *Status Quo of SHG Banking: Ground Realities*, GIZ Rural Financial Institutions Programme (RFIP) Newsletter 3/3, New Delhi: GIZ

Biehal, M. (1984): *Der Württembergische Sparkassenverbund 1916-1982*, Berlin: Duncker & Humblot

Birchall, J. (2013): *Finance in an Age of Austerity: The Power of Customer-owned Banks*, Cheltenham: Edward Elgar

-- (2013): *Resilience in a downturn: The power of financial cooperatives*, Geneva: International Labour Office

Blum, M. (2012): *Worldwide inequality, living standards and its determinants during the 19th and 20th Centuries* (Dissertation), Tübingen

BMZ - Bundesministerium für wirtschaftliche Zusammenarbeit (1982): *Querschnittsanalyse der Berichte zur Inspektion "Förderung von Entwicklungsbanken" in acht Ländern Afrikas, Asiens und Lateinamerikas* (unpublished), Bonn: BMZ

Böer, B. P. (1998): *Die Anfänge des Sparkassenwesens in den Freien Städten des Deutschen Bundes* (Sparkassen in der Geschichte, Abteilung 3: Forschung, Bd. 15), Stuttgart, Deutscher Sparkassenverlag

Boi, C. C. and D. Hung (1992): *Survey on Rural Credit in Vietnam*, Hanoi: Faculty of Banking and Finance, Economic University of Vietnam

Borchardt, K. (1984): *Tradition und Wandel, Strukturen des Kreditwesens in hundert Jahren deutscher Geschichte, 100 Jahre Deutscher Sparkassen- und Giroverband*, Stuttgart: Deutscher Sparkassenverlag

Born, K. E. (1976): *Geld und Banken im 19. und 20. Jahrhundert*, Stuttgart: Kröner

Bouman, F. J. A. (1977): Indigenous Saving and Credit Associations in the Third World: a Message. *Savings and Development*, vol. 1 (4), 181–219

–– (1994): ROSCA and ASCRA: Beyond the Financial Landscape, in: F. A. J. Bouman and O. Hospes, eds., *Financial Landscapes Reconstructed: The Fine Art of Mapping Development*, Boulder, CO: Westview Press, 375–394

Bouman, F. J. A. and O. Hospes, eds. (1994): *Financial Landscapes Reconstructed: The Fine Art of Mapping Development*, Boulder CO: Westview Press

Bracht, J. (2013): *Geldlose Zeiten und überfüllte Kassen – Sparen, Leihen und Vererben in der ländlichen Gesellschaft Westfalens 1830–1866*, Stuttgart: Lucius & Lucius

Brämer, P. et al. (2010): Der öffentliche Auftrag der deutschen Sparkassen aus der Perspektive des Stakeholder-Managements, *Zeitschrift für öffentliche und gemeinwirtschaftliche Unternehmen [Journal for Public and Nonprofit Services]*, 311–331

Braudel, F. (1979): *Civilization and Capitalism, 15th–18th Centuries*, translated by S. Reynolds, 3 vols., New York: Harper & Row

BRI – Bank Rakyat Indonesia (1990-2015): *Annual Reports 1989–2014*. Jakarta: BRI

–– (1990-2013): *BRI Unit (Desa) Reports*, Jakarta, http://www.ir-bri.com

–– (1995): *One Hundred Years Bank Rakyat Indonesia 1895 – 1995*, Jakarta

–– (2005-2016): *Financial Updates, Full Year, 2004–2014*, Jakarta, http://www.ir-bri.com

Brickley, J., C. W. Smith and J. L. Zimmerman (2008/1996): *Managerial Economics and Organizational Architecture*, 5th ed., Boston et al.: McGraw-Hill (1st ed. 1996)

Broadberry, S. and K. H. O'Rourke (2010): *The Cambridge Economic History of Modern Europe*, vol. 1, 1700–1870, Cambridge: Cambridge University Press

Brockhaus Konversationslexikon (1908), Leipzig: F. A. Brockhaus

Broens, N., and K. Slind (2013): *The Power of Mapping Financial Services Data*, Seattle: Bill & Melinda Gates Foundation

Brüggemann and Henrich (1896): Der Personalkredit des ländlichen Grundbesitzes im preußischen Saargebiet, *Schriften des Vereins für Socialpolitik*, vol. 74, 47–74, Düsseldorf

Bülbül, D., R. H. Schmidt and U. Schüwer, (2013): Caisses d'Épargne et Banques Cooperatives en Europe, *Revue d'Économie Financière*, vol. 111, 159–188 (An English version is available as SAFE White Paper Series No. 5, Goethe University, Frankfurt 2013)

Business Week (2005): *The ugly side of microcredit*, 24 December (US edition)

Butzbach, O. and K. von Mettenheim, eds. (2013): *Alternative Banking and Financial Crisis*, London: Pickering and Chatto

Catanach, I. J. (1970): *Rural Credit in Western India: Rural Credit and the Co-operative Movement in the Bombay Presidency, 1875-1930*, Cambridge, MA: MIT Press

Centenary Bank (2012): *Annual Report 2011*. Kampala, http://www.centenarybank.co.ug

Centralverein in Preußen für das Wohl der arbeitenden Klassen, ed. (1863): *Das Sparkassenwesen in Deutschland und den außerdeutschen Landestheilen Oestreichs und Preußens*, Berlin: Janke

CGAP (2007): *Sustainability of Self-help Groups in India: Two Analyses*. Occasional Paper 12, Washington, DC: CGAP

–– (2008): *Appraisal Guide for Microfinance Institutions: A Technical Guide*, by Jennifer Isern and Julie Abrams with Matthew Brown, Washington, DC: CGAP

–– (2009): *The Impact of the Financial Crisis on Microfinance Institutions and Their Clients: Results from CGAP's 2009 Opinion Survey*, Washington, DC: CGAP

–– (2012): *A Guide to Regulation and Supervision of Microfinance, Consensus Guidelines*, Washington, DC: CGAP

–– (2013): *Strategic Directions FY 2014 – FY 2018: Advancing Financial Inclusion to Improve the Lives of the Poor*, Washington, DC: CGAP

Chatfield, M. (1996): Tally Stick, in: M. Chatfield and R. Vangermeersch, eds.: *The History of Accounting. An International Ency-*

clopedia, New York and London: Garland Science
Chen, G., S. Rasmussen, X. Reille and D. Rozas (2010): *Indian Microfinance Goes Public: The SKS Initial Public Offering*, CGAP Focus Note No. 65, Washington, DC: CGAP
Christen, R. P., and J. Anderson (2013): *Segmentation of Smallholder Households: Meeting the Range of Financial Needs in Agricultural Families*, CGAP Focus Note 85, Washington, DC: CGAP
Christensen, C. M. (1997): *The innovator's dilemma: When new technologies cause great firms to fail*, Boston: Harvard Business Review Press
Chu, M. (2007): Commercial Returns at the Base of the Pyramid, *Innovation*, Winter/Spring 2007, 115–146
Collins, D., J. Morduch, S. Rutherford and O. Ruthven (2010): **Portfolios of the Poor. How the World's Poor Live on $2 a Day**, Princeton: Princeton University Press
CSFI – Centre for the Study of Financial Innovation (2011): *Microfinance Banana Skins 2011*, London: CSFI
Cuevas, C. E., and K. Fischer (2006): *Cooperative Financial Institutions: Issues in Governance, Regulation and Supervision*, World Bank Working Paper No. 82, Washington, DC: World Bank
Daley-Harris, S. (2002): *Pathways out of Poverty. Innovations in Microfinance for the Poorest Families*, Bloomfield, CT: Kumarian Press
Daley-Harris, S., and A. Awimboeds (2011): *New Pathways out of Poverty*, Bloomfield, CT: Kumarian Press
Darling, M. L. (1925/1928): *The Punjab Peasant in Prosperity and Debt*, London: Oxford University Press
−− (1930/2013): *Rusticus Loquitur, or The Old Light and the New in a Punjab Village*, London: Oxford University Press (reprinted 2013)
Demirgüç-Kunt, A., and L. Klapper (2012): *Measuring Financial Inclusion: The Global Findex Database*, Policy Research Working Paper 6025, Washington, DC: World Bank
Demirgüç-Kunt, A., L. Klapper, D. Singer, and P. Van Oudheusden (2015): *The Global Findex Database 2014: Measuring Financial Inclusion around the World*, Policy Research Working Paper 7255, Washington, DC: World Bank

Deneweth, H., O. Gelderblom and J. Jonker (2014): Microfinance and the Decline of Poverty: Evidence from the Nineteenth-Century Netherlands, *Journal of Economic Development*, vol. 39(1), 79–110
Derban, W. K. (2007): *Linking Indigenous Financial Systems to Banking: Barclays Bank and the Susu Collectors in Ghana*, New York: UNDP
Desai, A. V. (1968): *Real Wages in Germany 1871–1913*, Oxford: Clarendon Press
Deutsche Bundesbank, ed. (1976): *Währung und Wirtschaft in Deutschland 1876–1975*, Frankfurt: Knapp
Deutscher Sparkassenverlag (1951): *Zum Kunden gehen! Merkblatt über die Einführung und Technik des Abholverkehrs*, Stuttgart
−− (1982): *Handwörterbuch der Sparkassen*, 4 Bände, Stuttgart: Deutscher Sparkassenverlag
−− (1984): *Standortbestimmung. Entwicklungslinien der deutschen Kreditwirtschaft*, Stuttgart: Deutscher Sparkassenverlag
−− (1985): *100 Jahre Deutscher Sparkassen- und Giroverband*, Berlin
Développement International Desjardins (DID) (2008): *Project FIRST: Establishing a National Association for the PCFs Phase 2*, Quebec: DID
−− (2012): *The Cooperative Model in Microfinance: More Current and Pertinent than Ever*, http://www.did.qc.ca/media/documents/en/positionnements/COOP-highlights.pdf
Diaz-Alejandro, C. (1985): Good-Bye Financial Repression, Hello Financial Crash, *Journal of Development Economics*, vol. 19, 1–24
Dichter, T. and M. Harper (2007): *What's Wrong with Microfinance?* London: Practical Action Publishers
Dieckmann, R. (2007): *Microfinance: An emerging investment opportunity*, Frankfurt: Deutsche Bank Research
Dirninger, C. (2005): *100 Jahre Raiffeisenverband Salzburg 1905–2005*, Salzburg
−− (2007): *100 Jahre Raiffeisenbank Hallein 1907–2007*, Salzburg
−− (2010): *100 Jahre Raiffeisenbank Altenmarkt-Flachau-Eben 1910–2010*, Salzburg
−− (2012): *100 Jahre Raiffeisen in Michaelbeuern. Chronik der Raiffeisenbank Michaelbeuern*, Salzburg
Dohmen, C. (2011): *Good Bank, Bad Bank. Alternative Geschäftsmodelle im Bankensektor,*

radio broadcast: Deutschlandfunk, 09 January 2011, 6:40 – 7:00 p.m.
Domes, R. (1930/1999): *Sparkassenwandlungen*, Stuttgart: Deutscher Sparkassenverlag
Donald, G. (1976): *Credit for Small Farmers in Developing Countries*, Boulder, CO: Westview Press
Draheim, G. (1968): *Das Abholverfahren. Merkblatt WM 1 (by Hans Gundermann)*, Stuttgart
– – (1983): *Grundfragen des Genossenschaftswesens*, Frankfurt: Knapp
Drake, D., and M. Otero (1991): *NGOs: Alchemists for the Poor*, ACCION Monograph No. 1, Boston: ACCION
Drake, D., and E. Rhyne, eds. (2002): *The Commercialization of Microfinance*, Bloomfield: Kumarian Press
Dube, J. (1993): *Computer für Genossenschaften. Geschichte der genossenschaftlichen Rechenzentralen*, Wiesbaden: Deutscher Genossenschafts-Verlag
Duflo, E., R. Glennerster and M. Kremer (2007): Using Randomization in Development Economics Research: A Tool-Kit, in: T. P. Schultz and J. Strauss, eds. (2008): *Handbook of Development Econom*ics, vol. 4, Amsterdam: North-Holland, 3895–3962.
Easterly, W. (2001): *The Elusive Quest for Growth: Economists' Endeavors in the Tropics*, Cambridge, MA, and London: MIT Press
Eberle, J.C. (1959): *Dr. Eberle spricht; Schriften, Reden, Aufsätze zur Erneuerung der Sparkassen mit einführenden Beiträgen von F. Butschkau und J. Hoffmann*, Stuttgart: Deutscher Sparkassenverlag
Economist (2008): *Half-way from rags to riches – a special report on Vietnam*, 24 April 2008
Ehmer, J. (2004): *Bevölkerungsgeschichte und historische Demographie 1800–2000*, Munich: Oldenbourg
Eichengreen, B. (2008): *The European Economy since 1945. Coordinated Capitalism and Beyond*, 5th printing and first paperback printing, Princeton: Princeton University Press
Emmerich, N. (1995): *Geschichte der deutschen Sparkassenwerbung 1750–1995*, Stuttgart: Deutscher Sparkassenverlag
Erdmann, M. (1968): *Die verfassungspolitische Funktion der Wirtschaftsverbände in Deutschland 1815–1871*, Berlin: Duncker und Humblot

Fabry, P. W. (1986): *Bewährung im Grenzland. Genossenschaftsarbeit an der Saar*, Neuwied: Die Mitte
Fama, E. F., and M. C. Jensen (1983): Agency Problems and Residual Claims, *Journal of Law and Economics*, vol. 26, 327–349
Farbman, M., ed. (1981): *The PISCES Studies*, Washington, DC: US Agency for International Development
Faust, H. (1977): *Geschichte der Genossenschaftsbewegung. Ursprung und Aufbruch der Genossenschaftsbewegung in England, Frankreich und Deutschland sowie ihre weitere Entwicklung im deutschen Sprachraum*, 3rd ed., Frankfurt: Knapp
Federico, G. (2005): *Feeding the World: An Economic History of Agriculture 1800–2000*, Princeton: Princeton University Press
Fehr, E., and S. Gächter (2000): Fairness and retaliation: The economics of reciprocity, *Journal of Economic Perspectives*, vol. 14 (3), 159–181
Fischer, A. (1997): *Die Landesbank der Rheinprovinz: Aufstieg und Fall zwischen Wirtschaft und Politik*, Cologne: Böhlau
Fischer, B. (1986): *Sparkapitalbildung in Entwicklungsländern*, Munich: Weltforum Verlag
Fischer, W. (1995): *Lebensstandard und Wirtschaftssysteme*, Frankfurt: Knapp
Fishlow, A. (1961): The Trustee Savings Banks, 1817–1861, *Journal of Economic History*, vol. 21, 26–40
Florida, R. (2010): *The Great Reset. How new ways of living and working drive post-crash prosperity*, New York: Harper Collins
Flosbach, J. (2013): Profitability and Interest Rates: Does the Commercialization of Microfinance Institutions Lead to Higher Interest Rates?, *African Journal of Microfinance and Enterprise Development*, vol. 3 (1), http://www.microfinancegateway.org/sites/default/files/mfg-en-paper-profitability-and-interest-rates-does-the-commercialization-of-microfinance-institution-lead-to-higher-interest-rates-jun-2013.pdf
Fontane, T. (1963): *Aus England und Schottland. Sämtliche Werke*, vol. XVII, Munich: Hanser
Förderverein Schulze-Delitzsch, ed. (2008): *Hermann Schulze-Delitzsch. Weg – Werk – Wirkung*, Wiesbaden: Deutscher Genossenschafts-Verlag

Frankfurter Allgemeine Zeitung (2011): *Alternativen zur Mikrofinanzierung gesucht*, 17 June 2011

Friedman, T. L. (2007): *The World is Flat: A Brief History of the Twenty-First Century*, 2nd revised and expanded edition ("Further Updated and Expanded: Release 3.0"), New York: Farrar, Straus and Giroux

Fries, K. (1973): *Die Girozentralen. Überblick über ihre Entwicklung und gegenwärtigen Rechtsverhältnisse*, Stuttgart: Deutscher Sparkassenverlag

Führer, C. C. (1992): Das Kreditinstitut der Kleinen Leute. Zur Bedeutung der Pfandleihe im deutschen Kaiserreich, *Bankhistorisches Archiv*, vol. 18 (1), 3–21

Furubotn, E., and R. Richter (2005): *Institutions and Economic Theory*, 2nd ed., Ann Arbor, Michigan: University of Michigan Press

Gash, M., and K. Odell (2013): *The Evidence-Based Story of Savings Groups: A Synthesis of Seven Randomized Control Trials*, The SEEP Network, Arlington, VA, http://www.seepnetwork.org/the-evidence-based-story-of-savings-groups–a-synthesis-of-seven-randomized-control-trials-resources-1206.php

Geertz, C. (1962): The Rotating Credit Association: A "Middle Rung" in Development. *Economic Development and Cultural Change*, vol. 10 (3), 241–263

–– (1959): Form and Variation in Balinese Village Structure, *American Anthropologist*, vol. 61, 991–1012

Geiger, H. (1992): *Die deutsche Sparkassenorganisation*, 2nd ed. Frankfurt: Knapp

Genossenschaftsverband Bayern, ed. (1996): *Genossenschaften. Leitbilder und Perspektiven*, Munich: Vahlen

Geremek, B. (1994): *Poverty. A History*, Oxford: Blackwell

GIZ – Deutsche Gesellschaft für Internationale Zusammenarbeit (2011): *Revival, Reform and Beyond: Ideas for Future Capacity Building Initiatives for Primary Agricultural Cooperative Societies and the Short Term Cooperative Credit Structure*, New Delhi: GIZ

Gleber, P., B. Kubista and A. Bley (2012): *40 Jahre Genossenschaftliche Finanzgruppe Volksbanken Raiffeisenbanken*, Wiesbaden: DG Verlag

González-Vega, C. (1998): *Microfinance: Broader Achievements and New Challenges*, Economics and Sociology Occasional Paper 2518, Ohio State University, Columbus, OH

Gosden, P. H. (1996): Great Britain, in: J. Mura, ed.: *History of European Savings Banks*, Stuttgart: Deutscher Sparkassenverlag, 133–160.

Götzl, S., and J. Gros (2010): *Regional banks for 160 years: Co-operative banks in Germany – characteristics, structures, benefits*, Wiesbaden: Genossenschaftsverband Bayern

Gounot, M. (2001): *The efficiency of multi-layer savings and credit co-operatives*, Frankfurt: Lang

Greve, G. et al., eds. (2010): *Die Knappschaft als sozialer Pfadfinder: 750 Jahre Knappschaft. Soziale Verantwortung zu jeder Zeit*, Bochum: Knappschaft Bahn See

Güde, U. (1989): *Geschäftspolitik der Sparkassen*, Stuttgart: Deutscher Sparkassenverlag

Guemas, B. (1960): *Les caisses d'épargne et l'évolution de l'économie française*, Paris: Editions de l'Épargne

Guinnane, T. W. (1992): *A Failed Institutional Transplant: Raiffeisen's Credit Cooperatives in Ireland, 1894–1914*, Princeton: Woodrow Wilson School of Public and International Affairs

–– (1997): Regional organizations in the German cooperative banking system in the late 19th century, *Research in Economics*, vol. 51, 251–274

–– (2001): Cooperatives as Information Machines: German Rural Credit Cooperatives, 1883–1914, *Journal of Economic History*, vol. 61, 366–389

–– (2002): Delegated Monitors, Large and Small: Germany's Banking System 1800–1914, *Journal of Economic Literature*, vol. 40, 73–124

Guinnane, T. W. et al. (2013): *Die Geschichte der DZ Bank: Das genossenschaftliche Zentralbankwesen vom 19. Jahrhundert bis heute*, Munich: Beck

Haas, E.-J. (1976): *Stadt-Sparkassen Düsseldorf 1825–1972*, Berlin: Duncker & Humblot

Hahn, M. (1920): *Handbuch der preußischen Sparkassengesetzgebung*, Berlin: Galle

Hahn, O. (1980): *Die Unternehmensphilosophie einer Genossenschaftsbank*, Tübingen: Mohr-Siebeck

Handwörterbuch des Genossenschaftswesens (1980), Wiesbaden: DGV

Hardach, G. (2003): Optionen der Altersvorsorge im 19. und 20. Jahrhundert in

Deutschland, *Zeitschrift für Unternehmensgeschichte*, vol. 48, 5–28
-- (2006): *Der Generationenvertrag, Lebenslauf und Lebenseinkommen in Deutschland in zwei Jahrhunderten*, Berlin: Duncker & Humblot
-- (2008): Altersarbeit, Alterseinkommen und Altersstruktur in Deutschland seit dem neunzehnten Jahrhundert, *Jahrbuch für Wirtschaftsgeschichte*, vol. 49, 77–104
Hasselmann, E. (1968): *Die Rochdaler Grundsätze im Wandel der Zeit*, vol. 4, Frankfurt: Deutsche Genossenschaftskasse
-- (1971): *Geschichte der deutschen Konsumgenossenschaften*, Frankfurt: Knapp
Hatarska, V., and D. Nadolnyak (2007): Do Regulated Microfinance Institutions Achieve Better Sustainability and Outreach? Cross-Country Evidence, *Applied Economics*, vol. 39, 1207–1222
Hellmann, T., K. Murdock and J.E. Stiglitz (1997): Financial Restraint: Towards a New Paradigm, in: M. Aoki, H.-K. Kim and M. Okuno-Fujiwara, eds.: *The Role of Government in East Asian Economic Development*, Oxford: Clarendon Press, 163–207
Henze, W. (1972): *Grundzüge der Geschichte des Sparkassenwesens*, Stuttgart: Deutscher Sparkassenverlag
Hirschman, A.O. (1958): *The Strategy of Economic Development*, New Haven: Yale University Press
Hofmann, A., and H. Grossmann (2005): *Rural Finance in Conflict Environments: Experiences from Nepal's Small Farmers Cooperatives Limited (SFCL)*, Eschborn: GTZ, www.gdrc.org/icm/disasters/GTZ-Nepal.pdf
Hoffmann, J. (1991): *Deutsche Sparkasseneinheit. Geschichte, Aufbau, Leistungen des zentralen Sparkassenverbandes*, reprint from 1931, Stuttgart: Deutscher Sparkassenverlag
Hoffmann, W. (1915): *Die Arbeitsteilung zwischen Sparkassen und Depositenkassen*, Tübingen: Laupp
Hoffmann, W.G. (1969): Die Entwicklung der Sparkassen im Rahmen des Wachstums der deutschen Wirtschaft, *Zeitschrift für die gesamte Staatswissenschaft*, 125, 561–605
Hollis, A. and A. Sweetman (1998): Microcredit: What Can We Learn from the Past? *World Development*, vol. 26, 1875–1890
Holloh, D. (1998): *Microfinance in Indonesia: Between State, Market and Self-Organization*, Hamburg: Lit

-- (2000): *ProFI Baseline Survey: LPD – Lembaga Perkreditan Desa*, Denpasar: GTZ, ProFI
-- (2001): *Microfinance Institutions Study*, Jakarta: Bank Indonesia and GTZ
-- (2012): *Rural Cooperative Credit System in Orissa*, GIZ Rural Financial Institutions Programme (RFIP) Newsletter III (New Delhi), 4–5
Hollow, M. (2012): Pre-1900 utopian visions of the "cashless society", MPRA paper 40780, http://mpra.ub.uni-muenchen.de/40780
Holtmann, M., I. Rühle and A. Winkler (2000): Small and medium enterprise financing: Lessons from microfinance, *SME Issues*, vol. 1, No. 1, SME Department of the World Bank, Washington D.C.: World Bank
Horne, H.O. (1947): *A History of Savings Banks*, Oxford: Oxford University Press
Hörstmann, A. (1928): *Die Konkurrenz zwischen öffentlichen Sparkassen und Kreditgenossenschaften*, Celle: Pohl
Hulme, D., and P. Mosley (1996): *Finance Against Poverty*, London and New York: Routledge
Huss, B. (1924): *People's Banks or Use and Value of Co-operative Credit*, Natal: Mariannhill
Hüttl, L. (1988): *Friedrich Wilhelm Raiffeisen. Leben und Werk*, Munich: Genossenschaftsverband Bayern e.V.
IMF (1997): *Vietnam: Recent Economic Developments*, IMF: Washington, DC
Institut für bankhistorische Forschung, ed. (1982/83): *Deutsche Bankengeschichte*, 3 vols., Frankfurt: Knapp
Institut für Weltwirtschaft: http://www.ifw-kiel.de/forschung/p1fb1/globale-muster-des-strukturwandels
Intellecap (2010): *Indian Microfinance Crisis of 2010: Turf War or a Battle of Intentions*, http://intellecap.com/publications/indian-microfinance-crisis-2010-turf-war-or-battle-intentions
IPA – Innovations for Poverty Action (2012): *Savings Account Labeling for Susu Customers in Ghana*, Accra, http://www.poverty-action.org/project/0071
Jackelen, H., and E. Rhyne (1991): Towards a more market-oriented approach to credit and savings for the poor, *Small Enterprise Development*, vol. 2, 4–20
Javoy, E., and D. Rozas (2013): *MIMOSA: Microfinance Index of Market Outreach and*

Saturation, Part 1 – Total Credit Market Capacity, Paris: Planet Rating

Kähler, W. (1910): Der Aachener Verein zur Beförderung der Arbeitsamkeit. Ein Beitrag zur Geschichte des Sparkassenwesens und der Wohlfahrtspflege, *Jahrbücher für Nationalökonomie und Statistik*, vol. 39, 372–398

— (1912): Das Sparwesen im Regierungsbezirk Aachen, in: *Untersuchung über das Volkssparwesen*, Munich: Verein für Socialpolitik

Karlan, D., and J. Zinman (2010): Expanding Credit Access: Using Randomized Supply Decisions to Estimate the Impacts, *Review of Financial Studies*, vol. 23, 433–464

Kirsch, O. C., P.-C. Armbruster and G. Kochendörfer-Lucius (1983): *Selbsthilfeeinrichtungen in der Dritten Welt*, Munich: Weltforum Verlag

Klas, G. (2011): *Die Mikrofinanz-Industrie. Die große Illusion oder das Geschäft mit der Armut*, Berlin: Assoziation Verlag

Klein, E. (1973): *Geschichte der deutschen Landwirtschaft im Industriezeitalter*, Wiesbaden: Steiner

— (1982): Von den Anfängen bis zum Ende des Alten Reiches (1806), in: *Deutsche Bankengeschichte*, vol. 1, Frankfurt: Knapp

Klein, J. (2003): *Das Sparkassenwesen in Deutschland und Frankreich. Entwicklung, aktuelle Rechtsstrukturen und Möglichkeiten einer Annäherung*, Berlin: Duncker & Humblot

Klein, M. (2012): *Bankier der Barmherzigkeit: Friedrich Wilhelm Raiffeisen – Das Leben des Genossenschaftsgründers in Texten und Bildern*, 2nd edition, Neukirchen: Neukirchener Aussaat

Kluge, A. H. (1991): *Geschichte der deutschen Bankgenossenschaften: Zur Entwicklung mitgliederorientierter Unternehmen*, Frankfurt: Knapp

Klusak, G. (1969): *Die Raiffeisen-Kreditgenossenschaften*, Frankfurt: Knapp

Kluthe, K. (1985): *Genossenschaften und Staat in Deutschland*, Berlin: Duncker & Humblot

Knebel Doeberitz, H. von (1907): *Das Sparkassenwesen in Preußen*, Berlin: Deutscher Sparkassenverlag

Koch, P. (2012): *Geschichte der Versicherungswirtschaft in Deutschland*, Karlsruhe: Verlag Versicherungswirtschaft

Koch, W. (2000): *Und sie konnten zueinander nicht kommen. Das Verhältnis zwischen Schulze-Delitzsch und Raiffeisen*, Delitzsch: Förderverein Hermann Schulze-Delitzsch und Gedenkstätte des Deutschen Genossenschaftswesens

— (1991): *Der Genossenschaftsgedanke F. W. Raiffeisens als Kooperationsmodell in der modernen Industriegesellschaft*, Paderborn und Würzburg: Creator

Köhn, D., ed. (2013): *Microfinance 3.0, Reconciling Sustainability with Social Outreach and Responsible Delivery*, Heidelberg: Springer

Krahnen, J. P., and R. H. Schmidt (1994): *Development Finance as Institution Building: A New Approach to Poverty-Oriented Banking*, Boulder, CO: Westview Press

Kraus, T. (1877): *Die Raiffeisen'schen Darlehenskassenvereine in der Rheinprovinz*, Bonn: Strauss

Krauss, M., and W. Gerz (2012): *Zweimal 150 Jahre – Westerwald Bank eG. 1862–2012*, Heidelberg: Verlag Regionalkultur

Krauss, N., and I. Walter (2009): Can Microfinance Reduce Portfolio Volatility?, *Economic Development and Cultural Change*, vol. 58, 85–110

Kropp, E., M. T. Marx, B. Pramod, B. R. Quinones and H. D. Seibel (1989): *Linking Self-help Groups and Banks in Developing Countries*. Bangkok: Asian and Pacific Regional Agricultural Credit Association (APRACA), and Rossdorf: TZ-Verlag

Kropp, E., and B. S. Suran (2002): Linking Banks and Self-help Groups in India: An Assessment, in: Seminar on SHG-Bank Linkage Programme, New Delhi: National Bank for Agriculture and Rural Development (NABARD)

Kropp, E., and K. Osner (2010): *Systementwicklung und Entwicklungsfinanzierung: Die Geschichte der Förderkonzepte in der deutschen entwicklungspolitischen Zusammenarbeit von 1960 bis 2004*, Eschborn: GTZ

Kuiper, K. (2004): *Act or Accident? The Birth of the Village Units of Bank Rakyat Indonesia*, Eschborn: GTZ

Kulemann, W. (1922): *Die Genossenschaftsbewegung*, 2 vols., Berlin: Liebmann Verlag

Kunkel, C. R., and H. D. Seibel (1997): Microfinance in Laos: A Women's Business? *Asia Pacific Rural Finance* (Bangkok & Bombay), vol. (10), 87–96

La Porta, R., F. Lopez-de-Silanes and A. Shleifer (2002): Government Ownership of Banks, *Journal of Finance*, vol. 57, 265–301

La Porta, R., F. Lopez-de-Silanes, A. Shleifer and R. Vishny (1998): Law and Finance, *Journal of Political Economy*, vol. 106, 1113–1156

Latortue, A., and O.P. Ardic (2013): *Financial Inclusion: Blurred Lines, Sharper Vision*, http://www.cgap.org/blog/financial-inclusion-blurred-lines-sharper-vision

Lepp, A. (1996): *Finanzsektorpolitik und der Zugang klein(st)er Unternehmen zu Finanzdienstleistungen: Eine Untersuchung am Beispiel Peru* (Dissertation), Frankfurt: Goethe University

Levine, R. (2005): Finance and Growth: Theory and Evidence, in: P. Aghion and S. Durlauf, eds.: *Handbook of Economic Growth*, Amsterdam: North-Holland, 866–934

Levitsky, J., ed. (1989): *Microenterprises in Developing Countries*, London, Intermediate Technology Publications (now Practical Action Publishing)

Levy, M.J., Jr. (1966): *Modernization and the Structure of Societies*, Princeton: Princeton University Press

Lewin, K. (1947): Frontiers in group dynamics, *Human Relations*, vol. 1, 5–41.

Lippik, M., and T. Flöh (1991): *Entstehung und Entwicklung des Sparkassenwesens in Schleswig-Holstein*, Stuttgart: Deutscher Sparkassenverlag

Löber, H. (1985): *100 Jahre Deutscher Sparkassen- und Giroverband*, Stuttgart: Deutscher Sparkassenverlag

Lukas, H. (1972): *Der Deutsche Raiffeisenverband, Entwicklung, Struktur und Funktion*, Berlin

Lützenkirchen, C. (2012): *Microfinance in Evolution*, Frankfurt: DB-Research

Madan, G.R. (1994/2007): *The Co-operative Movement in India*, New Delhi: Mittal Publications (reprinted 2007)

Maes, J.P. and L.R. Reed (2012): *State of the Microcredit Summit Campaign Report 2012*, Washington, DC: Microcredit Summit Campaign

Mahajan, V., and T. Navin (2012): *Microfinance in India: Growth, Crisis and the Future*, Hyderabad: BASIX

Malchus, C.A., Freiherr von (1994): *Die Sparcassen in Europa*. Reprint from 1838, Stuttgart: Deutscher Sparkassenverlag

Martins, F., and A. Winkler (2013): Foreign Ownership in Latin American Microfinance Institutions: Evidence and Impact, *Journal of Business Economics (formerly Zeitschrift für Betriebswirtschaft)*, vol. 83, 665–702

McFadzean, J. (2008): *The Co-operators – A History of the Fenwick Weavers*, Kilmarnock: East Ayrshire North Communities Federation Ltd.

McKinnon, R.I. (1973): *Money and Capital in Economic Development*, Washington, DC: Brookings Institution Press

McNamara, R.S. (1973): *Address to the Board of Governors of the World Bank*, Nairobi

Mersland, R. (2011): The Governance of Non-Profit Microfinance Institutions: Lessons from History, *Journal of Management Governance*, vol. 15, 327–348

Mersland, R., and R. Strom (2009): Performance and Governance in Microfinance Institutions, *Journal of Banking and Finance*, vol. 33, 662–669

Meyer, R., and M. Zeller (2002): *The Triangle of Microfinance*, Baltimore: Johns Hopkins University Press

Milgrom, P. and J. Roberts (1992): *Economics, Organization and Management*, Englewood Cliffs, NJ: Prentice-Hall

Moody, J.C., and G.C. Fite (1984): *The Credit Union Movement: Origins and Developments, 1850–1970*, Lincoln: University of Nebraska Press

Morduch, J. (1992): The Role of Subsidies in Microfinance: Evidence from the Grameen Bank, *Journal of Development Economics*, vol. 60, 229–248

Morduch, J. (1999): *The Grameen Bank: A Financial Reckoning*, Working Paper, Princeton University

Moss, M. (1999): Henry Duncan and the Savings Bank Movement in the UK, in: *200 Years of Savings Banks: A Strong and Lasting Business Model for Responsible, Regional Retail Banking*. World Savings Banks Institute/European Savings Bank Group, Perspectives 63, Brussels

Moster, A., and B. Vogler (1996): France, in: J. Mura, ed.: *History of European Savings Banks*, Stuttgart: Deutscher Sparkassenverlag, 75–104

Müller, R. (2000): *Geschichte der Sparkasse Trier 1825–2000*, Stuttgart: Deutscher Sparkassenverlag

Mura, J. (1987/1995): *Entwicklungslinien der deutschen Sparkassengeschichte*, 2 vols., Stuttgart: Deutscher Sparkassenverlag

-- (1991): *Landesbanken, Girozentralen: historische Entwicklung und Zukunftsperspektiven*, Stuttgart: Deutscher Sparkassenverlag

-- (1994):*Sparkassenorganisation und Wirtschaftswachstum: historische Aspekte und Zukunftsperspektiven*, Stuttgart: Deutscher Sparkassenverlag

--, ed. (1996): *History of European Savings Banks*, Stuttgart: Deutscher Sparkassenverlag

Murdoch, C., and G. A. N. Wright (2011): *Successful Banking Correspondents Need a Compelling Product Mix*, MicroSave Focus Note 65, Delhi: MicroSave

Murken, A. H. (1995): *Vom Armenhospital zum Großklinikum. Die Geschichte des Krankenhauses vom 18. Jahrhundert bis zur Gegenwart*, 3rd ed., Cologne: DuMont

NABARD (1989): *Studies on Self-help Groups of the Rural Poor*, Mumbai: NABARD

-- (2007 – 2013): *Status of Micro Finance in India 2006-07 - 2012-13*, Mumbai

-- (2008): *Report of the Committee on Financial Inclusion*, headed by C. Rangarajan, Mumbai, http://nabard.org/pdf/report_financial/Full%20Report.pdf

-- (2012): *SHG2: Revisiting the SHG Bank Linkage Programme*, Circular No. 65(A)/MCID-04/2011 – 12 (27 March 2012), Mumbai

Nair, A. (2005): *Sustainability of microfinance self-help groups in India: would federating help?* World Bank Policy Research Working Paper No. 3516, Washington, DC: World Bank

Nair, A., and J. D. Von Pischke (2007): Commercial Banks and Financial Access, in: X. Barr et al., eds.: *Building Inclusive Financial Institutions: A Framework for Financial Access*, Washington, DC: Brookings Institution Press, 89 – 116

Nanda, Y. C. (1992): *Promotion of Linkages between Self-help Groups of the Poor and Formal Credit Institutions*. Mumbai: NABARD

-- (1995): *Country Report India. APRACA-GTZ Regional Workshop on the Linkage Program*, Bangkok: APRACA

NERI (2012): *Microfinance in the Lao PDR*, Vientiane: BoL, GIZ, MPI

Nielsen, K. B. (2014): *10 Useful Data Sources for Measuring Financial Inclusion*, Washington, DC: CGAP, http://www.cgap.org/blog/10-useful-data-sources-measuring-financial-inclusion

Nissen, F. (1926): *Die bankmäßige Betätigung der Sparkassen*, Stuttgart

Nitsch, M. (1997/2002): Systemische Intelligenz in Entwicklungsprojekten. Lehren aus dem Sparkassenprojekt in Peru, first published in a collection of essays in honor of Renate Rott, reprinted in M. Nitsch (2002), *Glaspaläste und Mikrofinanz*, Frankfurt: Lang, 165 – 192

North, D. (1991): Institutions, *Journal of Economic Perspectives*, vol. 5, 97 – 112

NRLM – National Rural Livelihoods Mission (2011): *NRLM Mission Document 031010*. New Delhi: Ministry of Rural Development

NRLM Planning Commission (2011): *Report of Working Group on National Rural Livelihoods Mission (NRLM)*. New Delhi: Ministry of Rural Development

Nsibambi, A. K. (2011): *Centenary Bank's Agriculture Lending: The Story*, in: AFYB 2011, 40 – 48

-- (2012): *Centenary Bank – World Bank Agri-Fin Project*, in: AFYB 2012,

Oliver, J. (2010): *Who's the Culprit? Assessing Finance in Andhra Pradesh*, CGAP Microfinance Blog 11/11/2010, http://microfinance.cgap.org/2010/11/11/who%e2%80%99s-the-culprit-accessing-finance-in-andhra-pradesh/

Oluyombo, O. O. (2012): *Cooperative Finance in Developing Economies*. Lagos: Soma Prints

Otero, M., and M. Chu (2002): Governance and Ownership of Microfinance Institutions, in: D. Drake and E. Rhyne, eds., *The Commercialization of Microfinance*, Bloomfield, CT: Kumarian Press, 221 – 245.

Otero, M., and E. Rhyne (1994): *The New World of Microenterprise Finance: Building Healthy Financial Institutions for the Poor*, West Hartford, CT: Kumarian Press

Ott, G. (2006): Die Sparkasseninstitute in Bremen und Hamburg, *Regionalgeschichte der Sparkassen-Finanzgruppe*, vol. 1, 51 – 69, Stuttgart: Deutscher Sparkassenverlag

Patten, R. H., and J. K. Rosengard (1991): *The Development of Rural Banking in Indonesia*, San Francisco: ICS Press

PCH – ProCredit Holding: Annual Reports (various years), Frankfurt, www.procredit-holding.com

Persson, K. G. (2010): *An Economic History of Europe: Knowledge, Institutions and Growth, 600 to the Present* (New Approaches to Economic and Social History), Cambridge: Cambridge University Press

Pix, M., and H. Pohl, eds. (1992): *Invention – Innovation – Diffusion. Die Entwicklung des Spar- und Sparkassengedankens in Europa*, Stuttgart: Steiner

Pohl, H. (1982): *WestLB – von der Hülfskasse von 1832 zur Landesbank*, Düsseldorf/ Münster, WestLB

– – (1982a): Die geschichtliche Entwicklung der Landesbanken, Girozentralen von den Anfängen bis 1908, in: *Deutsche Bankengeschichte*, vol. 2, Frankfurt: Knapp

– – (1982b): Das deutsche Bankenwesen (1806–1848), in: *Deutsche Bankengeschichte*, vol. 2, Frankfurt: Knapp, 13–140

– – (2000): Die Institute der Sparkassenorganisation als Wettbewerber, in: *Die Sparkassenorganisation in Wirtschaft, Gesellschaft und Region. Historische Aspekte und Zukunftsperspektiven*, Stuttgart: Steiner

– – (2001): *Die rheinischen Sparkassen. Entwicklung und Bedeutung für Wirtschaft und Gesellschaft von den Anfängen bis 1990*, Stuttgart: Steiner

Pohl, H. et al. (2005): Wirtschafts- und Sozialgeschichte der deutschen Sparkassen im 20. Jahrhundert, Stuttgart: Deutscher Sparkassenverlag

Pohl, M. (1983): Die Entwicklung des privaten Bankwesens nach 1945. Die Kreditgenossenschaften nach 1945, in: *Deutsche Bankengeschichte*, vol. 3, Frankfurt: Knapp, 207–276

Poullain, L. (1972): *Die Sparkassenorganisation*, Frankfurt a. M.

Puhazhendhi, V. (2013): *Microfinance India: State of the Sector Report 2012*, New Delhi: Sage Publications

Raiffeisen, F. W. (1970): *Die Darlehnskassen-Vereine*, 1st ed. 1866; translated as: *The Credit Unions*, Neuwied: Verlag der Raiffeisendruckerei

Rangarajan, C., et al. (2008): *Report of the Committee on Financial Inclusion*, Mumbai: NABARD http://nabard.org/pdf/report_financial/Full%20Report.pdf

Reed, L. R. (2011): *State of the Microcredit Summit Campaign Report 2011*. Washington D. C., http://www.microcreditsummit.org/SOCR_2011_EN_web.pdf

Reille, X., and S. Foster (2008): *Foreign Capital Investments in Microfinance*, Washington, DC: CGAP Focus Note 44

Reulecke, J. (1998): Die Vereinsbewegung für das Wohl der arbeitenden Klassen, in: O. Dascher and E. Kleinertz, eds.: *Petitionen und Barrikaden. Rheinische Revolutionen 1848/49*, Aschendorff and Münster 1998, Aschendorff

Reusch, R. H. (1935): Die Krisis des Jahres 1907 und die Sparkassen, in: *Sparkasse*, 8/1935, 149–151 and 9/1935, 169–175

Rhyne, E. (2009): *Microfinance for Bankers and Investors*, New York: McGraw-Hill

Robinson, M. S. (2001): *The Microfinance Revolution*, vol. 2: Lessons from Indonesia, Washington, DC: The World Bank

– – (2004): *Why the Bank Rakyat Indonesia has the World's Largest Sustainable Microbanking System*, International Seminar on BRI's Microbanking System, 01 December 2004, http://www.ruralfinance.org/fileadmin/templates/rflc/documents/1117473611572_Robinson_BRI_Paper_Revised_April_2005.pdf

Rockoff, H. (1993): *Geschichte der US-amerikanischen Sparbanken und Bausparinstitute*, Frankfurt a. M.: Bankhistorisches Archiv, vol. 19, 108–135

Rösner, H., and J. Schulz-Nieswandt (2007): *Zur Relevanz des genossenschaftlichen Selbsthilfegedankens*, 80 Jahre Seminar für Genossenschaftswesen der Universität zu Köln, Berlin: LIT

Roodman, D. (2012a): *Due Diligence: An Impertinent Inquiry into Microfinance*, Washington, DC: Center for Global Development

– – (2012b): *The German School of Institution Building in Microfinance*, David Roodman's Microfinance Open Book Blog, Center for Global Development (posted 17 October 2012)

Roodman, D., and J. Murdoch (2009): The Impact of Microcredit on the Poor in Bangladesh: Revisiting the Evidence, Center for Global Development, Working Paper Number 174, June 2009, updated in: *Journal of Development Studies*, vol. 50 (2014), 583–604

Rosenberg, H. (1967): *Große Depression und Bismarckzeit. Wirtschaftsablauf, Gesellschaft und Politik in Mitteleuropa*, Berlin: Springer

Rosenberg, R. (2007): *CGAP Reflections on the Compartamos Initial Public Offering: A Case Study on Microfinance Interest Rates and Profits*: CGAP Focus Note 42

Rosta, J. (2009): Trickle-Down Effect, *American Banker*, 01 September 2009, www.americanbanker.com/usb_issues/119_9/trickle-down-effect-1001271-1.html

Rostow, W. W. (1960): *The Stages of Economic Growth: A Non-Communist Manifesto*, Cambridge: Cambridge University Press

Rozas, D., and G. Erice (2014): *Microfinance and savings outreach: What are we measuring?*, E-MFP, Luxembourg, http://www.e-mfp.eu/blog/microfinance-and-savings-outreach-what-are-we-measuring; http://www.microfinancegateway.org/library/microfinance-and-savings-outreach-what-are-we-measuring

Rutherford, S. (2000): *The Poor and Their Money*, Oxford and New York: Oxford University Press

Sahlins, M. (1974): *Stone Age Economics*, Chicago and New York: Aldine Atherton

Sapundzhieva, R. (2011): *Funding Microfinance – A Focus on Debt Finance*, Washington, DC: Microfinance Information Exchange (The MIX)

Saul, K., et al., eds. (1982): *Arbeiterfamilien im Kaiserreich. Materialien zur Sozialgeschichte in Deutschland 1871–1914 [Workers' Families in the Kaiserreich. Materials on Social History in Germany 1871–1914]*, Dusseldorf, translation: Erwin Fink: Droste, 112–113

Schäfer, A. (1994): *125/145 Jahre Raiffeisengenossenschaften. Vom Flammersfelder Hülfsverein zur Raiffeisenbank*, Neuwied: Raiffeisenverlag

Schepers, V. (2003): *Internet Banking und sparkassenrechtliches Regionalprinzip*, Stuttgart: Deutscher Gemeinde-Verlag

Schmidt, R. H. (2013): Core Values of Microfinance under Scrutiny: Back to Basics?, in: D. Köhn, ed.: *Microfinance 3.0*, Berlin: Springer

– – (2010): Microfinance, Commercialization and Ethics, *Poverty and Public Policy*, vol. 2, 99–137

– – (2009): The political debate about savings banks, *Schmalenbach Business Review*, vol. 61, 366–392

– – (2005): Die Sicht der teilnehmenden Beobachter: Ein Abriss der IPC/IMI-Geschichte aus neoinstitutionalistischer Perspektive, in: B. Fritz and K. Hujo, eds., *Ökonomie unter den Bedingungen Lateinamerikas: Festschrift für Manfred Nitsch*, 95–122, Frankfurt: Vervuerth (English version available from the author)

– – (1998): The Current Status of the CERUDEB Project and the Roles of the German Savings Banks Foundation, Frankfurt: IPC (unpublished)

Schmidt, R. H., D. Bülbül and U. Schüwer (2013): The Persistence of the Three-Pillar System in Germany, in O. Butzbach and K. von Mettenheim, eds., *Alternative Banking and Financial Crisis*, London: Pickering and Chatto, 101–121 and 256–259

Schmidt, R. H., and E. Kropp (1987): *Rural Finance Guiding Principles*, Rossdorf: TZ-Verlagsgesellschaft

Schmidt, R. H., and N. Moisa (2005): Public Private Partnerships for Economic Development in Southeast Europe, in: I. Matthäus-Maier and J. D. Von Pischke, eds., *EU Accession – Financial Sector Opportunities and Challenges for Southeast Europe*, Berlin et al.: Springer, 251–275

Schmidt, R. H., and F. Noth (2013): Bewertung und Fehlbewertung von Mikrofinanzinstitutionen, in M. Dobler et al., eds., *Rechnungslegung, Prüfung und Unternehmensbewertung*, Stuttgart: Schäffer-Poeschel, 717–743 (an English version is available from the first author)

Schmidt, R. H., and I. Tschach (2002): *Microfinance as a network of incentives*, Finance and Accounting Working Paper 87a, Goethe University, Frankfurt (a German version was published in 2003 in a proceedings volume of the *Verein für Socialpolitik*, ed. by H. Ahrens, Berlin, 2003)

Schmidt, R. H., and C. P. Zeitinger (1996a): Prospects, Problems and Potential of Credit-Granting NGOs, *Journal of International Development*, vol. 8, 241–258

– – (1996b): The Efficiency of Credit-Granting NGOs, *Savings and Development*, vol. 20, 353–385

– – (1998): Critical Issues in Microbusiness Finance and the Role of Donors, in: M. S. Kimenyi, R. C. Wieland and J. D. Von Pischke, eds.: *Strategic Issues in Microfinance*, Avebury, 27–51

– – (2001): Building New Development Finance Institutions Instead of Remodeling Existing Ones, *Small Business Development*, vol. 12(2), 32–43

Schmit, L. Th. (1991): *Rural Credit between Subsidy and Market: Adjustment of the Village Units of Bank Rakyat Indonesia in Sociological Perspective*, Leiden: Leiden University Press

-- (1994/1999): *A History of the "Volkscredietwezen" (Popular Credit System), 1895–1935*, The Hague: Ministry of Foreign Affairs, Development Cooperation Information Department

Schrader, H. (1997): *Changing Financial Landscapes in India and Indonesia*, Hamburg: LIT

Schramm, B. (1982): *Die Volksbanken und Raiffeisenbanken*, Frankfurt: Knapp

Schulze-Delitzsch, H. (1853): *Associationsbuch für deutsche Handwerker und Arbeiter*, Leipzig: E. Keil

Schumpeter, J. (1912): *Theorie der wirtschaftlichen Entwicklung*, Leipzig: Duncker & Humblot; English version: *The Theory of Economic Development* (1934), Cambridge: Harvard University Press

Scratchley, A. (1860): *A practical treatise on savings banks*, London: Longman, Green, and Roberts

Seelmann-Eggebert, E. L. (1927): *Die Systeme im neuzeitlichen deutschen Genossenschaftswesen*, Stuttgart: Kohlhammer

Seibel, H. D. (1967): Labour Co-operatives among the Mano, *Liberian Studies Journal*, vol. 1(1), 47–60, Robertsport, Liberia: Tubman Center of African Culture; Arbeitsgenossenschaften bei den Mano in Liberia, *Afrika heute*, Special Issue 1968/10

-- (1970): *Indigenous Economic Cooperation and its Developmental Function in Liberia*. Cooperative Information, 7–53, Geneva: ILO – International Labour Office (also available in French and Spanish)

-- (1974): *The Dynamics of Achievement*, Indianapolis and New York: Bobbs-Merrill

-- (1978). Offene und geschlossene Gesellschaften. Überprüfung einer Hypothese im interkulturellen Vergleich: Melanesien und Polynesien, in: *Zeitschrift für Soziologie*, vol. 7, 273–298

-- (1980). *Struktur und Entwicklung der Gesellschaft*. Stuttgart: Kohlhammer

-- (1984): *Ansatzmöglichkeiten für die Mobilisierung von Sparkapital zur Entwicklungsfinanzierung*, Munich: Weltforum Verlag

-- (1985): Saving for Development: A Linkage Model for Informal and Formal Financial Markets, *Quarterly Journal of International Agriculture*, vol. 24, 290–298

-- (1989a): Linking Informal and Formal Financial Institutions in Africa and Asia, in: J. Levitsky, ed. *Microenterprises in Developing Countries*, London: Intermediate Technology Publications, 97–118

-- (1989b): Finance with the Poor, by the Poor, for the Poor: Financial Technologies for the Informal Sector, with Case Studies from Indonesia, *Social Strategies (Basel)*, vol. 3(2), 3–48

-- (1991): *Microfinance for Microenterprises: Some Practical Experiences of Linkages between Formal and Informal Financial Institutions in Indonesia*. International Symposium on Sharing Poverty or Creating Wealth? Access to Credit for Women's Enterprises, Amsterdam: Royal Tropical Institute

-- (1992a): *The Making of a Market Economy: Monetary Reform, Economic Transformation and Rural Finance in Vietnam*. Saarbrücken and Fort Lauderdale: Breitenbach

-- (1992b): *Self-help Groups as Financial Intermediaries: A Training Manual*, Saarbrücken and Fort Lauderdale: Breitenbach

-- (1996a): *Financial Systems Development and Microfinance: Viable Institutions, Appropriate Strategies and Sustainable Financial Services for the Microeconomy*, Schriftenreihe der GTZ No. 258, Eschborn and Rossdorf: TZ-Verlagsgesellschaft

-- (1996b): *Transforming Rural Finance in Africa: The role of AFRACA in Linkage Banking and Financial Systems Development*, AFRACA (Nairobi) Newsletter, 22 December, 8–16

-- (1997): *Upgrading, Downgrading, Linking, Innovating: Microfinance Development Strategies – A Systems Perspective*, Economics and Sociology Occasional Paper 2371, Columbus, OH: Ohio State University, www.econstor.eu/dspace/handle/10419/23668

-- (1998): *Enhancing the Resilience of Microfinance Institutions and Programs: Lessons Learned from the Asian Financial Crisis*, Cologne University Working Paper 1998-4, http://www.econstor.eu/handle/10419/23670

-- (2000): Agricultural development banks: close them or reform them? *Finance & Development* (International Monetary Fund), June 2000, 45–48

-- (2001): Mainstreaming Informal Financial Institutions, *Journal of Developmental Entrepreneurship*, vol. 6(1), 83–95

-- (2003): History Matters in Microfinance, *Small Enterprise Development*, vol. 14(2), 10–12

-- (2003): Centenary Rural Development Bank, Uganda: A Flagship of Rural Bank Reform in Africa, *Small Enterprise Development*, vol. 14(3), 35–46; cf. http://www.hf.uni-koeln.de/data/aef/File/PDF/AgDB%20Reform%20Case%20Studies/Uganda,%20Centenary%20RDB%20-%20A%20Flagship%20of%20Rural%20Bank%20Reform%20%28Seibel%202003%29.pdf

-- (2005): Bank Rakyat Indonesia: A Flagship of Rural Microfinance in Asia, in: M. Harper and S. Arora, eds., *Small Customers, Big Market: Commercial Banks in Microfinance*, New Delhi: ITDG Publishing, 7–20

-- (2005): *SHG Banking in India: The evolution of a rural financial innovation*. New Delhi, http://ideas.repec.org/p/zbw/uocaef/20059.htmlhttp://ideas.repec.org/p/zbw/uocaef/20059.html

-- (2006): *From Informal Microfinance to Linkage Banking: Putting Theory into Practice, and Practice into Theory*, European Dialogue No. 36, 49–60

-- (2008): *Economic Recovery and Microfinance in Aceh: Lessons learned in three years of post-Tsunami microfinance*, Eschborn: GTZ, http://www.hf.uni-koeln.de/data/aef/File/j%20Post-Tsunami%20Microfinance%20in%20Aceh%20-%20Lessons%20Learned.pdf

-- (2009a): *Restructuring State-owned Financial Institutions: Bidar District Central Cooperative Bank, India*, Manila: ADB

-- (2009b): *Restructuring of State-owned Financial Institutions: Lessons from Bank Rakyat Indonesia*, Manila: ADB, http://www.adb.org/publications/restructuring-state-owned-financial-institutions-lessons-bank-rakyat-indonesia

-- (2010a): From Self-Help Groups to Village Financial Institutions in Bali: How Culture Determines Finance and Finance Determines Culture, in: K. Wilson, M. Harper, and M. Griffith, eds., *Financial Promise for the Poor: How Groups Build Microsavings*, Sterling, VA: Kumerian Press, 29–37

-- (2010b): Old and New Worlds of Microfinance in Europe and Asia, in: A. Goenka and D. Henley, eds., *Southeast Asia's Credit Revolution: From Moneylenders to Microfinance*, London: Routledge, 40-57

-- (2010c): *Village Banks in Vientiane Capital, Laos: Roadmap Scenarios for a Sustainable Future*. Bonner Schriftenreihe zur Entwicklungsfinanzierung No. 4. Bonn, www.sparkassenstiftung.de/uploads/media/Laos_Village-Banks_Study.pdf

-- (2011): *SHG Sector Own Control (SOC): Evaluation of a Pilot Project of APMAS in Partnership with SERP, Andhra Pradesh*. Bonn: DGRV

-- (2012): An approach towards self-reliance and sustainability of the SHG sector in India: SHG Sector Own Control, *The micro Finance Review* (Lucknow), vol. 4(1), 1-16

-- (2013): Culture and Governance in Microfinance: Desa Pakraman and Lembaga Perkreditan Desa in Bali, in: J.-P. Gueyie, R. Manos, and J. Yaron, eds., *Microfinance in Developing Countries: Issues, Policies and Performance Evaluation*. London: Palgrave Macmillan, 107–126

-- (2014): Informal Finance and Development, *World Politics Review*, 01 July 2014, http://www.worldpoliticsreview.com/articles/13891/the-continued-relevance-of-informal-finance-in-development

Seibel, H.D., and G. Almeyda (2002): *Women and Men in Rural Microfinance: The Case of Uganda*. Rome: IFAD

Seibel, H.D., and F. Boschert (1997): *Aufbau eines Verbundsystems für ländliche Spar- und Darlehenskassen in Vietnam*, Eschborn: GTZ

Seibel, H.D., and U.G. Damachi (1982): *Self-help Organizations: Guidelines and Case Studies for Development Planners and Field Workers*, Bonn: Friedrich Ebert Foundation

Seibel, H.D., and H.R. Dave (2002): *Commercial Aspects of Self-Help Group-Bank-Linkage Programme in India*, Mumbai: NABARD

Seibel, H.D., Th. Giehler and S. Karduck (2005): *Reforming Agricultural Development Banks*, Eschborn: GTZ, http://www.gtz.de/de/dokumente/en-Reforming-Agricultural-Banks.pdf

Seibel, H.D., and S. Karduck (2007): Transaction costs of self-help groups: A study of NABARD's SHG banking programme in India, in: D. Alagiri, ed., *Financial Growth in India and China*. Hyderabad: IFCAI Univ. Press, 196–220

Seibel, H.D., and M.T. Marx (1986): Mobilization of Personal Savings through Cooperative Societies or Indigenous Savings and Credit Associations: Case Studies from Nigeria, in: *UN 1986*, 107–112

Seibel, H.D., and M.T. Marx (1987): *Dual Financial Markets in Africa: Case Studies of Linkages between Informal and Formal Financial Institutions*. Saarbrücken and Fort Lauderdale: Breitenbach

Seibel, H.D., and A. Massing (1974): *Traditional Organizations and Economic Development: Studies of Indigenous Cooperatives in Liberia*. New York: Praeger

Seibel, H.D., A. Rachmadi and D. Kusumayakti (2010): Reform, Growth and Resilience of Savings-led Microfinance Institutions: The Case of the Microbanking Units of Bank Rakyat Indonesia, *Savings and Development* (Bergamo), vol. 34(3), 277–303

Seibel, H.D., and B.J. Rohmann, eds. (2012): *Microfinance in the LAO PDR*, Vientiane: BoL, GIZ, MPI

Seibel, H.D., and N.T. Tam (2010): The People's Credit Funds of Vietnam: A Prudentially Regulated Credit Cooperative Movement, *Enterprise Development & Microfinance*, vol. 21(2), 137–153

Seibel, H.D., and N.T. Tam (2012): Growth and Resilience of Credit Cooperatives in Vietnam, in: O.O. Oluyombo (ed.): *Cooperative Finance in Developing Economies*, Lagos: Soma Prints, 179–197

Shaw, E.S. (1973): *Financial Deepening in Economic Development*, Oxford and New York: Oxford University Press

Sinclair, H. (2012): *Confessions of a Microfinance Heretic: How Microfinance Lost its Way and Betrayed the Poor*, San Francisco: Berrett-Köhler

Sinha, F., A. Tankha, K.R. Reddy and M. Harper (2009): *Microfinance Self-help Groups in India: Living up to Their Promise?* Bourton on Dunsmore: Practical Action Publishing

Smiles, S. (2002): *Self Help*. London 1859, reissued 2002, London: Oxford University Press

Sommer, A. (1934): *Sparkassen und Konjunktur*, Berlin: Heymann

Sparkassenakademie (1978): *Festschrift zum 50-Jährigen Bestehen des Lehrinstituts für das kommunale Sparkassen- und Kreditwesen 1928–1978*, Stuttgart: Deutscher Sparkassenverlag

Spiethoff, A. (1955): *Die wirtschaftlichen Wechsellagen. Aufschwung, Krise, Stockung*, vol. 2, Tübingen: J.C.B. Mohr

Spiethoff, B. (1958): *Ungewollt zur Größe, Die Geschichte der bayerischen Sparkassen*, Munich: M. Schmidt & Söhne

Spoo, H.H. (1999): *Das Bankgewerbe in Neuwied am Rhein im 19. und 20. Jahrhundert*, Cologne: Rheinisch-Westfälisches Wirtschaftsarchiv zu Köln

Srinivasan, G., and A. Tankha (2010): *SHG Federations: Development Costs and Sustainability*. New Delhi: ACCESS Development Services

Srinivasan, N. (2010): *Microfinance India: State of the Sector Report 2010*, New Delhi: SAGE Publications

— (2012): *Microfinance India: State of the Sector Report 2011*, New Delhi: SAGE Publications

Steel, W.F., and B.B. Tornyie (2010): Going downmarket: Ghana's rural banks adapt informal savings methodology, *Enterprise Development & Microfinance*, vol. 21, 154–167

Steiner, J. (1994): *Bankenmarkt und Wirtschaftsordnung. Sparkassen und Landesbanken in der Privatisierungsdiskussion*, Frankfurt: Knapp

Steinwand, D. (2006): *The Alchemy of Microfinance*, Berlin: Verlag für Wissenschaft und Forschung

Stiglitz, J.E., and A. Weiss (1981): Credit Rationing in Markets with Imperfect Information, *American Economic Review*, vol. 71, 393–410

Strickland, C.F. (1922): *An Introduction to Cooperation in India*. London: Oxford University Press

— (1934): *Report on the Introduction of Cooperative Societies into Nigeria*, Lagos: Government Printer

Strube, H. (1973): *Geschichte des Sparkassenwesens und der Sparkassen in Kurhessen 1819–1866*, Stuttgart: Deutscher Sparkassenverlag

Tankha, A. (2012): *Banking on Self Help Groups: Twenty Years On*, New Delhi: SAGE Publications

Terberger, E. (2012): The Microfinance Approach: Does it Deliver on its Promise? In *Die Unternehmung (Swiss Journal of Business Administration)*, vol. 66, pp. 358–370

Terberger, E., and A. Lepp (2004): Kazakhstan: Commercial Banks Entering Micro and Small Business Finance – The Kazakhstan Small Business Program, in: *Scaling up Poverty Reduction: Case Studies in Microfinance*, Washington, DC: CGAP, 125–138

Thomes, P. (1984): Die Kooperation zwischen der Bergwerksdirektion Saarbrücken und den öffentlichen bzw. genossenschaftlichen Spar- und Darlehenskassen im Arbeitereinzugsgebiet des Steinkohlenreviers an der Saar, in: *Zeitschrift für die Geschichte der Saargegend* 32, 50–63

-- (1985a): *Die Kreissparkasse Saarbrücken (1854–1914). Ein Beitrag zur Geschichte der öffentlichen Sparkassen Preußens*, Frankfurt a.M., Knapp
-- (1985b): Kooperation statt Konkurrenz: Der Konferenzbezirk der Sparkassen des Saarreviers, in: *Bankhistorisches Archiv* 11, 48–65
-- (1988): Sparkassen und Kreditgenossenschaften in der bayerischen Pfalz und im preußischen Regierungsbezirk Trier bis zum Ersten Weltkrieg, in: *Zeitschrift für bayerische Sparkassengeschichte* Bd. 2, 95–113
-- (1989): Verwaltete Krankheit. Die Industrialisierung als Wegbereiter des modernen Krankenhauses, in: van Dülmen, R. (Hg.): *Industriekultur an der Saar (1840–1918)*, 160–172, München
-- (1993): La diffusion des caisses d'épargnes en Prusse, in: Pix, M., Pohl, H. (eds.): *La diffusion de l'idée de caisses d'épargne au 19. siècle*, 227–252, Paris
-- (1995): German Savings Banks as Instruments of Regional Development up to Second World War; in: Cassis, Y., Feldmann, G., Olsson, U. (eds.): *Financial Institutions and Financial Markets in Twentieth Century Europe and North America*, 145–164, Cambridge
-- (1997): Sparkassen und kommunale Bindung – Die Sparkassen als Instrument der Kommunalpolitik, in: M. Pix, ed.: *Sparen, investieren, finanzieren. Gedenkschrift für Josef Wysocki*, Munich: Sparkassen- und Giroverband, 251–276
-- (1998): Das Kapital der Weiblichkeit. Die Kundinnen der Kreissparkasse St. Wendel (1859-1867), in: *Geld und Kapital. Jahrbuch für mitteleuropäische Banken- und Sparkassengeschichte* 2, 141–157
-- (2001): Industriekredit und Kapitalmarktfinanzierung in den Westzonen und der Bundesrepublik Deutschland von 1945 bis 1990, in: *Bankkredit oder Kapitalmarkt: Alternativen der Industriefinanzierung in Deutschland*, Stuttgart: Deutscher Sparkassenverlag, 39–54
-- (2002): Aspekte der Unternehmensfinanzierung zwischen Rekonstruktion und Globalisierung. Eine historisch-kritische Analyse der deutschen Nachkriegszeit, in: D. Krimphove and D. Tytko, eds.: *Praktiker-Handbuch Unternehmensfinanzierung. Kapitalbeschaffung und Rating für mittelständische Unternehmen*, Stuttgart: Schäffer-Poeschel, 15–46
-- (2007): Sparkassen und Banken im nördlichen Rheinland 1789 bis 1913; in: F. Irschinger, ed., *Geschichtlicher Atlas der Rheinlande*, Beiheft VII/16, Bonn
-- (2008): *Da, wo Sie zu Hause sind. 150 Jahre Sparkasse Saarbrücken*, Saarbrücken: Hager
-- (2010): *175 Jahre Sparkasse Aachen: Fair. Menschlich. Nah*, Monschau: Weiss
-- (2011): Is there an ICT Path in the German Savings Banking Industry? Circa 1900–1970s, in: Thomes, P. et al., eds.: *Technological Innovation in Retail Finance. International Historical Perspectives*, New York and London: Routledge, 119–136
Thomes, P., and F. Heesen (2013): Zwei Geschäftsmodelle – ein Ziel? Kreditgenossenschaften und Sparkassen im historisch basierten Vergleich, in: Rösner, H.-J., Schulz-Nieswandt, F., eds., *Kölner Beiträge zum Internationalen Jahr der Genossenschaften*, Berlin: 205–225
Thomes, P., and H. Bonin, eds. (2013): *Old Paternalism, New Paternalism, Post-Paternalism (19th-21st Centuries)*, Brussels: Lang
Thomes, P., B. Bátiz-Lazo and J.C. Maixé-Altés, eds. (2011): *Technological Innovation in Retail Finance. International Historical Perspectives*, New York/London: Routledge
Thomes, P., and J. Karbach (1994): *Vom Agrarland zum Montanrevier. Wirtschafts- und Sozialgeschichte der Saarregion (1792–1918)*, Saarbrücken: Selbstverlag Historischer Verein für die Saargegend
Toffler, A. (1980): *The Third Wave. The Classic Study of Tomorrow*, New York: Bantam Books
Trauth, D. (2012): Die Entstehung landwirtschaftlicher Vereine und Genossenschaften in Luxemburg (1874–1914). Mit einem komparatistischen Seitenblick auf den Regierungsbezirk Trier in der ehemaligen preußischen Rheinprovinz, in: M. Buchsteiner and A. Strahl, eds., *Thünen-Jahrbuch*, vol. 7, Rostock, 115–152.
Trende, A. (1957): *Geschichte der deutschen Sparkassen bis zum Anfang des 20. Jahrhunderts*, Stuttgart: Deutscher Sparkassenverlag
Tschach, I. (2002): *The Theory of Development Finance*, Frankfurt: Lang
Tucker, D.S. (1922): *The Evolution of People's Banks*. Longmans, Green & Co
UN – United Nations (1980): *General Assembly 35th Session*, Annex International Development Strategy for the Third United Nations

Development Decade (1981 – 1990), New York: United Nations

– – (1981): *Savings for Development: Report of the International Symposium on the Mobilization of Personal Savings in Developing Countries*, Kingston, Jamaica, 4 – 9 February 1980, New York: United Nations

– – (1984): *Savings for Development: Report of the Second International Symposium on the Mobilization of Personal Savings in Developing Countries*, Kuala Lumpur, Malaysia, 15 – 21 March 1982, New York: United Nations

– – (1986): *Savings for Development: Report of the Third International Symposium on the Mobilization of Personal Savings in Developing Countries*, Yaoundé, Cameroon, 10 – 14 December 1984, New York: United Nations

– – (2006): *Building Inclusive Financial Sectors for Development*, New York: United Nations

USAID – United States Agency for International Development (1973): *A.I.D. Spring Review of Small Farmer Credit*, 20 vols., Washington, DC: USAID

Vaidyanathan, A. et al. (2004): *Draft Final Report of the Task Force on Revival of Cooperative Credit Institutions*, New Delhi: Ministry of Rural Development, http://rbidocs.rbi.org.in/rdocs/Publication-Report/Pdfs/60190.pdf

Verband rheinischer Genossenschaften – Raiffeisen e.V. (1964): *75 Jahre Verband Rheinischer Genossenschaften e.V.*, Cologne

Vilar, P. (2011): *A History of Gold and Money: 1450 – 1920*, London: Verso (1976/2011)

Vogel, R.C. (1984): Savings Mobilization: The Forgotten Half of Rural Finance, in: D.W. Adams et al., eds.: *Undermining Rural Development with Cheap Credit*, Boulder, CO: Westview Press, 248 – 265

Vollert, G., and E. Hennigsen (1990): *Die Genossenschaften in der Bundesrepublik Deutschland*, Frankfurt: DG Bank

Von Pischke, J.D. (1991): *Finance at the Frontier*, EDI Development Studies, Washington, DC: World Bank

– – (2009): New Partnerships for Sustainability and Outreach, in: I. Matthäus-Maier and J.D. Von Pischke, eds.: *New Partnerships for Innovation in Microfinance*, Berlin et al.: Springer, 1 – 14

Von Pischke, J.D., D.W. Adams and G. Donald, eds. (1983): *Rural Financial Markets in Developing Countries: Their Use and Abuse*, Baltimore: Johns Hopkins University Press

Wagner, C. (2012): From Boom to Bust: How different has microfinance been from traditional banking?, *Development Policy Review*, vol. 30, 187 – 210

Wagner, C., and A. Winkler (2013): The Vulnerability of Microfinance to Financial Turmoil: Evidence from the Global Financial Crisis, *World Development*, vol. 51(11), 71 – 90

Wandel, E. (1998): *Banken und Versicherungen im 19. und 20. Jahrhundert*, Munich: Oldenbourg

Weber, W. (1985): *Die Entwicklung der Sparkassen zu selbstständigen Anstalten des öffentlichen Rechts*, Frankfurt: Lang

Wehler, H.-U. (2005 – 2008): *Deutsche Gesellschaftsgeschichte*, 5 vols., 4th or 5th print, München: Beck

Westdeutsche Genossenschaftszentralbank eG, ed. (1984): *1884 – 1984, 100 Jahre genossenschaftliche Zentralbank im Rheinland und in Westfalen*, Cologne: Westdeutsche Genossenschaftszentralbank eG

Westermann, D. (1935): *Die Glidyi-Ewe in Togo. Züge aus ihrem Gesellschaftsleben*, Berlin: de Gruyter

Williams, J. (1993): Democracy and the "Washington Consensus", *World Development*, vol. 21, 1329 – 1336

Wilson, P.H. (2009): *Europe's Tragedy: A History of the Thirty Years War*, London: Allen Lane

Wissenschaftsförderung der Sparkassenfinanzgruppe, ed. (2010): *Regionalgeschichte der Sparkassen-Finanzgruppe*, vol. 2, Stuttgart: Deutscher Sparkassenverlag

Woller, G., C. Dunford and W. Woodworth (1999): Where to Microfinance?, *International Journal of Economic Development*, vol. 1(1), 29 – 64

World Bank (1989): *Financial Systems and Development. World Development Report 1989*, Washington, DC: World Bank

– – (1993): *Transition to the Market*, Washington, DC: World Bank

– – (1995): *The World Bank, Lao PDR Agricultural Sector Memorandum*, 23 March, Washington, DC: World Bank

– – (1999): *Viet Nam. Transforming a State-Owned Financial System*, Washington, DC: World Bank

– – (2007): *Strengthening India's Rural Credit Cooperatives*. Appraisal Report No. AB3126, Washington, DC: World Bank

-- (2008): *Finance for All? Policies and Pitfalls in Expanding Access*, Washington, DC: World Bank

-- (2012): *Global Financial Development Report 2013: Rethinking the Role of State in Finance*, Washington, DC: World Bank

-- (2012): *Measuring Financial Inclusion: The Global Findex Database* (prepared by Asli Demirgüç-Kunt and Leora Klapper), Washington, DC: World Bank

WSBI – World Savings Banks Institute (2007): *From Social Commitment to Corporate Social Responsibility*, Brussels: WSBI

-- (2008): *Who are the clients of savings banks? A poverty assessment of the clients reached by savings banks in India, Mexico, Tanzania and Thailand*, Brussels: WSBI

-- (2011): *200 Years of Savings Banks: A Strong and Lasting Business Model for Responsible, Regional Retail Banking*, Brussels: WSBI

Wysocki, J. (1980): *Untersuchungen zur Wirtschafts- und Sozialgeschichte der deutschen Sparkassen im 19. Jahrhundert*, Stuttgart: Deutscher Sparkassenverlag

-- (1984): Eine utopische Sparkassenidee aus dem Zeitalter des frühen Absolutismus, in: M. Pix and J. Wysocki, eds.: *Historische Marktanalyse. Frühe Sparkassenideen: Utopie und Realität*, Neustadt an der Aisch: Eigenverlag des Arbeitskreises für Sparkassengeschichte, 95–120

-- (1993): *Essener Sparkassengeschichte – Beispiel einer mikrohistorischen Analyse*, Stuttgart: Deutscher Sparkassenverlag

Wysocki, J., and V. Wehrmann (1986): *Lippe, Leben und Arbeit 1786–1986*, Stuttgart: Deutscher Sparkassenverlag

Yaron, J. (1992): *Successful Rural Finance Institutions*, World Bank Discussion Paper No. 150, Washington, DC: World Bank

-- (2000): Efficient Rural Financial Intermediation: The Case of BRI-Unit Desa in Indonesia, in: UNDP: *Private Finance for Human Development*, New York: UNDP

-- (2006): State-Owned Development Finance Institutions (SDFI): The Political Economy and Performance Assessment, *Savings and Development* (Bergamo), vol. 30(1), 39–78

Yaron, J., M.P. Benjamin and G. Piprek (1997): *Rural Finance: Issues, Design and Best Practices*, ESSD Monograph No. 14, Washington, DC: World Bank

Yunus, M. (2007): *Poverty is a Threat to Peace*, Nobel Peace Prize acceptance speech of M. Yunus, held on 10/12/2006, published as an epilogue in M. Yunus: *Creating a World Without Poverty*, New York: Public Affairs

Zeidler, H. (1893): *Geschichte des deutschen Genossenschaftswesens der Neuzeit*, Leipzig: Nabu

Zeitinger, C.-P. (2008): *Delivering Products Irresponsibly*, speech given at the Frankfurt Forum on Development Finance on 18 February

Zeller, M. (1999): *The Role of Micro-Finance for Income and Consumption Smoothing*, Washington, DC: Inter-American Development Bank

Zweig, G. (1986): *Die deutsche Girozentrale – Deutsche Kommunalbank*, Stuttgart: Deutscher Sparkassenverlag